'As exhaustive and authoritative as you'd expect from a former *Times* Journalist of the Year'   *Arena*

'A valuable book for anyone interested in the current Anglo-American involvement in the Middle East'
                                             Contemporary Review

'[Hugh Miles] reveals the fascinating space Al-Jazeera occupies in the propaganda war raging around it . . . Miles illustrates that Al-Jazeera is a force for enlightenment and democratisation which may help to usher in a more moderate age, in the way the media played a role in the Czech Velvet Revolution. His compelling book should be read by anyone interested in the underside of current affairs'
                                             Sunday Business Post

'Miles, a young reporter who was born in Saudi Arabia and educated in Libya, litters his timely and readable account of "How Arab TV News Challenged the World" with illuminating detail about the strange world in which it operates'   *Word*

AL-JAZEERA

How Arab TV News
Challenged the World

Hugh Miles

ABACUS

First published in Great Britain in 2005 by Abacus
This paperback edition published in 2006

A CIP catalogue record for this book
is available from the British Library.

ISBN-13: 978-0-0349-11925-0
ISBN-10: 0-349-11925-2

Typeset in Bembo
by Palimpsest Book Production Limited,
Grangemouth, Stirlingshire
Printed and bound in Great Britain by Clays Ltd, St Ives plc

Abacus
An imprint of
Little, Brown Book Group
Brettenham House
Lancaster Place
London WC2E 7EN

A Member of the Hachette Livre Group of Companies

www.littlebrown.co.uk

For Mum and Dad

Contents

Acknowledgements

This book would not have been possible without the kind help of many people. I would especially like to thank Clare Alexander, Jihad Ballout, Julia Brickell, Dr Musa Keilani and his wonderful family, Thomas Jones at the *London Review of Books*, my wife, Dr Dina al Shafie, and my dad, Oliver Miles.

For their wisdom, support and time while I was researching this book, I would also like to thank Jon Alterman at CSIS, the American-Arab Chamber of Commerce, Rime Allaf, Dr Khaled Mohammed Al-Ali, Raghda Azizieh, Dr Ahmed Al Badi, Fay Bedoun, Jennifer Salan, and the staff at Arab–American Institute, Ahmad Berry, Sir Graham Boyce, Richard Beswick, Mahita El Bacha Urieta, Mahmoud Barhoum, Kirsteen Brace, Ben Campbell-White, Joel Campagna at the Committee to Protect Journalists, Séverine Cazes at Reporters sans Frontières Moyen-Orient, CNN, Richard Colvin, Richard Dawes, Yousuf J. Darwish, Mohamed el-Desouky, Ashraf Eissa, Dr Mamoun Fandi, Hannah Griffiths, Muhannad Haimour and all the staff at the Arab Community Center for Economic and Social Services in Dearborn, Michigan, Dr Michael Harmarneh, Imam Husham Al-Husainy, Ghassan Hajar, Khalid al Hatar, Roland Huguenin-Benjamin, Jon Hill, Abdul Rahman Hethen, John Harte, Mark Hernandez, Iain Hunt, Wally Jadan, Tony Jones at the British Council in Qatar, Dr Nabil Khouri, Sheikh Nasser bin Hamed Al Khalifa, Miriam Azar and the staff of the Qatari embassy in London, Rami G. Khouri, Dr Rinad el-Khatib, Professor Justin Lewis, Khalid Mannai, Molly McKew and the American Enterprise Institute, MEC International, Tom Miles, Joe Miles Secretarial Services, Julia Miles, Lucy Miles, Mohammad Al Mansoori, Maddie Mogford, Christian Parenti, James Peach, Sir Derek Plumbly, Mitchell Prothero, Christopher Prentice,

Jonathon Layfield, Rana Nejem, Deena Bitar, Hassan al-Ajrami and the staff at the British embassy in Amman, Steve Rendall at FAIR.org, Jamal Ar-Risai, Imad Saffarini, Dr Naomi Sakr, Brando Skyhorse, Charlie Stuart, Rory Stewart, Hada Sarhan, Dr Jamal Shah, Lieutenant-Commander Steve Tatham, Hazem Abdel Rahman Tawfik, David Wright, Professor Li Xiguang, Mwafac Yusuf, Dr Mohamad Zayani, and John Zogby. Thank you too, to the numerous interviewees – especially within the American administration – who chose to remain anonymous.

Also I would like to thank Walid al-Omary, Dr Faisal al-Qasim, Yosri Fouda, Muftah al-Suwaidan, Stephanie Thomas, Khaled al-Hroub, Abeer Kalla, Rania Khoury, Mostefa Souag, Abdul Rahim Foukara, Yasser Abu Hilala, Mohammed Ajloni and all the staff at Al-Jazeera for putting up with me while I snooped around and asked questions.

I have never received any payment from Al-Jazeera in connection with this book.

Introduction

Switch on Al-Jazeera any time of day or night and superficially it looks like any other news channel. The anchors look much like they do in the West. The men wear suits and the women wear make-up and no veils, and while some wear headscarves others have plunging necklines. When the news is rolling, straps, tags and ticker tape at the bottom of the screen are all used to convey information in an attractive and comprehensible way. Everything on Al-Jazeera is in classical Arabic, the lingua franca of the Middle East, and, being in Arabic, the ticker tape scrolls from left to right. The Al-Jazeera logo always remains superimposed on the screen whenever the news is on, a helpful indicator if you happen to be surfing at speed to find the channel. If another station uses Al-Jazeera's footage, it has no choice but to show the Al-Jazeera cartouche too. Forthcoming features are advertised using Greenwich Mean Time and New York time, but Al-Jazeera's principal operating time zone is Mecca time. Exactly the same, Al-Jazeera is broadcast all over the world at the same time – there are no regional differences.

Al-Jazeera's news mixes the anchors in Doha, in the field 'lives' from reporters around the world and pre-recorded video packages. Intermittently it is broken up by glossy, high-tech graphics, the swirling Al-Jazeera logo and thumping dramatic music. Viewers are teased with clips of what is to come on other shows and the occasional advertisement. In other words, Al-Jazeera's news looks and feels like any Western news station.

On the hour and half-hour, the news starts with a fast-paced montage of news clips followed by the bulletin. This cycle persists twenty-four hours a day, all year. The typical rundown of stories is similar to BBC News 24's and, like the BBC, Al-Jazeera reports from all over the world. Its news does not focus on events in just the Middle East: stories from elsewhere often make the headlines. For example, when a revolution happened in Haiti the Al-Jazeera correspondent from France went there and Haiti topped the rundown for days. Like all news agencies, besides depending on its own global network of correspondents, Al-Jazeera buys pictures from international news agencies, like Reuters and Associated Press (AP), as well from an Arab agency. As a result pictures are sometimes exactly the same as on other news channels.

If you watch Al-Jazeera for more than a few minutes you will notice one of the principal differences between it and other twenty-four-hour news networks: how few advertisements there are. It is possible to watch Al-Jazeera for an hour and not see any at all. When they do appear, they are brief and often conspicuously cheap. Al-Jazeera has only about forty to forty-five minutes of advertising each day, compared with about three hundred minutes of daily commercial advertising on CNN (Cable News Network).

Although news is Al-Jazeera's central focus, it is interspersed with talk shows and a diverse range of educational programmes throughout the day. Both of these strands deal with current issues, including technology, the environment or refugees, but sometimes the topics are more general, like the Second World War, alternative medicine or the *Titanic*. Al-Jazeera has bought a lot of footage from the BBC, so many of the educational programmes depend on dated and dubbed British footage, but Al-Jazeera does make its own programmes too. Many of these are on Middle Eastern topics, like the Lebanese civil war or Hamas. An economics and business report is broadcast daily from London and from the New York Stock Exchange, and every day there is a survey of the world press.

Sport, principally soccer, is covered too, and Al-Jazeera featured the first female Arab sports reporter. In November 2003 it launched a second channel, exclusively given over to sport, which has made respectable inroads into the competitive Arab sports television market. This early success is helped by the fact that the channel is free, although it hopes to become a sub-scription service when it goes twenty-four-hour. Its principal attraction so far has been its exclusive coverage in Arabic of the Spanish soccer league. Many other sports are featured too, but soccer, as the most popular sport in the Middle East, gets the most airtime. There has been talk of an Al-Jazeera English-language news channel for several years, and the launch date for this now looks set to be sometime in the summer of 2006. The Al-Jazeera Arabic language children's network was inaugurated in September 2005. An Al-Jazeera business channel and an Al-Jazeera documentary channel have also been mooted in the past, although no date has been set for their appearance.

My interest in Al-Jazeera started during the invasion of Iraq in 2003. At the time I was living in Earls Court, London, working freelance for Sky News. My job was watching several rival TV stations, monitoring the output so that we never missed any important pictures. It was especially important to watch the Arab stations as their reporters had better access inside Iraq than the Western networks and they regularly produced pictures that Sky wanted to use. Because I have studied Arabic and have lived and worked in the Middle East, it was my job to keep a close eye on three Arab stations: Al Arabiya, Abu Dhabi TV and Al-Jazeera.

When the second Gulf war started I switched to the night shift, working from 7 p.m. until 7 a.m. I spent three weeks sitting in a windowless, claustrophobic control room watching a wall of monitors screening pictures coming in live from Iraq. While some of the monitors showed output from rival networks, like the BBC and Al-Jazeera, others ran unedited pictures sent direct by cameramen in the field. Most pictures were not played out to air straight away, but were recorded and stored for making news 'packages' later. Since the cameraman's job was simply to film whatever he saw, without sparing a thought for the edit-ing process, the unedited pictures we received were often more gruesome than the pictures that made it on to the nightly news.

Watching twelve hours of war footage every night and then

catching an early-morning Tube train home, side by side with commuters on their way to work, drained me. As a freelancer I was supposed to be working on several other projects at the same time, unrelated to what I was doing at Sky. However, as the war progressed, I found my mind was so absorbed by everything I had seen the night before that all my other commitments were gradually slipping behind.

I owed the *London Review of Books* a four-thousand-word article on Piltdown Man, but every time I sat down at my computer to write, all I could see was images of war. I was wandering around zombified, unable to sleep, and when I did, my dreams were of night-vision-green tanks rolling across the Kuwaiti desert, Saddam Hussein saluting parades of Iraqi troops and F-18 Hornets taking off from the decks of US aircraft carriers.

After a week the editor began calling me, anxious to know when I was going to finish the Piltdown Man piece. After I explained that I was working the night shift and was physically unable to start researching Australopithecus dentition, he suggested I drop the article and write something about my experience watching the war on Al-Jazeera instead. That was how my investigation into the station began.

I have long been interested in the Arab world. My father was a diplomat and so I spent time in the Middle East when I was growing up. I was born in Saudi Arabia, went to school in Libya and worked as an au pair with a family in Cairo. I studied Arabic at Oxford and then later in the Yemen, and in recent years I have done consultancy work for companies and governments wishing to do business in the Middle East.

The article I wrote for the *London Review of Books* was restricted to how Al-Jazeera was covering the invasion of Iraq. As I researched it I realized that although there was a wealth of opinion and second-hand information on Al-Jazeera, accurate facts issued by the organization itself were scarce. Al-Jazeera seemed often to crop up as a third party in all sorts of news stories, but usually either as journalistic shorthand for 'the Arab media' or, even more vaguely, as something synonymous with that amorphous thing 'the Arab street'.

By the time I had finished my piece I had more questions than answers. Who had started the channel? Why now? How was it financed? What exactly was the channel's relationship with Osama bin Laden? Was it in league with the resistance in Iraq? Much of the Western press seemed to interpret Al-Jazeera's meteoric rise as a sign of an impending Islamic glasnost. But was that true? And what did the Arabs themselves think about it? Was satellite television news actually moving Arab countries towards real democracy or was it just some kind of substitute?

Trying to establish some of the facts, I found researching an Arab news network was not quite as straightforward as researching a Western one. Here, if we want to know something about a TV station, how many people in Britain have satellite TV or how much a thirty-second advertising slot during the Super Bowl costs, then we just look it up. But there is no reliable means, official or otherwise, of discovering this sort of information in the Arab world. We do not know what a Bedouin in the Sinai is watching on his satellite dish, nor what he thinks about it. In fact, asking these kinds of questions in Arab countries – even the more liberal ones – can land you in jail. Arab society is opaque and statistics and demography are not part of ordinary life. And the answers to my questions were not on the Internet.

The only way to find out how Al-Jazeera was being received in the Arab world, I realized, was to go out there and see for myself. But before I could do that I had to get permission from Al-Jazeera's management to meet their staff and visit their bureaux. So I flew to Al-Jazeera's headquarters in Qatar, in the hope that I might persuade the network's media relations department to help answer some of my questions.

Al-Jazeera is broadcast from its headquarters in the mitten-shaped country of Qatar, on a peninsula jutting from the Arabian mainland into the Persian Gulf. Qatar is about the size of Connecticut (4500 square miles) and, being almost entirely desert, is bleak even by regional standards. Lying between Iran and Saudi Arabia, like a mouse sharing a cage with two rattlesnakes, the little Emirate has had to learn to live on its wits. Remarkably, despite numerous wars and invasions in the Gulf region within the last twenty years, including the eight-year-long Iran–Iraq war and two US-led invasions of Iraq, Qatar has flourished.

Back in 1867 the Emir of Qatar signed a deal for protection with Great Britain. The Emirate remained a British protectorate until 1971, when it succeeded to independence. Before oil was discovered in 1939, the economy was based on pearl fishing. In the thirties, after a Japanese noodle salesman discovered how to culture freshwater pearls, the market for real ones collapsed and Qatar's economy atrophied to almost nothing. Oil revenue began to accumulate in serious commercial quantities in the fifties, but it was not until the spike in oil prices in the seventies that Qatar's fortunes really began to take off. At the same time the largest offshore natural gas field in the world, the North Field, was discovered in the sea between Qatar and Iran. For many years there was no adequate technology to exploit this extraordinary geological resource. Only in the nineties, after the development of new methods for gas liquefaction and transportation, could Qatar at last start to unlock the potential of this 2300-square-mile field.

Today Qatar's huge gas reserves – the largest known natural gas reserves of any country except Russia and Iran – bestow upon its people one of the highest per capita incomes in the world. Thanks to new technology, Qatar is experiencing a boom that experts predict will last for generations to come, maybe for two hundred years. As long as there is a buyer for its gas, Qatar is going to be rich. This is just as well, because apart from gas it has precious few natural resources. There are modest quantities of oil, but virtually all Qatar's food is imported and almost all its water is produced by desalination. Out in the desert, razor-wire fences keep intruders many hundreds of yards away from the precious refining and liquefying plants. The plants are as big as small towns and visible for miles around. Their metal towers exhale brown smoke which hangs over the desert sky like a pestilent cloud. At night the flares from the burn-off gas reflect off the miles of metal piping, making the whole structure look like a remote colony on some bleak and distant moon.

Doha, Qatar's capital, sits on the edge of the desert by the azure waters of the Persian Gulf. Central Doha is a noisy, neon-lit melting pot where the street signs are in Hindi, Arabic, English and Chinese. Hindi is a more practical language than Arabic for navigating your way around town and unless you have a business appointment, you could go for days without speaking with a Qatari. The total population of the country is only about 610,000 souls. Bearing in mind that at least four hundred thousand of these are migrant workers from Pakistan, India, Egypt and else-where, leaving only about eighty thousand adult Qataris, it is remarkable that the Emirate can field even the basic manpower that running a state entails – such as a government, an army and air-traffic controllers. Until Qatar became independent, it had been thought impossible that such a small country could even exist. Sheikh Zayed of the neighbouring United Arab Emirates (UAE) once quipped that Qatar's population was so small they could all stay in a hotel, which, in the Emirates, is probably true. Doha is so small it's no surprise if the same taxi driver picks you up twice in one day.

Since Qatar came into its immense wealth slightly later than its Gulf neighbours, it does not boast the same level of urban development as Abu Dhabi or Dubai. Still, it is hard to imagine that fifty years ago Doha was little more than a gravelly beach manned by pearl divers and just a handful of permanent build-ings. Today, on the edge of the city, a sprawl of gaudy new public buildings are lit up like casinos. Between all of them lie hundreds of yards of desert scrub, because this is a city that is largely yet to be built. Somewhere a modern-day Haussmann has a map on the wall of his air-conditioned office showing exactly what this city is going to look like when it is finished in ten years' time. Now all that remains is for the immigrant labourers to hurry along and complete it, square by square.

Each new edifice is a testament to Qatar's massive wealth. Mirrored skyscrapers of offices with Islamic-themed windows and luxurious hotel resorts with marbled, air-conditioned lobbies sprout out of the sand like so many daffodils. Great slices of desert have been requisitioned for wealthy new residential neighbourhoods. Shimmering white mansions are being thrown up, an Arab Bel Air. The residents cruise down long, wide boulevards lined with palm trees, so straight they might be Roman, so new the stripes on the road are still bright and clean, to reach the luminous green fairways of the eighteen-hole PGA-quality Doha Golf Club. The roads are tailored to fit the oversize SUVs that Qataris love to drive. A favourite local pastime is racing around the desert and, at the south of the peninsula, climbing sand dunes up to forty metres high. Despite the searing heat, the immaculately cropped grass by the verge is thick and lush, watered at night by sprinklers that pump water into the sky as if a fire hydrant has burst. After dark the palm trees light up with swirling psychedelic gold bursts, like giant Christmas decorations. A few yards beyond what man has created, the interminable desert starts.

Doha's new shopping mall, like most things in Qatar, is palatial and spanking new. Crisp and echoey, with sheer mirrored columns stretching upwards into the heavens, it is a monument to twenty-first-century living. It is also one of the most popular places for young Qataris to hang out and socialize. Even when it is nearly midnight, it is crammed with families. This is a country where half the population is under sixteen years old. Men in spotless floor-length white *dishdashas* and red *guthra* headdresses sip Starbucks coffee and shoot pool. Women in veils and full-length black *abayas* shop for underwear in designer boutiques or surf the Internet in the cyber café. But the sexes are as separate as the two sides in a chess game. Groups of men sweep past hand in hand, sometimes three or four abreast, swinging their interlaced hands. Kohl-lined eyes peep out from petite *abayas*, missing nothing. A black-and-white scrum of men and women push to get served at Kentucky Fried Chicken. Mums at the tables daintily remove their veils to eat, while their kids scream on the bouncy castle or tug demandingly at their *abayas*. Outside in the suffocating heat, a loyal line of parents hover in SUVs waiting to take exhausted loved ones home. This is modern life, Gulf style.

Life in Qatar, for Qataris at least, is easy. Even if you don't work, you are entitled to interest-free loans and a free plot of land from the government. Once you have spent your loan building your house, the government gives you $15,000 to furnish it. There is no income tax, and water, gas and electricity are free. Petrol is cheap and healthcare is also free, even if that involves flying you abroad for an operation.

Children born to the Emir's tribe – and there are thousands of them – get even more generous benefits, including monthly cash handouts from birth. Boys get more than girls. A Qatari government employee who retires continues to be paid the same annual salary as a pension for the rest of his life, so it is small wonder that after ten years studying abroad, followed by a sinecure at home, many Qataris choose to retire in their thirties.

Noticeable only by its absence is the huge American military deployment in this country. If you didn't know it, you could easily forget that somewhere out in the desert is the colossal Al-Udeid airbase, from which the invasion of Iraq was launched in 2003. There are no signs pointing it out and even if you know where you are going, the dun-coloured buildings behind the long wire fence are not easy to spot in the desert haze. The soldiers keep a low profile; they don't come into town much and when they do, they come plain-clothed in ones and twos. Many serve out their tour of duty within the confines of the base itself.

Coalition Central Command, where the daily war briefings were given to the world's press, is in a second military base, As-Saliyah. This camp is on the edge of Doha itself, in a windswept industrial zone, and is unmarked on the outside.

Appearances, it seems, are deceptive. America has invested hundreds of millions of dollars in its defence systems in Qatar and the two countries have a deep and binding relationship. In 2002 the Qatari Foreign Minister, Sheikh Hamad bin Jasim bin Jabr Al Thani, stunned everyone when he declared Qatar's relationship with America his country's 'first consideration'. While in the past Qatar looked to Britain for protection, now it has found a new 'big brother'. From the American perspective this benevolent Islamic country, which allows its resources to be exploited and its desert to be colonized, is its dream partner in the region.

Al-Jazeera's headquarters in Doha is a low, white building with a blue roof, next door to the compound that houses the Qatar Radio and Television Corporation. Satellite dishes and transmission masts loom overhead. It is easy to find, and taxi drivers know the dusty intersection simply as 'television roundabout'. A rickety fence runs around the sandy compound, edged with yellowing grass and palm trees. A lethargic security guard waves cars over the speed bump in the stifling desert heat. Next door a new office is under construction so that the current one can be used to house the forthcoming Al-Jazeera English-language channel. There is some consternation among the news staff about who has bagged the best spots.

Inside the headquarters building the principal newsroom covers barely 2500 square feet but is jam-packed with banks of computers, television screens and busy staff. It is a state-of-the-art news environment, built around a serial digital video infrastructure with analogue audio, although it is currently being upgraded. Fibre-optic cables connect it to the satellite uplink system, as well as to the studios and edit suites of nearby Qatar Television. Prominently displayed on the wall is Al-Jazeera's logo, a large, teardrop-shaped design based on the name 'Al-Jazeera' written calligraphically in Arabic. It means 'the island' or 'the peninsula', because, as Al-Jazeera's chairman, Sheikh Hamad bin Thamir Al Thani, once explained, Qatar is an important part

of the greater Arabian peninsula. Below the name is written, in
Arabic: 'The opinion and the other opinion.' In one corner of
the newsroom stands a conspicuous, larger-than-life photograph
of Tareq Ayyoub, the Al-Jazeera correspondent killed in April
2003 by an American missile during the invasion of Iraq.

During the spring of 2000 President Hosni Mubarak of Egypt
paid a state visit to Doha. While he was there he asked his hosts
if he might satisfy his curiosity about the new TV station which
had been causing him so much trouble. When he dropped by
unannounced after midnight at Al-Jazeera's little newsroom, the
bemused Al-Jazeera staff were happy to show him around. He
and his entourage were taken aback by the tiny scale of the operation. 'All this trouble from a matchbox like this?' the President
exclaimed.

Adjoining the main news floor are the edit suites, where
footage is spliced and assembled into packages before being
broadcast. Flimsy doors lead into individual offices which look
on to the central newsroom and inside you can see framed front
pages from the *Guardian* and *Time* magazine, with headlines
testifying to Al Jazeera's past glories. In the manager's office press
awards and trophies from international media organizations line
the walls.

Fortunately for me, Al Jazeera's management happily acquiesced to my request for help in researching this book. Since
Al-Jazeera had nothing to hide, they said, it was in their interest to let an independent observer have a snoop around, especially since the network was planning the launch of its
English-language channel.

Over the next few months, as well as returning to Doha, I
travelled to Amman, Cairo, Detroit, Geneva, Jerusalem,
London, Paris, New York, Ramallah and Washington, meeting Al-Jazeera's staff as well as a wide variety of other people
with insights or opinions on the Arab media. I talked with
academics, ambassadors, Qatar's Department of State, security
firms, non-profit organizations like the Committee to Protect
Journalists and Reporters sans Frontières (Reporters without

Borders, a Paris-based international organization committed to press freedom around the world), other television news organizations and magazines, politicians, think tanks, pollsters, doctors, hospital administrators, social workers, translators, an imam, economists, a historian, a lieutenant commander in the Royal Navy, businessmen of various persuasions, engineers and royal advisers, as well as numerous hoteliers, shopkeepers and students. While not exactly scientific, my research was at least random and as comprehensive as I could make it.

What I was not expecting to find was that the story of Al-Jazeera was not just the story of a news organization. Al-Jazeera has been so inextricably linked to tumultuous recent events in the Middle East – indeed at times it has been at the very eye of the storm – that the story of this news network is, in fact, the story of the upheavals that have taken place in that troubled region in recent years.

1

A Seed Planted in the Desert

Qatar is ruled by the Emir Sheikh Hamad bin Khalifa Al Thani and his tribe, the Al Thani. In proportion to the country's small size, the Al Thani family is the largest of all the ruling families in the Middle East. It also has a reputation for being the most argumentative. Transition from one ruler to another has rarely been smooth and the family's propensity for spilling one another's blood won them the title 'the thugs of the Gulf' from one pre-independence British administrator.

The previous Emir was Sheikh Hamad's father, Sheikh Khalifa bin Hamad Al Thani. He seized power in a coup immediately after Qatar's independence in 1971 and for the next twenty-three years presided over important developments in Qatar's infra-structure, domestic and foreign policies, effectively creating the modern state. In later years the old Sheikh developed a fine taste for luxury, spending more and more time out of the country, often on the French Riviera.

Today's Emir, Sheikh Hamad bin Khalifa Al Thani, is the eldest of Sheikh Khalifa's five sons. His first exposure to democracy was on a trip to London when he was still a boy and legend has it that the concept seemed so ridiculous to him that he had to be led in hysterical laughter from the balcony of the House of Commons after witnessing his first parliamentary debate. He later went to Britain's Sandhurst military academy, until he returned to Qatar in 1977, when he became Minister of Defence. He still has a house near Windsor, Berkshire.

In 1995 the elderly Sheikh Khalifa briefly returned to Qatar after one of his many trips abroad, demoted one son from his position as Prime Minister and promoted another in his place. Crown Prince Hamad was rattled by his father's habit of arbitrary promotion and dismissal. Thinking that one day this might put his own claim to the throne in jeopardy, he proclaimed himself the new Emir on 27 June that year, while the old Emir was in Switzerland on holiday. It is said that Sheikh Khalifa learned of the coup while listening to the radio in his hotel room in Geneva. Others say his son told him on the phone and then promptly hung up. If it had happened today he probably would have heard about it on Al-Jazeera.

The coup ushered in a year of strife and bickering between father and son. Sheikh Khalifa, who had every intention of clinging on to power, embarked on a tour of the Gulf to stir up dissent against his own son, whom he publicly disowned. Rumours of plots against the young Emir's life abounded, climaxing in a foiled counter-coup attempt on 14 February 1996. It was said that the Sheikh had taken many billions of dollars – possibly as much as twenty-five billion – out of the Qatari government coffers.

It was now Sheikh Hamad's turn to act. With the help of the Washington law firm Patton Boggs, he froze the money that his father had ladled out of the national reserve, thus ending his dream of a return to power. Sheikh Hamad quickly consolidated his position as Emir politically by ceding some of his power to a broader authority and by constitutionally safeguarding the role of Prime Minister.

On acceding to power Sheikh Hamad was, at just forty-four, the youngest ruler in the Gulf. The other Arab countries, with the exception of Oman, were governed by rulers in their sixties, seventies or eighties, many of whom had held power for a quarter of a century or more. The young Emir and his new political team of young, Western-educated technocrats belonged to a different generation, more open to political and social ideas from the West.

It was not long before it became clear that Sheikh Hamad had plans quite unlike his father's. He dispensed with the ritual and baroque finery of the court, and began instead to govern Qatar more like a managing director running a large corporation. Understanding the importance of privatization, he quickly turned many institutions in need of quick reform over to the private sector, among them Qatar's antiquated postal service.

Like any sensible hands-on manager, he developed good personal relationships with his trusted top staff and always kept a handle on the cash. Unlike other Arab rulers, who remained aloof from their subjects, the new Emir made a habit of explaining his policies and ideas, often speaking directly to the press. He shied away from the kind of ceremony typical of most Arab leaders and even made a point of working in the afternoons.

Nowadays he sometimes drives around Doha and if he sees a problem he calls the appropriate minister to tell him what needs to be fixed. He is known for showing up in Doha restaurants with no entourage except for a few security men and sitting down to eat with amazed diners. Although for security reasons no one is allowed to leave before him, he does not have the restaurant cleared, as other Arab leaders do.

Although Qatar has phenomenal natural gas reserves – a trillion cubic feet of gas and potentially a trillion-dollar economy – the old Emir had believed conservatively that Qatar's interests would better be served if the country never moved too far ahead of others in the region, culturally, economically or politically. The new Emir decided to abandon this policy. Rather than try to blend in with the other Gulf countries, he has done all he can to elevate Qatar's position on the world stage, inviting Bill Clinton and Al Gore to Qatar, hosting the World Islamic and World Trade Organization conferences and soliciting major sporting events like World Championship motorcycle racing and the Asian Games of 2006. Qatar, he has stated, should be 'known and noticed'.

Sheikh Hamad has plans to turn Qatar into an important

regional hub, a kind of Arab version of Switzerland: rich, neutral and secure. The massive airport that is currently being built, capable of carrying forty-five million passengers a year, shows that he is thinking big and long term.

Before any other Gulf country, the Emir introduced democratic elections for a number of establishments and authorities, delivered a new constitution, established an elected national body, the Municipal Council, and founded Al-Jazeera.

When I visited Doha, loyal Qataris assured me that the new Municipal Council, or Majlis Ash Shura, two-thirds of whose forty-five members are directly elected, the rest appointed by the Emir, had real political bite. When I asked my Qatari friends what kind of dramatic reforms it had helped implement recently I was told it had helped precipitate a major overhaul in the way the police calculate fines for traffic offences.

Although Qatar is often cited today as a paragon of virtue in the Middle East, it is important to keep this claim in perspective. Greater public participation in decision-making is a good start, but Qatar is still not a democracy. But then it is not a police state either: it is an autocratic state subject to the whim of one man, the Emir, who, although fortunately not a tyrant, is unelected, unaccountable and all-powerful. The Municipal Council may decide traffic laws but it does not discuss the military budget or the Emir's personal expenditure.

Political parties in Qatar are still outlawed, as is anything that vaguely resembles one: for example, an environmental lobby group, a consumer association or an association of professionals. Opposition is not tolerated and there is still no real debate about how the country is run. In 1998 local Qatari newspapers published a letter from a Qatari religious scholar called Abdul Rahman al-Nuaimi which criticized the emancipation of women in Qatar, one of the government's key policies. Nuaimi wrote that this trend was un-Islamic and that awarding women political rights risked turning them into men. He was arrested and jailed for nearly three years without trial.

With a word the Emir can change the course of the life of

any individual or family in Qatar, even powerful members of his own tribe, and all Qataris depend on his benevolence. On 5 August 2003 the Emir announced that his successor would no longer be his elder son, who had been in ill health, but would instead be his fourth son. In a moment one man's autocratic decision changed the future of Qatar for ever.

Nor is it only Qataris who watch what they say in Qatar. At an expat party during my first week in Doha, I was politely asked whether I had yet met anyone from the Qatari CID. The CID, so expat rumour had it, is the secret arm of the Qatari police and has the job of mingling with the expat community to gauge its disposition towards the state. Since there is no democratic forum for people to air their opinions, the government has to employ policemen to stay abreast of the mood on the street. It is the task of CID officers to spot seditious trends in behaviour before they start. If they stumble across anyone fishy among the expatriate community, they tip off the regular police, and the authorities, rather than hold a long and potentially embarrassing court case, simply expel suspect expats at once.

'This is why,' a veteran British expatriate policeman told me over a tray of sausages at an expat house party in Doha, 'there has been no terrorism so far in Qatar. The Qataris run a very tight ship. They know who goes into the country and who comes out, and if you want a long-stay visa they run a thorough background check on you. Not to mention AIDS tests, even for children. Any doubt at all, you get deported.'

Another highly unusual aspect of Sheikh Hamad's regime is that the second of his three wives, Sheikha Moza bint Nasser al-Misned, has an important role in running the nation's affairs. She is the chairperson of the Qatar Foundation for Education, Science and Community Development and sits on several other committees. Qataris see her as a sovereign in her own right. The royal couple rule almost as a partnership: sometimes she speaks in public with complete authority while he sits in the audience and watches. A glamorous mother of seven in her forties, Sheikha Moza possesses the positivity and self-confidence that characterize the Arab women's movement. One Qatari technocrat who worked for her told me he was impressed by her capacity for speed-reading lengthy technical documents and then asking intelligent, pertinent questions.

By the 1980s, when Qatar had become a seriously wealthy country, its Gulf neighbours, Dubai, Bahrain and Abu Dhabi, had already had a chance to establish themselves in the region as regional banking and commerce capitals. Unlike the other Emirates, Qatar traditionally had never been a trade hub, so the American-educated first lady, thinking laterally, decided that rather than compete with them she would concentrate on developing Qatar as a regional leader in education. Education has since become an obsession for both the Emir and his wife.

Buying wholesale into the American university system, the educational foundation which she heads paid $750 million for a branch of Cornell University to open a campus in Doha. At present the Weill Cornell Medical College turns out just sixty graduates a year, but, when it comes to royal projects, money is never a deciding factor, and Sheikha Moza has identified a regional demand for quality educational facilities. Virginia University, Carnegie Mellon, Texas A&M University and the prestigious American think tank the Rand Corporation have all recently opened branches in Qatar. According to one Qatari academic I spoke with, this has already had a positive effect far beyond anyone's hopes. With so many world-class institutions located on one block in Qatar's new science and technology park, the prospects for academic cross-fertilization during the lunch hour are enormous.

Academics have been given important roles in drafting Qatar's new democracy. For example, the President of the University of Qatar chaired the committee that drew up the new constitution. He had the final word over all the others who contributed, the Foreign Minister among them, so an academic took precedence over a minister.

Although women in Qatar still face discrimination, Sheikha Moza, who is a Unesco special envoy for education, has helped effect a dramatic improvement in their status. Women in Qatar vote, drive and make up 40 per cent of the workforce. Unlike in any Western democratic country, Qatari women were enfranchised at the same time as men. In March 1999 six women ran in the municipal elections. Although none of them won a seat, this was the first time that women had been allowed to stand for election in any of the six countries of the Gulf Cooperation Council (Bahrain, Kuwait, Oman, Qatar, Saudi Arabia and the United Arab Emirates), and more women voted than men.

Public education for women has reached a standard so high that women now account for nearly two-thirds of the University of Qatar's nine thousand students and win most of the academic prizes. The Dean of the University is a woman, many of the teachers are women and recently women's athletics were introduced for the first time. Increasingly, Qatari women can be found working in both public departments and commercial businesses. Paradoxically, because of the country's strict Wahhabi beliefs, photographs of Sheikha Moza were prohibited until very recently, and when she appeared with her husband for an interview on CBS News's *Sixty Minutes* the Arab world was astonished.

Besides representing Arab women, Sheikha Moza has also worked hard on behalf of children, and she chairs Qatar's Supreme Council for Family Affairs. Under her guidance the prodigious use of child labour in camel racing has come to an end. In Qatar camel racing is a traditional sport in which the jockeys are usually children. Being a jockey in a camel race is not like being a jockey in a horse race. Unlike horses, camels do not need a lot of goading: they run as hard as they can by themselves and just need someone to point them in a straight line. Since the jockey's job is simply to hold the reins, the principal prerequisite for the job is being small and light, so children are ideal. But this is not humane, ruled Sheikha Moza. Now Qatari technologists have pioneered a robotic camel jockey, and children are no longer needed. The camel, I was told, runs just as well.

In the West, Qatar's radical reforms have been hailed as a rare example of better Arab governance. Power had been passed down from one generation to the next peacefully, if not exactly democratically. But, in the Gulf, neighbouring cranky septua-genarian despots began to wonder if the same thing might happen to them. The little Emirate's sweeping new policies were seen as a wild and dangerous precedent.

The Qataris and the Saudis in particular have long been uneasy neighbours. Although Qataris practise the same brand of conser-vative Wahhabi Islam as Saudis, they are more moderate in outlook and more tolerant of the expatriate majority among whom they live. By Western standards, Qataris still seem very conservative, especially when it comes to sex, but alcohol is available and women are treated much better than in Saudi Arabia. There the sexes are forbidden to mix, women must be covered from head to toe when in public and other faiths are banned.

For years Saudi Arabia has seen itself as regional supervisor in the Gulf, owed respect and deference by all the smaller Emirates. From the Saudis' point of view, important regional decisions should not be embarked upon without consulting them first. On a personal level, the House of Saud thinks of itself as grander than the Al Thani, which the Al Thani strongly resent. In all, these two countries, like most Arab neighbours, have spent years nurturing a deep dislike of each other.

On several occasions in the early nineties the Saudis simply attacked the Qataris to remind them who was boss. In 2002 a new border agreement was signed to stop this, and since then Qatar's reforms have continued apace. Relations between the new Emir and the Saudis got off to a poor start because the Saudis were accused of sponsoring a failed counter-coup to put the deposed Emir back on the throne. Since then the Saudis have occasionally made a show of welcoming him back to the region, to snub the current Emir, his son Sheikh Hamad.

There are many things that irritate the Saudis about the Qataris. With its new democracy and new constitution, Qatar has underlined Saudi Arabia's backwardness; Qatar is the only country in the region with ties, albeit low-level ones, to Israel; at the end of the first Gulf war in 1991 Qatar offered Iraq the use of its capacious ports to handle commodities bought under the UN's oil-for-food programme; Qatar is much richer per capita than Saudi Arabia, with a per capita GDP of $21,500, compared with the Saudis' puny $11,800; and Qatar has gradually eclipsed Saudi Arabia as America's first choice of military partner in the Gulf.

But why, I wondered, are Qataris so different from their neighbours? When I visited Al-Jazeera's London bureau I met Muftah al-Suwaidan, its Qatari executive director, who had worked for Qatar Airways and Qatar National Bank in Paris before Al Jazeera, and I put this question to him. His response was, 'Until the end of the seventies Qatar was still a very conservative society. When the new Emir took over in 1995 and started to open society he brought new ideas and the people accepted it. Today in Qatar society is open. Qataris are not just open in the media, they are open in all aspects of Qatari life. But it is also to do with international changes: what is happening in the region. After Iraq invaded Kuwait and then there was the liberation of Kuwait, the Americans started demanding democracy and human rights in the region and this had an effect on Qatar before it did on our neighbours.'

Mostefa Souag, an Algerian and Al-Jazeera's senior correspondent in London, added other reasons. 'Qatar is a small country and change in a small country is easier than in a big one, as you can reach the whole population faster. Also, when a country is rich its fortune can reach everybody. People go abroad to study and then come back with new ideas.'

There are probably cultural reasons that they did not mention, like Qatar's colonial history and its long history of trading with Iran and the other Gulf states. The Saudis, by contrast, issue from the landlocked desert. But Qataris agree that it is their unusual royal couple who are primarily responsible for the country's progressive changes, including the establishment of Al-Jazeera.

'Qatar has a leadership that is willing not just to go hand in hand with the people, but prepared to go ahead and pull them,' explained Souag. 'If you have a leadership that is well educated, open-minded and know what the country needs, then they can go even further than the country and then bring them after. When the Emir took over, he came with ideas. He saw that one of the best ways to move forward was to modernize the media.'

Pulling the country forward whether it wanted to go or not didn't sound like very healthy governance to me. No, both Al-Jazeera men were adamant, this was genuinely a case of the leader knows best. 'Forty years ago, if you had said to Qataris, "Do you want to send your kids abroad to study?" most of them would have said no,' reasoned Souag. 'You have to make people open up.'

'Look, our leadership leads the people,' offered Al-Suwaidan. 'It is no different than when, during the [second] Iraqi war, a million people demonstrated in London against the war. Blair was asked, since a million people oppose it, why are you still going to war? And he said the leadership has to lead. Sometimes he does not have to listen to the public. Sometimes the leader can see further than the public.' It is a persuasive analogy.

Whether all Qataris agree is hard to gauge. In the run-up to the first Gulf war, while Americans in neighbouring Gulf countries, including Kuwait and Saudi Arabia, were being murdered, the Qataris' objections to the Emir turning their tiny country into a giant terrestrial aircraft carrier remained muted. If Qataris take issue with their Emir's decisions, they complain behind closed doors. There is occasional grumbling about some reforms, but as long as there is continued prosperity most people are too busy getting rich to complain much. The creation of Al-Jazeera was an act of liberalism, not one of democracy, and the channel could be unmade as quickly as it was made if one day the Emir changes his mind.

Not that Qataris are all holding on for democracy: many people told me they were very happy with the current system and liked what the Emir had done. 'Democracy would not work well in Qatar,' one Qatari told me. 'We have a small,

family-based country and if someone runs for a political position then, of course, their whole family backs them. This means
larger families can use the democratic system legitimately to
secure power for themselves, which is what has happened in
Kuwait, where families act like lobby groups. We have a strong
leader, with a moral conscience, good values and a pile of
money. Qatar is a special case. Democracy is not the best system
for us.'

Time will tell if Qatar is on the right course or not. The
country has already changed dramatically under the Emir's new
reforms. Qataris are now better educated and more politically
enlightened than ever before. The ratio of work to free time
has changed considerably and now that women have joined the
workforce there is a burgeoning middle class in which both
husband and wife work. In order to let the massive national
wealth trickle down, ordinary Qataris are being allowed to invest
in the economy, in security markets and companies mostly or
partly owned by the government. More social responsibility is
coming. Not long ago there were no taxes and all public services
were free. Now businesses pay limited taxes, as well as for water
and electricity and soon private users will do so too. The new
media, especially Al-Jazeera, have dramatically changed the way
Qataris see the rest of the world. People often call into
Al-Jazeera and complain about their Emir and life in Qatar, but
it is clear that the channel has made them feel Qatar is a player
on the world stage.

The Emir is laying foundations, like free speech and education, which will not bear fruit overnight. Probably the full
impact of the reforms will not be felt until a hundred years
from now.

As well as pursuing reform at home, Qatar has an ambitious
foreign policy that can be summed up as trying to get along
with everyone. It has had controversial ties with America, Israel,
Iraq and Iran all at the same time, it has welcomed exiled Hamas
leaders, given asylum to Saddam Hussein's wife, received visits
from high-level Al-Qaeda members (before 9/11) and sheltered

a Chechen Islamic leader wanted by the Russians. It practises a delicate balancing act that seems to have worked – so far.

In the context of Qatar's maverick tradition, Al-Jazeera perhaps does not seem such an extraordinary phenomenon after all. Nor is this the first time the Arab world has been overrun with exciting new media. Local newspapers first came to the Middle East in the nineteenth century and for years Egypt's *Al-Ahram* was generally considered to be the finest Arab newspaper in print. The Second World War saw the advent of radio in the Middle East in the form of Allied and Axis propaganda radio, after which came the BBC Arabic service, the Voice of America, Radio Moscow and, by far the most popular of all, the anti-imperialist Nasserite Voice of the Arabs.

The sixties brought transistor radios and then television. These were particularly important for the Arab world, since illiteracy rates are still well over 50 per cent in many countries, especially among women. The Iranian revolutionaries recognized this in the seventies, when they used audio-cassettes very effectively to spread their message; Islamic militants today disseminate sermons via CD, DVD or audio files on the Internet.

The seventies and eighties saw the rise of regional news-papers. After the civil war in Lebanon a growing number of Arab newspapers moved their headquarters to Europe. These decades also saw the rise of the Saudi media empires, as wealthy princes backed papers aspiring to promote a perspective on the Middle East sympathetic to the Saudi regime.

The problem with this abundance of media was that it was all controlled either by a Minister of Information or by the financial backers. Its main interest was in serving the govern-ment, which in practice meant much buffing of the ruler's ego. Newspapers and television broadcasts would typically dwell chiefly on what the Sheikh, Emir or President was supposed to be doing that day. Tedious national occasions would be celebrated at length and much airtime was given over to the shaking of hands, kissing of babies and cutting of ribbons. Until the 1990s the Arab media still followed, in spirit at least, a decree laid down in 1865 by the Sultan of the Ottoman Empire that required journalists to 'report on the precious health of the Sultan'.

Sometimes the press was used by the government for other purposes. In Saudi Arabia, for example, where all the press is state-controlled, it is well-established government practice to gauge public opinion on new issues by starting a debate in the newspapers. In the mid-seventies the Saudi newspapers debated whether or not cinemas should be legal for three months, before the King decided that those opposing cinemas were in the majority and banned them.

Unsurprisingly, Arabs learned to despise and distrust everything they heard, read or saw in the media. All the media came to be regarded, quite rightly, as appendages of the government, which only ever echoed, never investigated or criticized, what their leaders said. By way of a substitute Arabs shared news informally in the souk or at the mosque. The spoken word was always privileged over the written word and the person who told you something was often as important as the thing he told you. Although prioritizing the spoken word is anathema to Westerners, who feel happier trusting written documents, in the Middle East this tradition has its roots in Islam itself, where the sayings of the prophet Muhammad are transmitted orally. When Muslims recall these sayings, they do not reflect just on what was said, but on the chain of authority by which it has been remembered. This chain of trustworthy people, called the *Isnad*, is like a guarantee of authenticity stretching back through history.

The most determined in the Arab world looked abroad for news, and for years three major Arabic-language radio stations played a vital role in keeping Arabs in touch with world events: Radio Monte Carlo, which was French, the Voice of America and the BBC. Although these stations were extremely popular and offered a higher standard of news than anything produced domestically, they were Western and so still subject to some suspicion.

Whenever Arabs began to turn back to their state media, for example in times of war, their trust would be disastrously betrayed. The most famous instance of this was during the Arab-Israeli war of 1967, when Arabs everywhere were glued to the Sawt al-Arab radio station founded by Gamal Abdel Nasser, President of the United Arab Republic (Egypt). The beloved announcer Ahmad Said, a household name in the Middle East, declared that the Arab armies had crushed the Israeli army and that Israeli planes were 'falling from the skies like flies'. The rest of the Arab media went on to repeat this message until a week later, when Arabs found out from foreign sources that they had, in fact, been utterly defeated. Arab trust in the media was shattered. Since then the media has done little to win it back: in 1990, when Iraq invaded Kuwait, the Saudi media delayed telling the people for two days.

In May 2004 when Egypt was bidding to hold the 2010 soccer World Cup, the Egyptian Minister of Youth and Culture appeared on television. What he said gave the impression that the nation had indeed won enough votes from the FIFA Executive Board to become the host nation. This was it, thought millions of Egyptians; finally we have won something! Only later when the votes were officially counted did it emerge that South Africa had in fact been chosen, with fourteen votes; Morocco came second with ten; and Egypt was in a humiliating last place, with no votes at all. For many soccer-mad Egyptians, this was as much a hammer blow as being lied to about the progress of a war.

Satellite technology first came to the Arab world in the eighties – the Arabsat satellite was launched in 1985 – but for the first few years its potential was underused. The most important impact it had on the Arab media was in transmitting Arab newspapers edited in London, like *Al-Sharq al-Awsat* and later *Al-Hayat*, to Arab capitals for printing. It was not until after the first Gulf war, when regional governments noted the pivotal role played by CNN, that the strategic possibilities of satellite television were reconsidered. Arab satellite channels started to change and began to offer more round-the-clock news and current affairs programming.

The output was still blatantly self-serving, usually with a

heavy political bias. It steered clear of controversy and avoided anything that mixed religion and politics. The Egyptian Space Channel (ESC), for example, regarded its role as being that of ambassador for Egypt and strived to present a rosy picture of happy Egyptians in breathtaking locations. Lebanese Future TV, headed by Lebanon's billionaire Prime Minister, Rafiq Hariri, aimed to portray a vibrant picture of Lebanon well recovered from the war, in the hope that he might attract investors. Saudi Arabia's MBC (Middle East Broadcasting Centre) broadcast news and current affairs programming from London and became a popular family channel, but it strictly avoided anything that might infringe on the interests of the Saudi government. London-based ANN (Arab News Network), owned by the Syrian President's nephew, also had a strong political agenda. The fact that some of these new satellite chan- nels were based in Europe, out of reach of their own coun- tries' censorship laws, did not mean they offered a higher quality of commentary.

Even today, Egypt's Minister of Information telephones the Egyptian state news bureau every evening with a list of ministers and specific instructions as to the order in which each should appear. On his instructions, Egyptian news dedicates at least one bulletin every evening to the activities of the President's wife, Suzanne Mubarak, usually for several minutes. Extensive airtime is also given regularly to the activities of the President's favoured son, Gamal. Consequently the Egyptian national news still often looks more like the Mubarak family show.

Exactly what Sheikh Hamad had in mind when he decided so firmly to establish a satellite news channel – whether it was for political or financial gain, or out of a genuine yearning for democratic reform – is a matter of opinion.

Probably at least part of his intention was lateral thinking to stop his little country falling victim to a Saddam-style blitzkrieg, as when Iraq had invaded nearby Kuwait in 1991. From the moment he came to power, Qatar's security was always of para- mount importance to the Emir and since he knew from his

Sandhurst days that a military defence of his tiny country was always going to be impossible, he understood that if Qatar were to survive its troublesome neighbours then military self-discipline and planning would be crucial.

His solution was to embrace Arab public opinion. Rather than try and control the flow of information like King Canute's obsequious adviser – and all the other Arab rulers – he guessed correctly that hosting a popular television network would make Qatar much harder to sacrifice in the event of it being attacked. He foresaw that in the modern world, public opinion would be the most powerful shield of all. He first put forward the idea as early as August 1994, when his father was still on the throne. The initial plan had been to upgrade Qatari state television and begin transmitting it via satellite. Indeed in retrospect there are some signs that Qatari state television was a kind of Al-Jazeera prototype. In January 1996 a diplomatic row with Bahrain was ignited when two exiled Bahraini opposition leaders were interviewed on Qatari state TV. Although it was a regular terrestrial rather than a satellite broadcast, the signal carried easily across the water to nearby Bahrain and it miffed the Emir. The Bahraini Minister of Foreign Affairs accused Qatar of cooperating with Bahrain's enemies and deliberately attacking a sisterly state.

Despite, or perhaps because of this early row, the Emir issued a decree establishing a new channel called Al-Jazeera a month later. It was less than a year since he had acceded to power and it was evident that he had been planning it for some time. Preparations for the new channel were quickly underway. A three-man committee, consisting of a Qatari journalist, one of the Emir's close financial advisers and the under-secretary of the Ministry of Information, was appointed to recruit staff. The Qatari Council of Ministers, or Supreme Council, appointed a seven-man board of directors for Al-Jazeera, each of whom would sit for three years. Sheikh Hamad bin Thamir Al Thani, then a deputy Minister of Information, was appointed chairman. The Emir agreed with the editorial board that Al-Jazeera would be independent of his control and that if he were ever to break this pact the result would be their mass resignation.

Initially the plan had been for a channel that was part news and part entertainment, but after the Emir watched a six-hour pilot prepared by the committee in London, he settled on an all-news format. Nine months later, on 1 November 1996, Al-Jazeera began broadcasting.

To help it start up, the Emir gave Al-Jazeera five hundred million Qatari riyals ($137 million) as what was supposed to be a one-off payment. This funding was to cover five years, by which time, it was projected, Al-Jazeera would have achieved financial independence as a commercial operation. As with any other news channel, the plan was to generate sufficient income through selling advertising, programmes and exclusive footage, as well as hiring out equipment to other television stations. Al-Jazeera failed to raise enough revenue by these means, however, and is still receiving financial aid from the government. It has never had a single owner, some of the company's shares being owned by the Qatari government, some by private citizens. Executives have expressed the hope that one day the network might be incorporated as a private company and sell its stock to the general public.

Since Al-Jazeera's inception the Emir has continued to shape domestic policy to sustain the channel. Without his continued political and financial benevolence, it would have ceased transmitting long ago. The new Qatari constitution, overseen by the Emir, enshrined the freedom of the press and was a constitution which in later years he was to quote to the Americans when they pressured him to interfere with Al-Jazeera's output.

In March 1998 the Emir abolished the Ministry of Information, ending press, radio and television censorship. Overnight the government-owned Qatar Radio and Television Corporation, the Qatari Press Agency and the Department of Printing and Publications became independent public institutions. All the media in Qatar, including Al-Jazeera, found their horizons dramatically broadened in terms of whom they could employ and what they could broadcast or publish. Ironically, in Qatar at that time, as in many other Arab countries, satellite dishes were illegal. Al-Jazeera was still available free to Qataris via a terrestrial signal, but until a few years later satellite dishes were seen only on government buildings. Today large satellite dishes are still outlawed.

Even loyal Qataris confess they were astounded when they heard of the sweeping reforms. 'When we heard the Emir planned to abolish the Ministry of Information, we said to each other, this has got to be a joke,' recalled Mostefa Souag. 'This could not happen in the Arab world. When we first heard about Al-Jazeera, we thought this is another joke. Then we saw it and we finally realized that this administration, this elite which came with the new Emir, had genuinely decided to do something different. These are people who had been educated in the West, know what is going on in the world and wanted to apply their ideas in real life rather than be tied down by tradition.'

Seeking Arabic-speaking staff with television news experience, Al-Jazeera profited hugely at the very start from an aborted joint Saudi–BBC attempt to establish a similar kind of service. In the early nineties a prince, a cousin of King Fahd of Saudi Arabia, had set up a satellite television company called Orbit. To have access to European technicians and talent and avoid the kind of government interference that might arise if it were based in an Arab country, the prince decided to base Orbit's operations in Rome. In addition to offering nineteen television channels to paying subscribers, the company approached the BBC to supply an Arabic version of the BBC World Service news. For a long time the World Service had been available in the Middle East in English, but this was to be the first time that a television news channel of this sort had been available in Arabic.

Before agreeing to supply Orbit with its Arabic-language news channel, the BBC insisted the new channel should have the same values as the rest of the World Service. 'If someone wants the BBC they have to take it as it is. Culturally sensitive, yes; but journalism on bended knee, no,' said a BBC spokesman at the time. On 24 March 1994 the BBC and Orbit's Saudi backers signed a ten-year agreement which, on paper at least, looked set to benefit both parties. But there were suspicions that the cultural differences between them would result in disaster. The Arab press wrote off the whole project from the start, dubbing it 'the BBC's Petrodollar Channel'.

Broadcast from the BBC studios in west London, the new Arabic BBC news service grew incrementally from two hours of broadcasting a day at the start to eight hours by the end of 1994. But it was not long before the relationship fell apart over the perennially sticky issue of editorial control. There had been growing friction over what should be broadcast, before a blistering row in 1996 proved cultural differences in this instance to be insurmountable. Angry telephone conversations and board meetings revealed that what had been meant by 'cultural sensitivities' turned out to mean editing anything with which the Saudi royalty disagreed.

The final controversy came in two stages, and the first revolved around a Saudi dissident called Professor Muhammad Al-Mas'ari. Al-Mas'ari was the head of the Committee for the Defence of Legitimate Rights, an influential Islamic organization, banned in Saudi Arabia and based in Britain, which vehemently opposes the House of Saud. Since his expulsion from the kingdom, Al-Mas'ari had campaigned relentlessly against the Saudi royal family, calling for strict Islamic rule instead.

In January 1996 Al-Mas'ari debuted on Orbit's BBC Arabic service, but halfway through his interview a mysterious and timely blackout occurred, embarrassingly ending the transmission. Although Orbit denied it, besides the BBC they were the only ones who could have stopped the broadcast, by cutting the power from Orbit's central command in Rome. The BBC was furious, accusing Orbit of censoring its broadcasts and breaking their agreement, which had granted the BBC complete editorial control. The BBC was faced with the painful decision of pulling out of the deal with Orbit or compromising its editorial independence. It settled on the latter.

The Saudis were furious too, that Al-Mas'ari had been on Arab screens in the first place, and a storm erupted between the British and Saudi governments. The Saudi Ministry of Information instructed hotels in the kingdom not to broadcast any Orbit channels at all and the Saudi Ambassador insisted on Al-Mas'ari's immediate deportation from Britain, thus ending his media campaign against his homeland. If Britain refused, he warned, Saudi Arabia would terminate arms contracts worth billions of pounds, putting thousands of jobs at risk. Shamefully, Prime Minister John Major and Home Secretary Michael Howard acquiesced to the Saudis' demands and agreed to deport Al-Mas'ari to the Caribbean island of Dominica. But, to the deep embarrassment of the British government, Al-Mas'ari successfully appealed against the judgement in court. The British press condemned John Major for sacrificing Al-Mas'ari's human rights on the altar of Saudi arms deals.

The second and final blow to the relationship came a few months later when a BBC *Panorama* documentary entitled *Death of a Principle* was highly critical of Saudi Arabia's human rights record. Aired uncut in Arabic on Orbit's BBC service, the programme revisited the Al-Mas'ari affair and dynamited any chance of a reconciliation. It showed a Saudi funeral, a Filipina living in Saudi Arabia who testified in an interview to having been flogged for going out with male friends and, most controversially, a man about to be decapitated by a sword-wielding executioner. Although the actual moment of beheading was not shown, filming executions is illegal under Saudi law. 'This programme was a sneering and racist attack on Islamic law and culture,' said Orbit's president. The BBC Arabic service was abruptly switched off on the night of Saturday 20 April 1996, eighteen months after it had begun. A week later it was replaced with the Disney Channel.

At first the BBC thought that the show might go on, if only another rich but slightly more liberal Arab sponsor could be located. After all, the operation had been conducted from the BBC studios in London. But Orbit, it emerged, was determined to obstruct any new BBC Arabic project and was formidably placed to do so. Orbit's Saudi financiers were so influential that they had a stranglehold on any potential backer who ever wanted to do business in the Middle East again. Nor, after the recent scandal, was the British government in any hurry to help the BBC get the channel up and running again.

As if this panoply of obstacles was not enough, Orbit also owned all the computers and technical equipment that the BBC Arabic service had been using. The company had supplied the lot at the start, on the understanding that this was somehow more tax-efficient, and now it exercised its right to do absolutely nothing with it all, and not let anyone else either. The purpose-built digital studio was left empty and unused on the BBC's premises while executives spent a few fruitless weeks trying to strike a new deal.

The sudden closure of the Arabic channel left about 250 BBC-trained Arab journalists, broadcasters and media adminis trators out of a job. They were also out of a dream, for they had shared a vision that the Arabic service was going to make a difference in the Arab world by setting a higher standard than the tawdry and venal reporting of state television news. Offered the opportunity to work on a news channel without the same editorial reservations, 120 of them swiftly signed up with Al-Jazeera, which had just been established. Approximately a quarter of the total number of Al-Jazeera's employees were Qataris, the rest were drawn from all over the Arab world. Many were Palestinians, perhaps because Palestinians tend to be better educated and travel more than other Arabs. Palestinians are well represented among Arabs in other news organizations too, includ ing the BBC.

Many of these journalists went on to become some of the most familiar faces on Al-Jazeera. If the winner in this affair was Al-Jazeera, the losers, in the short term at least, were the tens of millions of Arab viewers who had just begun to acquire a taste for quality, independent news in Arabic when it was abruptly taken away from them.

'The BBC Arabic service was the beginning,' Mostefa Souag told me. He worked for the Arabic station from the day it opened to the day it closed. 'For the first time Arabs had the chance to watch Arab journalists doing the news and making programmes to the same standards as Western news channels.' Although the Arabic service was in part a foundation for Al-Jazeera, as Souag points out there were also some important differences between the two. 'The BBC project was different: the audience was very limited, because the channel was not free,' he explained. 'We were broadcasting just eight hours a day and it never ran long enough to create the kind of impact that Al-Jazeera has had. Al-Jazeera, on the other hand, broadcasts twenty-four hours a day, has a large audience and is free in most places, especially in the Arab world. It's broadcast from an Arab capital, in an Arab country and managed by Arabs themselves: the BBC was none of these things. Al-Jazeera was the first time Arabs discovered it was possible to have an Arab institution that they could respect.'

The collapse of the BBC Arabic service was an emotional time for its staff, many of whom were left in limbo. Souag, who had been a professor of English literary theory at Algiers University between 1985 and 1993 before working for Saudi Arabia's MBC, had dropped everything to be part of the BBC Arabic project. His story was typical: in October 1994 he had left a good job for the promise of a new life with his young family in London, attracted by the prospect of a career with the BBC, a company which carries tremendous prestige in the Arab world. All the staff were told they could expect to be employed for at least ten years. When the venture fell through after just eighteen months, many had already bought homes or were in the process of exchanging contracts on them. The dramatic demise led to huge personal problems. Many of the staff were no longer entitled to stay in Britain, while others, like Souag, had young children who were settled into school. No one at the time could have guessed that the ashes of the BBC project would turn out to be the most solid of foundations for Al-Jazeera.

★

Initially Al-Jazeera began broadcasting just six hours a day from just one satellite, the Arabsat satellite. In January 1997 this was bumped up to eight hours, then twelve hours daily. Arabsat, short for Arab Satellite Corporation, launched the satellite, which is jointly owned by twenty-one Arab states, in 1985. When Al-Jazeera first started broadcasting from it, the Arabsat satellite's global 'footprint' – the area on earth where its signal could be received – uniquely covered the Middle East. Today there are plenty of other satellites whose footprints overlap with this, but in those days when Arabsat was the only one, for a network to keep transmitting, it was crucial that it remain on good terms with Arabsat's management. Arabsat's headquarters and control facilities are in the Saudi capital, Riyadh.

Television satellites have a fixed number of transponders that are rented by TV stations so that they can broadcast their signals. In this case the Arabsat satellite's transponders were already virtually fully booked and Al-Jazeera had to settle for a Ku-band transponder, which had a weak signal. What Al-Jazeera wanted was a C-band transponder, which generated a much stronger signal receivable with an ordinary, small satellite dish. The terms 'Ku-Band' and 'C-band' refer to the frequency of the signal. To get a decent picture on the screen from a puny Ku-band signal you needed a very large satellite dish, six feet in diameter or bigger, which most of Al-Jazeera's potential audience did not have. With little or no reception in much of the Arab world, Al-Jazeera's first year slipped by without the channel making much impression. At the same time other new satellite channels were blossoming across the Middle East and Africa. Kenya, Uganda, Mozambique and South Africa all launched satellite ventures; two private Lebanese channels were expanding into satellite television; and Egypt was about to launch its very own satellite. Amid this scramble, Al-Jazeera, largely unreceivable in the Middle East, went almost unnoticed.

The leaseholders of the coveted C-band transponder on the Arabsat satellite were a French television channel called Canal France International (CFI). About 4 o'clock one Saturday after-

noon in July 1997, this channel was supposed to be broadcasting an educational programme for schoolchildren in the Middle
East. Unfortunately for CFI, a technical mix-up at France
Télécom meant that thirty minutes of a hard-core pornographic
film called *Club Privé au Portugal*, destined for customers in the
Pacific, was beamed in its place. Contemporary CFI broadcast
data suggested that a possible thirty-three million people across
the Middle East could have been watching, including plenty of
children expecting educational material. Predictably, the Saudis,
who controlled the satellite, were outraged, as CFI had offended
the most basic Islamic ideals. There would be no compromise:
despite protests from French diplomats, Arabsat tore up the
contract and expelled CFI from the Arabsat satellite, leaving the
coveted C-Band slot free. Al-Jazeera took the channel's place a
few months later. History does not record what happened to
the French technician who was responsible for the mishap. Only
when Al-Jazeera started transmitting from the C-band transponder in November 1997 was it in a position to compete
seriously with other satellite channels. At the same time as it
changed transponder, it increased its programming schedule to
seventeen hours each day.

Today Al-Jazeera is available all over the world, but its main
viewership is still to be found in the Middle East. From the
swankiest suburbs of Dubai to the poorest slums of the Palestinian
refugee camps, Arabs are watching Al-Jazeera. With the demise
of Saddam Hussein's regime in Iraq, satellite dishes are now
widespread in every Arab country and a growing expatriate
community is tuning in too. In Britain it is offered as part of a
subscription service on Sky Digital, or you can get it free-to-
air through certain satellites, like Hotbird. In the United States
and Canada around two hundred thousand subscribers pay the
Dish Network between $22.99 and $29.99 a month to receive
Al-Jazeera as part of a multi-channel Arabic package.

Because illiteracy rates are high in Arab countries, newspaper
circulation remains low and the printed media play only a
complementary role in how most people receive their news.

The television is the most important source of news. In Arab
countries Al-Jazeera is free, and all that is needed to receive it
is a satellite dish costing about $100. Dishes are now so common-
place that when impoverished desert Bedouin get married they
are no longer given jewellery but a satellite dish instead, so the
newly-weds can watch the news. In the remote desert you see
Bedouin tents made of goat hair, animals tethered outside, bare-
foot children all around – and a dish on the roof.

2

Making a Splash in the Arab World

Al-Jazeera was just one of a large number of new satellite channels flowering in the Middle East in the nineties. But the fact
that it was one of the few fully Arab news stations, run, staffed,
and financed by Arabs and broadcast from an Arab country, was
a significant development and continues to be a source of pride.
The network's longer schedule and greater availability, combined
with its liberal programming, meant that once it became more
widely receivable on the C-band transponder it would not go
unnoticed for long. Guests were deliberately selected to be as
controversial as possible and for the first time Israelis speaking
Hebrew appeared on Arab television. This was a major depart-
ure from anything done before and was truly shocking for the
Arab public. Many Arabs had never seen an Israeli speak before.
But what made Al-Jazeera's name in the Arab world first, long
before it became famous in the West, was its talk shows.

Political, social, economic and religious topics are all regularly tackled on Al-Jazeera's talk shows. They help draw a wider
audience to the station, although the average Al-Jazeera viewer,
as with news stations in the West, is still a man aged over twenty-
five. As the names of the shows suggest, most welcome viewers' opinions, by way of phone calls, faxes or emails. The audience
often plays an important role in the direction shows take and
plenty of heckling is not uncommon.

Among Al-Jazeera's best-known programmes is *More than One Opinion*, a political show presented from London by Sami Haddad. This is a live debate between invited guests. Normally there are more than two guests present, so it is more like a round-table discussion than a polemical debate. *Without Borders*, presented by Ahmad Mansur, is a gritty face-to-face interview, like Tim Sebastian's *Hardtalk* on BBC World, often with a politician who has made himself flavour of the month by doing or saying something controversial. *Top Secret* is a fearless documentary show that investigates a controversial topic and appears irregularly. Broadcast on Saturdays, *Open Dialogue* pits a group of ten or twelve members of the public against a guest. *Only for Women* is a ninety-minute programme about women's issues that runs on Mondays and is hosted by a bossy Syrian lady called Luna Shebel, who seems to provoke either love or hate in most of the women I spoke with. Other shows run for a set duration, for example during an election campaign, and then end. Weekly shows are usually aired live once and repeated later the same week.

Al-Jazeera's two most famous programmes, which have been running since its inception, are *Al-Ittijah al-Muakis* (*The Opposite Direction*) and *Al-Sharia wal-Hayat* (*Religion and Life*). Both these weekly talk shows feature guests discussing contemporary issues, while the host holds the ring.

The Opposite Direction, modelled on CNN's *Crossfire*, is a political show which airs every Tuesday for ninety minutes. It is anchored by Dr Faisal al-Qasim, a Syrian Druze who attended Hull University, where he studied, appropriately enough, drama. He is an unlikely-looking star, with spectacles and hair combed sideways over his bald spot. The show's formula is simple: two guests who have completely opposite opinions argue about a controversial theme, while Dr Al-Qasim stirs it up. Typically, an Arab dissident living in exile from his homeland is pitted against a representative from that same country's government, with incendiary results.

Al-Qasim's PhD thesis was a study of iconoclastic British

dramatists and he is enthralled by the idea that art and drama can change society. 'I like defrocking political and religious figures,' he told me. 'I like de-iconizing icons.' Besides being the presenter, Al-Qasim also writes and researches every show single-handedly and books all the guests himself with his mobile phone.

On one show Dr Al-Qasim posed the question 'Are Hezbollah resistance or terrorists?', which two doctors had been invited to debate, one Egyptian and one Lebanese. The broadcast was taking place before the Israeli military withdrawal from South Lebanon and the Lebanese Shiite Muslim guerrillas of Hezbollah were widely considered a respectable resistance movement against the Israeli occupation. Asking the question at all was scandalous to many Arabs, because they believed that to cast the slightest doubt on Hezbollah's legitimacy was a kind of betrayal.

Screaming, shouting, threats, insults, marching off set, *The Opposite Direction* has seen it all and consequently is, without question, the most popular show of its kind in the history of Arab television. Al-Qasim chooses topics with aplomb that ignite the most heartfelt reactions – and so the biggest arguments – between his guests. Sometimes he sides with one guest against another, but always his provocative comments and questions are aimed to extract the most explosive response. The show has been the source of numerous international disputes and instigated the severance of diplomatic relations with several neighbouring countries.

The Opposite Direction took some months to reach its zenith of popularity, because at first guests were unsure about participating in something so radical. Once it did, it was simply quite unlike anything ever seen before on television in Arabic. Saudi's Orbit had in the past run a more demure talk show, more like *Larry King Live*, which dared to feature some fairly risqué guests, but it was never as frank-talking as *The Opposite Direction*. Here, for the first time, Arab rulers would be openly slated as lackeys of the US and their policies blasted as sycophantic, treacherous and corrupt.

Still, some guests were nervous about the possible consequences of appearing on the show. On one occasion a Tunisian liberal went on air wearing a false moustache, so that Islamic militants might not be able to recognize him afterwards. Unfortunately, in the heat of the debate the moustache came unstuck, giving Al-Qasim the giggles.

The opportunity for members of the public to call in and join the mêlée was also something of a novelty in the Arab world. On Al-Jazeera, unlike most Arab networks, although an operator asks the callers what they want to say before they go on air, no protective time delay is used in their dialogue with the guests. Callers are aired completely live and often for much longer than on Western television. Each talk show continues to receive hundreds of calls.

In a region where free speech is scarce, the kind of free debate seen on *The Opposite Direction* was revolutionary. At first the Arab viewing public was sceptical that this was as simple as it looked. There were doubts that the callers were really ordinary members of the public, rather than the Mukhabarat, the secret police. Today the show is more or less accepted as genuine, although Arabs remain divided over its merits. Some believe it to be the first step towards democracy; others just think it's a shouting match.

Although still relatively unknown in the West, the show has made Dr Faisal al-Qasim one of the most famous faces in the Arab world and, simultaneously, the subject of deep suspicion. Although today there are plenty of imitators on other Arabic channels, still no other political talk show is anywhere near as popular. When Al-Qasim stepped down as presenter for a few weeks, the switchboard was inundated with calls from viewers complaining that the show had lost its edge. Without Al-Qasim, they said, *The Opposite Direction* might as well change its name to *The Same Direction*, since there were not any good debates any more.

When he appears in public, Al-Qasim is mobbed unless he wears a disguise, and it is often said that Arab cities go noticeably quieter when his show comes on the air. He has stood accused of being secular, a communist, a Freemason, a Zionist and an Arab nationalist all at the same time. 'I have also been accused of collaborating with the intelligence service of every country in the world except Togo and Burkina Faso,' he said.

He still receives piles of hate mail, though most of it now comes from the Mukhabarat, or secret police, he thinks. Years of practice mean he has become something of an expert at differentiating real hate mail from secret-police hate mail, which comes mainly from Syria and Egypt. It is strange to think there is someone in a police station in Damascus whose job it is to write letters to *The Opposite Direction* all day, but I don't doubt it is true.

Although he likes to make light of his fame and all the threats he receives, the truth is Faisal al-Qasim lives in fear for his life. His house is in a gated compound in Doha and whenever he leaves, he finds himself always looking over his shoulder. 'Every day I turn the key in the car, I thank God it doesn't blow up,' he told me. 'Every single day.' And God forbid, if one day he was blown up, I asked, where should we start looking for the culprits? He paused to think for a second. 'I have so many enemies . . .' he mused. Then it came to him. 'Governments, Foreign governments. The Mukhabarat.'

Religion and Life is another of Al-Jazeera's more famous regular shows. It is broadcast every Sunday evening at 9.05 Mecca time. The presenter invites Sheikh Yusuf al-Qaradawi to come on the show, except when the Sheikh has been called away on urgent Islamic business. Although something of an institution in the Arab world, Sheikh al-Qaradawi needs some explanation because he is certainly unlike anyone who might be a regular guest on a Western television network. In his seventies, he is a highly respected Islamic cleric and not actually an employee of Al-Jazeera. His ninety-minute show tackles the conundrums of modern life from an Islamic perspective. Anything goes, from politics to sex, and the Sheikh is renowned for his frank talking. Drawing on his encyclopedic knowledge of the Koran, he irons out problems for puzzled viewers on everything from extramarital sex to suicide bombings. *Religion and Life* draws thousands of enquiring letters every week from across the world and bootleg videos of old episodes are translated and sold in souks as far away as Indonesia and Malaysia.

It is hard for a secular Westerner to grasp how or why someone could hold as much sway as Sheikh al-Qaradawi. In Islam, great respect is vested in the most senior clerics, and their fatwas, or religious pronouncements, carry immense weight. Through the Internet and his Al-Jazeera TV slot the Sheikh's verdicts influence hundred of millions of Muslims all over the world, both Sunni and Shia. Most regard his opinions as a guideline. Some regard them as the unassailable truth.

The Sheikh is a passionate advocate of the Internet, since he believes its transnational nature protects the online Islamic community from pernicious government meddling. He has overseen the creation of the website Islam Online (www.islam-online.net), which serves as a database of fatwas pertaining to modern life. Advertisements run on other Arab television channels encouraging viewers with a religious query to log on to his website for advice. You can even email your chosen mufti for an online fatwa.

Sheikh al-Qaradawi is a religious exile, expelled from his native Egypt some forty years ago for membership of a religious organization called the Muslim Brotherhood that for decades opposed the Egyptian government. After a bungled assassination attempt on Egypt's President Nasser, many members of the Brotherhood were rounded up, imprisoned and tortured. After being jailed several times, tortured and banned from preaching in Egypt, the Sheikh left Egypt for the Gulf. He settled in Qatar, where he has lived for some thirty-odd years, teaching at the university and occasionally serving the interests of the state by conferring religious legitimacy on the Emir's new social policies. On occasions when Saudi clerics have condemned Qatar's liberalization on religious grounds, Sheikh al-Qaradawi has sprung to its defence. Over the years he has developed an extremely high media profile, writing books about progressive Islam and now guest-hosting *Religion and Life* on Al-Jazeera.

The Sheikh belongs to a school of Islamist thinkers who emerged in the nineteenth and twentieth centuries, when Arab countries were struggling to assert themselves as nations for the first time. Subject to Western power, these thinkers advocated interpretations of Islam that found ways to incorporate new social developments while simultaneously criticizing Arab leaders for their venality and incompetence. His flexible interpretations of the Koran contrast starkly with the Islamic conservatism still found in Saudi Arabia and Afghanistan. It goes without saying that he sees no contradiction in using modern technology – indeed he regards it as his duty – to spread his fatwas. Sheikh al-Qaradawi practises what he preaches: his daughters are highly educated, drive and work.

Although in the past his religious opinions have helped bolster support for the Emir's liberalization, opinions differ widely on whether the Sheikh is a moderate, a conservative or even a force for good at all. Certainly it helps anyone involved in Middle Eastern politics, from America to Al-Qaeda, when he arbitrates in their favour. The Sheikh's reputation in the West was scuttled and his American visa annulled after he passionately endorsed Palestinian suicide bombers, but his interpretations of the Koran keenly favour women's involvement in politics and he believes strongly that democracy and Islam are compatible. He helped the Americans by endorsing American Muslims who fought against Al-Qaeda in Afghanistan, but he opposed the invasion of Iraq and called for a jihad, or struggle, against France for banning headscarves in schools.

Unlike many Islamic leaders, the Sheikh strongly denounced 9/11, but at the same time pointed to the suffering of the Palestinians under Israeli occupation. He issued his fatwa 'despite our strong oppositions to the biased American policy towards Israel on the military, political and economic fronts'. Rather than support a military response to 9/11 he called for the criminals to be brought to justice in a court of law. One of the most memorable episodes of *Religion and Life* concerned Koran-sanctioned sex. The Sheikh shocked conservative viewers by saying the Koran makes it clear that parents cannot force their daughters to marry suitors they do not like. As concerns sex, he is decidedly liberal: as long as it is between consenting adults, more or less anything goes.

Sheikh al-Qaradawi is a one-off, a contradictory character who has become one of the most influential men of contemporary Islam. Although he condemns religious leaders who prostitute their authority to politicians and kings, he has, as his detractors point out, served Qatar well, largely because he shares with the ruling family an enthusiasm for educational reform across the Islamic world. His supporters claim he is a moderate who has promoted science, democracy and economic development strategies that aim to close the gap between rich and poor.

Besides America, the Sheikh's principal critics have been extremist Muslims living in London who have attacked his liberal attitudes towards women and his partiality to movies and music, which are regarded as un-Islamic. Without getting caught up in evaluating the merits or otherwise of the Sheikh and the New Islamist ideas he espouses, it is enough to say that if nothing else his opinions can be regarded as an important barometer of public opinion. Al Jazeera distances itself from his rulings, but he hosts one of the channel's most popular shows.

While Dr Faisal al Qasim and Sheikh Yusuf al-Qaradawi are two of the most famous faces on Al-Jazeera, it would be a mistake to think that they are the stars. No one person could be said to dominate its output, just as no individual dominates the BBC. But, just as in the West, viewers are loyal to shows, not channels, and many people tune in specially to see these two figures.

It did not take Al-Jazeera's talk shows long to whip up controversy. In November 1998 an episode of *The Opposite Direction* matched a Syrian writer against a former Jordanian Foreign Minister

to debate Jordan's current economic and political situation. The
Syrian argued that Jordan's 'warm peace' with Israel was at the
expense of its relations with Arab countries. The Jordanian
insisted that all Arab countries were gradually developing closer
ties with Israel and that there was nothing remarkable about this
relationship. As the debate heated up, the Syrian became increasingly derogatory about Jordan, referring to it as an 'entity' that
had been created solely to serve as a counterweight to Israel, to
help its expansion by absorbing Palestinian refugees. Jordan's very
existence, he said, was part of a greater Zionist plan and it was
common knowledge that Jordan had been conspiring with Israel
since the latter's foundation in 1948 to subvert the Palestinian
cause and commandeer the region's scant water supplies.

Less than twenty-four hours after the show had aired, Jordan's
Minister of Information, Nasir Judah, appeared on Jordanian
Television insisting that until the Qatari administration took steps
to stop the 'notorious' Dr Faisal al-Qasim 'spitting poison' in his
'intentional and repeated campaign against Jordan', the Jordanian
Ministry of Information would revoke the accreditation of all
of Al-Jazeera's six staff working in the bureau in Amman. This
would effectively close down the bureau. He said that only after
an official, public apology could Al-Jazeera's operations in the
Jordanian capital resume.

'We got a letter from the Jordanian authorities saying that our
office in Amman has been closed down,' said Al-Jazeera's managing director. 'The letter says, "You attacked the Jordanian people
and the Jordanian royal family." The Jordanian action is an over-
reaction to the programme. We are an independent channel
covering everything without bias or prejudice to anyone.' He
refused to send a letter of apology and the Al-Jazeera bureau in
Amman remained closed for the next four months.

This was a completely new development for Jordan. Although
what the Syrian had said on Al-Jazeera was the kind of thing
that Arabs had been saying to one another behind closed doors
for years, it was not the kind of thing that could be said on
television. Ties with Qatar had always been close and the

Jordanian Ministry of Information had never before made a fuss like this about a programme.

But they were not the only ones who objected to what was being discussed on *The Opposite Direction*. Taboos were being broken almost every week. Guests debated whether Islam was an obstacle to social progress, whether the House of Saud was corrupt, whether Kuwait was really a part of Iraq and whether Arab countries should allow America to station troops on their territory. One particularly scandalous episode about Islam had guests questioning the existence of God and comparing the Koran to the Declaration of Human Rights.

Walkouts and rows were becoming weekly fare. An Islamist Egyptian writer stormed off the set on air after a Jordanian feminist provoked him in a debate about polygamy. The former Algerian premier marched off in a huff when he lost an argument to an Islamic fundamentalist. Viewers were flabbergasted when a little-known Syrian intellectual told an eminent cleric that the reason the Arabs had been defeated in the Arab-Israeli war of 1967 was because Islam was a constricting and backward religion.

Sheikh al-Qaradawi's *Religion and Life* also got off to a flying start. The episode in which he pronounced that Koranic rules of moral conduct were compatible with fellatio was one of the most talked-about in years.

This kind of thing had simply never been seen before and Arab viewers were immediately spellbound, but it was not long before Al-Jazeera incurred the wrath of conservatives. Articles in the Saudi press heavily criticized Al-Jazeera. An article entitled 'Arabsat and another kind of Pornography' congratulated Arabsat on firing CFI for transmitting *Club Privé au Portugal* and went on to suggest that they should waste no time in firing Al-Jazeera for similarly outraging morality.

In December 1998 the Arab States Broadcasting Union (ASBU) decided to expand, going from being an organization made up solely of state-run broadcasters to include private Arab radio and television broadcasting institutions. This was part of a new policy which it had been developing throughout the nineties in an effort to free the Arab media from government control. An internal ASBU policy document written by its director-general in 1995 said that free media was a good thing as it gave broadcasters 'more credibility in citizens' eyes'.

All the private Arab radio and TV stations were invited to become members of ASBU, except Al-Jazeera, which was banned. The stated reason was that all members needed to demonstrate a commitment to Arab media principles and show respect to the Arab League Charter. Al-Jazeera was not the only offender: as one Qatari newspaper noted cynically, some channels 'which offer only nudity' had been allowed to join but only Al-Jazeera had been singled out for special treatment. The message was clear: if Al-Jazeera wanted to be in the club it had better start behaving.

Among the first to realize the potential of this new Arab platform for free speech were radical groups that had grown accustomed to censorship. During 1998, whenever the Palestinian Islamic resistance movement Hamas was invited on Al-Jazeera, it would seize the opportunity to announce policy or make threats. It was confident that every time it appeared it would find a large, transnational Arab audience and would never be edited. Hamas's founder and spiritual leader, Sheikh Ahmad Yasin, appeared several times and each time used the opportunity to make important points live. Other minority groups soon cottoned on to the idea. For example, Aslan Maskhadov, the President of Chechnya, seized his chance on Al-Jazeera and called on the US and the UN to intervene in his beleaguered homeland against the Russians. A sense began to develop among regional leaders that appearing on Al-Jazeera conferred credibility on what they had to say.

The mercurial Libyan leader Colonel Muammar Qadhafi used his appearance on Al-Jazeera in August 1998 to pull off a publicity stunt aimed at building bridges with America. This was just one in a series of unnoticed signs from Qadhafi, indicating his desire to come in from the political wilderness in which he had been languishing throughout the nineties at the behest of America. Keen to make amends for past crimes, he offered President Clinton the loan of a lawyer live on Al-Jazeera, to help tackle the political fallout arising from his affair with the White House intern Monica Lewinsky. 'I have no bad intentions towards [Clinton], and I was willing to send him a lawyer to defend him . . . Clinton is not Reagan, who was ridiculous, an idiot, aggressive and behaved like a cowboy,' said the Libyan leader afterwards.

In addition to the Israelis, various militant groups and Colonel Qadhafi, other regional pariahs who were surprised to find their opinions welcome on Al-Jazeera after years in exile were the motley cohorts of the Iraqi dictator, Saddam Hussein. In December 1997 Al-Jazeera began a relationship with Iraq's Ba'ath Party that was to provoke international censure for years to come.

Al-Jazeera, which had several Iraqis on its staff, some of whom had come direct from Iraq to start work in Doha, recognized that since no other international networks had a functional relationship with the Iraqi regime, there was a great opportunity in Baghdad. From 1997, when Al-Jazeera first opened a bureau in the Iraqi capital, the network covered events in Iraq more extensively than any other Arab news station. The biggest Arabic news channel, MBC, had no one at all in the country. In April 2000 Al-Jazeera's director-general even visited Iraq himself and met Saddam's son Uday, who was the owner and editor-in-chief of the Iraqi state newspaper.

Iraq was as friendless within the Arab world as it was in the West, and Al-Jazeera's sudden coverage provoked deep suspicions that the network had more than a professional interest in the regime. Suspicions that something fishy was going on were heightened by the Qatari Foreign Minister's vigorous condemnation of the coalition's persistent air attacks on Iraq and his appeals to the UN to lift the sanctions against the country.

This foresight by Al-Jazeera's management was soon to pay off with their first big international scoop. In 1998 tension was

mounting in Iraq because Saddam's regime had been refusing to
cooperate with UN weapons inspectors or to allow them to visit
so-called 'presidential palaces'. Iraq had accused them of passing on to America secret information uncovered during their
work – something the inspectors denied at the time but which
later turned out to be true.

On 16 December, at the start of the Muslim holy month of
Ramadan, Britain and America launched a punitive seventy-
hour military campaign against Iraq code-named Operation
Desert Fox. Some one hundred targets across Iraq were destroyed
to inhibit the production of weapons of mass destruction, or
WMD.

Al-Jazeera was the only news network to bear witness to the
successive waves of laser-guided bombs and cruise missiles as
they landed in Baghdad. Its cameras captured Republican Guard
facilities and suspected chemical and biological plants being
blown to smithereens. Fifteen minutes after the explosions
appeared on Al-Jazeera, they were on other networks all over
the world, as the exclusive footage was sold.

On 18 December the front page of *The Times* of London
carried a picture of a cruise missile exploding in Baghdad. It
was a still photo taken from television footage and at first glance
the logo in the corner of the picture looked like it had come
from CNN. Only on closer inspection could you see
Al-Jazeera's logo underneath CNN's.

Even though at this stage almost nobody in the West had
even heard of Al-Jazeera, the channel's staff in Doha regarded
Operation Desert Fox as the first landmark in its news coverage. This was, by any standards, a sensational scoop and it
ensured Al-Jazeera would become the Iraqi regime's news
network of choice. After covering the attack it found its operations in normally oppressive Iraq became easier. The regime
had learned a lesson about working with rather than against the
media, and senior Iraqi officials, including the Vice President,
the Deputy Prime Minister and the Foreign Minister, all came
forward offering interviews. From then on, whenever they had

the chance to appear on Al-Jazeera they grasped it, so that they could tell the world about their suffering under air strikes and sanctions, deny the existence of WMD and call for the impeachment of the American President. On Iraq's Army Day in January 2000, Saddam Hussein's speech was broadcast on Al-Jazeera even before it appeared on Iraqi state television – another coup for the channel.

In a telling display of the regime's new-found media awareness, during an interview with the Iraqi Deputy Prime Minister, Tariq Aziz, although both he and his interviewer were native Arabic speakers, when he came to condemn the bombing he would switch to English. By speaking in English, he hoped his remarks would be more widely quoted on Western radio and television and so maximize his chances of influencing Western public opinion against the air strikes. In the event, he was probably right.

The governments of the other countries in the region did not appreciate this sudden rash of Ba'ath Party gorillas on Al-Jazeera. Saudi Arabia, Kuwait and the free Kurdish community had all recently been menaced by Saddam Hussein and when he called for Arabs to rise up against them, calling their leaders 'stooges of American imperialism', this was viewed as unacceptable propaganda. Since there was nothing much that could be done about Saddam himself, according to regional logic the channel whose logo hovered behind his ear whenever he spoke would have to be targeted instead.

Kuwait's Minister of Information accused Al-Jazeera of doing all it could to rehabilitate the Iraqi regime. In Saudi Arabia, where the state speaks through its newspapers, one editorial dramatically asserted: 'The dangers posed by this channel are far more serious than the dangers posed by Western satellite channels. Simply speaking, the poisonous ideas that are conveyed via the Western satellite channels are easy to handle because the thought they are trying to convey is known to the viewer in advance. However, when this poisonous thought is conveyed via an Arab satellite channel, it becomes all the more dangerous because it is concealing itself behind our culture and claiming to be speaking for the sake of the overall Arab interest in general and the Arab Gulf region in particular.'

Al-Jazeera's director-general responded by denying that he was a mouthpiece, be it for Saddam Hussein or anyone else. He said he had given airtime to the regime's pawns simply because what they had to say was newsworthy. He accepted that they might have chosen to appear on Al-Jazeera because it was widely regarded as credible by a large audience in the Arab world, but that did not detract from their newsworthiness.

Western media analysts were less judgemental about Al-Jazeera's relationship with the Iraq regime. They did not necessarily suspect that Al-Jazeera was at fault because it gave airtime to the regime. It came as no surprise to most of them that Saddam should choose to make important speeches on Al-Jazeera; in fact, it seemed quite natural that he should seek to make speeches on this hot new network, in the hope that some of its popularity might rub off on him.

The screening of Saddam and his men had a galvanizing effect on the Arab street. Although Arab governments regarded the Iraqi dictator at best as a wild card and at worst as a danger, many ordinary Arabs thought of him as a hero. Al-Jazeera's coverage of Operation Desert Fox and the subsequent defiant speeches by the Iraqis sparked a ripple of protests in the Arab world against what many regarded as a foreign invasion of the Arab heartland.

Another adept self-publicist who made an early appearance on Al-Jazeera was Osama bin Laden. At that time virtually unknown in the West, he was already a famous and feared threat in the Middle East. Libya had been the first country to issue an official Interpol arrest warrant for the Al-Qaeda boss, along with three of his associates, in March 1998. America later played down Libya's alert, but a few months later bin Laden became the prime suspect in the August bombings of the American embassies in Kenya and Tanzania, which killed over two hundred people and injured thousands more. By Christmas 1998, when he made his debut on Al-Jazeera, he was already a wanted man. With what was to become recognizable as his characteristic dramatic timing, in a pre-recorded message on Christmas Day 1998 bin Laden urged Muslims to kill Americans, Britons and Jews in Palestine in response to the attacks on Iraq.

Bin Laden had been interviewed before by the American news network ABC, but never by an Arab news channel. So when, in June 1999, Al-Jazeera announced it had recorded an exclusive interview with him there was a flurry of excitement across the Arab world. The interview was heavily advertised well in advance. There was some speculation in the press about what he might have to say. Meanwhile, all the Gulf states neighbouring Qatar made it clear to Al-Jazeera that they did not want the interview to be aired at all. Bahrain, Kuwait and Saudi Arabia were frightened of bin Laden's popular appeal. To many Arabs he was a hero, someone who had escewed a life of luxury to live in a cave and fight imperialist America. In Saudi Arabia, possession of a copy of his speeches earned six months in prison.

Excitement swelled even more when, three days before the programme aired, the FBI announced it was adding Osama bin Laden to its 'Ten Most Wanted' list and offered a reward of $5 million for information leading to his arrest. On the day of the show many millions of viewers were glued to their seats to watch the ninety-minute special.

It was not clear when or exactly where the interview took place, but it looked as if it was coming from a hideout in Afghanistan. An Al-Jazeera spokesman said that it had been recorded months previously, but why it had not been broadcast sooner was not made clear. Wearing a camouflage army jacket and a white turban, bin Laden looked fit and well as he sat cross-legged on the floor, a Kalashnikov propped up by his side. His soft eyes and calm words belied his radical message: jihad against the United States.

For Saudi Arabia and Kuwait, televising bin Laden was an unforgivable offence. Both countries already had great internal problems with militant Islamists and the last thing they needed was someone so influential calling for jihad. Bin Laden's prime objective has always been ridding the Islamic holy land of American troops and implicit in his call for jihad against America was an exhortation to destabilize the Arab regimes most friendly to her.

Up to this point the Saudi authorities had not been making life easy for Al-Jazeera: the network's journalists were already banned from working in the kingdom, except when accompanying the Qatari Emir or covering the Hajj, the annual Muslim pilgrimage to Mecca. But after the network aired the bin Laden programme the Saudis decided that from now on they were going to clamp down on it in any way they could.

The authorities warned the public to look out for Al-Jazeera's pernicious influence and the state press derided its pro-Baghdad bias. Speaking about the network, the Interior Minister, Prince Nayif, declared: 'Saddam has started to make a breakthrough in the Gulf countries. That channel is a distinguished high-quality product but it serves up poison on a silver platter. We know that this channel is an offspring of the BBC and we know who stands behind it. The only difference is the location and the financier.'

A Saudi newspaper editorial in May 1999 accused Al-Jazeera of fabricating news coverage and interfering in the internal affairs of other countries. In the mosques imams denounced Al-Jazeera for corrupting Arab morals and passed a 'political fatwa' forbidding Saudis from appearing on the station's shows. The one Saudi journalist who worked for Al-Jazeera in Doha was put under pressure to quit his job.

Saudi magazines were banned from speaking with or interviewing Al-Jazeera staff, the network's reporters were no longer even allowed to cover the Hajj and watching satellite television in coffee shops was forbidden. Although Al-Jazeera was not expressly mentioned in the coffee-shop ban, it was clear that it was the target, because coffee shops are where young men socialize and debate issues, especially when they are watching the news. But little could be done to prevent viewers at home from turning their satellite dishes to pick up Al-Jazeera and videos of past episodes of *The Opposite Direction* continued to change hands in Saudi markets for as much as $100 each.

The Kuwaitis, who were marginally less perturbed by the bin Laden tape than the Saudis, managed to refrain from imposing the same kind of restrictions. At least they did until a few weeks later, when, in June, an episode of *Religion and Life* about women's rights prompted the immediate closure of Al-Jazeera's bureau in Kuwait. The Emir, Sheikh Jaber al-Ahmad Al Sabah, had recently granted Kuwaiti women the right to vote and to run for parliament, and the merits of this decision were being analysed, when an anonymous caller to the show, claiming to be an Iraqi in Norway, said something rude about the Emir. In Arabic, if you are speaking about someone important respectfully, it is customary to ask God to save him. Instead the caller suggested God should be called upon to kick the Emir out, since he was someone 'who embraces atheists and permits foreign armies to enter Kuwait', referring presumably to the coalition forces that had fought against Iraq in the first Gulf war.

Since the programme was live, there was nothing that could have been done to stop the caller, but being rude about the Emir is banned by the Kuwaiti constitution and so naturally the Kuwaitis were furious.

The Kuwaiti newspapers speculated that since the mysterious Norwegian-Iraqi caller had been allowed to finish his anti-Kuwaiti tirade without being cut off, this was proof that Al-Jazeera had a policy of targeting Kuwait, which is exactly what everyone had suspected since Al-Jazeera had started reporting from Baghdad.

The Kuwaiti Minister of Information was so appalled that he flew to Qatar at once to lodge his protest in person. Even if the caller could not have been simply cut off, he told the Qataris, the presenter could at least have done more to reprimand him for his seditious comments. Al-Jazeera, he said in a statement, had 'violated the ethics of the profession and harmed the State of Kuwait'. The Emir of Qatar explained that Al-Jazeera was an autonomous company responsible for its own editorial decisions and he had nothing to do with this process.

In the end the Kuwaitis revoked the press credentials of the single Al-Jazeera correspondent in the country and ordered the management in Doha to close the bureau. This remained shut for a month, before the Kuwaiti authorities cooled off and lifted the ban.

Saudi Arabia and Kuwait were not the only countries that complained about Al-Jazeera in these early years, but they were especially important because, as Al-Jazeera was soon to learn, between them they could control who in the region spent what on television advertising. It was commonplace for Arab rulers to refer to Al-Jazeera as the 'suspicious channel'. Its ideological sympathies were suspected at times of lying with Saddam's Ba'athists, bin Laden and his Islamic militants or even Israel. For years Al-Jazeera received almost daily complaints from neighbouring governments.

Al-Jazeera's charismatic manager of media relations, Jihad Ballout, deals with these incessant complaints. The network's media relations department is not in the same prefabricated bunker in Doha as the newsroom, sitting in its sandy compound. It is in a new office tower block with panoramic views of the Persian Gulf's sapphire waters. Jihad Ballout is perhaps the member of staff at Al-Jazeera that non-Arabic speakers are most likely to have come across, as occasionally in recent years he has appeared on Western television as the public face of the network. Suave and mustachioed, he has the air of a slightly haggard pop star yet has acquired a reputation for talking Al-Jazeera out of the stickiest of situations with the signature slickness of someone who has spent a life in PR. He weighs every word carefully when he speaks to the press and lets you know with sincere gravity if he is about to tell you something off the record. Before joining Al-Jazeera, he worked in PR for Phillip Morris, so I guessed his silver-tongued charm belied a readiness for a good scrap.

With Jihad Ballout, business is not business unless it is conducted with plenty of cigarettes and sweet black coffee. Having spent months trying to pin him down for two minutes, I was amazed when he gave me three hours of his time. Like all of the Al-Jazeera staff I met, his mobile phone rings ceaselessly, but when he gave me his attention it was formidably focused, save only for the occasional interruption by his deputies as they silently dropped off computer printouts of the latest attacks against Al-Jazeera that they had skimmed from the world press. Jihad furrows his brow as his eyes flick over the headline, momentarily drifting away from our conversation. 'O God! Why are these people so stupid?' he asks himself rather than me. 'I'm sorry I really have to refute this one.' Quickly he explains to his assistant in Arabic that this latest attack on Al-Jazeera, whatever it might have been, might call for a public statement when our meeting was over. 'I'm sorry, we're having a hell of a morning as usual,' he says, coming back to me.

'When we first started receiving complaints they were frustrating. In the same breath we were being accused of being anti-Israeli by Israelis, Islamists by seculars and Arab nationalists, Arab nationalists by Israelis, Americans and Islamists, funded by the CIA, funded by bin Laden and funded by Saddam Hussein. And then it just became funny,' he smirked, puffing on his cigarette.

Al-Jazeera did find it funny, but there were some serious diplomatic repercussions. Libya withdrew its ambassador 'permanently' after an episode of *The Opposite Direction* in which a Libyan dissident called Colonel Qadhafi a dictator; the Palestinian Authority accused Al-Jazeera of 'besmirching the Palestinian struggle and distorting the image of the Palestinian Authority' after it ran an interview with the leader of Hamas; the Egyptian and Algerian governments both took exception to the appearance of Islamic extremists; the Tunisians severed diplomatic relations with Qatar after members of the Islamic opposition criticized Tunisia's human rights record; an interview with a Bahraini opposition figure prompted fury from the capital, Manama; Iran objected to what it called 'false and biased reports' and 'imperialist propaganda' about Iran; Morocco recalled its ambassador from Qatar, claiming Al-Jazeera had 'led a campaign against Morocco, against its democratic evolution, its institutions and image'; the Syrians regularly insinuated that Al-Jazeera was a Zionist plot sent to sow discord.

Ironically, the only regional Arab ruler who did not complain about Al-Jazeera was the most reviled of them all, Saddam Hussein, who calculated that he had more to gain from Al-Jazeera's reporting of his people's plight under sanctions, than from any attacks on his repressive government. Only once, in May 2000, did he object to Al-Jazeera's coverage of his extravagant birthday celebrations, because the pictures of food undermined his case that UN sanctions were starving his country.

Within a year of becoming more widely available on the C-band transponder, Al-Jazeera stood accused of being pro-Iraqi, pro-Israeli, militant Islamist, an agent of the British and a pawn of the Qatari government. The contradictory nature of the complaints showed that there could be no substance to the allegations of bias. 'Ultimately it worked in our advantage, not because we were an enigma, but simply because it gave an indication that people did not want to believe that there could be a professional news organization in the Arab world,' said Jihad Ballout. For him, it was predictable that Al-Jazeera should be opposed in the Middle East; it was the Western criticism that bothered him. 'I can understand it in the Arab world. They had been living in virtual darkness for decades, being spoon-fed information. But the West, obnoxiously, felt an Arab couldn't produce a professional news bulletin, which was really frustrating.'

Arab ambassadors in Doha said they spent so much time complaining about Al-Jazeera that they felt more like ambassadors to a TV channel than ambassadors to a country. Occasionally, after an ambassador had lodged an official complaint he would add off the record that he thought Al-Jazeera was doing a great job. Nevertheless, the Qatari Foreign Minister, Sheikh Hamad bin Jasim bin Jabr Al Thani, who was a major shareholder in

Al-Jazeera, confessed that all the complaints he received whenever he set foot abroad gave him a monster headache.

Many of the complaints related directly to *The Opposite Direction*. The show's presenter, Faisal al-Qasim, shrugged this off as a good sign that he was doing his job properly and Al-Jazeera's official line never changed: that the station was completely independent of all groups and countries, that if it were found to be partisan then it would destroy its credibility for ever. Newsworthiness, accuracy and objectivity were always cited as essential ingredients for any story and Al-Jazeera denied it ever set out deliberately to embarrass or upset another country. The idea, spokesmen always maintained, was to present the Arab viewer with two sides of every argument, as per the channel's motto 'The opinion and the other opinion', and then let him make up his own mind.

Although it was acknowledged that Al-Jazeera was dependent on a loan from the Emir of Qatar, the channel denied this impinged on its journalistic integrity. There were no 'red lines' that could not be crossed. Al-Jazeera liked to compare itself to the BBC, funded indirectly by the state but free to say whatever it wanted. Neither the BBC nor Al-Jazeera was the official voice of its government and so it is wrong for complainants to persist in blaming the government of Qatar for Al Jazeera's programming.

The obvious solution for all these irate neighbours might seem to be to jam Al-Jazeera's satellite signal. One very effective means of banning unwanted television signals, which the Saudis have used in the past, is by transmitting endless recitation of the Koran. The Koran, which is recited twenty-four hours a day in Mecca, has an almost constant level of modulation and if its average picture level, or APL, is suitably high, it is ideal for use in jamming. The Saudis have portable, air-conditioned, medium-wave transmitting stations which they maintain for exactly that purpose. On receiving an unwanted signal, they can drive to the border to start broadcasting the Koran on a loop.

But jamming a satellite signal is technically more difficult than jamming a regular television signal. Also, it is almost impossible to do this over a large area for any practical duration. Authoritarian governments had tried occasionally in the past, but success had been partial and brief, if achieved at all.

Instead, Arab countries who felt maligned had to resort to more imaginative methods to obstruct Al-Jazeera, like harassing correspondents and obstructing visa requests. State-run television companies refused to share footage or facilities with the network, forcing it to become more technically independent than it might otherwise have chosen to be. Despite the obstructions, Al-Jazeera usually managed to air news with pictures from within all the countries in the region.

'It is easy to get footage with modern technology,' explained Ballout. 'Some of the time we got calls from people with tip-offs and information. The days are long gone when you can punish a news organization by keeping it out of a certain field of action or area. Banning us is detrimental, more so to the state or government or authority itself than to the media. The media can always get access – there are umpteen other ways the media can get access.'

Faced with the impossibility of jamming the Al-Jazeera signal or stopping the news-gathering operation, Arab countries sometimes resorted to extreme measures to obstruct Al-Jazeera's transmissions. To stop Algerians watching one particular episode of *The Opposite Direction* in January 1999, the Algerian government settled on a more radical approach. An exiled journalist was due to debate the country's long-running civil war with a card-carrying representative of the leftist government regime. Algeria's brutal civil war, which has claimed over one hundred thousand lives, has been marked by human rights abuses on a grand scale. Many of these deaths have been extrajudicial killings by government security forces. So the Algerian government, concerned that the debate might sooner or later touch upon these atrocities, shut down power to several major cities, including the capital, Algiers, ten minutes into the programme.

By the time the Algerians felt it necessary to take this dramatic step to inhibit Al-Jazeera's broadcasts, the network had become the scourge of the region's rulers. All the governments agreed that Al-Jazeera was biased, but there was no agreement on quite how, beyond the fact that each thought that the network targeted them.

There was a growing sense that Al-Jazeera did not analyse the Qatari regime as critically as it tackled its neighbours. In May 2000 a leading Tunisian newspaper, *Al-Sabah*, questioned the 'independence' of the station: 'If the Al-Jazeera TV channel really believes in freedom in general and freedom of expression in particular, why has it not mentioned, even once, the fact that dish antennas are banned in Qatar? Why has it not mentioned that citizens and residents of Qatar can only use cable television that transmits a few channels selected and approved only by the Qatari authorities?' This accusation was true, for until 2001 satellite receivers were forbidden in Qatar, although Al-Jazeera was free to all on cable.

Al-Jazeera's officials knew that the financial and political protection they received from the Qatari government was likely to raise questions about the network's partiality, but, while insisting that with a native population of only a couple of hundred thousand Qatar was hardly a news priority, they pointed to the occasions on which Al-Jazeera had criticized Qatari officials, policies and ministers. Al-Jazeera had featured jailed Qatari dissidents who accused the government of torture and in November 1997 had criticized Israeli participation in an Economic Summit Conference held in Doha, which was an implicit criticism of Qatari government policy.

Despite all the accusations and controversy, in its first four years Al-Jazeera succeeded in capturing the attention of viewers from the Persian Gulf to North Africa. In November 1998, only one year after the channel had become widely available on the C-band transponder, yet before the start of the twenty-four-hour service, the Dubai-based television-rating agency the Pan Arab Research Center estimated that Al-Jazeera was already one of the major news providers in the Middle East. Specific figures did not exist, but it was thought to be accessible in 60 per cent of homes under the satellite's footprint. Media analysts predicted financial independence by the year 2000, one year earlier than expected, as a result of anticipated higher advertising revenues.

On 1 February 1999 Al-Jazeera began broadcasting twenty-four hours a day from three different satellites, over the Middle East, North America and Europe. The channel now employed about five hundred people, up 150 from the year before, and had twelve bureaux, mostly in Arab countries but also in Europe and Russia. Preparations for two new digital channels were announced, one exclusively devoted to documentaries, the other a special channel in English that would transform Al-Jazeera into a fully international service, like the BBC. In May a deal was signed with Iranian Television and an office opened in Tehran. At the same time Al-Jazeera entered into a partnership with an Israeli cable TV company, which packaged Al-Jazeera together with other Arab channels for Israeli Arabs living in Haifa and Netanya. A partnership with BSkyB in Britain was on the table. In February 2000 Al-Jazeera and CNN were each invited by the oppressive Taliban regime to open a bureau in Afghanistan. CNN declined, but Al-Jazeera, having learned from its recent experience in Iraq the benefits of being the only news station in the country, went to considerable trouble and expense to establish itself, a decision that was to prove extremely significant in the future.

In September 2000 an opinion poll conducted by the Palestinian Central Bureau of Statistics for a Palestinian newspaper showed that nearly 75 per cent of Palestinians in the West Bank and Gaza chose Al-Jazeera for their first source of news, even though it was the only channel to let Israelis speak. Despite its controversial interviews and the ban imposed by ASBU, in 2000 Al-Jazeera won three international journalism awards and signed a cooperative deal with a major Russian news agency.

'No one paid any attention in 1996,' said Jihad Ballout. 'People just thought, another news organization that is financed and run by a Gulf country to raise its stature and its profile around the world.' For Ballout, Al-Jazeera came of age in 1998. 'During the Desert Fox operation in 1998, which was the birth of Al-Jazeera internationally, we were the only international news organization on the ground. No one else was there. We had detractors, Americans, but it was low-key because we had not become sophisticated enough to appreciate the value of our position – as simple as that. We had only been operating two years.'

After this important scoop, concerted efforts by regional powers, especially Saudi Arabia, to censor Al-Jazeera helped raise the network's profile. 'Only when we got down to real journalism did we become a destabilizing factor regionally,' said Ballout. 'When we started encroaching on taboos in the Arab world, be they social, political, religious or whatever, I think the regional status quo, all the way from Algiers to Yemen, started to feel threatened by Al-Jazeera. It was then that all these allegations started about being Israeli, being CIA-financed and so forth, especially when we took a professional decision to entertain Israeli spokespeople on our screens. They were not concerned about Israelis coming on television. It was the manifestation of everything Al-Jazeera had claimed.'

So hungry were Arabs for a reliable Arabic-language news service that they wolfed down Al-Jazeera's menu of accurate news and inflammatory talk shows as fast as they could. By June 2000 analysts suspected that Al-Jazeera had thirty-five million viewers each night, which would make it easily the most watched Arab news channel, knocking Saudi Arabia's MBC into second place and the London-based ANN into third. State news stations were left trailing.

The Opposite Direction became the most popular TV show in the Arab world and Faisal al-Qasim rose to cult status and collected thousands of articles about himself in the Arab press, most of them overwhelmingly hostile. 'This man's tongue should be cut out,' suggested one Jordanian columnist.

News channels like Al-Jazeera traditionally expect to make most of their money from selling advertising slots and at first glance the Middle Eastern market appears to be an advertiser's dream. Historically, the main obstacle to advertisers in the Arab world has been market fragmentation: different terrestrial TV channels covered different countries, each of which had to be handled in its own way. But with the advent of satellite television all this is a thing of the past. Transnational channels like Al-Jazeera can now tap an international marketplace stretching from the Gulf to North Africa and consisting of more than fifty million tele-vision-owning households, hundreds of millions of people, most of whom can be reached in one language – Arabic. In most Arab countries the majority of the population is under eight-een, watches a lot of television and is relatively susceptible to advertising. The Gulf countries and Saudi Arabia are the tradi-tional targets as their populations have large disposable incomes. Today satellite television also reaches the wealthy Arab expatri-ate market. The regional satellite television advertising industry, including Al-Jazeera's advertising office, is centred in Dubai.

But satellite technology has presented multinational marketers with problems as well as opportunities. The biggest problem for Al-Jazeera is that the way in which the advertising dollar is spent in the Middle East is a political decision and Qatar's rich Gulf neighbours have used this as a weapon to fight Al-Jazeera on commercial grounds.

Saudi Arabia is the dominant economic power in the region, Kuwait the second. The kingdom has the largest potential market in the region, about 90 per cent of its twenty million potential customers speak Arabic, which is far greater than the number who do so in the Gulf countries, which are largely made up of non-Arab expatriates. In addition, Saudi Arabia controls a large network of Arabic newspapers, magazines, press agencies and advertising companies. Advertising companies which might be tempted to advertise on Al-Jazeera have been coerced by their government into taking their business elsewhere. Initially all Al-Jazeera's adver-tising was managed by one Saudi company, the Al-Tuhama Advertising Company, which has close links to the Saudi royal family, but in February 1999 Al-Tuhama cancelled its contract.

Al-Jazeera suspected this was because of pressure from the Saudi authorities. The affair wound up in court.

'You have to understand how the economic situation in the Gulf operates,' Jihad Ballout explained. 'Let me give you an example: a luxury car dealership is controlled by one family in Saudi Arabia. Usually to be successful in business in any Arab country you have to be close to the high echelons of power. No one will get the dealership of any international brand if they are not close to the ruling power. So the boss in Munich calls the dealership and says he wants to advertise on Al-Jazeera because they understand that Al-Jazeera is the best vehicle for advertising. The dealership goes back to Munich, saying, "Listen, this is going to jeopardize a tender that we have for 650 vehicles or motorcycles and cars for the police force."

'So the regional advertising budget – and Al-Jazeera is deemed to be a regional medium – is really controlled by regional merchants and dealerships and the most powerful by far are the Saudis. For every two cars sold in Bahrain seventy may be sold in Saudi. If I wanted to put it diplomatically I would say that the powers that be in the region have convinced major advertisers of the wisdom of not using Al-Jazeera as an advertising medium.'

Nor is this the only mechanism of control the Saudis have over where the advertising dollar goes. Technically, satellite dishes are banned in the kingdom. In practice this ban is not enforced, but the Saudi authorities have made it clear to big-name advertisers that if they gave custom to Al-Jazeera they could implement the ban and in future permanently deny those same advertisers access to the large Saudi market.

'My belief is ultimately economic common sense will prevail and stakeholders will start wondering why money is being thrown away, but this needs a shift in social attitudes. How long it will take, I don't know – I hope it is in my lifetime,' said Ballout mournfully.

But even if the Saudis did loosen the restrictions on regional advertisers doing business with Al-Jazeera, there are still other

problems. For example, there is a serious dearth of accurate viewing data in the Middle East and this makes advertisers nervous.

Measuring audience statistics is nearly impossible and is calculated by analysing so-called 'viewing points', which means hotel
rooms and coffee shops, as well as private homes. Subscription
rates to pay-TV channels, like adult channels, are not divulged
and so evidence is largely anecdotal. Many people in the Middle
East watch satellite television sourced from illegal dishes or via
illegally shared satellite connections. Cheap satellite dishes and
smuggled reception devices found their way into every country
in the region except Iraq. In Algeria, Morocco and Lebanon
informal networks were set up so many households could share
one dish. In 1999 it was estimated that access to satellite television in Lebanon increased fivefold in one year, but most
Lebanese households were watching satellite television illegally.
A whole street could share one subscription by running a wire
from house to house. In Morocco satellite dishes became known
as 'couscous dishes' because they were considered such a basic
household staple.

Viewer statistics from Iran and Saudi Arabia were particularly
misleading. In Iran satellite dishes are technically illegal, although,
as in Saudi Arabia, this law is not enforced. After the first Gulf
war Saudis bought dishes in droves despite the ban. In 1999
analysts estimated that 60 per cent of Saudi households had
access to satellite television, but since most of the dishes were
on private property there could be no proper accounting for
them. Dishes were legalized in Syria only after the regime decided
they were apolitical, but a glance at the Damascus skyline revealed
that this law had been long ignored anyway. A Syrian estimate
in 1999 concluded that nearly a third of homes in that country had a dish.

Even if the number of dishes could be calculated it was almost
impossible to know what anyone was watching on them. Modern
viewers are loyal to a programme, not a channel, and once a
commercial break starts they tend to zap to another channel. In
the Middle East commercial breaks can be fifteen minutes long,

so a commercial in the middle of a break is unlikely to be seen by many people at all. Advertisers trying to assess who might be watching their ad at any given time now have to calculate where in the slot it might be placed and what would be showing on all the other channels at the same time.

'It is extremely difficult to do any kind of census in the Middle East and that is to do with cultural considerations as well as technical considerations,' said Jihad Ballout. 'Firstly we are free-to-air in the Middle East, so it is virtually impossible to know how many people are tuning in to your station at a certain time. Secondly, Arabs, or Muslims in general, are a little bit apprehensive about people knocking on their door and asking them intrusive questions.'

With so many problems and variables it is hardly surprising that different monitoring bodies have often come up with data that varies dramatically. For example, the Dubai-based monitoring service Ipsos-Stat estimated in 1999 that terrestrial television in the Middle East had made $240 million in advertising revenue. By contrast, the Pan Arab Research Center estimated that terrestrial television had made just $100 million from advertising, while a third body, the trade magazine *ArabAd*, estimated it had made only $55 million.

Despite the confusion, during the late nineties the amount of money spent on Arab satellite television advertising grew enormously. In the 1980s, before satellite television, Middle Eastern advertisers had a straight choice between spending their money on TV, radio, print or outdoor advertising. In 1996 just over $100 million in advertising revenue was available to pan-Arab satellite stations. According to the Pan Arab Research Center, despite an economic downturn, this figure almost doubled between 1996 and 1997. In 1998 the figure grew again, and just over $355 million in advertising revenue was available to be split between all the various satellite TV channels.

But as the advertising market grew, so did the number of satellite channels competing for a slice of the cake. By the end of 1999 the Middle East had one of the most crowded commercial television markets in the world. Besides pay-TV channels, in most of the Middle East you could receive at least sixty terrestrial and free-to-air satellite channels in Arabic, around five more in English and another six in Hindi. Competition was so fierce that television channels were offering steep discounts to advertisers, and with a growing number of channels and a finite number of advertising dollars to go around, industry analysts predicted some of them would have to go bust. In 1998 MBC, traditionally the biggest Arab television news channel, with forty million viewers, laid off 120 employees in an effort to make the station financially independent before its main sponsor, King Fahd of Saudi Arabia, died.

From Al-Jazeera's point of view this all spelt trouble. Live news coverage is an expensive business which involves transporting people and valuable equipment to remote and sometimes hostile environments. Opening new bureaux around the world is not cheap either, and the benefits take years to come through. The price of additional shifts and new staff and equipment all added up.

So, despite its success, at the start of 2000 Al-Jazeera was still in the red, but confident that it would be making money by 2001. Its annual running costs were estimated at about $25 million, but being blacklisted by the Saudis had cost the network a hefty $10–13 million.

Although Al-Jazeera's running costs were comparatively low by regional standards – Iran's state television network Voice and Vision broadcast about 70 per cent of Al-Jazeera's output yet employed an army of sixteen thousand permanent and twelve thousand contract staff – its management decided to start looking for other avenues of income besides regional advertising, including more American and European sponsorship, as well as syndicating their documentaries and programmes to other Arab networks. Operation Desert Fox had been a lucrative scoop, but to do this again meant beating the Western news stations at their own game. In the meantime Al-Jazeera's oil-rich patron would have to continue to supply vital financial support.

3

The Second Intifada

The second Palestinian intifada, or uprising, began in October 2000, when Palestinians rose up against the Israelis' presence in the Occupied Territories. It continues to this day and thousands have since been killed. Most of the dead have been Palestinian civilians. The first few weeks and months of the intifada were an important time in Al-Jazeera's history. The network's reporting of events in the Occupied Territories had social and polit ical consequences not just in Israel and the Occupied Territories but also in the rest of the Middle East.

Before the events of October 2000 Al-Jazeera had affected politics inasmuch as it had caused diplomatic rows, upset autocratic regimes and stirred up fierce internal debate within Arab countries. During the second Palestinian intifada Al-Jazeera became a forum for those involved in the uprising and a window for those outside. For the Israelis this was a shock. Their traditional hegemony over the media came to an end and they realized that they had to develop new strategies to win world public opinion. Even the Western television stations, long accustomed to their superior position, began to sit up and take notice of Al-Jazeera during the autumn of 2000. As the Arab public followed the events of the intifada hour by hour, Al-Jazeera became a household name across the Arab world, although it remained still largely unknown in the West.

In late 2003 Al-Jazeera's bureau in Ramallah, in the West Bank, moved into a smart new office, but its bureau chief remains the same man it has always been: Walid al-Omary. He has one of the most dangerous jobs in the world, but he faces it fearlessly because he believes passionately that he has a duty to bear witness to what has happened to both sides under the Israeli occupation. Tall, with a slouch and an endearing crooked smile, Al-Omary has kind, red eyes that have seen thousands of bodies since the intifada began. Conversations with him never last long before being broken by a call on one of his three mobiles or his pager. One phone is for Israel, one for Palestine and the third for international calls. He needs three because there is no connection between the Israeli and Palestinian ones. 'The telephones round here are like the people. They don't talk to each other,' he explains. His pager carries information from the Israeli press office, schedules from the Israeli parliament, called the Knesset, and special announcements from the Israeli Defence Force.

Al-Omary's patch is the West Bank, Gaza and Israel. Getting his story has often nearly cost him his life. A month before the intifada, during clashes in Hebron, he took a rubber bullet in the leg. Israeli settlers have attacked him and his crew on several occasions, not because they were journalists but just because they were Arabs. Once, when he was covering a news story in an Israeli settlement, settlers surrounded and attacked his car. The police told him to leave for his own safety, saying there were not enough soldiers in the surrounding area to protect him. In Hariya, after a suicide bomb, furious onlookers attacked Al-Omary and his cameraman, again simply because they were recognizable as Arabs. On another occasion, in a settlement near Bethlehem, he was tailed by a settler in a jeep with a gun, but rescued by an Israeli news crew from Channel 2 TV.

Walid al-Omary is from a small village in Israel, near Nazareth. He studied international relations at the Hebrew University in Jerusalem, followed by media and communications at Tel Aviv University. In his second year in Tel Aviv he started working as a translator and journalist to pay for his education, translating

Hebrew to Arabic. Today he is still Al-Jazeera's simultaneous live translator for important Knesset speeches. Al-Omary's in-depth knowledge of both Palestinian and Israeli society, his language skills, bravery and hack's obsession with a good story ensured he had plenty of work as a stringer long before Al-Jazeera was established. It takes special skills to cover news in Israel and the Occupied Territories, not just because it is dangerous and there is a shortage of basic facilities but also because journalists have to understand how to satisfy two quite different authorities, one Palestinian and one Israeli. The conflict today is between two societies, between and within which a journalist must be able to navigate if he is to make any headway at all, which is an extremely sensitive business.

When Al-Omary graduated from Tel Aviv University he became the Head of Israeli Affairs at the Palestinian press office in East Jerusalem, at the same time working as a correspondent for a Palestinian magazine based in Cyprus. In 1989 he began reporting for a Paris-based radio station and worked as a correspondent for a Palestinian magazine based there. Four years later he began work as a freelance journalist for various American stations, reporting on the return of the Palestinian authority after the Oslo peace agreements. For the next two years he worked freelance, while occasionally appearing as a consultant on Israeli TV. He started a full-time job at NBC in 1995 but left the following year after he was offered work on the first Al-Jazeera pilots. He was never involved with the BBC Arabic service.

Several other Arab satellite channels approached him at the same time as Al-Jazeera, but, disenchanted by the prospect of churning out more bland Arab news, he decided to take his chances with the then unknown Qatari newcomer. He was attracted by Al-Jazeera's promise of a free-speech Arab television news channel. The executives at Al-Jazeera promised him this was going to be unlike any news channel ever seen before in the Arab world, so he agreed to give the channel a three-month trial, which was then extended to six months, after which he had a feeling Al-Jazeera was going to take off. Since then he has been on call for Al-Jazeera in the West Bank twenty-four hours a day every day of the year. He has been on holiday only once, to Australia for a month, because his wife, who is Vice President of the West Bank's Birzeit University, is Australian. Besides reporting for Al-Jazeera, he lectures at Birzeit's Institute of Media and has published several books about the news, Israeli policies and the media. When he can find the time today, he is writing a book about his experiences covering the intifada.

The Arabic word 'intifada' is usually translated as 'uprising' but it also has connotations of 'shaking off'. The first intifada was sparked in 1987 after an Arab summit meeting in Jordan when the Arab leaders effectively abandoned the Palestinian cause. It lasted six years, although the social and political conditions that underpinned the uprising had been years in the making. Both the first and second intifada were born out of deep-seated, bitter, pent-up frustration with both the Israeli occupation and the ineffectual Arab leadership.

During the second intifada Al-Jazeera played an important role in fomenting some of the discontent, by fearlessly investigating the failings of Yasser Arafat's Palestinian Authority (PA). Within three months of the start of transmission Al-Jazeera had the first in a long series of confrontations with the PA's Legislative Council, Arafat's inner office, over a report by the channel on the denial of human rights to Palestinian prisoners held in PA jails. Over the next few years Al-Jazeera and the PA were constantly at loggerheads. In 1998 the PA threatened Al-Omary with arrest for what it called 'unbalanced reporting', which it said was undermining its authority. On several occasions during 1999 and 2000 Al-Jazeera journalists were harassed and denied access to Arafat's compound. Once three PA heavies in Gaza severely beat up an Al-Jazeera reporter.

The biggest bone of contention between Al-Jazeera and the Palestinian Authority was the network's exhaustive coverage of the power struggle between the PA and the popular militant Islamist group Hamas. Hamas had been founded at the start of the first intifada with the short-term aim of driving Israel out of the Occupied Territories. Funded in part by Saudi Arabia and Kuwait, Hamas had enough money to provide a basic welfare service to the Palestinian poor, which soon made it extremely popular. The PA, by contrast, had a bad reputation for corruption and had failed to impress the rule of law on either Gaza or the West Bank. While Hamas leaders enjoyed a reputation for austerity and justice, the PA's leaders were known for their nepotism, flashiness and hordes of hangers-on. Contrary to popular belief in the West, most Palestinians do not support Hamas because it is violent: they support it because it is kind.

Al-Jazeera's reports on the inefficiency and corruption of the PA provoked frequent denouncements that the channel was the lackey of Hamas. The PA often accused Al-Jazeera of being funded by Israel and strongly objected to its policy of interviewing Israelis. Sometimes it even complained about Al-Jazeera labelling Israel as Israel on the regional map the channel sometimes showed on the screen.

In the years leading up to the second intifada, the Palestinian people had grown to trust Al-Jazeera's judgements in the frequent disputes between it, Hamas and the PA, and they had grown correspondingly disillusioned with their government. By September 2000 their political disenchantment had reached breaking point. Frustration since the collapse of the Oslo peace talks in 1993 had been compounded by another round of failed peace talks in the summer of 2000 at Camp David in America. As the world dithered, the Palestinians saw their leaders becoming more corrupt while the Israelis continued to build more settlements. They could see no end to their daily privations and humiliation.

The spark that ignited the second intifada was a visit to a holy site in Jerusalem sacred to both Jews and Muslims by the right-wing General Ariel Sharon, who was then the Israeli opposition leader. The site is known to the Jews as Temple Mount and to the Muslims as Al-Haram al-Sharif. Sharon was already notorious among the Arabs for the role he had played in the invasion of Lebanon in 1982, when he had let his Christian militia allies slaughter between eight hundred and two thousand (depending on whose figures you believe) Palestinian men, women and children in refugee camps in a four-day killing spree. His visit to the Temple Mount was regarded by Arabs as a deliberate provocation and led immediately to spontaneous violent demonstrations. These quickly became known as the 'Al-Aqsa intifada', after Jerusalem's Al-Aqsa mosque, where they began. Unlike during the first intifada, this time many of the Palestinians were armed with guns and sporadic shoot-outs occurred.

Two days after the intifada began a news crew captured on camera the shooting of a twelve-year-old Palestinian boy by Israeli soldiers. A firefight had been underway between Palestinian militia and Israeli troops in Gaza when Jamal al-Durra and his son Muhammad were caught in the crossfire. Muhammad was filmed being shot in the abdomen. Pinned down by fire and unable to get help, he died in his wounded father's arms. The pair had not been demonstrating, nor armed or throwing stones: they had just been walking home. This grim vignette went into heavy media rotation around the world and in the Arab countries Muhammad al-Durra immediately became a *shaheed*, a martyr, which is the controversial title awarded to anyone who dies for the Palestinian cause. A graceless initial response by the Israelis to the accidental killing added to Palestinian fury and ensured Muhammad al-Durra would become the poster boy of the intifada.

Al-Jazeera ran repeatedly the clip of the boy being shot, and for several days the picture of his dying became the network's emblem of the intifada. This had a deeply galvanizing effect on the wider Arab public. Arabs everywhere became desperate for bulletins from the Occupied Territories, but state-run Arab news providers were slow to give good coverage. In the first days of the intifada, when Palestinians had begun fighting in the streets, Jordanian TV was still running its usual fluffy programme schedule of saccharine music and vapid talk shows, interspersed with dreary staged monologues by government spokesmen.

Underpaid producers and editors knew what they were missing, but the wheels of Jordanian bureaucracy turned so slowly that when a request to break with the official state schedule was logged it took days for a decision to come back from the top.

From the very start Al-Jazeera's live coverage from the front line far outstripped any other network's coverage. Bulletins about confrontations between the Palestinian stone throwers and the Israeli army soon gave way to images of Palestinian corpses and ghastly operating-theatre scenes. The only guidelines were that close-ups of the dead were not shown and the faces of the Palestinian fighters would be obscured, so that the Israeli security forces could not identify them from news footage. The names of the dead would not be mentioned on camera until there had been confirmation that their parents knew, so that no one found out their relation had died by watching the news. Normally this was not an issue as names were rarely mentioned. Only when an important leader was killed was it important, for example when Al-Jazeera broke the news that Abu Ali Mustafa, the leader of the radical Popular Front for the Liberation of Palestine, had been assassinated by an Israeli helicopter.

Al-Jazeera was not the only choice available to viewers. By now there were some thirty pan-Arab satellite television channels, broadcasting from almost every Arab country and reaching all twenty-two Arabic-speaking nations. These included MBC and Abu Dhabi TV, as well as a Palestinian channel, Orbit, Rafiq Hariri's Al Mustaqbal from Lebanon and Hezbollah's Al-Manar. This last, whose name means 'the lighthouse', had begun broadcasting the previous month, and so was the newest Arab satellite news channel. Al-Manar remains one of the most popular militant news stations in the region. The BBC and CNN were also widely receivable in English.

Al-Jazeera consistently had the best footage of the intifada and one important reason was that the Palestinian people were acting as its news gatherers. The channel had spent years winning the trust of the Palestinian people through its fearless exposés of corruption within the PA, and in the very first days of the intifada Walid al-Omary's Palestinian mobile phone number was distributed on paper and by word of mouth throughout the whole of the Gaza Strip and the West Bank. Anybody at all could contact him with news stories and many did. Members of the public would call him and let him know whenever something important had happened. His methodology was always the same no matter what the situation: his first priority was to check out every tip with his contacts within both authorities, Israeli and Palestinian. Usually the next step was to call his Israeli journalist colleagues to see if they had heard the same story, and they often reciprocated if they heard something unsubstantiated.

Once Al-Omary had run the story by them, the third step was to start calling around his extensive network of trusted local sources to see what they knew. In his battered little black book are scribbled the names and numbers of the people, officials and institutions that he trusts as reliable sources of information. Every town and village in Israel and the Occupied Territories is listed alphabetically and Ramallah, for example, has more than ten pages of names. Arab names and phone numbers, written in Arabic, start in columns at the back of the book. Israeli names and numbers, written in Hebrew, are at the front. He would usually call three or four contacts to compare accounts before setting off to cover a story. Al-Jazeera has a portable uplink in its van stationed in Ramallah which it can use to transmit live from the field.

The support of the Palestinian people benefited Al-Jazeera in other ways too. Sometimes, when Israeli curfews meant venturing outside brought the risk of getting shot, the Al-Jazeera team would spend days and nights stuck inside the office. During one strict curfew, when the Israelis invaded Ramallah for the first time at the start of the intifada, tanks had been parked in the entrance to the Al-Jazeera bureau, so there was no chance of getting in or out unnoticed. All the shops were closed. Inside the bureau the staff had very little food and after Israeli snipers shot the water tanks on the roof of the office, they had very little water too. Since no one could go outside to find out what was happening in the rest of the town, Al-Omary was reduced to transmitting bulletins about the deteriorating humanitarian situation inside the office. This situation lasted seven days, without anyone being able to either leave or enter the building, and by the seventh day the conditions inside the office, as everywhere else in Ramallah, had grown desperate. The water had run out and the food was almost finished. Al-Omary filed a report about life in the Al-Jazeera bureau: how the eight Al-Jazeera staff had one can of tuna and three bread rolls left each.

The next day the Israeli tanks rolled away from the entrance to the bureau for a few hours. A local woman who had heard Al-Omary's TV report the night before seized the opportunity and risked her life to break the curfew and deliver a huge tray of food to the front door of the bureau. Then a man and his son came with four gallons of water in big plastic drums. 'We started crying, all of us. It was amazing,' Al-Omary told me.

It did not take long for Arabs outside the Occupied Territories to realize that Al-Jazeera was the channel to watch to follow the intifada. 'A piece of hot news to Jordanian officials: Jordanians have zapped to Al-Jazeera and they're never coming back!' ran a piece in the *Star*, a political English-language weekly based in Jordan. Within days Walid al-Omary had become a household name throughout the Arab world. It was the first time that the full tragedy of what was happening in Palestine had been beamed directly into the homes of millions of Arabs. Al-Jazeera's powerful pictures prompted Arabs in many other countries to take to the streets in solidarity with Palestine before rushing home each night to watch themselves on television. As the insurgency spread, the network dropped its usual schedule to broadcast hour-long news programmes showing running battles between Palestinian protesters and Israeli security forces. Each death brought another funeral, which in turn brought an emotional demonstration, with crowds of mourners chanting for revenge.

One of the first steps the Israeli army took after the intifada had been declared was to separate the West Bank into sixty-four separate areas, accessible only through 270 military checkpoints. Sometimes there would be as many as twelve checkpoints between Ramallah and Jenin, turning what would normally be a two-hour car journey into a day trip. Ramallah to Nablus is normally a forty-minute journey by car, but now, with checkpoints, it could take six hours. This was intended as a measure against the Palestinian people generally, but it was particularly problematic for Al-Jazeera.

New regulations concerning the necessary documentation Palestinians needed to pass these checkpoints were passed. Palestinian journalists wanting to travel around the Occupied Territories now needed an Israeli press card from the Israeli government press office, which they would have to present at each checkpoint. The type of press card each journalist received depended on his or her town of origin: Palestinians from Ramallah, where most of Al-Jazeera's West Bank bureau staff come from, were not allowed to travel outside Ramallah. Only Israeli Arabs, meaning Palestinians whose villages of origin are within Israel itself, were issued Israeli press cards allowing them to travel anywhere in the Occupied Territories. Only Walid al-Omary and three other Al-Jazeera staff fell into this category.

Even for those with the pertinent identification, checkpoints presented a serious logistical obstacle to news gathering. Often, after a three- or four-hour wait, the news team would be refused passage without explanation. But, when the intifada began, Al-Omary's background ceased to merely facilitate his work; it became the *sine qua non* for travelling in the Occupied Territories and Israel.

Checkpoints were such an insidious daily problem that sometimes the only way to tackle them was through subterfuge. When the Israeli soldiers prevented all traffic from entering or leaving the West Bank town of Nablus, Al-Omary, after several vain attempts to talk his way in, bought a donkey and smuggled his camera equipment over the mountains and into the town on it while he and the Al-Jazeera cameraman walked alongside. They successfully managed to penetrate Nablus and transmit their exclusive story about what was happening inside.

Covering the Gaza Strip presented a different set of problems from covering the West Bank. While the West Bank is heavily militarized, with Israeli checkpoints and settlements, the PA governs Gaza. Gaining entry to the tiny strip is a basic problem, because since the intifada began the Israelis have surrounded the 1.4 million people who live there with a tight security cordon, allowing only certain people to go in or out. Before the intifada about forty thousand Gazans worked each day in Israel, but this dropped to six thousand after the security cordon was erected. A press card could usually secure entry to Gaza for three days at a time, but not always. Once inside, moving around was relatively easy, as the whole area was under the control of the PA and there were no military checkpoints. Only occasionally did the Israeli military swoop in, divide Gaza into three sections and completely prohibit travel between them.

Covering the intifada presented some very personal challenges to all the Al-Jazeera staff in the West Bank bureau. All are from the area and often they found themselves covering events that might place their own families at risk. When suicide bombers struck a restaurant in Haifa where Jews and Arabs ate together, Al-Omary lost two close friends. 'We try to keep balance in our coverage and just try to give the people the facts and let them judge what is happening, but it is not easy at all – not easy at all for us – and I am living in this society,' he told me. 'At the same time Al-Jazeera is not the UN and it faces and suffers the same dangers as the people.'

Once, while covering a shoot-out at night out from the roof of his office, Al-Omary saw Israeli aircraft arrive and start firing missiles into the centre of Ramallah. As viewers watched on TV as each missile exploded in the town below, he narrated off camera what was happening, which neighbourhood or house he thought had been hit and where the worst fires were burning. Suddenly one of the missiles seemed to land directly on his house, where his wife and daughter were sleeping. Immediately he stopped talking and moved away from the microphone to call his wife and check that she had not just been hit. Although it only took a couple of minutes, by the time he got back his three mobile phones and two office lines were ringing off the hook as concerned viewers across the Arab world were calling in demanding to know what had happened to Walid al-Omary. The next day he found a missile had landed in the entrance to his house, but his family were unhurt.

The pictures coming out of the intifada were brutal. Two weeks after the death of Muhammad al-Durra an Italian news crew captured the lynching of two Israeli soldiers in a Ramallah police station. Beaten then shot, the Israelis were thrown dead out of a window while an exultant Arab mob cheered. Then a young Palestinian man appeared at the window, palms dripping with blood, smiling broadly. Al-Jazeera showed and denounced the mob murder, but minutes after it had happened, Al-Omary, who was in the Al-Jazeera bureau in Gaza City at the time, received instructions from the Israeli military to warn the PA that they should evacuate their offices and police stations immediately. Shortly after he had delivered this message on Al-Jazeera, he saw Israeli helicopters flying overhead. Grabbing his cameraman, he ran up to the roof of the office, where he breathlessly told viewers that this was the first time he had seen helicopters used in the intifada. As he was speaking, the camera watched the helicopters launch rockets into a police building near the rooftop from which Al-Omary was reporting. The first missiles landed just seventy metres from him, well within killing distance. The explosion was so close that the cameraman dropped the camera and ran for cover, leaving Al-Omary to report alone for more than fifteen minutes. When students in Cairo heard the news of the first helicopter raid in Gaza, they immediately demonstrated.

Television coverage of the intifada provoked international fury at Israel. Traditionally, Israel has cultivated a media image as David besieged by an Arab goliath, but now the roles were becoming reversed. Israel could no longer claim to be using reasonable force to suppress the Palestinians, when Al-Jazeera showed otherwise. The Israelis no longer looked like the underdog, they looked like bullies, and a week after the fighting started the UN Security Council condemned Israel for its use of excessive force.

This was not the first time that television had been the battleground for world public opinion. Israel had been concerned about its media image in conflicts since the country had first been founded in 1948. In those days it was only the written press that was of concern – the first televised Arab-Israeli confrontation was the Six-Day War of 1967 – but from that time the Israelis have always been deeply conscious of the pictures that have emerged from the continuing conflict.

The intifada of 2000 was the first time the formidable Israeli press machine had faced Arab competition. Within the Israeli media there was a great deal of soul-searching as to who was responsible for letting this happen and it was decided that special countermeasures would have to be taken.

Israel enlisted Nachman Shai, director-general of its Science, Culture and Sports Ministry, to set up a special media team to manage the country's television image. Shai was familiar to many Israelis from the first Gulf war, when his soft, bookish approach had forestalled public fears of an Iraqi scud-missile attack. Together with his 'special information team', Shai distributed five-minute videos of the Palestinian lynching to the international press, as well as footage of Palestinian children learning how to load guns. He blamed television for inciting the intifada. 'This war,' he said, 'is a television war. And in some cases it is a war on television. This is completely different from the Gulf war. It has become a daily struggle over which side will have the most airtime; which side will have won the latest propaganda war.'

Specifically, Shai blamed Al-Jazeera and Palestinian television for inciting Israeli Arabs to rise up in solidarity with the Palestinians. The time when Al-Jazeera had been accused of being pro-Israeli for the interviews it had run with Israeli spokesmen now seemed a distant memory. 'Palestinian television brought about more riots,' said Shai. 'Of that I have no doubt.' A few days after he made this pronouncement the Israelis destroyed the Palestinian radio transmitters with missiles and bombed the Palestinian television headquarters. Al-Jazeera, broadcast from Doha but available to anyone with a satellite dish, was not so easily silenced.

It was not to be long before Al-Jazeera's coverage was to provoke a powerful international response. In the first week of the intifada Al-Jazeera conducted a telephone interview with the President of Yemen, Ali Abdullah Saleh, in which he called for volunteers and military support for the Palestinians. 'All Arabs are urged to support the Palestinian intifada through various political and economic means and in the defence field,' Saleh said from Paris. 'What has been taken by force can only be retaken by force,' he added. He also called on Arab leaders to break off diplomatic relations with Israel.

Saleh's very public call to arms ran contrary to Hosni Mubarak's appeal for calm a few days earlier. The Egyptian President wanted a 'wise reaction' to escalating tension. 'Declaring a war is not something simple . . . It's not a game,' he had said. When Al-Jazeera's Cairo bureau chief, Hussein Abdul Ghany, asked Mubarak at a press conference whether Egypt would go to war against Israel he turned to him and asked in disbelief, 'You want me to take Al-Jazeera to war? Let Al-Jazeera go to war. We are not going.' Mubarak's words may have struck a chord with the older generation, who remembered the calamitous Arab defeat of 1967, but Saleh was more in touch with the mood on the Arab street. In demonstrations everywhere Arabs began calling on their leaders to start arming the Palestinian people and declare a jihad against Israel.

Saleh had used Al-Jazeera as a platform to score political points. He knew that Egypt, with a population of around seventy-six million, more than double that of any other Arab country, and dependent on substantial American financial aid, had much more to lose than any other Arab nation in a war with Israel. Consequently, it was in no hurry to stick up for the Palestinians. Saleh used Al-Jazeera to make a popular case and Washington's Department of State spokesman Richard Boucher knew it. 'We are indeed aware of those statements and we were going to take them up with the government,' he said. 'At this point, certainly we have concerns about statements like that.'

Many Arab leaders who appeared on Al-Jazeera at this time seized the opportunity to call for war against Israel. Two of them were Sheikh Nasrallah, the charismatic head of Hezbollah, and Iran's Foreign Minister, Kamal Kharazi. Both used appearances on Al-Jazeera to lambast Israel and warn it against any further military action in Lebanon. Hezbollah's stated aim was to escalate the intifada by any possible means and its deeper intervention was a fearsome prospect. The group commands great respect from Palestinian fighters and had been involved in the intifada from the start.

Some saw interviews at this time with such polemical figures as Sheikh Nasrallah and Kamal Kharazi as incitement. Certainly their comments injected vitriol into the intifada and popular demonstrations in other Middle Eastern countries swelled in support of the Palestinians. Protesters in Egypt and Jordan called on their governments to sever diplomatic ties with Israel and in Cairo effigies of President Clinton were burned. Crowds shouted slogans that dated back to the 1967 Arab-Israeli war, including 'Wake up, wake up, Egyptians, the Zionists are coming' and 'The one who hits Palestine today will strike at Ras el-Tin [Alexandria] tomorrow'. In Jordan, usually a relatively tranquil Arab nation, violent demonstrations after Friday prayers left sixty-nine policemen injured.

In Saudi Arabia a television fund-raising campaign raised 150 million Saudi riyals ($40 million) for Palestine in two weeks. King Fahd personally donated thirty million Saudi riyals ($8 million) to 'the heroes of the Al-Aqsa intifada' and Crown Prince Abdullah arranged for wounded Palestinians to be flown to the kingdom for medical treatment. He also issued an oblique warning to Israel that an escalation of the conflict would provoke a Saudi retaliation. 'Let no one be under any illusions that the Kingdom of Saudi Arabia would stand by watching with folded arms,' he said. Al-Jazeera did not run a telethon for Palestine, but its reports undoubtedly fuelled those on other channels.

As the crisis grew, President Mubarak called an emergency Arab summit in Cairo for 21 and 22 October. Such emergency summits had been held before, for example when Saddam Hussein invaded Kuwait. This time Saddam was in much better standing on the Arab street, having made much cheap political capital with his outspoken anti-American comments. To many Arabs he looked like a man unafraid of taking strong action against Israel and his image had become ubiquitous at demonstrations. America had tried to dissuade Egypt from inviting him to the summit, but so strong was the anti-American feeling at this time that Egypt felt it would do better to ignore America and do so. Even Kuwait felt unable to object. Saddam Hussein was not the only leader to have profited from the intifada. It had proved to be a cohesive force for Iraq, Iran and Libya, who had all moved closer to one another in their mutual antagonism towards the US and Israel.

During the week of the Arab summit the Arab public's mood was virulent. There was widespread hope that Arab leaders would take this opportunity to break off diplomatic relations with Israel. Oman and Morocco had already done so, but the all-important Egyptian administration feared sanctions against Israel, because in one swoop this would take the whole region back a decade to before the launch of the peace process at the Madrid conference in October 1991. The recurrent appearances of radical spokesmen on Al-Jazeera, like Hezbollah's Sheikh Nasrallah, made it increasingly difficult for Egypt to stick to a moderate course.

On the Tuesday before the summit the Libyan leader, Colonel Qadhafi, dramatically made a mockery of the whole event when he read out resolutions the summit was supposed to have reached live on Al-Jazeera, before the delegates had even sat down. A draft copy of the resolutions had been given to all the Arab leaders beforehand and although the document he read was supposed to be only a draft to be debated, Qadhafi made it look as though the Egyptian hosts had fixed the result in advance. To all the world it looked like the Arab leaders had connived to stitch up the Palestinians.

Qadhafi had leaked the draft because he wanted to pressure Egypt into adopting a more militant stance against Israel, but in doing so he had detonated a political bombshell. He chose to use Al-Jazeera for his stunt as he thought it would be broadly trusted, and he was right. The Arabs were convinced their leaders were deceiving them and conspiring to abandon the Palestinians. The summit became a fiasco.

The draft Qadhafi read out on Al-Jazeera, which was addressed to each conference attendee, said: 'Participants agreed to firmly resist Israel's attempt to infiltrate the Arab world under any pretext, to halt the establishment of any new relations with Israel and to cancel all relations that were established during the peace process, which has been suspended due to recent developments and their impact on the Arab and Islamic arenas.' What this meant in practice was that, besides some empty rhetoric, Egypt and Jordan would keep diplomatic relations with Israel, because their two peace treaties were signed in 1979 and 1994 respectively, while other, smaller Arab countries would have to break off relations and suffer the economic consequences. More importantly, there was absolutely no tough message to Israel that if it didn't stop the occupation then the Arabs would retaliate.

Understandably, the Egyptians were mortified that Qadhafi had made them look duplicitous and pathetic on international television. The situation was made even worse when, midway through the maverick Qadhafi's broadcast bombshell, a caller phoned in from Cairo to denounce his government as American lackeys. 'We have a generation of paralysed rulers who cannot respond to the demands of the furious masses and who are trying to subdue this awakening nation,' he told thirty million viewers.

Such overt criticism of the regime would never have been allowed on Egyptian state television.

Qadhafi's media moment made it abundantly clear that the Arab leaders were trailing, not leading, public opinion. The Egyptian Foreign Minister, Amr Moussa, tried in vain to explain to a deeply sceptical Arab public that the conference was not a put-up job. 'The draft statement is an initial document and not a final document, and it's not right to make it public,' he blathered, but this distinction was lost on the seething Arab public.

Furious that Al-Jazeera had been the instrument of their humiliation and powerless to do anything about Qadhafi, the Egyptians decided to take revenge on Al-Jazeera. Egyptian officials starting accusing the channel of having militant Islamist tendencies and of being a tool of the Qatari administration. By letting the public make baseless accusations on satellite television, they said, Al-Jazeera was distorting the case for war and leading the Arabs – and specifically Egypt – into a trap. 'They take one angle and press all their weight on it,' said Egypt's chief of foreign relations on the state-owned Egyptian television channel. 'As an Egyptian, I don't believe we should go to war. The Israelis crossed a red line. The Arab street was angry. I was angry. But we have different ways of managing it.'

Al-Jazeera responded that it was merely giving Arabs an opportunity to say what they otherwise could not. 'People start to think, what kind of leadership do we have?' said Al-Jazeera's Walid al-Omary. 'We don't do it to incite or provoke people, but events here have been very harsh.'

As predicted in the communiqué Qadhafi leaked, no Arab nations at the summit volunteered to fight for Palestine, but they did pledge a billion-dollar fund for food and medicine, of which an estimated $693 million was actually committed. Public pressure, shepherded largely by Al-Jazeera, was an important factor in raising such a substantial sum. Mubarak also eventually recalled the Egyptian Ambassador from Israel, because, he later told his advisers, he couldn't stand the television images of young

Palestinians battling Israeli soldiers. 'I had to do something,' he reportedly said.

After the summit and throughout the rest of October there was no let-up in Al-Jazeera's blood-drenched coverage of the 'Al-Aqsa intifada'. On its talk shows the word *khawana*, 'traitors', was bounced around with increasing frequency as opposition commentators and Palestinian Islamists attacked Egypt's 'soft stance' on Israel. A Lebanese singer called Julia Boutous recycled Al-Jazeera's image of Muhammad al-Durra in her music video for a song called 'Where are the Millions?', which was a rallying call for the intifada. The number of pro-Palestinian demonstrations around the world grew and Egyptian flags and pictures of Hosni Mubarak were added to the list of things that were burned.

Within Egypt at this time, it seemed as if the country was edging towards a revolution. Throughout that October, each week after Friday prayers street protests and demonstrations flared in universities, as well as in secondary and even primary schools. Protesters bemoaned Egyptian government inaction, calling out, 'Where is the Egyptian army?' and shouting praise for Hezbollah. Professional associations of all kinds, unions, NGOs, famous celebrities and newly formed grass-roots organizations all vied to cry support for Palestine, while proponents of 'normalization' of relations with Israel hid from the media in fear. The Arab press each day extolled Egypt's 'democratic intifada', which had arisen in response to the Palestinian one. Egyptians began to boycott Israeli and American goods and well-known US companies, including McDonald's and Coca-Cola, reported a substantial drop-off in business.

Although the demonstrations in Egypt were spontaneous, Islamist demagogues tried to harness them and take credit for the unrest. Observers were struck by the cosmopolitan make-up of the protests, which reflected the breadth of public opin-ion behind the Palestinian cause. No one social group or political party was in charge. Young people played a predominant role, the so-called 'generation of peace', who had never known defeat in war. Until now it had been assumed that this generation considered the Palestinian question merely an abstraction, not a burning political issue. Now it became apparent that, despite years of Sadat's Egypt-first nationalism, pan-Arabism still meant something to Egyptian youth. There was a religious dimension to the protests too: many young Egyptians demonstrated because the Zionists were threatening the holy sites of Islam.

What the Egyptian government feared most at this time was that its inertia over Palestine would be regarded as part of a wider policy of American appeasement. Egyptian society is repressive and bureaucratic and the 'Egyptian intifada' dovetailed with long-running social problems. Hundreds of thousands of educated but unemployed youth had already grown disillusioned with their illegitimate, impotent government and its useless domestic policies. Mubarak had long promised to tackle widespread corruption in Egypt, but nothing perceptible had been done. Coincidentally, Egyptian parliamentary elections were being held at the same time and Mubarak's National Democratic Party suffered slightly in the polls. It would have suffered more had Egypt been a democracy. During the parliamentary elections an Egyptian cameraman who worked for Al-Jazeera had his arm broken when he was beaten up by plainclothes policemen and policewomen wielding metal bars. He had filmed them illegally locking a polling station in a Cairo suburb earlier. There were numerous cases of Egyptian police intimidating other journalists too.

At the end of October 2000 many international commentators thought the Middle East was on the verge of a new regional conflict. The Arab street was screaming for war, but Mubarak, knowing that the Arab countries were no match for Israel's conventional army, let alone its nuclear capabilities, was hanging on to what he called the 'strategic option', which meant peace. Guests on Al-Jazeera routinely denounced the Egyptian government for failing the Arabs and there is no doubt these voices added to the destabilization in the country. Only by exercising all the power of the state, from rigging the elections to waging an aggressive media campaign against Al-Jazeera, could Mubarak's supporters hope to weather the storm.

Al-Jazeera became a scapegoat for the civil disorder in the state-controlled Egyptian press. One such newspaper ran a cartoon depicting the Al-Jazeera news anchors as Jews wearing yarmulkas and Egypt's Minister of Information consistently accused Al-Jazeera of deliberately undermining Arab unity. 'The Jazeera channel's campaigns against Egypt are a big mistake, poisoning Arab society and ripping it apart,' the minister told state television. 'We have to know who's trying to break up the Arab ranks,' he added. 'I may . . . stop all dealings with the Jazeera channel concerning studios . . . satellite feeds or correspondents.'

'Egypt has offered the souls of its martyrs,' the Minister of Information complained, 'Its president brings the Arab nation together, seeks to stop the Palestinian bloodshed and responds to all international calls for mediation, and after all that, this noisy campaign is waged.' A warning was issued that unless Al-Jazeera changed its editorial policy towards Egypt within forty-eight hours, the Ministry of Information would stop Al-Jazeera from using Egyptian studios, block its satellite feed and prevent its correspondents from working anywhere in Egypt.

As usual, many of the most vehement anti-Egyptian voices had been issuing from the guests on the political discussion programme *The Opposite Direction*, hosted by Dr Faisal al-Qasim. His younger brother, Magd al-Qasim, is a pop star in Egypt, who, although he had no connection to Al-Jazeera besides his brother, had for some months been the subject of a hate campaign in a Cairo weekly paper. Because his brother was a controversial Al-Jazeera host, the paper had been calling for his deportation. After much campaigning, on 27 October the Egyptian authorities snapped. The Egyptian police went to Magd al-Qasim's house in the middle of the night and told him he must go at once with them to the airport, because he was being deported. He was given no time to collect any cash, his pyjamas or even his mobile phone, before being bundled into a car and driven away. When they arrived at Cairo airport, the police gave him a choice: there were two planes leaving and he had to get on one of them. One was going to Sudan, the other to Iran. Magd al-Qasim begged for clemency: he did not know a soul in either place and he did not even have any money or possessions. Taking pity on him, the police let him wait two hours so he could get on another plane, to Jordan, instead. He stayed in Jordan just twenty-four hours before flying on to Doha to stay with his borther, Faisal, the presenter who had landed him in trouble in the first place.

By way of justification, a few days later the Egyptian state daily newspaper *Al-Akhbar* announced that the musicians' guild of Cairo had decided to expel anyone who worked for Al-Jazeera. Singers and performers in Egypt need a permit from the guild to perform. 'Any singer, musician, or composer working with Jazeera will be struck from the list of the union, which will stop dealing with this person permanently,' the paper reported. The guild's chairman warned 'any singer, Egyptian or Arab, who is a guild member or benefits from a work permit or agreements between the guild and its colleagues in other countries, against working with the channel'. *Al-Akhbar* carried the Minister of Information's pronouncement and called Al-Jazeera 'this Zionist and dubious channel, which has no other goal than to harm the reputation of Egypt and the Arab world'. Magd al-Qasim was allowed back into Egypt three months later. As it turned out, his temporary exile did his career a power of good, not least because he was interviewed by CNN upon his return.

After four weeks of mayhem over 130 people, mostly Arabs, had been killed and the intifada was still showing no sign of abating. On the Arab street people were queuing up to give their blood for Palestine. In Palestine itself the public were strongly united. Differences between Fatah, Hamas, the Democratic Front for the Liberation of Palestine, the Popular Front for the Liberation of Palestine and other militant groups had been largely eliminated. Peace talks brokered by Bill Clinton between the Israeli and Palestinian leaders were held at Sharm el Sheikh, but the

Palestinian militant factions declared that the intifada would go on anyway. It was clear that the peace process, with all its hard-won agreements, annexes and treaties, lay in tatters. Israel now termed it 'a frame of reference'.

The discrepancy between the anger of the Arab people and their leaders' inertia prompted commentators in the Arab media to start asking one another if the Arab giant was finally awakening. It was clear the emergency summit had done nothing to resolve the troubles. Arab regimes who had committed themselves to a peace process with Israel, like Morocco, Jordan, Tunisia, Saudi Arabia and the Gulf states, were faced with a stark choice of ignoring their people and risking civil unrest or taking decisive steps against Israel and America.

Demonstrations stretching across the Arab world in solidarity with the Palestinians resulted in the temporary closure of twenty one American embassies. In Morocco between half a million and a million people took to the streets. In tiny Oman thousands marched. The Pakistani press reported that twenty thousand Pakistani Muslims had pledged jihad against Israel. In Jordan thirty thousand Palestinians clashed with police as they tried to cross one of the bridges connecting Jordan and Israel. The Jordanian Prime Minister felt under such intense pressure to show his solidarity with the intifada that he even paid a visit to Saddam in Baghdad – the first by an Arab premier since Saddam's withdrawal from Kuwait in 1991.

The dangers of civil disorder were felt particularly keenly in the countries of the Gulf Cooperation Council (GCC): Oman, the United Arab Emirates, Qatar, Kuwait, Bahrain and Saudi Arabia. These countries, usually politically dormant, had in 1991 sought shelter from Saddam under the American military umbrella. Some, Saudi Arabia among them, had allowed the US military to use their land and facilities. Now that Washington and Israel had been equated as the dual opponents of the Arab world – their flags burned alongside one another on satellite TV – these regimes risked being found guilty by association. Social conditions, corruption and rising unemployment made these states ripe for unrest. Masses of disaffected youth in Saudi Arabia, where half the population is aged under fifteen, were brought to a new level of media consciousness by watching the intifada on Al-Jazeera. Its powerful visual messages politicized young Saudis and prompted them to interrogate their government about its relationship with America.

The Saudi authorities were caught off guard when hundreds of men launched a protest in the city of Sakkaka, near the Jordanian border. Again observers were struck by how representative of the general population the protesters were. The protests were suppressed and arrests were made, but since the movement was spontaneous and unorganized there were no leaders who could be publicly humiliated or imprisoned. More unrest followed when a football crowd in Riyadh turned into a rally for Palestine. When a group of affluent and well-connected women demonstrated for Palestine in Jeddah, Saudi society was shocked. The demonstrators were taken to police stations and, in the presence of male relatives, made to sign a promise not to protest again. Such a lenient punishment reflected the deep public sympathy for the intifada, by contrast with the fate of women who had held an illegal driving demonstration in Riyadh during the first Gulf war. They had been fiercely condemned as un-Islamic and a fatwa had been passed banning women from driving. These demonstrations by ordinary Saudis and the state's tolerant response were unprecedented and sent shivers down Western spines. Given that the Saudis were the custodians of the mosques at Mecca and Medina, the holiest sites for a billion Muslims, as well as the world's biggest suppliers of oil, the West could not afford to ignore their opinion.

In the furnace of the first weeks and months of the intifada, a new Arab political awareness was forged. For the first time Arabs made their autocratic leaders defend their decisions and policies. The television pictures of the intifada transcended national boundaries, reaching into homes, offices and cafés beyond the Middle East and North Africa, into small villages as far away as

Indonesia and Pakistan. There was no need to be literate to understand what was happening. Some media critics have since compared Al-Jazeera's role in the intifada to that of the reporters who had covered the Vietnam War thirty years earlier. On both occasions the audience acquired a strong sense of immediacy to the events through the medium of television. Both conflicts changed the way future wars would be covered.

'We made a revolution in Arabic media,' said Muhammad Jasim al-Ali, Al-Jazeera's general manager. 'You can't hide anything from the audience. The mentality has changed. It will change more.' The Arabs had not been so united since the fifties and sixties, when Nasser's Sawt al-Arab radio stirred up dissent in the Arabian Peninsula. Then, as now, a powerful message dovetailed with economic uncertainty and social problems, but then the result had been that Egyptians had turned out on the streets to demonstrate for the liberation of Egyptian territory. Now Egyptians were demonstrating for Palestine. Then it had been one man's character and convictions on the radio that had united the Arabs. This time it was a plural expression of opinions coming through a visual medium.

Al-Jazeera made Arab state television networks realize that they could no longer carry on broadcasting news they way they always had. Midway through the intifada, two of its rivals, the London-based Arab News Network and Abu Dhabi TV, conspicuously began to copy its news format in an effort to win back some viewers. Like Al-Jazeera, they began to run regular news editions and hourly bulletins that opened with the most spectacular news story. This may seem basic, but in the Arab world it was an innovation. The Arab audience finally shed its dependency on CNN and the BBC. Israelis criticized even the Israel Broadcasting Authority for failing to show the Palestinian side of the intifada and for failing to report attacks on Israeli Arabs by Israeli Jews.

One key difference between Al-Jazeera and the other Arab channels was its policy of interviewing Israelis. It was still the only Arab channel to do this. Other Arab channels still either spoke for the Israelis or ignored them completely. This policy drew severe criticism from the Arab world, especially from Syria, and shortly before the intifada began a group called the Organization of Revolutionary Cells had even blown up a Qatar Airways office in Beirut in protest at Al-Jazeera's perceived Zionism. A statement faxed to Agence France Presse (AFP) in Amman accused the Emir of Qatar and his Foreign Minister of being 'protégés of the Zionists and their American protectors'. The group said it was acting against the 'traitorous Qatari regime and its apostate diplomatic chief' and that Al-Jazeera was 'a tool of the Zionists which spreads all that serves this malignant tumour called Israel'.

Al-Jazeera was defiant, saying that, in keeping with its motto, the Israelis had to be given a voice. 'We respect the intelligence of the people and they have to hear the Israeli point of view from the Israelis and not through third parties like what has happened since the establishment of Israel, where somebody tells you what the Israelis said or are going to say,' Walid al-Omary passionately explained to me in his office in Ramallah. 'Before Al-Jazeera started this policy many people in the Arab world had never heard an Israeli voice.' It was not long before all the other networks were doing it too.

According to the Pan Arab Research Center, during the intifada about half of all Arab viewers deserted their local state news networks in favour of satellite news. Jordanian officials estimate that around thirty thousand dishes were purchased in Jordan in the days immediately after the intifada began. For Al-Jazeera this dramatic switch in viewing habits held the promise once again of huge advertising revenue. Overall, Middle East advertising expenditure was on the increase. The advertising market in the Arab world was now estimated to be worth a billion dollars and Al-Jazeera was confident it would get a slice of the cake, since during the intifada the network claimed a nightly audience of thirty-five million.

But the violence of the intifada was hardly the ideal backdrop for many big advertisers and popular Arab opposition to products with a perceived American or Jewish link muddied the waters further. Coca-Cola, McDonald's and the Cairo Sainsbury's were all boycotted in protest at the American government's support of Israel. McDonald's in Saudi Arabia moved fast but in vain to offset the boycott by promising to send one Saudi riyal to intifada charities for every five spent in its restaurants. The intifada prompted many advertisers to hold back on major entertainment-led campaigns until the violence had stopped. The main consumers of Al-Jazeera were the Palestinians themselves – about 78 per cent of them used it as their news channel of choice, according to Nabil Khatib, director of the Institute of Media at Birzeit University, but they were not in a position to buy much of what was being advertised.

The intifada raged on in 2001 despite international efforts to broker peace. By the end of March more than four hundred people had been killed, the vast majority of them Palestinians. Al-Jazeera's footage, which was widely syndicated around the world, continued to be a major factor in mobilizing support for the Palestinians. Another Arab summit was held and the Arab nations drifted towards finding a policy. Al-Jazeera's prestige grew daily on the strength of its coverage. Walid al-Omary was awarded a prize for Arab Visual Media Personality of the Year at the first Arab Media Award ceremony held in Dubai.

The international media would now cite Al-Jazeera's West Bank reports daily with the same respect granted to Western news agencies. The network even began to make the first ripples in the West. Dr Faisal al-Qasim was interviewed on *Sixty Minutes* as part of an investigation into what presenter Ed Bradley called the 'tiny television network with a big mouth'.

US government officials made positive noises about Al-Jazeera. Department of State spokesman Greg Sullivan claimed he tuned in in his office every day. 'We recognize it as a powerful voice with a wide viewership in the Arab world,' he said. 'It is a media outlet of importance in the Arab world.' The US government-funded Voice of America broadcasting service, keen to expand its presence in the Arab world, asked Al-Jazeera's managers in Doha if they would broadcast its programmes, but they declined.

The Israelis, still stunned at how Al-Jazeera had turned the
tables on them in the media war, were determined not be caught
out again. Israeli government officials took every opportunity
to tell Western reporters that Al-Jazeera misrepresented events
on television by showing them out of context and that the channel failed to recognize the role of Palestinian incitement in the
intifada. In May 2001, during a visit to Washington, the Israeli
Foreign Minister, Shimon Peres, declared, 'I think Israel has a
problem with the way things have been shown [on] television.
It shows a picture. It does not tell a story.'

Al-Jazeera never denied that its footage had rallied support
for the Palestinian cause, but maintained that this was a natural
but unintended consequence of the facts being shown, rather
than any deliberate attempt at propaganda. At least, an Al-Jazeera
spokesman pointed out, Israelis officials, including the President
and the Foreign Minister, could be seen and heard on Al-Jazeera
in an unaccented way, unlike on any other Arab channel. The
network even carried Peres's Washington speech in which he
complained about its coverage. If the Israelis tried to prevent
Al-Jazeera doing its job, the network argued, it was only because
they had something to hide, for its reports were not one-sided.
When a suicide bomber killed Israeli civilians, for example,
Al-Jazeera would emphasize that these were civilian, not military,
victims. 'We're not interested in officials, we're interested in
people,' Al-Omary said. 'There is no denying that the Palestinians
are under occupation, and that they are suffering. That is what
we show.'

Many Israelis disagreed with Peres, regarding Al-Jazeera as an
important new democratic Arab forum and an agent for change.
Two of Al-Jazeera's regular Israeli guests were Gideon Ezra,
former deputy head of the General Security Service (GSS), and
Yigal Carmon, former counter-terrorism adviser to Prime
Ministers Shamir and Rabin. Following a satellite-linked discussion with West Bank Fatah chief Marwan Barghouti, Ezra told
the *Jerusalem Post* that he had been received courteously and
given a fair hearing. 'I wish all Arab media were like Al-Jazeera,'

he said. 'There I was in Jerusalem, with [Barghouti] in Ramallah, and the moderator was sitting in Al-Jazeera's London studio, and they were hearing me out, even though little of what I said could have been agreeable to them. All of a sudden, an Israeli called in claiming to be a former GSS man who quit because he could no longer stand coercing Palestinians into becoming collaborators. Now that's what I call a free discussion.'

There had been occasions on which Al-Jazeera's coverage had actually been of palpable benefit to the Israelis. When three hooded Palestinians were shown firing a mortar at a Jewish settlement, this solved some unanswered tactical questions. Hamas had claimed responsibility for dozens of mortar attacks and boasted about its use of home-made explosive shells, but until then there had been some doubt as to exactly how the attacks had been carried out and whether Hamas really was responsible. Several other Palestinian groups, competing for popular approval, had claimed responsibility and Palestinian Authority officials had refused even to acknowledge the existence of mortar shells in Palestinian areas. When a video with a twenty-second clip of mortars in action was delivered to Al-Jazeera's bureau in Ramallah, it cleared up this particular mystery. It was played over and over on the evening news and was even syndicated to Israeli channels. 'The tape of the footage arrived on our desk,' said Al-Omary, 'and we showed it, because it was important to do so.'

Some Arabs suspected that the Israelis were using Al-Jazeera footage to coordinate attacks. Sometimes it was almost tempting to believe this was true. One evening in October, for example, Al-Omary was sitting in his office in Ramallah, when dozens of Israeli armoured vehicles started to roll into town. From inside there were good views of much of Ramallah as well as an outlying town, and the main road on which most of the vehicles were travelling passed near the bureau. The cameraman captured some dramatic footage of Israeli soldiers swarming all around, clambering on the roofs and inside the neighbouring mosque, and before long numerous firefights had broken out. Israeli soldiers officially closed the bureau down, but Al-Omary surreptitiously set up a camera looking out of the window of his office and, unnoticed, this transmitted live footage which was broadcast. Palestinian and Israeli gunmen were fighting so close by that it might almost have seemed possible that the footage could have been used militarily, but in practice it is extremely doubtful that something someone saw on Al-Jazeera could have ever helped them coordinate troops in a gunfight.

Two thousand and one was an election year in Israel and the furore over Al-Jazeera had been so intense that the way in which the media covered the intifada was destined to become a campaign issue. In January, in an unprecedented move by an Arab news channel, Israeli Prime Minister Ehud Barak gave a lengthy interview on Al-Jazeera during which he answered questions about the intifada and called on PA chairman Yasser Arafat to halt the violence. Al-Jazeera won praise from both Palestinians and Israelis for this interview, but it did not stop Barak losing the election to Ariel Sharon a month later. Despite, or perhaps because of, his hard-line reputation, Sharon's victory rally was given live coverage on Al-Jazeera.

The new Israeli administration was acutely aware that it had been losing the media war to Al-Jazeera, so it was not long before the Ministry of Finance issued funds to found a new English- and Arabic-language television channel to compete with Al-Jazeera. The aim was to increase Israel's broadcasts in these two languages, in order to put its case to the Middle East and beyond. Israeli Minister without Portfolio Ra'anan Cohen, who was in charge of the Israel Broadcasting Association, said, 'Arab countries are flooded currently with dozens of land- and satellite-based channels operating twenty-four hours a day. The Arab-Israeli conflict is an issue that takes up a significant amount of time on those channels. The Arab channels provide a distorted view of the Israeli reality, so quality Arabic broadcasts are a must.'

English-language programming on the Israel Broadcasting Authority's television channels was stepped up and plans for three new channels, including one devoted to English- and Arabic-language broadcasts, were drawn up. This channel would broad-

cast news and current events via satellite to countries throughout the Middle East and Europe. Nachman Shai, by this time
head of the Israel Broadcasting Authority, acknowledged that
this was part of a new Israeli media policy in the light of the
intifada. 'The importance of it is greater in the current situation when there are military tensions and a serious security
conflict,' he said. Faced with this escalation in the media war,
the Arab Ministers of Information convened in Lebanon to dither
about what they should do in response. They decided to set up
an Arab satellite channel that would broadcast in English and
present the Arab point of view. Lebanon's Minister of
Information suggested that Arab television broadcasts should
begin in Hebrew as an additional countermeasure.

As the media war began to take shape, the Palestinian Authority
scored a spectacular own goal when it shut down the Al-Jazeera
bureau in Ramallah. This was the climax of Al-Jazeera's feud
with Yasser Arafat's authority, after which the PA climbed down
and finally accepted that Al-Jazeera was here to stay.

Arafat's security chiefs were angry about what they regarded
as an offensive image of the Palestinian leader shown in a promotional trailer for a fifteen part documentary on Lebanon's civil
war. The daring and uncompromising documentary, called
simply *The War of Lebanon*, had been two years in the making
and was the first Arab documentary to explore the fifteen-year
conflict. Produced and shown on Al-Jazeera, it was filmed in
eight cities across four continents and cost several hundred thousand dollars, which, while nothing special by Western television
standards, is a lot of money in the Middle East.

From the promotional point of view, it was fortuitous for
Al-Jazeera that Ariel Sharon had been recently elected as the
Israeli Prime Minister, since he had such an infamous role in
this war. Not only had he masterminded the Israeli invasion of
Lebanon personally, but after the war an Israeli inquiry had found
him indirectly responsible for the massacre of Palestinian refugees
at Shatila and Sabra. It was thought at the time that this would

signal the end of Sharon's political career and now there was talk that Al-Jazeera's forthcoming documentary might reveal previously unknown information about the new Israeli Prime Minister which might reignite interest in the massacres.

The series came with a warning that in one episode there were disturbing pictures of a massacre. Some critics complained that, coming so soon after the war had finished, the documentary would only open wounds that had not yet had time to heal. Voices from all sides in the conflict were featured, as well as interviews with Arab, Israeli and international players, and the series tried hard to give as full a portrait as possible of events both inside and outside the Lebanon. Many new and troubling details about how the war had been conducted were revealed for the first time and there was plenty of graphic footage, heart-rending testimonies and explicit photographs. Although no new light was shed on Sharon's role, the weekly series became increasingly popular.

Ironically, the trailer was to become more famous than the series itself. It featured some archive footage of Lebanese guerrillas holding a poster showing Palestinian President Yasser Arafat with a shoe dangling in front of his head, which to Arabs is a deeply insulting gesture. Shortly after the trailer was broadcast, Walid al-Omary received a telephone call from the PA saying it was horrified that Al-Jazeera could broadcast such a disrespectful gesture towards the elected Palestinian leader and that it wanted him to close the office and hand over the tape of the trailer immediately. Such a seemingly inappropriately zealous response came because this incident was not the first time Al-Jazeera had broadcast something that the PA found disagreeable. Al-Omary refused.

A couple of hours after the telephone conversation a gang of armed heavies from Yasser Arafat's Fatah organization arrived at the Al-Jazeera office and threatened Al-Omary that if he did not close the office at once, they would demolish it. When some officials from Arafat's office also showed up, he had no option but to comply.

It says much about the PA's priorities that, for fear of Al-Jazeera's reports into its corruption and ineptitude, it was prepared to close down a news network that had helped rally massive international support for Palestine. Its heavy-handed intervention also demonstrated remarkable ignorance as to how news is broadcast. Al-Jazeera's Ramallah bureau had nothing to do with the Lebanon series, which was being transmitted from Qatar, and so, as the Al-Jazeera staff tried to explain, they could not hand over the offending tape. But, faced with intransigent senior Palestinian officials and armed security men, they could do nothing but close the bureau and temporarily move operations to West Jerusalem. Palestinian security men took up positions outside the closed bureau and insisted they would allow it to reopen only when the trailer featuring Arafat and the shoe had been pulled and Al-Jazeera had issued an apology.

No apology was forthcoming and the trailer continued to be aired, so for five days the bureau remained closed. During this time a growing international chorus called for the PA to reconsider its decision. High-profile Palestinian spokeswoman Dr Hanan Ashrawi and international media organizations like Reporters sans Frontières weighed in to condemn the PA on behalf of Al Jazeera. The New York-based Committee to Protect Journalists (CPJ), a non-partisan, non-profit organization of journalists that works to defend press freedom worldwide, issued a statement saying: 'The Palestinian National Authority's closure of Al-Jazeera and restrictions on its reporters are a crude attempt at censorship that violates basic international norms for free expression.' One senior PA official told the *New York Times*, 'We are not just shooting ourselves in the foot, we are shooting ourselves in the nose.'

Yasser Arafat was in Saudi Arabia the day the Ramallah bureau was closed, but returned two days later. On arriving back in Ramallah he passed a message to Al-Omary through Ashrawi that he wanted to meet. Ashrawi picked up Al-Omary from his temporary office in West Jerusalem in her car and they drove to Arafat's compound, where it was understood the President was awaiting. When the car drew up inside Arafat's compound Ashrawi got out, but when Al-Omary tried to follow her, Arafat's guards told him that he was *persona non grata* and should leave at once. Al-Omary explained that he had received word that Arafat wanted to see him, but the guards were adamant: Al-Jazeera and especially Walid al-Omary were not welcome at PA headquarters. While Al-Omary talked, still seated in the car, Ashrawi, the consummate peacemaker, dashed inside to find Arafat and tell him what was going on. Permission from Arafat to enter the compound received, Al-Omary was grudgingly allowed out of the car.

Inside the compound he was greeted by Abu Mazen, then an important member of the Palestinian Legislative Council, who led him into a room and told him to wait for Arafat. A few minutes later Abu Mazen arrived back, leading Arafat by the hand. Standing in the doorway, he gestured to Al-Omary, saying to Arafat, 'This is the tiger!' Arafat fell upon his guest, shaking his hand and kissing him many times, as he was prone to do with everybody, but as he kissed him he reached under his jacket and pinched a roll of fat on his belly so hard that tears came into Al-Omary's eyes. Then they sat down to talk.

Abu Mazen, Arafat, Ashrawi and Al-Omary, plus other members of the Palestinian Legislative Council, were present. Nabil Amr, the Palestinian Authority PR strategist who was at that time very close to Arafat, began the discussion with a tirade about Al-Jazeera's insolence. He demanded that Al-Omary explain to the assembly what he thought he was doing by repeatedly airing a trailer for a documentary with a shoe dangling on Arafat's head. Arafat hushed him, saying that the trailer was really not so important. He said that he did not know that the Al-Jazeera bureau had been closed because he had been away.

For forty-five minutes they sat in the rubble of Arafat's office and talked about Al-Jazeera. Al-Omary told Arafat that he was not going to change his line no matter what happened. He explained to Arafat that if he stopped reporting negatively about the PA he would lose his credibility with the Palestinian people and once that had happened it could never be regained. The Palestinian people, he argued, trusted Al-Jazeera more than they trusted any other source of information, simply because Al-Jazeera was honest with them. If Al-Jazeera was closed down or inhibited or tainted in any way, it would be catastrophic for the Palestinians. Arafat listened to Al-Omary at length and when he had finished speaking, he called over one of his bodyguards and told him to go and open the Al-Jazeera office straight away.

Since this showdown Al-Jazeera's Ramallah bureau has remained open, although that is not to say that its reporters never had any more trouble from the PA. A few days after the bureau had reopened Al-Omary received a menacing phone call from General Tawfiq Tiwari, the head of the Palestinian Mukhabarat, the intelligence wing of the Palestinian Authority. He told Al-Omary that although he knew the office had been reopened on Arafat's instructions, as head of the secret service he wanted him to understand that he was against the reopening and against Al-Jazeera generally. Al-Omary politely told Tiwari that if he had a problem he should address it directly to Arafat, who, as the democratically elected leader of the Palestinians, would be happy to hear from him.

Today Al-Omary maintains good relations with both the PA and the Israeli government. Both sides have come to respect his work, since he has acquired a reputation for telling the truth. Israelis still accuse him from time to time of bias towards the Palestinians, and Al-Jazeera still has occasional run-ins with the PA. When Abu Mazen became Prime Minister of Palestine, Arafat's office accused Al-Omary of bias towards Abu Mazen, while at the same time Abu Mazen's people were claiming the opposite. Since the shoe incident the PA has arrested Al-Omary only once, for five hours in Gaza. When a senior Palestinian official in the Legislative Council verbally attacked Al-Omary in public, he was bombarded with calls on his mobile phone from members of the Palestinian public telling him to leave Al-Jazeera alone. Al-Omary is stoical about his relationship with the authorities. 'We have had a lot of problems with the PA but I can tell you that I don't change anything in my coverage. I continue doing the same thing. First of all we have to tell the people the truth and if it is important then we cover it. We are not going to cover what makes the authorities feel comfortable. This is the last thing that is important to us. The authorities mean nothing to us. We are just working. We won't break the law but will cover everything that is important, even if it is dangerous.'

For its part the PA has come to understand that Al-Jazeera is more popular than it is and that it had better think twice before trying to push the network around. When Palestinians have a problem they call Al-Jazeera before they call the PA, and unfortunately for Al-Omary it isn't only with news tips. Sometimes they call simply because they think he personally might be able to help them with a problem. Many times he has arrived at his office to find people camped outside, ranging from those hoping he might be able to orchestrate a meeting with Arafat for them, to those who have come to request money. He sometimes gives them money out of his own pocket, especially students, but he cannot help them all. Sometimes the requests are bizarre. Once a woman called from a remote village just before the Ramadan holiday, telling him that she had recently divorced her husband and needed his help to arrange a meeting with her daughter during the holiday.

The PA has also come to understand that sometimes a camera can solve a problem sooner than a gun. It often employs Al-Jazeera's pictures as evidence in disputes and tips off Al-Jazeera with information. Al-Omary and his news team have a reputation among the Palestinians for the courage and wherewithal to go out and start reporting anywhere at any time. Because they are always on call and the action usually takes place at night, this places great strain on their personal lives.

Since the second intifada began it has achieved little good. Thousands of people have died, hundreds of homes have been demolished and there is still no peace. But what little good has come out of these terrible events can perhaps in part be attributed to Al-Jazeera. After the violent events of the winter of 2000, global awareness of the crisis in the Occupied Territories increased dramatically. The international community decided that no matter how intractable, this was a conflict that needed to be resolved. In June 2002 President George W. Bush became the first American president to acknowledge the inevitability of an independent Palestinian state and a 'road map to peace' was drawn up by the US, the United Nations, the European Union and Russia, which, although still far from fully implemented, envisaged among other things the creation of a Palestinian state by 2005. 'There is no evidence that the Israelis would have been moved by any other means than the struggle,' British Member of Parliament and Arab rights advocate George Galloway told Al-Jazeera in an interview. This is a conflict that, unlike some, has not been ignored and Al-Jazeera played a key role in making this happen.

The intifada propelled Al-Jazeera to fame in the Middle East and this had a rub-off effect on Qatar, which suddenly found itself famous for something other than pumping gas. It began to take a more pronounced role in regional and even global affairs. The Qatari Foreign Minister, Sheikh Hamad bin Jasim bin Jabr Al Thani, visited Washington, where, in an effort to revive the peace process, he met the Israeli Foreign Minister, Shimon Peres, and the US Secretary of State, Colin Powell. The meeting attracted a flurry of press attention that peaked when the Qataris proposed to host a peace conference in Doha. The Emir began to take to the world stage, making and receiving several state visits, including from the Taliban and the Cuban leader, Fidel Castro. He even invited the new Israeli Prime Minister, Ariel Sharon, to come to Doha, but nothing came of the invitation. In April 2001 he arranged a meeting between visiting US congressmen and a passing Taliban delegation.

Qatar began developing some of its own modest media ambitions. It held its first Film Festival, sponsored by Al-Jazeera. The network now had 350 staffers in Doha and thirty international correspondents, but it had plans to expand. In March it announced plans to start two new twenty-four-hour channels, one documentary and the other economic. In May CNBC announced talks with Al-Jazeera to launch a business-related news service and in June Al-Jazeera's test transmissions in Britain on BSkyB began. The plan was to offer a subscription-only service on Sky Digital to Britain's four hundred thousand Arabic speakers, before moving to other markets across Europe, and that autumn Al-Jazeera launched a direct-mail campaign targeted at the British Arab community in preparation for its imminent release.

However, despite combined revenue from cable subscriptions, programme sales and advertisements, Al-Jazeera was still not breaking even. This was because the Saudi government was still making concerted efforts to obstruct advertisers doing business with the network. In August the Swedish telecom manufacturer Ericsson withdrew a multi-million-dollar advertising campaign on Al-Jazeera shortly after it won a contract for a much larger advertising campaign from a Saudi telecommunications company. Al-Jazeera's marketing chief blamed Ericsson's change of heart on the Saudi government.

Al-Jazeera was also expanding its operations in North America. Already 200,000 Al-Jazeera subscribers in the US and Canada paid around $25 a month for a package of seven Arabic-language channels which included Al-Jazeera and this number was increasing by 2500 weekly. To increase its US profile Al-Jazeera stepped up coverage from Washington.

In January 2001 Al-Jazeera launched its Arabic-language website, http://www.aljazeera.net, which carried audio clips and complete transcripts from the discussion programmes, all for free, as well as opinion polls tying in with issues discussed on the talk shows. Like Al-Jazeera's television broadcasts, the website is in classical Arabic, the lingua franca of the Middle East. By May aljazeera.net was receiving three hundred thousand daily page views, about 25 per cent of which came from the US. After seven months the site had received more than nine million visits and forty-six million page views. In July alone, the site received more than 1.5 million visits and ten million page views.

In August the pro-Israeli American hawk Daniel Pipes and the terrorist expert Steven Emerson, then director of the Middle

East Forum and director of the Investigative Project respectively, co-authored an article in the *Wall Street Journal* suggesting that the US government should shut down websites related to terrorism that were hosted by servers in America. This was part of a bigger strategy the pair were presenting to the US government to push it to intervene more dynamically on behalf of Israel in the Palestinian conflict. 'One has to admire the Israeli restraint, then and over the past eight years,' they wrote, 'but one also has to wonder: when is the government going to begin more actively to defend its citizens? . . . The time has also come for the US to support Israel in rolling back the forces of terror . . . It doesn't take a genius to figure out what the US government should do . . . the federal authorities should use the tools it already has for closing down these Web sites and organizations.'

A few weeks after the article was published, a week before 9/11, eighty members of the elite North Texas Joint Terrorism Task Force, made up of the FBI, the Secret Service, the US Customs Service and the US Office of Foreign Assets Control, raided Al-Jazeera's web host, based in Dallas, Texas. The FBI declined to reveal what it was looking for, but copied masses of files over three days, saying the search was 'one aspect of a more than two-year investigation that is ongoing'. The Al-Jazeera website was shut down, as were five hundred other customers who shared the same web host, including another Arab newspaper.

Several American Islamic groups blamed the raid on Israeli lobbyists in Washington and denounced it as an 'anti Muslim witch-hunt'. This was strenuously denied by the US authorities. 'We were executing a search warrant as part of a criminal investigation. It had nothing to do with anti-Islamic or anti-Palestinian or anti-Middle East issues or anything like that,' said special agent Lori Bailey, spokeswoman for the Dallas FBI office. Besides hosting Al-Jazeera, the Web host sold Internet domain names with Arabic or Islamic themes, including 'jerusalem-palestine.com,' 'islamicfund.org' and 'ilovepalestine.net'.

4

September 11

'I stress that I have not carried out this act, which appears to have been carried out by individuals with their own motivation,' said the statement read out by an Al-Jazeera announcer.

In the wake of 9/11, Osama bin Laden immediately became the US administration's prime suspect. On Sunday 16 September Al-Jazeera received the statement, signed 'Sheikh Osama bin Laden', that was to propel the station to instant notoriety in the eyes of the West. In the faxed statement bin Laden insisted that while he was in Afghanistan he would obey the laws of the ruling Taliban regime, a regime that he said would not allow such an attack. He pledged allegiance to the Taliban leader, Mullah Muhammad Omar, saying: 'On this occasion, I affirm that I did not carry out this act. I live in the Emirate of Afghanistan and I have pledged allegiance to the emir of the faithful, who does not allow such acts.' He was used, he added, to the United States accusing him every time 'its many enemies strike at it'.

Washington rejected the denial. 'No question, he is the prime suspect, no question about that,' President Bush said, returning after the attacks from the Camp David retreat in Maryland's Catoctin Mountains. Speaking from the South Lawn of the White House, he ratcheted up the war rhetoric. 'People have declared war on America and they have made a terrible mistake,' he said. 'They have roused a mighty giant and, make no mistake about it, we're determined.' The President vowed to launch a 'crusade to rid the world of evildoers' and that: 'We will find 'em, get 'em running and hunt 'em down.'

Domestically, new laws to combat 'terror' were quickly railroaded into action. Vice President Cheney spoke of 'a lot of evidence' linking the nineteen suspected hijackers with bin Laden's Al-Qaeda network and he named Afghanistan as a potential target for retaliatory action. But the Taliban, citing both international and Islamic law, said on Al-Jazeera that they would not hand him over for trial until firm evidence had been produced by the United States connecting him with the attacks on that country.

This was not the first time that Osama bin Laden had appeared on Al-Jazeera. In 1998, at a time when Washington was threatening Baghdad, the channel had interviewed him for almost an hour, during which he had reminisced about his childhood and said that Muslims had a duty to wage religious war 'targeting all Americans', thus precipitating a protest by the US Embassy in Doha to the Qatari authorities.

A year before 9/11, in September 2000, after the attack on USS *Cole* off the coast of Yemen, Al-Jazeera had aired another chilling tape of bin Laden in which he had threatened to 'move forward' against American forces in the Persian Gulf. Looking very thin, he was shown surrounded by his lieutenants, including his operational commander Ayman al-Zawahiri, and Assad Allah Rahman, son of Sheikh Omar Abdul Rahman, the blind cleric who had orchestrated the first World Trade Center bombing.

After bin Laden had listed his grievances against America, Al-Zawahiri said, 'Enough of words; it is time to take action against this iniquitous and faithless force which has sent its troops all over Egypt, Yemen and Saudi Arabia.' All the men applauded before Assad Allah Rahman concluded: 'It's time to move forward and shed blood.' This tape had been part of the evidence that had prompted President Clinton to launch missile attacks on bin Laden's hideout and training camps in Afghanistan.

In January 2001 an Al-Jazeera correspondent, Ahmad Zaydan, was the only journalist present at the wedding of bin Laden's son Muhammad to the daughter of one of his aides. Exclusive footage was broadcast of bin Laden sitting on the carpeted floor of a tent in the southern Afghan town of Kandahar, smiling and shaking hands with wedding guests. Already at this time he had a $5-million bounty on his head, having been indicted in the US for allegedly masterminding the August 1998 bombings of the American embassies in Kenya and Tanzania, which killed more than two hundred people – a charge he had always denied. He also denied American allegations that he financed the bombing of an American military complex in the Saudi city of Dhahran in June 1996.

Besides hundreds of Al-Qaeda fighters and members of the Taliban, present at the wedding were bin Laden's mother, his two brothers and his sister. His family had flown in from Saudi Arabia aboard an Afghan plane that had come to pick up pilgrims for the Hajj. Bin Laden made a wedding speech – in which he seemed to steal the groom's limelight – reciting a romantic poem in praise of the Palestinians who had been killed in the intifada and those who died during the attack on the *Cole*.

Al-Jazeera also aired an exclusive video clip a few months before 9/11 of the Taliban destroying the Bamiyan Buddhas. The camera shook and thick clouds of smoke billowed upwards as viewers saw the smaller of the two ancient statues of the Buddha in the city of Bamiyan blown to smithereens by dynamite. Although the footage appeared first on Al-Jazeera, it had been shot by the Taliban themselves, following a diktat by their Supreme Leader, Mullah Muhammad Omar, that all statues in Afghanistan should be destroyed, regardless of their historical significance, to prevent idolatry. The two colossal statues had been carved into sandstone cliffs at Bamiyan more than fifteen hundred years ago and their destruction drew international condemnation. An international group of scholars, including Al-Jazeera's Sheikh al-Qaradawi, had travelled to Afghanistan in a vain attempt to persuade the Taliban to change their mind, arguing that the statues had been tolerated by the early Muslims and that non-Muslims had always been free to worship under Islam.

Nine days after the attacks on New York and Washington, on 20 September 2001, Al-Jazeera reran the December 1998 interview with Osama bin Laden. At the start of the ninety-minute tape bin Laden was introduced as a 'gun-wielding millionaire turned into a legend by the West'. Pictures showed him riding a horse, firing an AK-47 and even driving a bulldozer. Then came an interview conducted at an undisclosed location in Afghanistan by Al-Jazeera's correspondent in Pakistan, Gamal Ismail. Bin Laden explained at length why it was every Muslim's duty to participate in the jihad against the 'infidel' America and Israel. Clearly well versed in the Koran, he drew on the teachings of the prophet Muhammad as well as classical Arabic poetry in his argument. 'Every Muslim should seek a place to fight the Jihad . . . to please God,' said a bearded bin Laden, wearing traditional Afghan robes under a camouflage military jacket. 'What is wrong with resisting aggressors?'

It was important to air the interview a second time, Al-Jazeera explained, to give viewers an insight into the ideology of the alleged terrorist mastermind. World television networks queued up to pay for the pictures. Al Jazeera later ran sections of the tape several more times.

Then, on 24 September, there rolled off the fax machine in Al-Jazeera's Qatar office a message which, had it appeared anywhere else in the world at that time, might have seemed like a sick joke. It was a typewritten note, hand-signed with bin Laden's full name, Osama bin Muhammad bin Laden. The Al-Jazeera announcer read the note, as a still picture showing a copy of bin Laden's statement occupied the entire screen. It was a 'message to the Muslims of Pakistan', in which bin Laden urged them to mobilize all their resources to 'push away' what he described as 'the US crusader troops' and prevent them from invading Afghanistan and Pakistan.

This was a direct response to Bush, who had used the same term. There had been international concern about the word

'crusade', which the President had used several times, most
noticeably while standing on the White House lawn on 16
September. He had said, 'This is a new kind of, a new kind of
evil . . . and the American people are beginning to understand.
This crusade, this war on terrorism, is going to take a while.'

The word 'crusade' has historical connotations in the Middle
East and Europe that it does not have in America. It conjures
images from the Middle Ages of bloody Christian military
campaigns against the Muslims in an effort to capture the Holy
Land. The President's terminology was picked up and debated
in much of the Arab and European media, including on Al-Jazeera.
Now it was being thrown back at him by Osama bin Laden.

'We incite our Muslim brothers in Pakistan to deter with all
their capabilities the American crusaders from invading Pakistan
and Afghanistan,' the statement read. 'The new Jewish crusader
campaign is led by the biggest crusader, Bush, under the banner
of the Cross.'

The note ended with a quote from the Koran: 'If God helps
you, none can overcome you. If He forsakes you, who is there
after that, that can help you? In God, then, let believers put
their trust.'

It was now clear that the suspected terrorist had chosen Al-
Jazeera as his favoured conduit to the outside world. *Time* magazine's 'most wanted man in the world' stood accused by the US
of masterminding the attacks and the whole world wanted to
hear what he had to say. Al-Jazeera was the sole means by which
pictures from Afghanistan could reach the wider world.

The fax was headline news and so was the station that broadcast it. Speculation was rife about the relationship between bin
Laden and Al-Jazeera. Although it was widely assumed that bin
Laden himself had not sent the fax – a fax was too traceable –
the apparent cooperation between them suggested complicity.

Interestingly, apart from one or two radical Arab newspapers
which had also received messages from bin Laden in the past,
the rest of the Arab press did not print his picture or the full
contents of the fax. Conservative Arab governments regarded

him as too pernicious an influence and they had long exercised pressure through their respective information ministries to make sure press coverage about him was sparse. Bin Laden had sent videos to Arab news stations in the past, before the existence of Al-Jazeera, but had been consistently ignored. The Arab States Broadcasting Union obliges member states not to broadcast anything that prejudices or annoys another member state and that would certainly include footage of bin Laden. On this occasion the London-based Saudi-owned daily paper *Al-Sharq al-Awsat* accused Al-Jazeera of foolishly publishing a note that was clearly fabricated.

Al-Jazeera was bin Laden's 'mouthpiece', declared British tabloids, and was run by Palestinian and Syrian extremists. The *Daily Telegraph* called it 'Bin Laden TV'. 'All News Channel bin Laden Loves,' read the *New York Post*'s headline on 4 October. Inside was a mock quote from Osama bin Laden: 'People say I don't watch TV – but what do they know? It's obvious that I watch Al-Jazeera, the Arab world's all-news channel, because when I want to get a message to the outside world, I fax my statements to them.'

A pattern of suspected communiqués from Al-Qaeda was fast emerging. A week after 9/11 a man called *The Opposite Direction* claiming to be a spokesman for Al-Qaeda in Kuwait. He said US policy towards the Middle East was to blame for the suicide attacks. Shortly after bin Laden's fax, a second fax arrived from the reclusive Taliban leader, Mullah Muhammad Omar, urging Muslims to help finance the war against the West in the event Afghanistan was attacked. 'Merchants and owners of capital, your prime duty is to spend in the way of God,' the statement said. Broadcast on Al-Jazeera, all this added fuel to Western claims that Al-Jazeera was nothing but a mouthpiece for terrorists.

Hafez al-Mirazi, Al-Jazeera's bureau chief in Washington, denied any special connection with Al-Qaeda. He insisted bin Laden did not choose Al-Jazeera to make his pronouncements because of any perceived loyalty to his cause. 'It's the same reason that the Unabomber would send a letter or a fax to the *New*

York Times,' said Al-Mirazi. 'It's a matter of credibility with the audience and the same reason that [Secretary of State] Colin Powell gave us an interview, the same reason the White House calls us if there is any meeting between the President and Arab leaders. They want us to cover it,' he told the *New York Post*. When accused of only representing one side, he insisted he was frustrated that more American officials did not respond to his requests for interviews. 'We are desperate to find any officials,' he said. 'We say every day, "Please, come talk to us. Exploit us."'

Veteran anchorman Jamil Azar, one of many BBC-trained Al-Jazeera journalists, had already been vilified in the Egyptian press as an agent of both Mossad and Britain. When asked the day after the fax arrived what he knew about bin Laden's whereabouts, Azar replied simply, 'Things arrive on the fax machine. They could be coming from Pakistan or Tajikistan – we simply don't know.' He told AFP he believed that 'frank, objective and very intrepid' reporting combined with worldwide coverage was what had attracted bin Laden. 'In a professional way, we're flattered by this sort of attention from him. It means he thinks we are influential. If we were to be described as a mouthpiece for any regime, let alone bin Laden, it would be far from the truth and would worry us.'

Despite the widespread condemnation, the Western press was still extremely keen to use Al-Jazeera's pictures. With the channel now widely dubbed 'the Arab world's CNN', Sky was the first British station to strike a deal that enabled Arabic speakers in Britain and elsewhere in Europe to watch Al-Jazeera. Subscribers to BSkyB in Britain, a company part-owned by Rupert Murdoch's News International, could now watch Al-Jazeera for free. Al-Jazeera said it preferred to be compared to the BBC rather than CNN.

As President Bush warned the American public to brace themselves for a long fight, the world's media were waiting to move into Kabul to cover the imminent US assault on the Taliban.

Before 9/11 the only journalists in Kabul were three Afghan nationals working for three international news agencies – AFP, AP and Reuters. After the attacks all foreigners were asked to leave and no others were allowed in.

But, as it became apparent that a US invasion was brewing, international media organizations scrambled to get a position both in Afghanistan and in wider Central Asia.

On 1 October AP reported that 450 international journalists had registered in Pakistan, although the real number was estimated to be more than seven hundred, since many would have slipped in unofficially. They waited impatiently in Islamabad, hoping to get an Afghan visa to enter the country, but the beleaguered Mullah Muhammad Omar had decided to close the borders to foreign journalists. Faced with hostile Soviet propaganda during the Cold War, the Taliban leader had become suspicious of the media and on 3 October a Taliban radio broadcast attacked the BBC's output as enemy propaganda. Despite the Taliban, the BBC's John Simpson and cameraman Peter Jouvenal famously managed to cross the border briefly from Pakistan into Afghanistan and then back again, by wearing extra-large blue burkas. The *Sunday Express* journalist Yvonne Ridley, who later worked for Al-Jazeera, was not so lucky, and was arrested by the Taliban as a suspected spy when she crossed over the border.

The only way into Afghanistan for foreign journalists was by enlisting the help of the Northern Alliance, foes of the Taliban, who provided passage from neighbouring Tajikistan and by 1 October some 250 foreign journalists, mostly Westerners, were in Northern Alliance-held areas.

Although international phone lines had been cut, the three agency reporters in Kabul were each equipped with a satellite phone, with which they could communicate with their nearest bureau, in Islamabad, four or five times every day. This they did despite the Taliban decree that anyone found using a satellite phone would be hanged. Fortunately, since most of the Taliban did not know what a satellite phone looked like, this law had never been put into practice. Al-Jazeera had the only camera crew in the country and so the channel's news team was the only one able to transmit pictures, although technically photography and filming, along with lobsters, wearing shorts and flying kites, were banned too. The Taliban regarded television as a 'source of moral corruption' and music as suspect.

Al-Jazeera's correspondents in Afghanistan were Taysir Alluni in Kabul and Muhammad al-Burini in the southern Taliban stronghold of Kandahar. They delivered regular live broadcasts to the Doha studio via their uplink in Kabul. An uplink is the point on earth from which the satellite signal is transmitted up to the orbiting satellite. Uplink facilities have very large dishes, as much as ten or twelve metres in diameter, so the satellite can get the best possible reception.

No other network had anything approaching the same set-up or the same access. Abu Dhabi TV, Al-Jazeera's closest Arabic-language news rival, was currently covering events in Afghanistan from Peshawar and Islamabad in Pakistan. 'We are the only [television] present in the Taliban-controlled zone,' Al-Jazeera chief editor Ibrahim Hilal told AFP with pride.

Al-Jazeera's serendipitous position meant it had a monopoly on all the pictures, stories and interviews coming from Afghanistan. Almost daily interviews with Taliban officials as the international situation deteriorated were each a valuable exclusive. Taysir Alluni's bulletins about how the Taliban's heavy machine guns had brought down an unmanned American plane or how Afghan demonstrators had stormed the US Embassy in Kabul were all quickly devoured by analysts trying to make sense of the situation inside a country which few people knew much about. At the gathering of Taliban clerics to discuss handing bin Laden over to the US, Al-Jazeera's live coverage was broadcast to Doha and then syndicated around the world.

As the doors of diplomacy swung shut, those in Afghanistan who had any comprehension of the magnitude of 9/11 began to anticipate a massive American retaliation. Taysir Alluni told how people were starting to flee Kabul, leaving the Taliban to erect missile batteries and take anti-aircraft precautions in the capital.

As an American-led war against Afghanistan became inevitable, it was starkly obvious that Al-Jazeera was about to scoop the whole thing. This was of grave concern to the American administration, who, in the wake of 9/11, had become particularly sensitive about how the 'War on Terror' was covered. Already, in the run-up to the war, the American administration had knocked heads with the network over a story that Afghan security forces had seized five members of the US Special Forces on a reconnaissance mission near the border with Iran. The Americans vehemently denied this was true – the US Ambassador in Doha even lodged a formal protest with the Qatari Foreign Minister – but Al-Jazeera stuck by its story, saying it had come from the same Taliban source who had invited the channel's reporter Ahmad Zaydan to bin Laden's son's wedding.

This spat did not augur well for the US administration, but there was little it could do at this stage to temper the network's output. Steps could be taken, however, to prevent the retransmission of Al-Jazeera's footage in America. On 10 October the White House announced it had asked the five major US television networks, ABC, CBS, CNN, Fox and NBC, to censor Al-Qaeda footage, which meant in practical terms material from Al-Jazeera, since it was the only network in a position to deliver it. In a thirty-minute conference call National Security Adviser Condoleezza Rice urged all the American network chiefs not to screen videos of bin Laden.

Shamefully, all five network executives conceded they would vet all their clips from Afghanistan and not use any of Al-Jazeera's footage live. 'Pre-recorded statements from representatives of Al-Qaeda could be communicating hidden messages to their members,' said Walt Disney Co.'s ABC News. NBC would 'apply journalistic judgement before deciding which portions, if any, we will broadcast', said a spokesman. 'We'll do whatever is our patriotic duty,' said Australian-born media mogul Rupert Murdoch, whose company News Corp owned the Fox News channel, Fox Television, Twentieth Century Fox, other television stations and a large stable of newspapers. 'Our policy is to avoid directly transmitting any report we think will facilitate any terrorist action,' reasoned CNN in a statement. 'To determine what should be transmitted, CNN will take the advice of the pertinent authorities.'

The US First Amendment, it was stressed, was not at stake in this instance because Rice had phrased her concerns as a request and not as an order, but the pressure from the White House was obvious. The next day White House press secretary Ari Fleischer asked America's newspaper editors not to publish full transcripts of bin Laden's or Al-Qaeda's statements.

Britain, America's most loyal ally in the War on Terror, also tried to exert pressure on the press. Tony Blair summoned the top British broadcasters, the BBC, ITN and Sky News, to Downing Street, where his media adviser, Alastair Campbell, gave them a stern lesson on what would constitute acceptable reporting. He told them that they had to be 'more sceptical' of Taliban claims about civilians killed in the bombing and that they should avoid seeking out extremist Islamic voices. Any more bin Laden footage which materialized, the three networks were told, would have to be censored, for there was a 'real danger that they could be sending out messages to terrorists members of their network'.

British broadcasters were unimpressed. The BBC, ITN and Sky News issued a joint statement which read: 'As responsible broadcasters we are mindful of national and international security issues and the impact reports can have in different communities and cultures. But we will retain the right to exercise our own independent, impartial editorial judgement . . . the provision of independent and impartial news is a fundamental part of a free society and the democratic process.'

These calls for censorship demonstrated a dim appreciation of Al-Qaeda's proven ability to manipulate modern telecommunications. Britain and America both claimed Al-Jazeera's footage should be censored in its retransmission on other networks to thwart bin Laden's attempts to pass secret messages through news clips. This was a patently ridiculous argument. After all, if the members of an Al-Qaeda sleeper cell were expecting a secret tip-off from bin Laden, would they really be watching the BBC or CNN? Surely they would just subscribe to Al-Jazeera itself and watch the unedited version? If they were banking on getting their orders from a retransmission of bin Laden's speech on the BBC they might have a problem, as the clip the BBC ran lasted less than a minute and bin Laden's full speech had been twenty-five minutes long. The chance of catching the message would have been slim.

Any American household with a satellite dish and a view of the sky could sign up with EchoStar Communications Corporation's Dish Network and order Al-Jazeera straight away for around $25 a month as part of their seven-channel 'Arabic Enhanced Pack'. In October 2001 EchoStar Dish Network had more than six million subscribers, but only about one hundred and fifty thousand of these chose to subscribe to Al-Jazeera. The American administration did not ask EchoStar to stop carrying Al Jazeera for two reasons. The first was that American intelligence probably depended on EchoStar to watch bin Laden's speeches on Al-Jazeera, like everybody else. The second was that, even if EchoStar had broken its contract and dropped Al-Jazeera, most American households would still have been able to receive the signal via satellite.

In 2001 Al-Jazeera footage arrived in America like this: a signal was transmitted from the Kabul uplink to a satellite above Afghanistan. The signal would be retransmitted from the satellite's on-board transponders back towards Doha, where a jumbo parabolic receiving dish was waiting to collect it. In Al-Jazeera's headquarters in Doha the footage was assembled and edited into news, before being broadcast back out again to the Arabsat 2A satellite, owned by the Arab League and controlled from Saudi Arabia, which was positioned above Africa. The Arabsat 2A satellite sent the signal back down to earth, at the major European satellite station in Fucino, Italy. From there the signal was uplinked again, to half a dozen satellites around the world, including the large PAS 9 satellite, owned by the PanAmSat Corporation, which had a geostationary position above North America. The PAS 9 satellite sent the signal back down to earth a third time, where it was received by Wyoming-based EchoStar, which in turn pumped the signal back up to one of its own smaller satellites above America. This small satellite fed the signal into American households via their domestic satellite dishes.

Such a decentralized route meant that it was virtually impossible to stop Al-Jazeera being received. If the US government stopped EchoStar transmitting Al-Jazeera, then the signal from PAS 9 would still be receivable in America, although viewers would need a larger satellite dish, two metres in diameter. Nearly a million American households have one. If the government pressured PanAmSat to stop relaying Al-Jazeera from PAS 9, viewers with large dishes could still receive Al-Jazeera through one of the other half-dozen satellites that received the signal from Fucino. If the government persuaded the Italians to stop transmitting the signal, then viewers under the footprint of Arabsat 2A – which covers Europe, Africa and the Middle East – could still watch Al-Jazeera.

Only in this rather complicated and no doubt politically tortuous way could the American authorities stop the Al-Jazeera signal arriving in the US. However, a potential terrorist could still be watching unedited Al-Jazeera footage retransmitted on one of countless other international news television stations which often showed Al-Jazeera, including Filipino, Indonesian and Chinese stations. Since Al-Jazeera had become so important at this critical time, it was being carried by plenty of international news channels around the clock.

Nor did the coalition's plans for censoring Al-Jazeera make any allowance for the Internet. All of bin Laden's messages were available unedited online to anybody with a computer and a dial-up connection. If that failed, Al-Qaeda operatives could always pick up a telephone. In short, government efforts in the twenty-first century to stop a determined Al-Qaeda sleeper cell from receiving a message from bin Laden, through technical means alone, were destined to fail.

Bin Laden himself pointed this out in another video, released in January 2002. 'They made hilarious claims. They said that Osama's messages have codes in them to the terrorists. It's as if we were living in the time of mail by carrier pigeon, when there are no phones, no travellers, no Internet, no regular mail, no express mail and no electronic mail. I mean these are very humorous things. They discount people's intellects.'

All these undemocratic calls for censorship did achieve was to limit the Western public's ability to evaluate the War on Terror. Fantasies about Al-Qaeda sending secret messages through the television were so acute that the White House was prepared to reinterpret the constitution to control the media. What was really at stake had nothing to do with Al-Qaeda operatives, but was a concern by the coalition authorities that they were about to lose the media war to Al-Jazeera.

During the months following 9/11 patriotism consumed America. New legislation to control the media was drafted, in the form of the Patriot Act. For the first time the government was allowed to subpoena generic information – like a name and a billing address – from satellite content providers if it suspected someone was involved in terrorist activities. It could not tell from this information whether someone was watching Al-Jazeera or anything else, but the new law certainly contributed to the climate of stringent self-censorship in the American press.

The American media was timid in interrogating its own administration about the war. Journalists depended heavily on government spokesmen from the Department of Justice and the Pentagon for information, whom they rarely cross-examined with independent sources. Everyone from the *Daily Mail* to Tony Blair and US Defense Secretary Donald Rumsfeld was accusing anyone critical of the US government's new actions of being anti-American.

Although the country was gearing up for war the media

refrained from publishing pictures of troop movements, in part because it was denied access to all but a few military points. It did not worry unduly about the more than eight hundred people who had been detained in custody, in murky legal circumstances, either on alleged immigration violations or as material witnesses for grand juries. Nor did it object when the US Attorney General, John Ashcroft, rescinded a government-wide directive supporting the Freedom of Information Act. The abundance of American flags, fluttering in newsreaders' lapels and during commercial breaks, did not suggest a particularly independent frame of mind, nor was the media climate in America conducive to debate.

One media outlet made life particularly difficult for Al-Jazeera. The network's Washington bureau had been planning to move into a new building in Virginia, next to a liberally minded American press organization called the Freedom Forum. 'The Freedom Forum, based in Arlington, Va., is a nonpartisan foundation dedicated to free press, free speech and free spirit for all people,' its website proudly declares. 'The foundation focuses on three priorities: the Newseum, First Amendment and newsroom diversity.' The Newseum is an 'interactive museum of news'. Among other things, the Freedom Forum hands out a million-dollar annual prize to one individual deemed to have demonstrated 'exceptional free spirit'. On World Press Freedom Day it commemorates journalists who have died covering the news by adding their names to the Freedom Forum Journalists Memorial, in Freedom Park.

In the weeks before 9/11, the Freedom Forum had agreed to allow Al-Jazeera to move into its offices. 'We were subleasing through them,' Al-Jazeera's Washington bureau chief, Hafez al-Mirazi, explained to me. 'Then, after 9/11, when everything was done and we were moving, they said, "No, you can't, because we are worried about some of the other tenants and we cannot have it." "Worried about what?" I asked. "What's going to happen?" And they said, "No, we cannot." And I said, "This is very funny and sad, that you are Freedom Forum, who would like us to be killed so that next year you can put our names in your records here in Freedom Forum [Freedom Park] but you won't let us share your office now.'"

There were, of course, exceptions to this trend of patriotism. For example, the Voice of America, an independent agency funded by the US government, was asked by the Department of State not to air a story that included an interview with Mullah Muhammad Omar. Since there was no doubt that what the Taliban leader had to say was newsworthy, despite government objections that a public broadcaster had become a platform for 'terrorists', the programme went ahead.

The Emir of Qatar, Sheikh Hamad bin Khalifa Al Thani, was invited to Washington, where he met President Bush and Colin Powell, among others. The official reason for the Emir's visit was that he was chairman of the Organization of the Islamic Conference, the largest Islamic organization in the world, but Washington was on a mission to petition Islamic support for its War on Terror. By courting its Islamic allies, the White House hoped to show that this new war was not targeting Muslims. Colin Powell decided to use this opportunity to have a quiet word with the Emir about Al-Jazeera.

Exactly what transpired is unclear, but it was well known that US officials were unhappy with the reruns of the old bin Laden television interview and felt Al-Jazeera had given too much airtime to analysts hostile to the US in the aftermath of the attacks on Washington and New York. The White House thought that Al-Jazeera had encouraged anti-American sentiment in the Middle East and disliked terminology like the 'US-named war against terrorism'. Colin Powell asked the Emir if the station could moderate the tone of its coverage of Afghanistan. The Emir told the press.

The Americans, he announced, had asked him to 'influence' Al-Jazeera to 'tone down' their reporting. 'We heard from the US administration, and also from the previous administration,' he was quoted as saying by CNN. 'Naturally we take these things as a kind of advice.' The Emir dismissed the notion that

Al-Jazeera's coverage was unbalanced, saying the network had given both US and Afghan officials equal airtime since the attacks. 'We are balanced and objective and never interfere in the news. We give all opposing views,' he said. Bin Laden 'is a party to the conflict and his opinions must be heard'. He said he had no intention of interfering with Al-Jazeera 'because parliamentary life requires you have free and credible media and that is what we are trying to do'.

'These accusations are not strange', Al-Jazeera's general manager, Muhammad Jasim al-Ali, told Reuters. 'We have been accused of being the voice of Iraq because of our coverage, and now as we are the only people with access in Afghanistan, we're accused of being pro-Afghani.' He added: 'At one point, we were accused of being agents of the Americans, the Zionists and the Iraqis at one and the same time. It was even alleged that Saddam Hussein is a shareholder in Al-Jazeera. We have correspondents in the United States and we have correspondents in Kabul and Kandahar. We give equal coverage to both sides and that is our role. We present both sides.'

Shortly after the Emir's bombshell, US Department of State spokesman Richard Boucher reiterated Powell's remarks in a press briefing. 'We've expressed our concerns about some of the kinds of things we've seen on their air, particularly inflammatory stories, totally untrue stories, things like that . . . We would certainly like to see them tone down the rhetoric.'

Qatar's Foreign Minister, Sheikh Hamad bin Jasim bin Jabr Al Thani, responded by claiming the United States had not yet presented any clear evidence of bin Laden's involvement in 9/11. He said that although Al-Jazeera may have made mistakes there was no reason to shut it down.

Criticizing Al-Jazeera boosted the network's notoriety and flew in the face of something in which the United States once took considerable pride: the freedom that the American media enjoys from government interference. It was ironic that the puritanical Taliban tolerated Al-Jazeera, but the United States would not.

The Committee to Protect Journalists condemned the interference. 'The US administration is effectively urging Qatari
authorities to interfere with what is essentially an independent
news station,' said CPJ executive director Ann Cooper. 'Arab
government attempts to influence Al-Jazeera have garnered widespread attention over the years. We are disheartened to see US
officials adopting similar tactics.'

'Because this comes from the United States, which considers
itself the strongest advocate of freedom of expression, it comes
as very strange and unacceptable,' Al-Jazeera news editor Ahmad
Sheikh told AP in a telephone interview from Doha. 'We believe
in objectivity, integrity and presenting all points of view – which
includes both Osama bin Laden and George W. Bush.' Mr
Powell's request, he said, 'revealed the true face of [Washington's]
hypocrisy. Would they have dared to violate the US constitution and also tried to censor CBS?'

In an open letter to Colin Powell, the International Press
Institute (IPI) called on the Secretary of State to stop pressuring media organizations and 'to allow them to report freely based
on their own editorial policy'. 'In the opinion of IPI,' wrote its
director, Jonathan Fritz, 'the attempt to curtail the news reporting of an independent television station, based in another
country, is an infringement of editorial independence.' Fritz also
expressed concern that America was developing a 'two-tiered
approach' which 'enables balanced news stories to be reported
in Western countries while trying to prevent similar news stories
being aired in the Middle East'.

Media commentators in the Arab world were even more
assertive in their criticism of America's attempt to interfere with
Al-Jazeera. Arab newspapers, including Lebanon's *Daily Star*, the
London-based *Al-Hayat*, Jordan's *Al-Arab al-Yawm* and Qatar's
Gulf Times, criticized its attempts to influence the channel. They
argued that Washington was trying to pin anti-American sentiment on Al-Jazeera, when, in fact, it had only itself to blame
for disregarding human rights issues committed by pro-American
regimes in the Middle East. 'This is truly appalling,' said Majed

Alalawi, deputy head of the Bahrain Center for Studies and Research. 'I would have expected Powell to ask for more liberalization, for more freedom of speech in the region, not for more censorship.'

The Palestinian newspaper *Al-Hayat al-Jadidah* sprang to the vigorous defence of Al-Jazeera. 'Al-Jazeera is now accused of promoting hatred against the United States . . . We reassure our colleagues in Al-Jazeera that they have a huge credit in the Arab street. We congratulate them on the anger of America and Israel at their respected channel.'

An article in the Jordanian newspaper *Al-Arab al-Yawm* said:

> There is nothing surprising in the attempt on the part of the United States and certain Western nations to suppress Al-Jazeera Satellite Television Channel insofar as its coverage of the current developments is concerned. What is surprising, though, is the boldness with which these attempts were disclosed. If this is emblematic of anything it is of the disdain in which the Arab intellect and will, and for that matter the burgeoning democratic experiments in our part of the world, are held . . . It is to be regretted that these 'democratic' rules are not good for consumption outside the borders of the United States, more so in the Third World nations than any place else.

The message from the White House made no impression on Al-Jazeera's editorial policy, but it did cause an upsurge of interest in the channel in the West. It was not long before Al-Jazeera screened another video from Al-Qaeda. This one, said Al-Jazeera in a statement, was a 'couple of weeks old'. The television reporter told viewers, 'Al-Jazeera satellite channel has obtained what is believed to be the latest video clips taken of Osama bin Laden and Dr Ayman al-Zawahiri. The footage was reportedly filmed during a ceremony held to announce the unification of Al-Qaeda Organization led by bin Laden, and Al-Jihad Organization led by Al-Zawahiri.'

Pictures showed an unsmiling Osama bin Laden, flanked by masked guards, attending a celebration in a camp in a remote mountain location. Al-Qaeda gunmen were firing shots into the air and singing militant songs. Later the pair reviewed a platoon of hooded guerrillas holding assault rifles at the ready. The video was probably filmed before 9/11 because since then the Afghan mountains had been subjected to intense scrutiny by US spy planes and a big outdoor gathering like this would almost certainly have been spotted. The video graphically underlined Qatar's rejection of America's demand, but unlike the next bin Laden video Al-Jazeera broadcast, this one had little significant political impact on the unfolding situation.

On 7 October, twenty-six days after the attacks in New York and Washington, the air war started. Al-Jazeera dramatically interrupted its regular programming schedule to go live to Afghanistan. The announcer said, 'In Afghanistan, there seems to be fresh developments as the Taliban movement cut off electricity from the capital Kabul and explosions are being heard in the Afghan capital while ground defences have started, it seems, to confront the planes. This is what we are watching from the Afghan capital, Kabul, directly right now.'

Then the studio in Doha launched into a live two-way interview with its correspondent Taysir Alluni, conducted from the corrugated-iron roof of his 'office' in Kabul. About 8.57 p.m. local time the first Tomahawk cruise missiles arrived, launched from American and British vessels in the Arabian Sea. Just after nightfall the Taliban cut off the electricity throughout Kabul and the lights blinked out. Large explosions shook the city, followed by the chatter of anti-aircraft fire. During the interview one missile landed so close to the Al-Jazeera team that it blew the cameraman off the roof. 'I am sorry the cameraman has disappeared and I don't know where he is,' Alluni told the studio.

Then he set up a spotlight on the roof of the office, explaining as he did, 'I don't want to be a target too or you will be without news. The city's power has been cut, I'm in the dark, and will become a sitting duck if the missiles zero in on me.' When the cameraman reappeared he shot footage of planes flying overhead, while thunderous explosions could be seen and heard in the sky.

It was the start of the American-led assault on Afghanistan. In Washington, President Bush confirmed US and British military action had begun. 'The battle is now joined on many fronts,' he said in a televised address. 'We will not waiver, we will not falter, and we will not fail. Peace and freedom will prevail.'

As the first bombs fell, Muhammad Kicham, the Qatar-based anchor, heard a voice come through his earpiece: 'Muhammad, you're now on CNN . . . and BBC . . . and Sky News.' In that instant a sizeable proportion of the world's population saw Al-Jazeera for the first time. Alluni's footage of the attacks on Kabul was shown that night on TV stations worldwide. As it was sent by videophone, there was not much to see, and hazy night-vision shots in phosphorous green made for a grainy tableau that looked more like the bottom of an aquarium than a night sky. 'It is not obviously,' decided CNN's Aaron Brown, 'a television war.'

The next night a second wave of bombing swept over Kabul. A world away in newsrooms in America, evening was approaching. The anchors and reporters explained almost apologetically that they would have to wait until daylight in Afghanistan for satellite images of the devastation, because, apart from the Al-Jazeera footage, none of them had any pictures. 'If we could see pictures tonight, how awesome would the American firepower be, do you think?' the Sky news anchor asked.

On the first night of the bombing, a few hours after an address to the nation by Bush and only minutes after Blair had addressed Britain, Taysir Alluni announced that he had just received a video from Al-Qaeda which he would transmit live immediately, although he did not yet know what it contained. 'It was sent to us by one of the individuals, who appears to be from the Taliban movement leadership,' he said. It was a new pre-recorded video message by Osama bin Laden and his first verified statement made after the 9/11 attacks. It was to be his most powerful message yet.

All the US networks were monitoring Al-Jazeera closely, and when the announcement was made that a new message was about to be broadcast, network executives scrambled to go across to Al-Jazeera at once, instead of using their normal footage. Three US networks and two cable all-news channels hastily cut across to Al-Jazeera in time for the speech. Live sports coverage of a World Cup soccer qualifier, a NASCAR race and a Giants game were all interrupted. Other networks, caught by surprise and unsure of the authenticity of what they were about to see, only managed to broadcast the speech later. Fox News did not have an English translation ready in time. None of the networks was exactly sure what was going on or what they were looking at, because at the beginning of the tape only bin Laden's henchmen were visible. NBC, CBS and Fox all heavily qualified what viewers were about to see, saying they had no idea where it was taking place or when it was shot.

The fact that the American administration took absolutely no steps to prevent American networks transmitting this message, less than three weeks after it had expressly called for a ban on all live, unedited videotaped messages issued by Osama bin Laden, reflected the administration's ill-thought-out, hand-to-mouth media policy in the wake of 9/11. First it warned of secret messages. Then it realized that nothing would seal its case for war better than a live Al-Qaeda confession.

The tape showed bin Laden dressed in combat fatigues and an Afghan headdress, kneeling in a stone cave and flanked by two aides armed with automatic rifles. After a statement by Sulayman Abu-Ghayth, identified by a caption on the screen as 'official spokesman of the Al-Qaeda organization', came bin Laden, holding a microphone and staring at the camera with his languid eyes. He did not claim responsibility for the September 11 attacks but expressed support for those who carried them out.

'America has been filled with horror from north to south and east to west, and thanks be to God what America is tasting now is only a copy of what we have tasted,' he said in reference to 9/11. In a soft voice he concluded with a pledge: 'I swear to God that America will not live in peace before peace reigns in Palestine'. After bin Laden had spoken, his chief lieutenant, Ayman al-Zawahiri, stated that the attacks had been prompted by America's support for Israel.

When the tape had finished rolling, the Al-Jazeera anchorman in Qatar said, 'So, these were clips from a tape that has just been transmitted to us from our office in Kabul. This tape was recorded during daytime. It seems that arrangements were made to show the tape after the strike.'

These pictures are 'live on Middle Eastern television', said the presenter on Britain's ITN; Channel 5 credited 'Afghan television, Al-Jazeera'; the presenters at Channel 4 did not attribute the pictures at all. The BBC, in keeping with its policy of not naming other television stations, mentioned Al-Jazeera just once by name later that same evening, in a report by John Simpson on the *Ten O'Clock News*. During a live two-way conversation with the studio in London, Simpson spoke from Afghanistan, saying he had been 'at that station, Al-Jazeera in Kabul' only 'a couple of weeks before,' adding, 'it has very close links with Osama bin Laden and they have been very careful to foster those links'. The BBC's Stephen Sackur said simply that the pictures came from 'an Arab station', but the pictures shown on the BBC came via its sharing agreement with ABC, which had plastered the caption 'Courtesy of Al-Jazeera' across the screen, so the connection was made for British viewers.

The eerie video was replayed again and again on all the networks over the next few days, partly because all the other pictures coming out of Afghanistan were so poor. Both the content and timing of this latest tape were deeply chilling. As US warplanes and missiles had begun pounding Kabul, suddenly to see Osama bin Laden calling for a holy war on satellite TV was dramatic timing *par excellence*.

This was, in fact, bin Laden's fourth call for jihad, but it exhibited a greater degree of media manipulation than in the past. By linking the fate of Al-Qaeda with the fate of the Palestinians, he aimed to appeal to the greatest number of Arabs. He understood and envied the much deeper appeal the Palestinian cause had to the Arab public and so was trying to align himself accordingly.

Bin Laden was deftly using the most widely distributed and trusted Arab network to pit Arab domestic populations against their rulers. This manipulation of modern media and technology was becoming his signature. First he hijacked airplanes, now he had hijacked the airwaves. By appearing on Al-Jazeera, a global platform with a reputation forged in the intifada, bin Laden was profiting from Al-Jazeera's respected reputation in the Middle East. His symbolism was as epic as could be, suggesting the clash of two mighty civilizations was at hand. UN sanctions against Iraq, Palestine and Western corruption, all topics in his speech, were close to the heart of every Arab. Linking the war against America with the struggle in Palestine was to play upon heart-felt Arab sentiments. America's hypocrisy struck a loud chord with Muslims around the world.

Saddam Hussein was to try the same trick when the American-led coalition invaded Iraq two years later, but coming from a man who had turned down a life of luxury to live in a cave for a cause, Osama bin Laden's message seemed deeply credible to many. The effect his words had on the Arab street was hard to quantify, but one indicator was the plethora of admirers that sprang up online in Arabic political chatrooms.

Addressing the world so soon after Bush and Blair, bin Laden looked defiant. Wearing battle fatigues and a white Muslim headscarf, he seemed like a holy warrior ready to die. Unflinchingly facing the camera, when he spoke of punishing America for the decades of 'humiliation and disgrace' which it had inflicted on the Muslim world, he wanted to look like an Islamic hero.

The pressure to deliver good pictures when everyone was

depending on Al-Jazeera resulted in squabbles between the networks. CNN had signed a deal with Al-Jazeera by which it could broadcast Al-Jazeera's pictures for six hours before anyone else could touch them. Anticipating scoops from Afghanistan, some days earlier CNN bosses had faxed a letter to all the other networks, reminding them about this. In broadcasting the bin Laden speech direct from the Al-Jazeera satellite feed, the other networks had flagrantly disregarded that warning and now CNN was furious.

'We felt there was an overwhelming public interest in seeing these important statements which far outweigh any commercial interest CNN may have been pursuing,' said Jeffrey Schneider, vice president of ABC News. CNN backed down. 'Although this usage is considered an act of piracy, CNN and Al-Jazeera made a decision to ignore it for one day only,' said Al-Jazeera's managing director in a letter addressed to the other American networks.

This graphic first salvo of the media war was Al-Jazeera's most sensational scoop yet and from now on the news channel was viewed with renewed suspicion in the West. Many thought its links with the Taliban were much too close and the perfect timing of the last tape suggested complicity. There were suggestions that bin Laden had instructed Al-Jazeera to play it at the most opportune moment, possibly when the bombing started. The channel's explanation was that this latest tape had simply been left at its satellite uplink station in Kabul, but this was widely disbelieved.

In an interview with AFP on the day of the scoop, Al-Jazeera's chairman, Sheikh Hamad bin Thamir Al Thani, said Western speculation did not bother him:

> We will never change our strategy of covering news wherever it is. The viewers are our only judge. We are accused of putting forward the viewpoints of the Taliban or bin Laden. That is not true.
> We are looking for big news. And today we are lucky

to be in Afghanistan. During the Gulf war in 1991, CNN was the only satellite channel to broadcast to the world the speeches of Iraqi leaders, and it was not accused of being turned into a mouthpiece for Saddam Hussein.

Why do people hold against this freedom which Western media benefit from? We are giving the version of all sides. We have always been a target for accusation. We have been called pro-Iraqi, pro-Israeli and today pro-Taliban.

Bin Laden knew that Al-Jazeera, unlike other Arabic channels, operated in an atmosphere of freedom, independent of governmental influence. He could be confident when he sent them his speech that it would not be edited and that it would reach a wide audience. Tony Blair was the first Western leader to realize that the best way to stop bin Laden from winning the war of words in the Middle East would be by counter-attack. He had learned in domestic politics the importance of a fast rebuttal and having just read the Koran during his summer holiday, so becoming perhaps the third British Prime Minister since Gladstone to make any serious attempt to understand Islam – the others being Anthony Eden and Winston Churchill – Downing Street quietly let it be known that the Prime Minister would welcome a call from Al-Jazeera about the possibility of doing an interview.

'So I called the press officer and said, "I hear that you are interested in doing an interview with Al-Jazeera,"' Muftah al-Suwaidan recalled. 'They said yes, it is very important his message goes out to the Arabic audience. No time was agreed but it was understood it would be in the next three or four days.'

A couple of days later, at two o'clock in the afternoon, Al-Suwaidan received a call from the Prime Minister's press office telling him to be in Downing Street in an hour. So he scrambled a cameraman and immediately summoned Sami Haddad, the presenter of the political talk show *More than One Opinion*, who was once part of the ill-fated BBC Arabic project.

'What was strange was, within five minutes of hanging up

the phone to the press office, everybody knew,' said Al-Suwaidan. 'Sky, the *Guardian*, everyone started calling saying, "I hear you are doing an interview with the PM . . . what are you going to ask him?" I was so surprised. When we got to Downing Street there were photographers everywhere taking pictures of us. They had all completely forgotten about the Prime Minister.'

Appearing in a dark suit and tie inside Number Ten, Blair explained to millions of Arab viewers why he had ordered the strikes on Afghanistan, his interview with Sami Haddad being simultaneously translated into Arabic. Bin Laden had enjoyed an open microphone, but Haddad, the BBC-trained Al-Jazeera interviewer, did not make things so easy for the Prime Minister.

Blair emphasized that he was after justice, not revenge, and that this was not a war between civilizations. Haddad accused him of being 'hawkish' towards Arab states compared with other European countries and pointed out that the traditional legal concept of innocent until proven guilty seemed to have gone out of the window in this instance. He suggested the coalition's policy of dropping food aid to the Afghan people was 'a way to kill the father and feed the son'.

'We are certain the Al-Qaeda and Osama bin Laden are responsible for what happened,' replied Blair. 'Bin Laden praised on your television the perpetrators of the attacks, saying that these acts are right and that they should have been done.' He warned that if bin Laden were to prevail then he would impose a fundamentalist Islamic regime across the world. 'I don't believe that anybody seriously wants to live under that kind of regime.' Then he said that bin Laden's fundamentalist 'version' of Islam was 'a million miles away from the reality'. Haddad retorted, 'Isn't it the task of the Muslim world to see to that, not the Western Christian world?'

Although Blair adequately set out the coalition's position on the War on Terror, his answers on other issues, including about Iraq and possible further attacks on other Arab countries, were scorned by Haddad. The Prime Minister was accused of abandoning the Afghan mujahadeen to their fate at the hands of the Soviet Union and leaving a 'million children to die' in Iraq. Haddad compared Hezbollah, Hamas and Islamic Jihad to the French Resistance fighters who fought the Nazis. 'Well, some people may consider them to be freedom fighters,' Mr Blair replied haltingly, but 'blowing up innocent civilians' deserved to be universally condemned.

Significantly, he stopped short of supporting Palestinian rights under international law. Haddad said to him: 'You always talk about weapons of mass destruction as if Iraq is the only country which has had weapons of mass destruction. What about Israel? They have weapons of mass destruction. You don't talk about that.'

Despite the grilling, Blair's effort as spokesman for the coalition, to win hearts and minds in the Middle East, was commendable. He was certainly well liked by the Al-Jazeera team who met him.

'The Prime Minister was very nice,' Al-Suwaidan, who was the producer that day with Sami Haddad, told me. 'He is really a very nice guy, but what's his name, Alastair Campbell? He was standing right there next to Tony Blair as the interview was taking place. Oh!' Then Al-Suwaidan, who is Qatari, continued in a tough-sounding Irish accent, in imitation of the Prime Minister's fearsome press secretary, although Campbell is not Irish. 'Sami! Sami, your time is up!' he cried, tapping his wristwatch fiercely to indicate that time was up long ago. 'I said, "Sami, don't listen to him!" Sometimes when you have a hot issue if they tell you you've got fifteen minutes, take half an hour. Just act like you can't hear. It's a game, isn't it?' Then, in his best Alastair Campbell voice again, now apoplectic and pointing at his watch: 'Sami!'

'After we came out,' he went on, 'I had the tapes in my hand and everybody was waiting for us and they took photos of us. It was a big thing for us. You know how the Western media make small things a big deal? For us we are not used to this. I swear to God! We were in the papers and everything, me and Sami.'

Blair's direct appeal to the Arab street was part of a tactical diplomatic offensive to sustain the fragile international coalition behind the military strikes. He chose to deliver his message on Al-Jazeera for the same reasons that bin Laden did. It was impossible to tell how well his speech was received in the Arab world, but the Arabs I met told me they tuned in because he was the British Prime Minister, not because they were particularly interested in his political message. It did little to make Arabs accept the invasion of a Muslim country.

In most Middle Eastern newspapers Blair's speech never received as much coverage as bin Laden's, which was printed side by side on front pages next to Bush's. The President's simplistic message – that you were either on America's side or the terrorists' – and bin Laden's Manichean vision, which divided people between 'the camp of the faithful and camp of the infidel', gave the reader the choice. Blair had tried to win hearts and minds, but Bush's speech had turned the coalition's position into a mockery.

Before Blair's interview the White House had promised Al-Jazeera an interview with President Bush. It would have been his first interview with an Arab network. Al-Jazeera was asked to send a fax to the White House confirming its interest, but after the Blair interview the fixture was postponed and then cancelled.

History has taught us that wars made television channels. The Second World War made *Time* magazine and in January 1991 the world learned the names Peter Arnett, Bernard Shaw and the Al-Rashid Hotel. This time the world learned about Doha, Qatar and Al-Jazeera. 'During the Gulf war CNN was in the right place at the right time,' said Muftah al-Suwaidan proudly at the time. 'Now it's our turn. We are the only channel with a reporter in Kabul.'

For the first time reams and reams of op-ed pieces in newspapers and magazines all over the Western world ran articles on every aspect of Al-Jazeera, from its effect on the Middle East

peace process to personal details about its staff. Through reporting, Al-Jazeera itself had become embroiled in events, both the
conduit and subject of the news.

The same networks that criticized Al-Jazeera for having an
anti-American bias were happy to broadcast its exclusive footage
of US strikes on Kabul and the video of Osama bin Laden.
CNN exercised its exclusive deal with Al-Jazeera energetically,
running plenty of Al-Jazeera footage. CBS news anchor Dan
Rather denied that running this footage was tantamount to
broadcasting enemy propaganda, but acknowledged that it was
the responsibility of both CNN and CBS, as news organizations, to 'pass it along. You can make your own judgements
about it.' Professionally speaking, Al-Jazeera had done the same
thing, but it was denied the same explanation. Bin Laden had
chosen to deliver his home-made videos to the station's Kabul
office, partly because transporting them out of the country would
have been difficult, but any network would have capitalized on
its exclusive position in Afghanistan without a moment's hesit-
ation. Any network would have interviewed bin Laden if it had
been given the opportunity and in 1997 CNN's Peter Arnett
was the first to do exactly that. Al-Jazeera's management had
just been far-sighted – or lucky – enough to open a bureau in
Kabul.

Deliberately inflammatory or simply controversial, Al-Jazeera
seemed to be winning fame in the nick of time. The Emir's
$137-million subsidy was due to run out in November 2001
and the channel needed to be able to stand on its own two feet
if its persistent claim that it was independent of the Emir was
to hold water. Although the cost of covering the war in
Afghanistan was considerable, revenue from subscriptions and
footage fees was increasing. The pictures of the air strikes in
Afghanistan were being sold both directly to networks, like the
BBC, and also to news agencies who distributed them all over
the world. Footage of the world's most wanted man was selling
to networks all over the globe for up to $20,000 a minute. A
three-minute clip of the 1998 bin Laden interview was sold for

$250,000. There was an exponential increase in the number of American and Australian cable-based subscriptions and intense demand in Britain prompted Al-Jazeera to start encrypting its service on BSkyB in the hope it could charge fees to some of the country's four hundred thousand Arabic speakers.

Al-Jazeera was being intensely courted by Western broadcasters who wanted to sign cooperative agreements to share its footage and save their own spiralling overheads incurred by covering the war. NBC had an agreement with Al-Jazeera, which was terminated when Al-Jazeera signed up with CNN, but in October 2001 Al-Jazeera signed a non-exclusive agreement with ABC News agreeing to share video feeds and other information. Viacom Inc.'s CBS network confirmed it was in discussions about signing a similar agreement with Al-Jazeera.

At Al-Jazeera's headquarters in Doha, the mood was buoyant and advertising was looking up. There was talk of plans for a new spin-off documentary channel in Britain, featuring independent Arabic filmmakers. This was seen as a natural follow-up to the success of the Qatar International Film Festival, which Al-Jazeera had sponsored. There were even rumours of floating the company. But US intelligence forces were keeping a close eye on Al-Jazeera and its staff and routinely monitoring communications between Qatar and Kabul. They were increasingly unhappy with the direction Al-Jazeera was taking and the political will to do something about it was beginning to crystallize. In the meantime the royalties from Afghanistan kept pouring in.

5

Afghanistan

Before 9/11, the UN estimated, war had displaced more than a million people in Afghanistan. Hundreds of thousands of people with inadequate food, water and medicine were already on the move. As the war began winter was rapidly approaching and the UN predicted that to prevent a humanitarian crisis up to 7.5 million Afghans would need aid soon.

After 9/11 the American administration drummed up a fragile coalition of countries from around the world to participate in its War on Terror. Muslim countries were especially important to the coalition, not only for strategic reasons, but also because their collaboration was evidence that the war was not a crusade against Islam. But Muslims themselves were extremely wary about allying themselves with America. After all, until 9/11 America had usually ignored Muslims or assumed that autocratic Arab regimes could be coerced. Most Muslims viewed the war as a crusade against a defenceless, Third World, Islamic country. Many would have preferred to subscribe to anything, including the Taliban, other than Washington's war.

As the situation in Afghanistan deteriorated, the wavering countries in the coalition needed growing reassurance that the war would be short, humane and justified. The coalition would soon disband if the Afghan people were seen to be suffering unduly. Keeping the loyalty of Muslim allies, like Pakistan, Egypt and Saudi Arabia, was going to require the delicate handling of hearts and minds. With Al-Jazeera monopolizing all the television pictures coming out of Taliban-controlled Afghanistan – which at the start of the war was nearly 90 per cent of the country – the stage was set for a public relations battle as fierce as the shooting war.

The domestic press in Afghanistan – newspapers and a national news agency – were all tightly controlled by the Taliban. A fear of the media engendered by the Cold War, when the Taliban fought the Soviets, had led to the imposition of strict controls on the media. Once it had been possible to find a wide selection of the Western and Pakistani press in Kabul, but books and magazines published abroad had been outlawed in 1997. Television, a suspected source of moral corruption, had been banned in 1998, along with photography, filming, the Internet and chess. Press freedom had been non-existent for years. The country had fallen so far off the world's radar it did not even have an international telephone dialling code.

When the bombing began, journalists from all over the world rapidly deployed in northern Afghanistan, which was controlled by enemies of the Taliban called the Northern Alliance. Getting into the area controlled by the Taliban from the north meant crossing the perilous front line. Without access to what was happening inside Taliban-controlled Afghanistan, the coalition press formed a 'press pool', which shared what little information they had, while compensating heavily with news from the Pentagon. The Pentagon was very secretive. 'Our goal is not to demystify things for the other side,' explained Defense Secretary Rumsfeld.

Short on information, but long on warnings, the American administration had its eyes skinned for unpatriotic news reporting. Ari Fleischer, the White House press secretary, warned Americans that they should 'watch what they say' about US military, intelligence and police operations. He warned all five major American television networks, as well as the wire services, not to carry any advance information about Bush and Cheney's schedule, nor use the names of military personnel engaged in combat missions.

The network chiefs all acquiesced to the Pentagon's demands. The problem was, a few reporters would not stop asking questions. 'It's not what government officials are saying that's the issue,' Fleischer said. 'It's the type of questions that reporters are asking that's the issue. The press is asking a lot of questions that I suspect the American people would prefer not to be asked, or answered.'

The Pentagon had done an impressive job of taming the American media. When the bombing began, the American news networks knew in advance, but delayed their reports. NBC journalists who witnessed the B-2 stealth bombers taking off from Whiteman Air Force Base in Montana in the small hours of the morning did not report it until sixteen hours later.

Not satisfied with rigorous self-censorship, some American network executives decided to go one step further in the name of patriotism. Walter Isaacson, CNN's CEO and chairman, issued a memo asking his staff to slant the news in America's favour. 'As we get good reports from Taliban-controlled Afghanistan, we must redouble our efforts to make sure we do not seem to be simply reporting from their vantage or perspective. We must talk about how the Taliban are using civilian shields and how the Taliban have harbored the terrorists responsible for killing close to 5000 innocent people,' he wrote. If CNN reporters found themselves covering civilian deaths it was important that they not 'forget it is that country's leaders who are responsible for the situation Afghanistan is now in'.

A senior executive at CNN sent a follow-up email suggesting some sample reports: 'We must keep in mind, after seeing reports like this from Taliban-controlled areas, that these US military actions are in response to a terrorist attack that killed close to 5000 innocent people in the US' or, 'The Pentagon has repeatedly stressed that it is trying to minimize civilian casualties in Afghanistan, even as the Taliban regime continues to harbor terrorists who are connected to the September 11 attacks that claimed thousands of innocent lives in the US.'

'Even though it may start sounding rote, it is important that we make this point each time,' stressed the executive. Later in the war, when a CNN correspondent filed a report from a bombed medical facility in Kandahar, CNN anchors added a disclaimer stating that CNN was not on the side of the Taliban.

Unlike virtually all the other news networks covering the war, Al-Jazeera was not a member of the press pool, nor was it beholden to the Pentagon for access. It was also the only foreign television broadcaster in Taliban-controlled Afghanistan at the start of bombing and had the only uplink facility, with which it could do live two-way communications with Al-Jazeera head-quarters in Doha. One Al-Jazeera correspondent was in Kandahar; the other in Kabul, and each of these two corre-spondents had established a working relationship with the Taliban. Since 9/11 they interviewed Taliban officials almost every day, but once the bombing began, this changed. Al-Jazeera's relationship with Taliban officials remained cordial, but they declined to be interviewed as often and access to military instal-lations became more limited. Gathering news became a daily challenge. In the opening days of the war Alluni told Doha, 'We get information through personal contacts and by travelling on the street and asking some people . . . When a great number of people confirm a certain report, we relay it to Al-Jazeera. There are times when we receive so many conflicting reports. We find it really difficult to get news, especially since the phone service here is very bad, and our contacts have now been cut, especially with the officials.'

The only other witnesses to what was happening inside Taliban-controlled Afghanistan were the Afghan population, the Taliban themselves, the Pentagon, observing through orbiting spy satellites, and three journalists from international news agencies who had satellite phones but no cameras. With its monopoly on information coming out of Afghanistan, Al-Jazeera was in an unrivalled position. America's war was now hostage to a maverick Arab news network.

After the first night of bombing and Tomahawk missile attacks the world waited with bated breath for news. The Pentagon announced it would be several days before accurate results could be ascertained. Without footage, Western television networks were stuck. 'We're just whistling in the wind about the extent of the bombing, until we get an official briefing from the Pentagon,' admitted ABC's anchor Peter Jennings. Then the Pentagon released some high-tech gun camera video shots of things exploding which were heavily rotated. Waffling military analysts were hired to pad out the news. Reactions were taken from within the White House and the Pentagon, and from leaders of the US Congress. CNN reported some responses from around the world, from Rudolph Giuliani, Shimon Peres and Jacques Chirac.

The next morning Al-Jazeera's Taysir Alluni was wandering around the rubble in the streets of Kabul assessing the damage caused by the air assault and interviewing bewildered citizens whose homes had been destroyed. The camera showed one old man squatting in the ruins of his house, throwing fistfuls of dirt into the air in anguish. Another was helping his neighbour make repairs.

Despite the bombing, Alluni reported, Afghans were doing their best to continue with their normal daily lives. Not many people had been killed, he assessed, because the raids had been so accurately targeted, but this was only day one and who knew what was yet to come? The American government had urged patience, but these people were poor and hungry, without enough food for the winter.

During the second night of bombing Alluni stayed on air, guessing how many planes or missiles there were and what they might be targeting. He surveyed the damage again the next day. This time a missile apparently destined for a short-wave radio tower had gone off target and blown up a civilian house, killing four UN employees working on a mine-clearance project. Alluni told America all about it when he was interviewed live, through a translator, by CNN's Paula Zahn. He also told her how Afghan civilians were now fleeing Kabul in droves for the mountains nearby, which could soon result in a humanitarian crisis.

Over the coming weeks Al-Jazeera reported a string of stories that presented the coalition's assault as anything but humane. Often its account was starkly at odds with that of the Pentagon. When Al-Jazeera reported the Taliban claim that US bombers had killed a hundred doctors, nurses and patients in a military hospital on the outskirts of Herat, the Pentagon denied it. AFP also reported this claim. When Al-Jazeera ran a story that the Taliban had shot down a US helicopter near the southern city of Kandahar, the Pentagon denied this. Then the Taliban produced two sets of charred and punctured landing gear, brandishing them in front of Al-Jazeera's cameras like a war trophy. They claimed these were from the downed helicopter. The undercarriage appeared to come from a Chinook transport helicopter and the model number and the manufacturer's name, Boeing, were clearly stencilled on the side. Donald Rumsfeld still described the claim as 'false'. A week after the war started, Al-Jazeera reported that an America bomb had struck a hospital in Kandahar, killing five people. At first the Pentagon denied it, and Rumsfeld called the reports of civilian casualties 'ridiculous', but this time Al-Jazeera showed pictures of badly burned Afghan children, injured in the bombing, lying in hospital, crying in pain.

Al-Jazeera's reporters in Kabul and Kandahar had Taliban minders and were consequently under constant pressure to pay lip service to the regime. At the end of each bulletin they would always note that they were reporting from the Islamic Emirate of Afghanistan – the Taliban name for the country. Although this protocol provoked accusations of partiality, two of the international correspondents in Kabul, from AFP and Reuters, both filed damning reports of their own, reinforcing Al-Jazeera's stories about Afghan civilian casualties. AFP reported how American warplanes had bombed Afghan civilians trying to escape to Pakistan, killing at least twenty people, nine of them children.

As the war wore on, the relationship between Al-Jazeera and the Pentagon became increasingly antagonistic. The Pentagon accused Al-Jazeera of giving too much credence to unsubstantiated reports from the Taliban, while insisting the press believe their own unsubstantiated reports. Both sides were generating their own propaganda, with each side trying to turn the fog of this under-reported war to its advantage. Al-Jazeera's graphic reports of civilian casualties took a heavy toll on the morale of America's more sceptical allies. The coalition risked being undermined.

The British government also made no secret of its antipathy towards Al-Jazeera. In a parliamentary written answer, Tessa Jowell, the Culture Secretary, announced that the Independent Television Commission (ITC) was monitoring the channel's output. If it were deemed to be in breach of the EU Television Without Frontiers directive, the purpose of which is to 'ensure that broadcasts do not contain any incitement to hatred on grounds of race, sex, religion or nationality', Al-Jazeera would be banned from broadcasting in Britain. 'It is open to the government,' said Jowell, 'on the advice of the ITC, to proscribe a television broadcaster which broadcasts from another member state where the broadcasts contain material which manifestly, seriously and gravely infringes this prohibition, on at least two occasions in a 12-month period.'

The problem for Jowell was that Al-Jazeera's licence to broadcast in the European Union had been granted by the French broadcasting authority, the Conseil Supérieur de l'Audiovisuel (CSA), and under EU rules it was up to the CSA whether it chose to take it away again. Following a complaint from the British Embassy in Paris, the CSA warned Al-Jazeera that if it failed to respect its contractual obligations by transmitting any more unedited statements from bin Laden, it would be taken off the air.

This was the gravest threat the channel had ever received,

because if the French regulator retracted its licence, all the bureaux in Europe, including the key London hub, would have to cease transmitting. The president of the CSA, Dominique Baudis, ruled that Al-Jazeera had breached its licence agreement by broadcasting live images without providing proper context and by broadcasting false information without subsequently providing the necessary corrections. This second charge related to a comment made by Dr Faisal al-Qasim, presenter of Al-Jazeera's *The Opposite Direction*, who, in the context of a debate, had referred to the conspiracy theory that had mushroomed in the Arab world since 9/11, that four thousand Jews who worked in the World Trade Center had not turned up for work on the morning of September 11, without making it clear that it was not true. The source of this conspiracy theory was believed to have been the Hezbollah television station website, Al-Manar. Baudis said the CSA would prefer to try to make Al-Jazeera respect its licence agreement rather than just ban it outright and a letter was addressed to Sheikh Hamad bin Thamir Al Thani, Al-Jazeera's chairman, explaining as much. The channel stood warned.

Reporters sans Frontières wrote to the French authorities protesting about their judgement against Al-Jazeera. In the letter the secretary-general of Reporters sans Frontières condemned the 'openly discriminatory measures' which had been instituted against Al-Jazeera by the CSA, and said: 'It is not surprising that the British authorities have sought the means to better control a media outlet that is impossible to ignore in the current conflict. We ask you to avoid any discriminatory targeting of information broadcast by the Al-Jazeera channel, and that you treat them exactly the same way as other conventional foreign channels.'

Tessa Jowell apparently failed to mention her concerns about Al-Jazeera to her colleague, Labour MP Harry Cohen, who asked the House of Commons authorities to make Al-Jazeera available free in all MPs' offices on a spare channel on the Parliamentary Video Network. His request was turned down and the proceedings of the Scottish parliament were broadcast instead.

To drive home the government message that Al-Jazeera was under surveillance, MI5 officers paid several visits to the network's London bureau in Westminster Tower, which has magnificent views of the Houses of Parliament from just across the river on the Albert Embankment.

'I had too many visitors,' recalled Muftah al-Suwaidan, the bureau's executive director. 'They came and asked questions. They were very smart, they said they were here just to say hello, but they asked lots of questions. They would say, "Somebody told us they heard somebody mention a name in your broadcast, Muhammad Al so-and-so, and he was threatening to do a terrorist act against the Americans." I knew right away who they asked for did not exist. You knew they were making the name up as it made no sense. But I had to show them I was trying to find out, so I called the producer in Doha and asked if he knew this guy.'

Al-Suwaidan believes the visits were a way the security services had of letting Al-Jazeera staff know they were being watched. 'After the bit about the name, they started to talk. "If there is anything you guys need, if you have any problems, just let us know,"' Al-Suwaidan said. '"Who comes here, who goes there, what do you do, can we come and see your live programmes?"'

Yosri Fouda, presenter of Al-Jazeera's investigative news show *Top Secret* and executive producer at Al-Jazeera's London bureau, was equally nonchalant about living under surveillance. 'I always assume that somebody is watching and I have to make an understanding for this. And if you are watched it is probably not because you are under suspicion, it is probably because you are a point of contact for so many people. It makes the lives of our friends here or our friends there [gesturing out of the window to the Houses of Parliament and Thames House, MI5's headquarters] much easier to watch someone in my position, which is fine by me. The only difference between me and them is that perhaps we are after the same piece of information, but they are after it to suppress it and I am after it to let it out. The area of common interest between journalists and security agencies is much larger than the area of conflict.'

Across the Atlantic, Hafez al-Mirazi, the network's Washington bureau chief, was also dimly aware that he was under surveillance:

I think I am fortunate or unfortunate that nobody from the FBI needed to sit down with me. I considered this a sign that they didn't need any more information, since they had everything on me 24/7 anyway. When I talk to Arab-Americans and they tell me the FBI came and paid them a visit, I tell them this is good news because they didn't know anything about you and they needed to know something. My life is transparent. [Laughs] If you started your life as a journalist in the Arab world, you think those people are not doing their job if they are not keeping an eye on you.

Once someone called at the office checking about a cameraman who went to the Justice Department news conference and then left abruptly. Like any other news agency, the story had not been that important and we had another place we had to rush him to. The producer had sent him to the White House or somewhere – it was a typical day.

Two or three days later the FBI showed up asking us, 'Who is this guy? Give us information about him.' I said, 'What are you worrying about? It's two days later and nothing has exploded.' But he was just a guy doing his work. You can't blame them. So I said, 'Listen, we will give you what you need. If you want something more formal, you need to file something formal.' And he was getting married and they insisted on calling him on his wedding [day], at night.

Due to Al-Jazeera's exclusive position, other news networks were not able to verify the network's reports. NBC had a reporter forty miles from Kabul who gave vivid reports of 'some flashes of anti-aircraft fire a long way to the south of us'. CBS's man was on 'a mountain path about twenty miles north-east of Kabul'. The nearest Western reporter to Kabul was from CNN. His pictures of bombs exploding at night were taken from a great distance with a videophone looking through a telescopic scope. Videophone pictures taken at night are green and pixelated, so the resulting footage normally needs a good deal of explanation and no small amount of imagination if you are to understand what you are looking at. By the time the Pentagon censors had finished their strict inspection and delay process, his pictures would not appear on television in America until over twelve hours later. When they finally appeared, CNN was proud of its 'exclusive', but its competitors scorned their quality, comparing them at times to an Etch-a-Sketch and a Rorschach ink drawing.

For weeks any half-decent pictures were so precious to the American news networks that they ran them over and over. When they could do that no longer, an arsenal of experts was on hand to explain what might be going on, with the aid of high-tech computer-generated maps. Most of the twenty-four-hour news cycle was filled with rambling and speculative dialogue, more like a play by Samuel Beckett than headline news.

In the West, a combination of limited-quality pictures and a pernicious climate of self-censorship made Al-Jazeera's coverage seem especially vivid. Brutal accounts of civilian deaths contrasted starkly with what was shown on American news networks. Filtered once by the Pentagon and then a second time by the editors and journalists themselves, fleeting pictures of civilian casualties, sandwiched between smarmy pundits and frequent images from 9/11, were all that American viewers saw. The anchor at CNN diligently followed his CEO's memo, reminding viewers about the dead of the Twin Towers, whose 'biggest crime was going to work and getting there on time'.

It was at this time that Al-Jazeera became a household name in America. Clips of its news coverage were on the air night

after night and the network became very famous, very fast.
When American networks ran Al-Jazeera footage, presenters
would warn that what was about to be shown 'could not be
independently confirmed', as if to imply lingering, unanswered
questions about Al-Jazeera's professionalism. This tag, which was
never applied to exclusives from other American or international
networks, came with more than a hint of racism.

On Western talk shows Al-Jazeera was condemned as a mouthpiece for terror or the Islamic media wing of the 'Axis of Evil'.
In the press it was compared to the former organ of Soviet propaganda, *Pravda*, and Nazi propaganda newspapers. Its immediate
closure or destruction was advocated as a top national priority.
The *New York Times* decreed that Al-Jazeera 'slants its news with
a vicious anti-Israel and anti-American bias'. Its 'deeply irresponsible reporting reinforces the region's anti-American views'.
National Public Radio warned listeners that Al-Jazeera's coverage should 'come with a health warning'. CBS's celebrity news
anchor Dan Rather wondered whether perhaps bin Laden might
be behind Al-Jazeera. Was there 'any indication that Osama bin
Laden has helped finance this operation?' he mused. The *New
York Daily News* summed up concerns about Al-Jazeera and
offered a violent final solution:

Al Jazeera is the favorite network of bin Laden . . . It is
one of the most potent weapons in the Islamic Axis arsenal
. . . Even a legitimate news organization shouldn't have
monopoly coverage of a war. But Al Jazeera is far from
legitimate. It is an Arab propaganda outfit controlled by
the medieval government of Qatar that masquerades as a
real media company. Since the start of the American bombing, Al Jazeera has transmitted grainy pictures of the Afghan
sky. But that will change. Soon the actual fighting will
intensify, and we will be shown scenes of death and destruction and hear the cries of children. Men on the street will
deplore the terrorism the Great Satan is visiting on innocent civilians . . . Al Jazeera's role is to present that killing

as an unjustified slaughter, to bring the war into American living rooms as a horror show of satanic cruelty, starring President Bush as Dracula . . . Dealing with Al Jazeera is a job for the military. Shutting it down should be an immediate priority because, left alone, it has the power to poison the air more efficiently and lethally than anthrax ever could.

Although American television networks were busy vilifying Al-Jazeera in public, behind the scenes executives were competing fiercely to befriend the channel so that they might use its footage more cheaply. The tension between Al-Jazeera and the American networks was palpable. When CNN's Paula Zahn interviewed Hafez al-Mirazi, then Al Jazeera's Washington bureau chief, on 5 December 2001 about Arab press coverage of the Israeli-Palestinian conflict, there were signs of this tension spilling over into the public domain. Salama Ahmad Salama, senior columnist for Egypt's *Al-Ahram*, was also at the discussion, via a live link-up from Cairo, but could not get a word in edgeways.

PAULA ZAHN: Mr Al-Mirzari, I think we could all agree this morning we are products of our culture.

HAFEZ AL-MIRAZI, AL-JAZEERA: Al-Mirazi.

ZAHN: But as you know, your station has been accused of using anti-American language, of running graphics that feature and glorify Osama bin Laden. Even Secretary of State Colin Powell denounced the station when you repeatedly aired Osama bin Laden's statement and Colin Powell said that that was vitriolic, irresponsible kinds of statements. What is your defence to his criticism?

AL-MIRAZI: Well, Secretary Colin Powell gave interviews to Al-Jazeera and later also said good words about Al-Jazeera, as well as Dr Condoleezza Rice and other US officials. They respected the credibility of Al-Jazeera and the objectivity. The problem actually is with the American media and the Western media, who instigated the government, and they always instigate against an independent media like Al-Jazeera, because they do what the American media cannot do, which is not to mix patriotism with journalism. We cover a war in Afghanistan by putting both sides of the story, the side coming from Kabul at that time and . . .

ZAHN: Well, Mr Al-Mirzari, I have to stop you there . . .

AL-MIRAZI: It's Al-Mirazi.

ZAHN: I think that charge is blatantly ridiculous.

AL-MIRAZI: Well, I'll tell you what is ridiculous . . .

ZAHN: I think if you watch the majority of the coverage in this country . . .

AL-MIRAZI: Paula, what is ridiculous . . .

ZAHN: We do question the policies of our government.

AL-MIRAZI: Well . . .

ZAHN: I think we constantly put the leaders of our government on the spot when we question . . .

AL-MIRAZI: Only on domestic policies.

ZAHN: . . . the progress of this campaign.

AL-MIRAZI: Only on domestic policies. But in foreign policy, you are just rubber-stamping whatever the government do.

ZAHN: Oh, Mr Al-Mirzari, you're not being honest at all.

AL-MIRAZI: It's Al-Mirazi.

ZAHN: Look at the debate in this country about the Israelis' retaliatory strikes in . . .

AL-MIRAZI: OK . . .

ZAHN: . . . in the Middle East. I mean you have read the editorials in this country.

AL-MIRAZI: Paula, let me . . .

ZAHN: You've seen the front-page headlines.

AL-MIRAZI: Let me just remind you of the CNN coverage of what happened Saturday night, last Saturday. For two hours, CNN was doing exactly what people were criticizing Al-Jazeera of doing, footage of ten minutes coming out of Jerusalem, terrible footage, of course. Nobody would allow or accept the killing of civilians. But ten minutes of footage have been kept repeating all over for more than two hours with commentators from your own reporters like Leon and others, and adopting the rhetoric and the argument of the Likud, not only the Israelis or the Labor, but the Likud, and giving a podium for Mr Netanyahu and all the Israeli right . . .

ZAHN: I think, sir . . .

AL-MIRAZI: . . . to bash the Arabs.

ZAHN: I have to tell you, I beg to differ with you.

AL-MIRAZI: That is not creative reporting.

ZAHN: I can't say that I watched every minute of our four hours of coverage that night, but I will tell you that as with all news organizations, one would hope that you get on the phone and you try to find differing points of view. We, of course, had Palestinian representation on our air. That is absolutely absurd.

AL-MIRAZI: But you give them a tough time the same way that you are giving me a tough time. Had you had an Israeli journalist with you, you would have been pampering him or showering him with praise, very easy softballs. But the only problem with that, you get Arabs only to grill them. And this is the problem.

ZAHN: No, sir, that is not true.

AL-MIRAZI: There is no way . . .

ZAHN: I had the former Prime Minister . . .

AL-MIRAZI: Well, you did that with Hanan Ashrawi.

ZAHN: . . . of Israel on yesterday . . .

AL-MIRAZI: You did that with Hanan Ashrawi.

ZAHN: We also had Mr Barak on . . .

AL-MIRAZI: Yes, and . . .

ZAHN: . . . and we asked him the question, why is it Shimon Peres walked out of this meeting when the vote was taken to possibly try to in some way topple the government of Yasser Arafat?

AL-MIRAZI: Exactly . . .

ZAHN: Shimon Peres, we well reported the story that there is a rift within the Israeli government, that not all Israelis supported . . .

AL-MIRAZI: OK. You are defending Sharon.

ZAHN: That is absolutely not true.

AL-MIRAZI: You were defending Sharon . . .

ZAHN: There are . . .

AL-MIRAZI: You were criticizing the liberal, Paula.

ZAHN: There are people, as you well know, within the Israeli government that do not support these retaliatory strikes. I think our coverage is fair and balanced.

AL-MIRAZI: Wait . . .

ZAHN: A final thought, sir, this morning on what the goal of Al-Jazeera's coverage is.

AL-MIRAZI: The goal is the motto of Al-Jazeera, to cover both sides of the story, the view and the other point of view, to make sure that we would have an Israeli journalist or an Israeli official with us in the interview, deal with him with respect the same way we would interview Arabs. And we would also remind people with that word that you called ancient, Paula, yourself when you interviewed Hanan Ashrawi. The word is occupation. And this is the word that we should always remember.

Occupation is an ancient word, I agree with you. That shouldn't have been, that shouldn't have stayed in the twenty-first century and it is the responsibility of credible journalists like you and journalists in the US to remind people that the occupation of the Palestinian land should be ended.

ZAHN: Mr Al-Mirzari, we're going to leave it there this morning. But I do once again need to remind you in our coverage with various guests we've had representing the Israeli government this week we asked questions, as we have over the last couple of weeks, about

the settlement issue, which is deeply important to the
Palestinians, and also the whole issue of refugees and
their potential return if a Palestinian state ends up being
created.

So we . . .

AL-MIRAZI: When was the last time . . . ?

ZAHN: Our coverage has been fair . . .

AL-MIRAZI: Paula, when was the last time . . . ?

ZAHN: I've got to leave it there because we are hitting a
business news break . . .

AL-MIRAZI: OK, thank you.

ZAHN: . . . that is a sponsored segment and someone's
got to pay for these conversations, Mr Al-Mazari and
Mr Salama Salama. Thank you for your time this
morning.

The war in Afghanistan was also the first Internet war. Most
major news channels had no website until 1995, so during the
first Gulf war the Internet was not yet a factor. Online news
had been an important news source during 9/11 and now more
people than ever turned to Aljazeera.net, expecting more of the
same kind of exclusives that were appearing on the Al-Jazeera
television channel. Al-Jazeera.net had proved a runaway success
since its launch a year earlier. In one month after 9/11, it received
seventy million page views. In total, in 2001, it received in excess
of thirty-eight million visitors and had some 265 million page
views. The site had become increasingly sophisticated over the
year and now it offered live video streaming of major press
conferences from the White House or the Pentagon, transcripts
of television debates and plenty of archived audio and video
clips, and served as a forum for further discussion of topics
touched on in talk shows. It enjoyed a first-class reputation
among the educated Arab expatriate community, especially journalists, businessmen and diplomats.

In the first week of the war a forum set up on Al-Jazeera
Online heavily criticized the American attack on Afghanistan.

The forum, entitled 'America's war', described American policy
in the Middle East as 'absolute support for Israel' and questioned
Bush's motives and connections with the Zionist lobby. The
website referred sarcastically to America's fight against 'what it
calls terrorism', a fight that was really directed 'against Arab and
Islamic groups and countries' and 'without evidence and without considering implications in terms of economic and human
loss'. News stories on the forum detailed alleged massacres of
Afghan civilians by the coalition and were accompanied by
shocking photographs. None of the stories featured American
accounts of the strikes.

This kind of unchallenged, subjective presentation of the
facts, available to anyone, anywhere, at any time and for no
charge, was exactly the kind of inflammatory threat to the unity
of the coalition that America wanted to stamp out. It was clear
to the coalition that something needed to be done about
Al-Jazeera, but it was cautious because the last American attempt
to temper the channel's reporting, when Powell had a word with
the Emir, had disastrously backfired. The White House had
simply sent a message to the Arab world that a free press in the
Arab world – and by implication Arab democracy – was an
intolerable threat to the West.

There was a growing awareness that it might be better to try
to work with, rather than against, Al-Jazeera. Tony Blair said
himself that the coalition needed to 'upgrade considerably our
media and public opinion campaign'. President Bush confessed
at a prime-time press conference to have been completely ignorant of the depth of hatred for America: 'How do I respond
when I see that in some Islamic countries there is a vitriolic
hatred of America? I'll tell you how I respond: I'm amazed. I'm
amazed that there is such misunderstanding of what our country is about. We've got to do a better job of making our case.'
Defense Secretary Rumsfeld agreed: 'They are trying to manipulate world opinion in a way that is advantageous to them and
disadvantageous to us and we need to do everything we can to
make sure that the truth gets out.'

To counter Al-Jazeera's influence, the US Department of State launched a massive propaganda campaign to plug American policy throughout the Middle East. A Boston PR firm won a lucrative Pentagon contract to market the War on Terror to seventy-nine countries and the Coalition Coordination Center was set up, better to communicate the coalition's message to the world press. Blair's top spin-doctor, Alastair Campbell, flew to Washington for two days of transatlantic brainstorming with his opposite number in the White House.

A group of writers, producers and studio executives were wheeled out of Hollywood to help the 'information offensive'. Called 'Hollywood 9/11', this loosely associated entertainment industry group began by enlisting America's most famous Muslim, former world champion boxer Muhammad Ali, to do a one-minute public service announcement. It was to be broadcast in several languages, over several Arab networks, including Al-Jazeera. This was the first in a planned series of public service programmes about American life, aimed at Muslims around the world.

A former Madison Avenue advertising executive named Charlotte Beers, once known as 'the most powerful woman in advertising', was sworn in as the new Under Secretary of State for Public Diplomacy and Public Affairs. Beers, the only executive to have chaired two of the top ten ad agencies, had made her name in the industry marketing Uncle Ben's Rice and eating dog food to impress marketing men. Now she was working for Uncle Sam and her brief was to craft a 'public diplomacy' campaign to win hearts and minds for military action in Afghanistan and the War on Terror. She had to make the Arab world understand that the war in Afghanistan was being conducted humanely and that America was not at war with Islam, whatever 'Spin Laden' – as he had become known in the British press – might claim.

Beers told *Ad Age* magazine she intended to 'reignite the understanding of America' and she kicked off her 'information offensive' by lining up six appearances on Al-Jazeera of top-ranking US officials, including the Assistant Secretary of State for Near Eastern Affairs William Burns, Secretary of State Colin Powell, chairman of the Joint Chiefs of Staff General Richard B. Myers, Defense Secretary Donald Rumsfeld and the President's National Security Adviser, Condoleezza Rice.

During her sixteen-minute interview, dubbed into Arabic, Rice stressed to Arab viewers that America's war was against terror, not Islam, and that the Bush administration hoped soon to find peace in Palestine. She spoke at length about the Middle East peace process and asked Israel to relieve economic pressure on the Palestinians. She avowed several times that before any peace talks with Israel, Palestinian violence would have to stop. At the end of the interview she was asked whether she had a special message for Al-Jazeera's audience. She told them, 'The President of the United States understands Islam to be a faith of peace, a faith that protects innocents, and the policy of the United States is to do the same.' The White House distributed a transcript of the interview. Within a few hours Al-Jazeera showed American-made Israeli tanks rumbling into Palestinian towns. Neither the Arab press, nor viewers, missed the irony.

Donald Rumsfeld used his appearance on Al-Jazeera to deny the claims of civilian casualties made by Taliban officials. After two weeks of bombing, in a videophone interview with Al-Jazeera one Taliban spokesman had claimed that between six and nine hundred people had been killed or were missing. 'And don't ask me about the number of wounded, because it is in the thousands and I don't have a figure for that,' he said.

The Defense Secretary dismissed talk of carnage as 'ridiculous', but acknowledged some civilian casualties would be inevitable owing either to falling Taliban anti-aircraft fire or fighting between Afghan factions. He confirmed only four cases of accidental civilian deaths so far. Like Condoleezza Rice, he reiterated that the War on Terror was not a crusade against Muslims, but 'a matter of self-defence'. 'This effort is not against Afghanistan's people,' he said, 'it's not against any race or any religion, it is against terrorism, and terrorists, and the senior people that are harbouring terrorists.'

British Foreign Secretary Jack Straw and the Archbishop of Canterbury, the latter looking rather spectacular in archbishop's full regalia, also made appearances on Al-Jazeera around this time. The White House refused the channel's request to interview the President. Perhaps giving Al-Jazeera such a huge scoop over its rivals was one step further than the White House was prepared to go or, more likely, there were concerns that he would simply be humiliated by being asked embarrassing questions he could not answer.

In Afghanistan, the Voice of America, which had previously had a mere 2 per cent audience share in the region, began an expanded news service in the local languages of Dari and Pashto. A gigantic US Air Force EC-130 cargo plane, called *Commando Solo*, was converted into a $70-million flying radio and TV station which broadcast propaganda as it circled high above Afghanistan. Its fuselage was stuffed with radio and TV production equipment, including transmitters and jammers so powerful that the crew could block any radio or TV broadcast and replace it on the same frequency with their own. Hundreds of thousands of propaganda leaflets were dropped, one showing a man in Afghan clothes shaking hands with a Western soldier, under which was written the message: 'The partnership of nations is here to help.' Afghan illiteracy rates were so high that radio and pictures were the most effective way of distributing information. US air strikes cleared the airwaves a day after bombing started when they blew up the Taliban's main radio station around Kabul, Radio Voice of Shari'ah.

Beers had her work cut out. America had spent years frittering away Arab trust. It had slashed its public diplomacy programme and had few cultural organizations in the Middle East. Years of under-investment in Arab media, compounded by a shortage of Arabic speakers, meant that, despite America's genius for popular culture of its own, its message to the Muslim world was off-key. Only a fraction of the CIA's Near-Eastern department spoke Arabic and many other Arab experts had been marginalized by the administration as suspicious or unnecessary.

Since 9/11 a catalogue of PR gaffes had helped spoil the coalition's image abroad. America's initial name for the Afghanistan campaign, Operation Infinite Justice, faithfully translated into Arabic to mean something along the lines of 'divine retribution', sounded incredibly blasphemous. Bush's 'crusade' goof pigeonholed him immediately as the leader of a ragtag band of mercenaries on their way to the Middle East to pillage and plunder.

Over the next year Beers created an ad campaign called 'Shared Values', which used a combination of speaking tours, town-hall meetings, print publications, radio broadcasts, cultural-exchange programmes and other social policy programmes to win Arab support for the War on Terror. The campaign kicked off with a $15-million television advertising campaign, including screening on Al-Jazeera, which featured Muslim Americans talking about their positive experiences of living in the United States.

In December 2002, after the feedback was assessed, it was decided the ads had been an umitigated disaster. Arabs in the Middle East, it turned out, could not care less what life was like for Arabs in America. Several Arab nations, including Egypt, had simply refused to run them. In Jordan a focus group was so scathing about their appeal that they were immediately discontinued. Beers left the Department of State in March 2003, citing health reasons. In the interim, international sympathy for America's War on Terror had largely been squandered. As for *Commando Solo*, its efforts in Afghanistan also seemed to have been a flop. 'Most of the people here listen to this station just for a laugh,' reported Al-Jazeera's correspondent in Kandahar. 'When we asked them why they listen to it, they said that they do so only to laugh. So, they only consider it a means of passing time. That is what they told us.'

Nevertheless, the appearance of top-ranking American officials on Al-Jazeera less than a month after Colin Powell had asked the Emir of Qatar to tone down the station was a sea change in media policy.

★

The White House's 'media offensive' had no impact on Al-Jazeera's guests, who continued to lambast American policy. There were growing concerns internationally for the fate of more than six hundred Arab-Americans who had been detained by the FBI since 9/11. It had become apparent that once they had been arrested, these people had been systematically denied basic civil liberties, including access to legal counsel. None of them had been charged with any offence relating to the attacks. Most had been held on technical violations of immigration law or traffic charges, which would never normally have led to jail sentences. Egypt's most popular TV commentator joked that bin Laden had so many right-hand men that he must be a strange-looking monster. Speculation was rife as to which Arab country would be attacked next.

A Gallup poll of Pakistani urban opinion after two weeks of bombing suggested that 83 per cent had sympathies with the Taliban, while only 3 per cent said they were rooting for America. Al-Jazeera's pictures of bombed villages and hospitals intensified fears that hundreds of civilians were dying. Radical preachers across the Muslim world had been accusing the coalition of massacring children and now television seemed to be corroborating this. Ordinary Muslims remained unconvinced that this was not a war against Islam. Like many other newspapers, the *Pakistan Observer* published still photographs from Al-Jazeera of Afghan children wounded in the American bombing, accompanied by the blaring caption 'Children Among Scores Killed in US Attacks'. Demonstrations seemed to be attracting ever more moderate members of society and Pakistan's President, General Pervez Musharraf, who had signed up to the coalition believing the attacks would be short and sharp, was worried this lingering air campaign would destabilize the country. Lethal sectarian violence against Christians had broken out and police had to be stationed full-time at churches, schools and hospitals to prevent a bloodbath.

President Musharraf warned America on CNN's *Larry King Live* that if the bombing did not end soon, he might not be able to stop a popular uprising. 'One would hope and wish that this campaign comes to an end before the month of Ramadan,' he said, 'and one would hope for restraint during the month of Ramadan, because this certainly would have some effects in the Muslim world.'

Sheikh Yusuf al-Qaradawi, Al-Jazeera's resident religious agony aunt on *Religion and Life*, epitomized the moderate Arab point of view. As the gruesome pictures played out, he hardened his stance against the war, telling viewers that America's indiscriminate bombing was the characteristic behaviour of a bully. He compared Bush to bin Laden, both of whom, he said, punished many innocent people while they fought their cause. He blamed the Western media for turning bin Laden into a much bigger monster than he otherwise might have been and, although he stopped short of advocating jihad against America, as many clerics did, he did not favour collaborating with the coalition either.

As tension in the Arab world mounted, NGOs were warning that hundreds of thousands of Afghans were in peril if they did not receive emergency food aid deliveries soon. Relief organizations now estimated that there were approximately seven million 'internally displaced' refugees in Afghanistan. With the cruel Afghan winter just weeks away, a humanitarian catastrophe – maybe the deaths of hundreds of thousands of Afghans through famine or cold – could be awaiting.

Meanwhile, Al-Jazeera's harrowing footage kept coming. On 23 October the network reported the deaths in a US air strike of ninety-three Afghan civilians in the village of Chukar, including eighteen members of one family. Al-Jazeera's Kandahar correspondent showed videophone pictures of a row of corpses wrapped in white shrouds lined up against the wall inside a room. At least one was a child.

Following an Al-Jazeera report about a US AC-130 airplane pounding an Afghan village with gunfire, the Pentagon was criticized by the US human rights organization Human Rights Watch. The massive, slow-moving 'Spectre' gunship annihilated at least ten civilians with its cannons, machine gun and howitzer. A handful of survivors who made it to Pakistan to tell the tale denied that any Taliban had been in the vicinity when the attack occurred. 'We've seen a sharp rise in civilian casualties in the past week that we have been able to document,' said a Human Rights Watch spokesman. 'It adds to the urgency of our call that the Pentagon take the necessary precautions to prevent casualties. This rise in the number of casualties that we've seen is totally unacceptable.'

Consistent reports of Afghan civilian casualties were weakening public support for the war, even in America. 'US Appears To Be Losing Public Relations War So Far,' ran a *New York Times* headline. In a CNN phone-in during the *Talk Back Live* show, viewers were asked to consider the heavily loaded question: 'Is it unpatriotic to speak out against the war?' The poll showed that although the vast majority of Americans still supported military action in Afghanistan, in the past two weeks support had slightly waned. The American public was becoming tetchy about the lack of good news and, more importantly, the lack of good television pictures, coming out of the war. In terms of dramatic impact, coalition reports of bombed-out, empty caves and demolished Taliban training camps did not compare with Al-Jazeera's grisly pictures.

A survey in the *Economist* magazine showed that British support for the war had fallen from around three-quarters of the population to two-thirds. French support dropped from two-thirds to a half and in both Germany and Italy well over half the population wanted the war to end right away.

At the start of November Al-Jazeera broadcast another letter it had received from Osama bin Laden. This was the second bin Laden tape since 9/11 and it had been sent to Al-Jazeera seven days earlier. At first Al-Jazeera bosses had hesitated over broadcasting it, because they thought it was of questionable news value, but eventually that decision had been reversed.

In the letter, bin Laden called on Muslims in Pakistan to stand up to what he called this Christian crusade. 'Muslims in Afghanistan are being subjected to killing and the Pakistani government is standing beneath the Christian banner,' the Al-Jazeera newsreader read out. A picture of the letter appeared on the screen, handwritten in Arabic, and bits could be made out. 'The crusader war against Islam has intensified,' the newsreader went on, 'the world is split into two. Part of it is under the head of the infidels Bush, and the other half under the banner of Islam.'

In the seven days between receiving the letter and broadcasting it, Al-Jazeera was approached by the American administration and asked for an opportunity to refute the letter's contents when it was eventually aired. Just as the British authorities had been keeping an eye on Al-Jazeera's London bureau, the Americans had been routinely eavesdropping on all the communications between the Kabul bureau and Doha. When Taysir Alluni had transmitted the tape off air via the Kabul uplink to studio bosses in Doha, the Americans had intercepted it.

When the letter was read out the American spokesman was at hand to present the American side of the case. So short was the Department of State of Arabic speakers fluent enough to appear on Al-Jazeera that it was obliged to summon Christopher Ross out of retirement, the former US Ambassador to Syria, who had left the service in 1998. He read a long prepared statement which reiterated the same message heard before about the war not being against Islam and he presented America as a friend of the Arabs. He mentioned how Americans had protected Muslims in Bosnia and Kosovo and reminded viewers that food was being dropped in Afghanistan. The anchor then quizzed Ross about Palestine, asking why, if America was a friend of the Arabs, it backed the Israelis in contravention of international law. His uninspiring reply was that America had been the only power that had brought the two sides to the negotiating table. 'He sounded like a POW reading a prepared statement,' John Zogby, the leading Arab-American pollster, told me later.

★

America lost the PR war, but there was never any doubt it would win the real thing. Three weeks and more than three thousand bombs after the war began, the Taliban were on the run. As the jubilant Northern Alliance, supported by US Special Forces, finally approached Kabul, scores of television journalists were intent on bringing Al-Jazeera's picture monopoly to a close.

Fearing retribution and chaos when the Taliban fled, network executives in Doha called Taysir Alluni in Kabul and told him he had better leave the city at once, before the Northern Alliance arrived. The Northern Alliance were known to have a vendetta against Arab journalists after two suicidal assassins posing as a Tunisian television crew had blown up their leader, Ahmad Shah Mas'ud, two days before 9/11 with a bomb concealed in a camera. Alluni assured Doha that he was on his way out of Kabul to a safe house. Afterwards he changed his mind. He was in touch with the Northern Alliance himself and after they assured him he would come to no harm, he decided it would be better to stay. He omitted to tell Doha about his change of plan.

At about 1.30 that morning two American five-hundred-pound (227 kilograms) bombs landed on the Al-Jazeera bureau in Kabul. Only one detonated, but it was enough to level the building. No one was inside at the time, as the technical staff had left a few hours previously. The bureau had sat in a residential part of Kabul and there were no obvious military targets nearby, although the Ministry for the Suppression of Vice and the Promotion of Virtue was across the street. It was easily recognizable, with its three large satellite dishes sprouting at the top, and was well known to residents throughout the city.

The Arab media were indignant at what was widely regarded as a vengeful and deliberate strike against Al-Jazeera. The Pentagon denied it had been on purpose. 'The US military does not and will not target media. We would not, as a policy, target news media organizations – it would not even begin to make sense,' said a spokesman from Coalition Central Command. But America had deliberately targeted the press before: in April 1999

NATO laser-guided missiles ploughed into the Serbian television headquarters, killing dozens. Over a hundred civilian staff had been working inside at the time. The attack had been intended to prevent state-run broadcasts of Serb propaganda, but instead drew international condemnation and bolstered Serbian resolve.

The Western media barely covered the attack on Al-Jazeera. Although they had all been relying on Al-Jazeera's pictures, they were unwilling now to speak up on the network's behalf. Britain's ITV and Channel 4 did not mention the incident at all and the only American news network to mention the attack was CBS, saying the network might have been 'damaged' by an accidental missile strike.

Al-Jazeera's bureau had been operating for twenty months before it was blown up, but the network and the Pentagon differed over whether Al-Jazeera had officially notified the Pentagon of the bureau's exact location. Al-Jazeera claimed that it had passed on the coordinates several times, through its partner CNN. The Pentagon denied ever having received them.

US intelligence had, however, been routinely monitoring Doha–Kabul communication, so one might assume they knew where the bureau was. The Pentagon would have known from Alluni's phone call to Doha that he had been ordered to flee, but not that he had decided to stay. Its officials were fortunate he had not been in the building when it had blown up.

'The office sits in a residential area. We cannot say for sure that it was deliberately targeted, but the Americans know exactly where the office is. I can see no other reason why a bomb would land in that section of Kabul,' said the station's managing director. Its chief editor, Ibrahim Hilal, believed that bombing Al-Jazeera's Kabul office had been the Pentagon's plan since the start of the conflict, but it had not wanted to bomb the bureau while it had the only uplink in the city. Otherwise nobody, including the Pentagon, would have been able to see what was going on in Taliban-controlled Afghanistan.

Later, following a BBC investigation, the Pentagon confirmed that the missile strike had, in fact, been deliberate. Deputy

Assistant Defense Secretary for Public Affairs Rear Admiral Craig Quigley told BBC World's presenter Nik Gowing that the Pentagon had no regrets about the incident because the bureau had 'military significance'. It was, according to Quigley, 'at the time, a facility used by Al-Qaeda'. 'It is not relevant for us to know that it was a broadcast facility.' Any target that was 'directly relevant to prosecuting the war' was permissible.

General Tommy Franks, commander of US operations in Afghanistan, wrote a letter about the incident to the Committee to Protect Journalists, in which he confirmed that the bureau 'had been monitored for a significant time and had repeatedly been the location of significant Al-Qaeda activity'. No evidence was offered to support this claim. Franks also claimed that one of bin Laden's deputies, Muhammad Ataf, had been killed in the attack. The BBC, who visited the building a few hours later, found no trace of blood or body parts. A few weeks later Ataf was reported killed a second time, this time by a Hellfire missile launched from a CIA-operated unmanned drone.

While working under the rule of the Taliban, Taysir Alluni had indeed kept in close contact with the regime. This included operating a radio handset tuned to the same frequency that they used, so he could communicate with officials and occasionally eavesdrop on their chatter. After 9/11 Alluni frequently interviewed Taliban officials in the bureau and perhaps this is what Franks meant by 'military significance'. Al-Jazeera executives denied there had been any other contact with Al-Qaeda apart from when couriers dropped off the infamous tapes, although the line between who was Taliban and who was Al-Qaeda was a fine one.

What the BBC investigation concluded was that the American military did not differentiate between targeting satellite uplinks belonging to legitimate news organizations and targeting satellite communications belonging to the enemy. In the eyes of the Pentagon both had 'military significance'. Evidently this placed in mortal danger all news organizations working behind what the Pentagon viewed as enemy lines.

Many Americans saw the attack on Al-Jazeera as a legitimate extension of the War on Terror. They thought it reasonable that Al-Jazeera should be targeted, for the same reason Serb television had been during the war in Bosnia: because it was the propaganda wing of the enemy war machine.

Even though the Pentagon gave reassurances at the time that the US authorities would investigate the incident, no investigation took place and no one was charged with the bombing.

Immediately after the bureau had been blown up, Doha executives could not locate Alluni and they feared the worst. He reappeared on Arab screens two days later, with a tale of lucky escapes, starting with leaving the bureau only minutes before the missiles struck. 'It seems that only a few minutes after we left, the office was bombed by American planes,' he told viewers. 'I don't know the extent of the damage, but from what I was told . . . I assume it was a mistake.'

After the attack Alluni had tried to make his way east out of Kabul, to the province of Paktia. On the way he was stopped, beaten and robbed by anti-Taliban Afghans. 'We had a big problem that endangered our lives . . . There was a barrier manned by irresponsible young people who opened fire on us, took our car, stripped us of everything we had and searched our pockets.' Later other tribesmen retrieved and returned his stolen equipment, but with the bureau demolished he was obliged to use CNN's facilities to transmit and receive from then on. 'My experience has been bitter . . . I can't speak about it,' he confided to viewers. 'I have seen things I never dreamed of seeing. What I saw is indescribable. I confess I am psychologically shocked.' Meanwhile, Al-Jazeera's other correspondent, working in Kandahar, escaped over the border into the Pakistani city of Quetta.

Later Alluni was pragmatic about the attack: 'During my work in Afghanistan I felt that the US was obsessed by the idea of what's called "Third World", and tried to have full control over the media, because the US knows that a media war could be more dangerous than a military war.

'We were expecting a hostile action against us, specially after the harsh US officials' press releases against Al-Jazeera, but attacking our office in that brutal way never crossed our minds. I consider this attack as an assassination attempt by the US Pentagon.'

Ironically, Alluni said later that he thought that, if anything, Al-Jazeera had been pro-American during the war: 'On the contrary, we feel we were biased towards the US during the war in Afghanistan, and statistics prove it. The amount of information we broadcasted about the US and its officials is way more than what we broadcasted about Taliban or Al-Qaeda or their officials. So, the American reaction was totally imbalanced and unexpected from a superpower like the US, which is supposed to have more confidence in its actions, and not to deal with Al-Jazeera the way it did.'

Asked about the similarities and differences between Al-Jazeera and CNN, Alluni gave a telling reply: 'I believe that CNN and Al-Jazeera before the war in Afghanistan were identical. Both stations were aiming to provide fair, qualitative news coverage to its audience. However, my experience in Afghanistan proved to me that CNN inclined away from this aim. Based on what I watched on CNN during the war in Afghanistan, I can say that out of the material we provided to CNN, based on a mutual agreement we had with them, very important material was disregarded while only the material serving US interests was broadcasted.' Whether or not important material was disregarded, CNN, in common with other American media, was criticized in the press for reporting the news in a partisan way.

The war in Afghanistan was not a particularly humane one. Six thousand uranium-based guided missiles and bombs, used to bust open bunkers, caves, water pipes and fuel stores, left a fearsome radioactive legacy behind for the civilian population. When the war was over, humanitarian organizations reported Afghan children suffering from pathological radioactive poisoning in their respiratory systems and bodies. In July 2002 an American

B52 heavy bomber dropped a two-thousand-pound laser-guided bomb on an Afghan wedding ceremony. The bomb, which was primed to detonate after landing, for maximum effect, was uranium-based. Besides killing scores at the time, people who visited the site suffered nosebleeds, radiation sickness and burns months later. Villagers living nearby can expect their next generation of children to be disfigured.

Afghanistan was also the moment when the American administration realized that they did not even have a horse running in the Arab media derby. After a startling U-turn, the Bush administration worked out it was better off working with, rather than against, Al-Jazeera. Top American policy makers appearing on Al-Jazeera was certainly a step forward, even if Arabs still felt the important questions had been left unanswered. As it turned out, the worst American fears were not realized: the vast majority of Arabs did not heed bin Laden's call. They just watched then changed the channel.

Two weeks after the bureau was destroyed, Al-Jazeera returned to Afghanistan with fresh correspondents. It was not long before they began receiving more tapes from Al-Qaeda. The third Al-Qaeda tape the network screened showed four young men who may have been bin Laden's sons. The price on bin Laden's head was bumped up to $25 million and when no more news arrived, rumours of his death began to spawn. These hopes were confounded when he popped up again on a fourth tape on Boxing Day, looking tired and ill, but alive. The half-hour Hi-8 tape had arrived in Doha via courier from Pakistan, but had lain unnoticed on a secretary's desk for two days before anyone realized what was on it.

References bin Laden made in his speech showed the tape had been made within the last few weeks. He still stopped tantalizingly short of confirming clearly that he had orchestrated the 9/11 attacks, but he spoke affectionately about the hijackers, mentioning some of them by name. 'This is nothing more than the same kind of terrorist propaganda we have heard before,' the White House spokesman told reporters in Crawford, Texas, where President Bush was enjoying his Christmas holidays. Al-Jazeera received at least six or seven other tapes from Al-Qaeda that it did not air, because it deemed them not to be newsworthy.

The war in Afghanistan cemented Al-Jazeera's reputation as a world-class news network. The gamble of setting up a bureau in a news backwater had paid off handsomely. Maintaining a presence in Afghanistan for nearly two years had given the network unique access to its factions and warlords. Al-Jazeera had scooped Afghanistan, as it had scooped Operation Desert Fox in 1998. Now, in an effort to pull off the trick a third time, the network opened bureaux in other potential hotspots around the globe, among them Somalia and Ethiopia.

Many international news organizations lauded Al-Jazeera for its war coverage. Among people who worked in the Western media it was now regarded as a leading source of breaking news. The deputy director of BBC news commented that the rise of Al-Jazeera had 'brought something fresh to the table'. 'It reminds everyone they can do a better job than others in news gathering,' he said.

Al-Jazeera's new higher profile brought problems too. Its correspondents were now much more conspicuous and, consequently, more often harassed. Swiss authorities jailed Al-Jazeera's Brussels correspondent without charge when he tried to enter Geneva to cover a World Trade Organization meeting. He was detained overnight and in the morning expelled from the country. Al-Jazeera's Moscow correspondent was stopped from entering China. A third correspondent was detained at Waco airport in Texas because the credit card he used to buy his ticket was traced to Afghanistan. Several Arab countries – Saudi Arabia, Algeria, Bahrain and Tunisia – still denied Al-Jazeera the relevant licences necessary to open a news bureau.

According to unofficial estimates, during the war Al-Jazeera's audience had swelled from thirty-five to forty-five million viewers worldwide, but this could not be verified as accurate data in several recipient countries was unavailable. Eight million of these viewers were in Europe, 150,000 in America. Revenues from subscriptions and footage fees had grown, and cooperative agreements to share information and resources were now in place with CNN, ABC, NBC, Fox News, the BBC and Germany's ZDF. The United States had seen an exponential increase in the number of Al-Jazeera subscriptions and in Britain plans were afoot to encrypt its satellite TV service so that it could become a paid subscription service.

A deal was signed with a major Japanese satellite television provider to make Al-Jazeera available free of charge in Japan for the first time. A Japanese press release said the company 'firmly believes it has a social responsibility' to air Al-Jazeera in addition to its existing channels, which included CNN, BBC and Fox News.

Promotional forays were also made into China. The western province of Xinjiang has a Muslim population of eight to ten million, which was regarded by network chiefs as a potential opportunity. The problem was that the Chinese authorities treat their Islamic minority with deep suspicion and made it clear that they would want to exert close control over Al-Jazeera's broadcasts to prevent sedition.

Malay television audiences responded positively when Al-Jazeera was transmitted for a few hours each day in Arabic and Malay, on a private satellite TV station. Malaysian Muslims were particularly interested in following the war as well as the situation in Israel and Palestine, which had once again begun to deteriorate. Malaysian Al-Jazeera also found an audience in the large number of Middle Eastern tourists who had visited the country since 9/11, in lieu of going to America. Opening a bureau in Australia was also now being planned.

Executives were now seriously engaged in developing an English-language Al-Jazeera channel. This would make the network a fully international operation, like the BBC or the Voice of America. Al-Jazeera's chairman, Sheikh Hamad bin Thamir Al Thani, told the press that initially the new channel would divide the twenty-four-hour news day into two sessions of twelve hours, one in Arabic, the other in English, and for half the day the Arabic would be translated live into English. Al-Jazeera Radio, an eponymous news magazine and two new Al-Jazeera channels in Arabic, one dealing with finance and the other with business news, were also in the pipeline for 2002.

Although analysts had expected that the network would start making a profit in December 2001, Al-Jazeera announced instead that it would need to draw another $130 million from the Qatari government to tide it over for another five years. Economists attributed the network's continued insolvency to the long-running Saudi campaign to have potential advertisers boycott it. The Saudis resented the coverage bin Laden had received even more than the Americans. *Forbes* magazine estimated that Saudi obstruction had cost Al-Jazeera $4 million in lost advertising fees, which could amount to as much as a quarter of its total annual revenue.

Fortunately for Al-Jazeera, the wealthy Emir had no qualms about tiding it over. The network's director told a Qatari newspaper that although the station would take another handout he was optimistic that advertising, subscription and rebroadcasting revenue would see it soon paid back. Already a trickle of documentaries was being sold and there were a few rinky-dink advertising contracts from local Qatari car dealerships and oil industry subcontractors. More significantly, in every part of the world except the Middle East, Al-Jazeera was operating a paid subscription TV service and individual video clips from Afghanistan were selling for as much as $250,000 apiece.

6

Media War

America's new policy to promote itself in the Islamic world seemed beset with problems. International sympathy following 9/11 drained away alarmingly fast after Al-Jazeera's pictures showed the extent of collateral damage inflicted on Afghan civilians by the coalition's bombing. Although many Arabs had sympathized with America's loss, most felt the war in Afghanistan had been executed heavy-handedly and the key irritant in the relationship, America's foreign policy in Israel and the Occupied Territories, remained unchanged.

The American administration made some thoughtless mistakes. When the Department of Defense issued a clearly doctored photograph of a clean-shaven bin Laden wearing a suit, hoping to show that the terrorist leader had deserted the Arab cause, it reinforced America's reputation for habitually doctoring evidence. In February, amid a storm of criticism, the Department of Defense was obliged to close its new media unit, the Office of Strategic Influence (OSI), which had been set up in the wake of 9/11 to drum up support for the War on Terror. Damaging leaks indicated that its purpose was deliberately to supply false information to foreign journalists and media organizations as part of a dishonest propaganda strategy. American and international media watchdogs slammed the office as just the latest in a string of attempts to manipulate the media. 'The office is done. What do you want – blood?' said Defense Secretary Rumsfeld at the closing press conference.

As America struggled to manage its image, radical Muslim preachers across the Middle East were busy doing all they could to undermine it, distributing cassette recordings of fiery sermons that canonized bin Laden as the defender of Islam and vilifying the American-led assault on Muslim Afghanistan. Owing to concerted efforts by Arab governments to suppress any national conversation about bin Laden, it was impossible to gauge how much support Al-Qaeda really had, but anecdotal evidence, on the Internet and elsewhere, suggests that a substantial minority viewed him as a folk hero righteously standing up to America.

Despite these setbacks, the American administration persevered in its attempt to win hearts and minds in the Middle East and a steady stream of American officials were now appearing on Al-Jazeera, as they had done since Tony Blair first appeared, a month after 9/11. Most of them spoke in English and were translated. Only a few, like former ambassador Christopher Ross, spoke Arabic.

The Department of State was busy drawing up comprehensive plans for an Arabic-language radio and television network, in the hope that this might in future break Al-Jazeera's spell over the Arab audience, but polls indicated that America was facing an unenviable struggle against popular public opinion. The White House advertising mogul Charlotte Beers travelled to Egypt and Morocco to conduct consumer research, where she met local journalists and other 'opinion formers' to discuss what could be done about America's image problem. A gulf of misunderstanding between Beers and her hosts quickly became evident and her task was made even harder by President Bush's State of the Union address in which he spoke at length about the War on Terror without once mentioning the Palestinians.

Arabs told Beers that they were still frustrated at the double standards they perceived in US foreign policy. Why, they asked, were UN sanctions and obligatory nuclear disarmament not being forcibly applied on Israel, as they were on other countries?

As her campaign bogged down in the desert sand, she came under fire at home as well as abroad. 'Ms Beers expressed herself like President Bush in every way. No matter how hard you try to make them understand, they don't,' was the conclusion one Cairo newspaper editor came to. American critics denounced her Madison Avenue jargon about 'brand America' as naive.

In this climate of suspicion, frustration and mutual misunderstanding, a mysterious new video of Osama bin Laden appeared, not on Al-Jazeera this time, but on CNN. The ensuing scandal led to a major bust-up between the two networks and left a cloud of suspicion hanging over the American administration.

In October 2001, a few days after the coalition began bombing Afghanistan, CNN announced that a contact of Al-Jazeera, who claimed to represent bin Laden, had invited the two news channels to submit a list of questions to the terrorist leader. Naturally, this was seen as a great opportunity to interview the world's most wanted man, but to avoid any accusations of complicity, CNN knew the arrangements would have to appear entirely transparent. CNN dutifully contacted the other major American television networks to let them know that it had been presented with the offer and promised that if anything came of this, it would share the footage. The network stressed to viewers that it had no connection with bin Laden, did not know even if he was alive or dead and was communicating with Al-Qaeda in Afghanistan solely through Al-Jazeera's contacts. It warned that bin Laden's response would not be shown unless it was genuinely newsworthy. 'If he spews off just propaganda, there's no reason for us to air it,' said CNN's CEO and chairman, Walter Isaacson. 'We'll only report it if it is news.'

A group of senior editorial staffers at CNN drew up six questions for bin Laden, about Al-Qaeda's role in 9/11 and about the recent spate of anthrax attacks in America. Al-Jazeera drew up another twenty-five questions of its own. CNN gave its list of questions to Al-Jazeera, who faxed the two lists from Doha to Kabul, where Al-Jazeera's correspondent read the questions over the telephone to his Al-Qaeda contact. The ethics of this stunt were hotly debated in the American press. CNN was criticized for offering questions in advance, since this is usually considered bad form for journalists. Some said the network was only serving to publicize Al-Qaeda. Fox News announced that it would never participate in such a stunt, but was later embarrassingly contradicted by the managing director of Al-Jazeera. 'I assure you they contacted me to send more questions of their own,' he said. 'I got calls and emails from them.' A Fox News spokesman said later that a Fox correspondent had made contact with Al-Jazeera asking to be considered, but only if bin Laden agreed to a regular interview.

After the questions had been submitted there was nothing to do but wait. A week later, nothing had happened. 'There has been nothing,' said Al-Jazeera's managing director. 'We are still waiting.' He hypothesized that bin Laden either might have rejected the questions as being too critical or else he might have been physically incapable of delivering the answers. After all, Al Qaeda's positions in the Afghan mountains were being heavily bombed every day. CNN's chief news executive, Eason Jordan, concurred: 'That it's taken a few days doesn't surprise me. And if we never get the response, I would not be shocked.'

In time the whole attempt was overtaken by other events and the questions soon slid from public attention. Anyone who remembered assumed that, for one reason or another, they had not been, nor ever would be, answered. But, in fact, Taysir Alluni met Osama bin Laden on 20 October 2001 in his den, and in a face-to-face interview had a chance to put all these questions to bin Laden. Afterwards Al-Jazeera did not tell CNN that the interview had taken place, despite the fact that the two networks had a comprehensive sharing agreement.

Only when the *New York Times* declared that a tape of the interview existed did CNN demand of Al-Jazeera whether there had, in fact, been any answers to the questions the channel had put to bin Laden. Al-Jazeera now admitted there had, but the tape was not going to be aired because it did not meet its editorial standards. And that was the end of the affair until, three months later, an unknown party gave a copy of the tape to CNN. On Thursday 31 January, Taysir Alluni's interview with bin Laden was aired for the first time.

When the interview was being set up, Alluni had no inkling that he was about to meet bin Laden. He had been contacted by Al-Qaeda in Kabul and told simply that he was going to be led to a good story. He was driven from Kabul blindfolded in the back seat of a car which drove round and round in circles to disorient him. When it finally stopped, armed men led him to an unknown place, still blindfolded and still under the impression that he was being taken to cover some kind of news event. When the blindfold was removed he found himself face to face with bin Laden in his lair. 'The correspondent . . . was surprised by bin Laden's presence,' said an Al-Jazeera statement released later, somewhat mildly.

The interview was conducted in Arabic and shot against a canvas backdrop. Bin Laden wore camouflage fatigues and had a sub-machine gun close at hand as he talked about 9/11. He spoke ambiguously, seeming first to deny, then confirm, his involvement in the attacks. 'America claims it has convincing evidence of your collusion in the events in New York and Washington. What is your answer?' asked Alluni. 'America has made many accusations against us and many other Muslims around the world,' he asserted. 'Its charge that we are carrying out acts of terrorism is unwarranted.' But then a few seconds later he declared: 'If inciting people to do that is terrorism, and if killing those who kill our sons is terrorism, then let history be witness that we are terrorists.'

Bin Laden invoked Islam to justify attacking civilians: 'We kill the kings of the infidels, kings of the crusaders and civilian infidels in exchange for those of our children they kill. This is permissible in Islamic law and logically.' Here Al-Jazeera's reporter stopped him. 'They kill our innocents, so we kill their innocents?' he asked. 'So we kill their innocents,' bin Laden replied. When asked whether he was responsible for the anthrax attacks in America bin Laden answered vaguely: 'These diseases are a punishment from God and a response to oppressed mothers' prayers in Lebanon, Iraq, Palestine and everywhere.' 'I tell you, freedom and human rights in America are doomed,' he went on. 'The US government will lead the American people and the West in general into an unbearable hell and a choking life.'

Al-Jazeera was furious that CNN had aired the tape without its permission. The network's director-general released a fiery statement saying he had expected CNN to 'respect its special relationship with Al-Jazeera by not airing material that Al-Jazeera itself chose not to broadcast . . . Al-Jazeera will sever its relationship with CNN and will take the necessary action to punish the organizations and individuals who stole this video and distributed it illegally.'

CNN and Al-Jazeera had a cooperative agreement, signed at the start of the Afghan conflict, which CNN believed entitled it to use the tape as if it were its own. 'CNN did nothing illegal in obtaining this tape, and nothing illegal in airing it — our affiliate agreement with Al-Jazeera gives us the express right to use any and all footage owned or controlled by Al-Jazeera, without limitation,' read a statement on CNN's website.

CNN refused to explain who had given it the tape, confirming only that it was not from a government source. The network's Eason Jordan defended his decision to air it, while simultaneously casting doubt on Al-Jazeera's reasons for suppressing it: 'Once that videotape was in our possession, we felt we had to report on it, and show it because it is extremely newsworthy . . . And we really were dumbfounded as to why Al-Jazeera would decide not to air or even acknowledge the existence of the videotape . . . The only television interview with Osama bin Laden since 9/11 was not something we could ignore or sweep under the rug,' Jordan maintained, 'it not only absolutely warrants being seen, it must be seen.'

The implication coming out of CNN was that Al-Jazeera had deliberately tried to cover up the interview, possibly to protect bin Laden in some way, perhaps because it contained the crucial admission which would finally turn the Islamic world against

Al-Qaeda for good. When Peter Bergen, author and CNN's terrorism analyst, was asked, on CNN's *American Morning with Paula Zahn*, why he thought Al-Jazeera chose not to air the tape he said, 'You know, I'm frankly very puzzled. You know, this was the only television interview that bin Laden ever gave and frankly if he was reading out of the telephone book it would be newsworthy. And the fact is that there is quite a lot of . . . it is very indicting. I mean he, on a couple of occasions he basically seems to take responsibility for the events of 9/11. He sort of ducks the question of anthrax. But this is all very interesting. So frankly I'm just perplexed why they chose not to air it. I mean I'm not part . . . privy to all the facts of the case. But it's a very puzzling episode.'

Then Paula Zahn asked him, 'What was the incentive in holding this back from the American public?' Bergen replied 'Well, Paula, I mean, again, I'm just really, really perplexed and, you know, Al-Jazeera bills its reputation as being a sort of independent broadcaster in the Middle East, different from some of the other broadcasters that are basically government entities. Perhaps they came under some pressure from their own government, the government of Qatar, not to broadcast this. But I think there's some facts that we don't know yet which will elucidate this funny and rather strange episode.'

Jihad Ballout, Al-Jazeera's manager of media relations, later explained to me why the channel had withheld the tape. 'We refused to air the interview for two reasons. One, because it was done under duress, meaning Taysir Alluni was given a list of questions by the interviewee. He was in an environment of intimidation. Two, bin Laden was using Al-Jazeera to give out a very edited and sanitized statement to his people. It was a message, a pure message.'

Al-Jazeera also contradicted CNN story's about how the interview had been set up in the first place. 'Bin Laden's people wanted their man to go on air with an interview,' Ballout told me. 'There was a choice between CNN and Al-Jazeera. We were both approached independently and submitted questions and Al-Jazeera was chosen by Al-Qaeda.' Just because Al-Jazeera had the only bureau in Afghanistan did not mean CNN could not communicate with the Taliban, he reminded me. 'Telephones are there,' he said. 'The Taliban, as has been proved so far, are quite adept at using high technology.' What doubly vexed Al-Jazeera was that, having used its footage without permission, CNN was presenting Al-Jazeera as the go-between and now had the gall to cast aspersions on the integrity of Taysir Alluni, who, Al-Jazeera believed, had done nothing but behave in accordance with the highest professional standards.

'Some news organizations are sometimes paranoid and I think that is the result of 9/11,' Ballout told me in his office in Doha. 'They are paranoid of going out to do their job. I am a journalist. I will contact the devil if there is a story that is going to satisfy my professional desire and be of service to my audience . . . You know, some news organizations are wary of saying they received a call from somebody who purports to be representing bin Laden or Saddam Hussein or whatever. I think there are double standards at work here. They would not make contact with bin Laden but they would give their right arm to broadcast an interview with him.'

Al-Jazeera was livid; CNN would not back down. The row escalated. Eason Jordan blasted what he called Al-Jazeera's 'lies and deceptions'. 'Now we are at a point where we cannot believe anything that Al-Jazeera has to say on the subject,' he surmised.

So who did give the bin Laden tape to CNN? After the interview, bin Laden's aides had, as usual, made a copy of the tape. Bin Laden and his lieutenants make a point of keeping copies of all their interviews so that they can pass them along to their affiliated production company, Al-Sahab. The company, whose name means 'the cloud', makes no secret of its affiliation with Al-Qaeda. Al-Sahab is a veritable cottage industry, turning out propaganda videos, often featuring snippets of past interviews as well as the last will and testament of several suicide bombers. These videos sometimes include clips that have never been aired

before, which are often of great interest to various security services around the world.

But if Al-Qaeda had given CNN the tape, it would have had
to transport it out of Afghanistan, in the middle of the war,
which, although not impossible, would have been far from easy.
'I think that is a little bit more difficult than picking the phone
up and calling a contact,' commented Ballout drily.

Besides Al-Qaeda, one other party also had a copy of the
interview: the Pentagon. Although this tape had never been
broadcast before, since 9/11 the American secret service had
made it their business to know all of Al-Jazeera's internal affairs.
They had evidently known about this one for some time. Tony
Blair had certainly seen the tape before it was broadcast on
CNN, because he had cited bits of it in a speech to the House
of Commons three months previously, when he was justifying
the case for war against Afghanistan. 'Bin Laden himself said on
20 October in a broadcast videotape that, and I quote, "If aveng-
ing the killing of our people is terrorism, let history be a witness
that we are terrorists." Mr Speaker, they are terrorists and history
will judge them as such.'

Ballout is non-committal. 'There were rumours that the US
administration was putting pressure on Al-Jazeera to air or not
to air, or to pass on certain communication before it was aired,'
he said discreetly. So might, I asked him, this have been an
attempt by the American administration to smear Al-Jazeera by
implicating the network in a cover-up? 'I think this question
should be posed to the American administration of the time
rather than to Al-Jazeera,' he answered coolly.

There is only circumstantial evidence that it was the American
administration who gave the video to CNN, albeit through a
third party. Despite the recent stern rebuke from Condoleezza
Rice that bin Laden's speeches were not to be aired unedited
for fear of transmitting secret messages, CNN was not admon-
ished by the White House for airing this tape, although it admitted that it had not asked for any kind of permission first. Editorial
restraint had been practised, CNN determined, since the tape's

full length ran to over an hour and less than eight minutes had been broadcast. No transcript of the interview was published. Despite promising to share the results of the questions put to bin Laden with other networks, in the end CNN never did. 'Given the legal circumstances, we cannot give away this kind of material. I don't think it is our place to give it away,' ruled Eason Jordan.

It never emerged for sure who had given CNN the tape. In the American media it was widely insinuated that the affair had been an attempt by Al-Jazeera to cover up bin Laden's confession of responsibility for 9/11. In retrospect, it looks more like a smear campaign by the coalition, bitter at Al-Jazeera's coverage of the war and desperate to have bin Laden's near-confession on air, to prove their vengeful war was justified. American media policy had gone full circle in the space of a few months. From desperately trying to suppress bin Laden's announcements for fear of secret messages, now they were handing out tapes to their own news networks. There is no point muzzling sheep.

Whatever the truth of this insalubrious affair, it did not take long for CNN and Al-Jazeera to patch up their differences. Ruffled feathers were soon smoothed with so much at stake between the two news organizations. Charlotte Beers missed blackballing bin Laden over his fast and loose interpretation of the Koran justifying the murder of civilians, but in the long run only the pride of the American secret service was hurt. Taysir Alluni, under deep surveillance, had met their quarry face to face and they had never even known.

Over the coming months Al-Jazeera's and the American administration's perspectives on events became increasingly antagonistic. The rift deepened when the BBC published the results of its damning investigation into the bombing of Al-Jazeera's Kabul bureau, in which it branded the Pentagon as remorseless.

The Taliban vanquished, for now at least, Afghanistan quickly faded from public attention. The world's media shifted its gaze elsewhere and attention began to focus on the plight of inmates

in the US naval base at Guantánamo Bay, Cuba. The prison was
to be the subject of a documentary on Al-Jazeera's intermittent
investigative show *Top Secret*, which is fronted by Yosri Fouda.

Tall and rake-thin, with long, slender hands and angular
cheekbones, Yosri Fouda has presence. He once taught mass
communication at the American University in Cairo before
leaving to do a PhD at Glasgow University. After that he became
the roving reporter of the BBC Arabic project for the full eighteen months before the Saudis pulled the plug. Afterwards, unable
to make the move straight to Doha, he worked for the Associated
Press television network for a year.

Since starting at Al-Jazeera this Egyptian sleuth has almost
single-handedly pioneered the Arab tradition of investigative
journalism. His investigations have taken him to some of the
most God-forsaken parts of the planet, where he has met some
of the most maniacal terrorists, and he has been arrested many
times, but so far at least, has always managed to come back
unscathed. An impeccable dresser with eyes like the palace cat,
he is the sort of man you are very glad decided to work for the
forces of good, rather than evil.

In this latest episode of *Top Secret* Fouda followed in the footsteps of an unfortunate group of Pakistani men who left home
seeking adventure in Afghanistan and wound up lags in Camp
X-Ray in Guantánamo Bay. Having escaped death at the hands
of the Americans, they were handed over by their own government when they got home. From Pakistan, they were flown to
Cuba, where they found themselves indefinitely detained without charge and without access to their lawyers or family. Fouda's
report did not stint from depicting life in a hot cage with rats
and mosquitoes, miles from home, as hellish.

Al-Jazeera had an employee in Camp X-Ray, a real-life
prisoner in the media war. A Sudanese assistant cameraman called
Sami Muhyi al-Din Muhammad al-Haj had been arrested in
December in southern Afghanistan and carted off to Cuba on
'suspicion of involvement with Al-Qaeda activities'. 'Apparently
an error in his passport number and the possibility that his name

might be on the list of wanted suspects by the American authorities led to his arrest,' said Al-Jazeera in a statement. Al-Haj had
had his passport stolen two years previously and it was suggested
that he might be the victim of some kind of identity fraud.
Al-Jazeera only discovered he was in Guantánamo Bay when his
wife received a letter saying so, and then she let them know.
Since Al-Jazeera had only hired Al-Haj on a freelance basis a
matter of days before he was arrested, network executives have
been wary about championing his cause as vocally as they might.

Despite the network's best efforts to discover what became
of Al-Haj, three appeals to the US Embassy in Doha and letters
to Washington were left unanswered and no explanation was
forthcoming. After nine months the press watchdog Reporters
sans Frontières, fearing that Washington might use the detention to exert leverage on Al-Jazeera, stepped in on Al-Jazeera's
behalf.

'It is quite irregular for the US authorities to refuse to tell
the journalist's family and friends what the charges are against
him,' said Reporters sans Frontières in an open letter to US
Attorney General John Ashcroft. 'Without questioning why he
was arrested, we think this continued silence is especially unfortunate because it could be seen as an intention to harass
Al-Jazeera, which has already been the target of US State
Department pressure,' it said. 'We don't think this could happen
to any other news organization,' said Reporters sans Frontières'
Americas Desk in a separate email. Five years later Al-Haj is still
imprisoned without charge in Cuba.

That winter the Israelis launched an incursion into the West
Bank and the world media, hungry for red meat after Afghanistan
had quietened, quickly refocused its attention on Palestine.
Al-Jazeera resumed its heavy coverage from the Occupied
Territories, still anchored by the indomitable Walid al-Omary.

As the Israeli army tightened its steely grip around the West
Bank, all eyes turned to the Israeli Prime Minister, Ariel Sharon,
to try to guess what he was going to do next. And so when

Sharon's press office quietly let it be known that he would like to be interviewed on Al-Jazeera to send an important message to the Arab world, Al-Jazeera agreed at once and the bureau in Ramallah began feverishly making arrangements. The logistics of organizing the interview in the face of the occupation, especially with regard to security, were devilish. When the Palestinian Authority found out Al-Jazeera was planning to interview Sharon it sharply objected, as did many important Arab journalists, but Al-Jazeera was determined.

It took two months to plan the Sharon interview and Al-Jazeera depended heavily on the help of its colleagues in the Israeli media. As it became clear that it was really going to happen, Al-Jazeera started running a heavy advertising campaign. At such a sensitive time, when Palestinians were dying almost daily at the hands of the Israeli occupiers, this caused, predictably, a wave of controversy in the Arab world. In Lebanon demonstrators took to the streets calling for the interview to be stopped.

Anger at the forthcoming interview was focused in Lebanon, partly because during the week that the interview was scheduled to take place, the Arab summit was convening in Beirut. The opening ceremony was on the Wednesday and Sharon's media adviser telephoned Walid al-Omary and said Sharon would like to be interviewed that same day. Al-Omary explained that the opening of the Arab summit was a key media event which Al-Jazeera would have to cover at length and he asked whether it might be possible to reschedule the interview to any other time or day that week that would suit the Prime Minister. A new time was agreed: 5 p.m. on Tuesday, the day before the Arab summit began.

As part of the deal, Al-Omary wrote to Sharon's press office well in advance and laid out every detail of the interview. It was going to be live, with the anchor in Doha asking the questions which Al-Omary had written. Sharon would sit in the Israeli Cabinet office and hear the questions via an earpiece. As part of the elaborate security precautions surrounding the interview, every member of the Al-Jazeera news team who was going to be present had to be vetted in advance. They were obliged to send their names and personal details well ahead of time, so that the press office would have an opportunity to veto anyone unsuitable.

On the day of the interview Al-Jazeera's news crew left Ramallah for Tel Aviv at 1 p.m. Knowing security would be tight, they wanted to leave plenty of time before the 5 p.m. interview, so that they could set up their equipment and make all the necessary final preparations. While they were on the road to Tel Aviv, Sharon's press officer called Al-Omary on his mobile and asked whether he would be asking the questions there in the office or whether Sharon would hear the questions from the anchor in Doha via an earpiece. Al-Omary explained that it would be the latter. The press officer said that this was not suitable, because Sharon was an old man who did not hear so well and that an earpiece would not agree with him. So Al-Omary asked his technician what else could be done instead. The technician suggested that instead of Sharon hearing the questions via an earpiece, they could play the questions out of a loudspeaker right there in his office. They did not have a loudspeaker with them, so they stopped at an Israeli hi-fi store on the way and bought one.

After they had reached the Knesset and gone through all the security checks, the team were led into the Cabinet Room, where the interview was due to take place. Having set up all the equipment, including the loudspeaker, they checked everything was in order and that the Prime Minister would be able to hear the questions from Doha.

When Sharon's press officer saw what they had set up, he raised a new objection. Sharon, he said, must be speaking to a human being: he could not just address himself to the camera. Al-Omary explained to the press officer that many world leaders did interviews like this – including President Bush – and that the reason the questions were being asked from the studio in Doha was that this was such an important interview for

Al-Jazeera. Moreover, it would be impossible to do a live interview with Al-Omary right there in the Cabinet Room, because
that would require substantially more equipment, including a
second camera and a mixer, which the team had not brought
with them.

A compromise was found: Al-Omary and Sharon would sit
face to face as if the former were the interviewer and the camera
would be positioned next to his head looking at Sharon.
Al-Omary would wear the earpiece through which he would
hear the questions from Doha in Arabic and he would then
translate them into English for Sharon. Sharon would then reply
to Al-Omary in English, but to the viewers it would look like
he was speaking to the camera.

Both parties agreed that this was an agreeable solution. With
minutes to go, Al-Jazeera set up the camera and Al-Omary called
the chief editor in Doha and explained that the interview was
on course as planned and that he should be ready. Sharon himself
had not yet appeared. The arrangement was that he would arrive
two minutes before the interview was due to start, do the interview and then leave at once.

With just minutes to go, Sharon's press officer said that he
had changed his mind again. This set-up was not agreeable, after
all, he had decided. Al-Omary had to be asking the questions
without the aid of the studio. Doha must not be involved at all.
Al-Omary called his boss in Doha again and explained the new
hitch. His boss asked him what he thought they should do.
Al-Omary, who had in the past interviewed other senior Israeli
officials without problems, suggested that at this stage he thought
the whole thing should be cancelled. He felt Sharon's press office
had treated him disrespectfully, objecting to details that they had
known about and agreed to weeks in advance. It was clear to
Al-Omary that, for whatever reason, the Israelis were determined to obstruct the interview come what may.

At this point Sharon arrived in the Cabinet Room. Al-Omary
turned to him and said, 'Mr Prime Minister, there is no interview.' Without a word Sharon turned on his heel and walked

out. A few moments later the press officer appeared and told Al-Omary to have his team remove all the lights and speakers and camera equipment from the Cabinet Room at once. When they had finished, all the Al-Jazeera news crew were to leave, except Al-Omary, because the Prime Minister wanted to speak with him alone, in private. 'Really I was afraid,' recalled Al-Omary. 'I know that Israel has laws, but I was afraid.'

When these instructions had been carried out, the press officer led Al-Omary into the Prime Minister's office, where Sharon, looking stern, was waiting for him. Al-Omary sat down meekly across the table from Sharon, not knowing what to expect. Sharon began to speak in a very serious tone. 'This interview was important to me,' he told Al-Omary. 'I had a message that I wanted to deliver to the Arab leaders meeting at the summit in Beirut tomorrow. I want to tell them they must forget the idea that there will be no peace until Israel withdraws to the 1967 borders.' Then he changed his tack. 'As you know, Walid, in your village their sacks are full with onions and tomatoes,' he began telling a completely bemused Al-Omary. It was clear from what he was saying that he knew every detail about Al-Omary, his family, his friends and all his personal details. Al-Omary hails from a farming village in Israel, near Nazareth.

Sharon talked to him for fifteen minutes, without stopping or asking a single question, about the rich harvest that had been collected in his village that year. He expounded at great length about Israeli agriculture policy and how this had helped villagers benefit from the land. When Sharon had finished speaking, Al-Omary was collected by the press officer and led out of the building.

Outside were waiting banks of camera crews from Israeli TV stations and international news agencies hoping to interview Al-Omary about what had transpired. Everyone wanted to know why Al-Jazeera's well-publicized and controversial interview had had to be cancelled. Dodging the press, Al-Omary climbed into the waiting Al-Jazeera van with the rest of his television crew and headed back to Ramallah. Disappointed at not getting his interview, he was nevertheless intrigued by the strange and slightly intimidating lecture he had received from Sharon about nature's bounty.

The day after Sharon's speech fiasco the Arab summit was opening in Beirut. Al-Jazeera was due to broadcast Arafat's speech to the delegates live from his besieged office in the West Bank. Because of the siege conditions, passage in and out of Arafat's compound was extremely difficult. To make sure they had adequate time to set up, Al-Jazeera's news team, rather than try to arrive early that morning, decided it would be safer to get there the previous evening and spend the night in Arafat's office.

That morning Al-Omary had left his home in Ramallah at 7 a.m. to give a media lecture at Birzeit University as he regularly did, when he received an urgent call from the news team who were supposed to be interviewing Arafat, urging him to come at once. Inside the compound he found his colleagues had been up most of the night making preparations, in very adverse conditions. By contrast with Sharon, who had made his dramatic entry only at the last minute, Arafat had been wandering around in his pyjamas all night, chatting with the news crew and taking peeks through the eyepiece of the camera to see what he could see. He had spent much of the night lecturing the Al-Jazeera news team about the virtues of eating honey, which, they had learned, he held in the highest regard.

'It was then I realized the problem we have in this region,' Al-Omary told me. 'These two nations are run by two old men. For one, the most important thing is the benefit of onions; for the other it is honey. The problem is not just the militants on either side, it is the leadership. As you say in English, "You cannot teach old dogs new tricks."'

The saga of the aborted interview torpedoed the trust between Sharon's press office and Al-Jazeera. The Prime Minister never offered to give another interview. Each side blamed the other for the failure. The Israelis say that the problem lay in Al-Jazeera's technical failings on the day. Al-Omary believes that Sharon's press office deliberately sabotaged the interview for fear of telling comparisons between the Sabra and Shatila massacres of the 1980s, for which Sharon had been found indirectly responsible, and the current methods he was using to suppress the intifada.

That spring, under cover of the War on Terror, the full force of the Israeli army was unleashed in the Occupied Territories. The West Bank was burning and Arabs everywhere instinctively turned to Al-Jazeera for the news. It was accurate and fast, and rather than watch once each day, people began to follow events hour by hour. Televisions were left on in shops, cafés and homes.

Al-Jazeera's importance as a news source locally was elevated dramatically after the Israelis blew up the offices, studios and equipment of the popular local Palestine radio station the Voice of Palestine. When Israeli troops took the largest Palestinian city, Nablus, all five FM radio stations in Ramallah and all six TV channels and radio stations went dead. Palestinians turned to Al-Jazeera for news. In Hebron and Bethlehem the radio stations that remained on air took their audio feed direct from Al-Jazeera.

When the Israelis invaded Jenin, soldiers encircled the town and for days no press could get in. Telephone reports from people in Jenin said that hundreds had been killed. So urgent were the reports of a massacre that the UN Security Council called an emergency meeting and the UN Secretary General, Kofi Annan, appointed a special investigating committee to find out what was going on. Al-Omary and his team were also desperately trying to get into the town to see the situation for themselves. For four days they tried to gain entry but each time were turned back at the security cordon. On their first two attempts the Israelis confiscated their videos as well as kicking them out. Eventually they made it inside and Al-Jazeera gave the first television reports of what had been happening in Jenin.

Within minutes of their arrival Al-Omary met a Palestinian doctor who insisted that he and his crew come to the hospital at once to see the casualties with their own eyes. Al-Omary suggested to the doctor that he send his cameraman, but the doctor insisted that they must all come. At the hospital Al-Omary was led straight to the mortuary, where he saw the corpses. An Israeli tank had killed seven Palestinian policemen, their bodies destroyed almost completely. Two of the hospital staff had collected the body parts of the seven men and laid them out like a ghastly jigsaw on steel tables.

'Many times people try and show me a very shocking death in order to try and use Al-Jazeera to make a shocking statement,' he told me. 'One woman whose son had been killed wanted to show me his body. She was crying and screaming that I had to see. The face of the corpse had been completely destroyed. I could not show pictures like this, but it was important to the relatives and medics that I had at least witnessed what had happened. Showing pictures of the dead serves neither the dead nor the living.'

Al-Omary's report from Jenin comprehensively dispelled the stories of hundreds dead. Although hundreds of houses had been demolished, there had been tens of casualties, not hundreds. By telling the truth about what had happened inside Jenin, Al-Jazeera cleared up the rumours. The UN special investigating committee appointed by the Secretary-General was unceremoniously disbanded. Because Arabs heard it from Al-Omary on Al-Jazeera, they believed it too.

Broadcasters who wanted to compete with Al-Jazeera for its audience were obliged to emulate its professional style. The news marketplace was becoming increasingly competitive. Other types of media were now available as a source of news, notably the Internet and text-messaging services. In Jordan a local mobile phone service provider offered free text messages to over sixty thousand subscribers as a convenient way of keeping abreast of events in Palestine. It suited those who did not have the time or inclination to sit near a television or radio all day.

By April the conflict in the West Bank had intensified to such a degree that the international community feared that it might spill over once again into other countries in the region. From Morocco to the Gulf, tens of thousands of Arabs demonstrated in the streets against their leaders' inaction over Israel. Marchers in Morocco carried placards that read, 'We are all Palestinians.' Worryingly, Amman and Cairo bore witness to the largest protests, capitals of two countries that were supposed to have made their peace with Israel.

Once again the Arab world was riveted to its seat, spellbound. Women and children trapped in demolished buildings, disfigured corpses in the street, bulldozers knocking down houses with people inside while US-made Apache gunships hovered overhead, a torrent of horror was pouring out of the West Bank. When Sharon threatened to exile Arafat once and for all, Arafat appeared on Al-Jazeera declaring he would rather die than leave. Feelings of desperation saturated daily lives across the Middle East, permeating religion, advertising, entertainment and sport. The same message was heard across the region: solidarity with Palestine. Once again telethons raised millions of dollars for West Bank victims and deep resentment at American foreign policy reverberated through the Arab media. In the West analysts once again compared the Arab experience of this conflict to when the bloody drama of Vietnam had been beamed into America's living room. A new and uncomfortable intimacy with the intifada was beginning.

Al-Jazeera's loquacious tele-sheikh Dr Yusuf al-Qaradawi appeared as a guest on the live discussion programme *Religion and Life* to talk about why the Arabs found themselves in such a dreadful condition. Dr Al-Qaradawi staunchly defended the right of the Palestinians to fight with any means necessary against the Israeli occupation. 'The Israelis might have nuclear bombs but we have the children bomb and these human bombs must continue until liberation,' he said. When the host of the show told Al-Qaradawi that several viewers had phoned in calling for peace rather than jihad, he replied that any Muslim who called for peace at this time was guilty of treason. He blamed America as one of the principal reasons why Arabs today were in despair. When the host picked him up on this, saying that many Arab countries enjoyed good relations with America, Al-Qaradawi dismissed this out of hand. 'It is not a friendly relationship but one that is based on cursing deep inside and smiling on the surface,' he said. 'The real position is the one that is expressed by the Arab street but the official position does not express the true feelings of these peoples.' Life for Arabs during the Cold War had been better, he insisted, as at least there had been a balance of power. 'It is in people's interest if there is disagreement among the oppressors,' he determined.

Capitalizing on the inflamed passions of the intifada, Al-Qaeda sent a new video to Al-Jazeera. It featured bin Laden and his lieutenant, Ayman al-Zawahiri, as well as, on a separate portion of the tape, one of the 9/11 hijackers reciting his 'will'. This way, Al-Qaeda hoped, the tape would receive maximum publicity. Al-Jazeera would not say how it had received this latest tape, but confirmed that it had not come through the network's correspondent in Afghanistan because it knew he was under surveillance.

Since it was unclear when this tape had been recorded it could not be regarded as evidence even that bin Laden was still alive, but the timing of the tape's release – in the heat of the intifada – lent it a particular significance. It was a deliberate attempt by Al-Qaeda to associate itself with the situation in Palestine.

The Saudi press, long-time state-sponsored critics of Al-Jazeera, speculated that this might be a conscious effort by the channel to equate Al-Qaeda and Palestinian militant groups, thereby turning the West Bank into just another theatre in the global War on Terror and legitimizing the Israeli tactics. Arabs were already uncomfortable that Israelis were allowed to speak on Al-Jazeera, the prospect of an interview with Sharon had caused uproar and now this latest tape, which played straight into the hands of Sharon, was seen as further evidence that Al-Jazeera was a Zionist instrument. The Saudi press speculated that Al-Jazeera might even have fabricated some of the tape, or at least timed its release deliberately to make all Arabs look like terrorists, to the detriment of the Palestinian cause.

The besmirching of Al-Jazeera at this depressing time by the rest of the Arab media was an understandable reaction to the crisis. When the news is too ghastly to bear, shoot the messenger. When Al-Jazeera's bureau in Amman starting being harassed for allegedly disseminating Zionist propaganda, the network's chief editor, Ibrahim Hilal, decided that it would be better to confront the rumours head on.

Hilal made an announcement in defence of the network's decision to broadcast the tape. He explained Al-Jazeera's policy and its motto, 'The opinion and the other opinion', and said, with regard to the timing, that although the tape had been deemed immediately newsworthy, its release had been postponed ten days lest it overshadow events in Palestine. The announcement did little to quash the conspiracy rumours. Word on the Arab street was that Al-Jazeera was purposefully linking Palestinian militants with Al-Qaeda to tar them as terrorists. Despite this, a few days later Al-Jazeera went ahead and broadcast the whole tape.

This incident marked the start of a steady decline in Al-Jazeera's relations with its Arab neighbours. The pressures of the War on Terror had changed what Arab regimes regarded as acceptable levels of free speech and now that America was cracking down on the press in the name of patriotism, Arab regimes thought they could do the same.

The trend that had been developing before 9/11, towards more freedom of the press in the Arab world, was thrown into reverse. Al-Jazeera, however, did not change its style. It still featured the same steady throughput of guests glad of the opportunity to lay into Arab regimes. On the network's talk shows Arab rulers were still routinely branded as tyrants or slaves to Western masters. Arab dissidents living in the West who appeared on Al-Jazeera still presented themselves as refugees in exile from nightmare regimes. In the newly buttoned-up media culture after 9/11, it was clear this kind of talk could not go on indefinitely without consequences.

In May, after a Bahraini dissident appearing on *The Opposite*

Direction called the ongoing democratization process in the king-
dom 'only cosmetic', Al-Jazeera was banned from reporting from
within Bahrain. The Bahraini Minister of Information accused
Al-Jazeera of seeking to 'harm Bahrain' and of having ties with
Israel. 'It is a Zionist channel, penetrated by Zionists,' he ruled.
'As long as I am minister, Jazeera will not have an office in
Bahrain.' Even the sports news, he raged, was offensive and delib-
erately targeted Bahrain.

Al-Jazeera was nonchalant about the ban, but it was obliged
to close its bureau in Bahrain. Remarkably, this did not stop the
network obtaining new footage of the Bahraini elections.
Bahraini citizens spontaneously called in to Al-Jazeera headquarters in Doha and offered their own VCR and digital home
video recordings of what was going on. This phenomenon was
repeated in several other countries in the region and it demonstrated how the information age had rendered conventional
means of censorship irrelevant. So close are the ties that bind
the Gulf countries together, information passes freely from one
to another despite what rulers say or do. It is telling that, despite
the Bahraini government's condemnation of Al-Jazeera as
Zionist, Bahrainis still saw fit to call that network first to offer
their pictures, free of charge, rather than call a competitor.

At the Arab summit in Cairo, Ministers of Information from
thirteen Arab countries decided to do more about this Zionist
propaganda. The Arab League resolved to launch a new
$22-million Arab media campaign against Israel. Its job was to
denounce what they called Israel's racist policy towards the
Palestinians and to counter Western portrayals of Arabs as terrorists. The new channel featured two hours each day of rather
dry current affairs programmes in Hebrew and could not have
won many viewers. Israelis themselves were not allowed to
appear.

Qatar, the only Arab country with no Ministry of
Information, was not represented at the Cairo conference. In its
absence, plans were drawn up to combat Al-Jazeera's suspicious
policy of interviewing Israeli officials, as well as the channel's

other perceived Zionist tendencies. Two aljazeera.net journalists had recently written articles for an Israeli website, which had prompted Palestinian journalists to complain to the Arab Journalists Association in Cairo that Al-Jazeera was guilty of 'normalization' with Israel. The association had a strict policy of boycotting Israeli publications. One of the Al-Jazeera journalists expressed support in his article for a US attack against Iraq and the other criticized Palestinian suicide attacks.

Resolutions in Cairo were drafted aimed at counteracting 'Israeli and US attempts to portray the Palestinian national struggle as unjustified terrorism'. The draft clearly had Al-Jazeera in mind when it urged 'Arab media not to allow Israeli officials to address Arab public opinion in their attempt to justify aggression'. Al-Jazeera showed what it thought of this action when, a few months later, Al-Omary interviewed the Israeli President Moshe Katsav, its highest-ranking Israeli official yet.

Al Jazeera's determination to pursue its own editorial policy, no matter what, put the network on a collision course with other Arab countries. The channel's sickly relations with Saudi Arabia took another blow when a Saudi dissident on the ever-controversial *The Opposite Direction* denigrated the Saudi peace plan for Palestine and accused King Fahd of treachery. The host, Dr Faisal al-Qasim, let the comments pass without reprimand and for a few weeks it looked like the Saudis might let the incident slip.

Then, while touring the Gulf and in a deliberate snub to the Qataris, the Saudi Foreign Minister pointedly visited all the regional capitals except Doha. It soon emerged that a decision had been taken at the highest level to stamp out Al-Jazeera for good. The Saudis had consistently been doing their best to make life difficult for Al-Jazeera in a covert way and had even denied the network permission to cover the Hajj festivities. Now the gloves were off.

Saudi Arabia had long held that Qatar was treating the regional hierarchy with disrespect. By denigrating Saudi Arabia on television while presenting itself as the most reliable ally in the region, the little upstart now looked as if it was hoping to usurp the Saudis' position as America's principal regional partner.

Saudi Arabia's relationship with America had been badly damaged when it emerged that fifteen of the nineteen 9/11 hijackers had been Saudis. The relationship suffered another blow when Saudi Arabia refused America permission to use Saudi territory as a springboard from which to attack Afghanistan. Now, as the Americans prepared for an assault on Iraq, they had decided, rather than risk being rejected by the Saudis again, to throw their lot in with the Qataris. In March, the Emir of Qatar, Sheikh Hamad bin Khalifa Al Thani, announced the existence of a massive, super-high-tech American airbase in the desert, called Al-Udeid. It was America's new $1.4-billion operational regional hub and would be ready in December. For the Qataris, having a huge American presence nearby was the ultimate insurance. As the Emir once put it to his advisers, 'The only way we can be sure the Americans will answer our 911 call is if we have the police at our house.'

As the Saudis and Qataris rowed about Al-Jazeera, the Kuwaitis were called in to mediate. But the Kuwaitis sided with Saudi Arabia against Qatar. 'I regret that Qatar is gaining enemies instead of friends, especially from Jazeera and what it broadcasts,' Kuwait's Foreign Minister, Sheikh Sabah al-Ahmad Al Sabah, told the Kuwaiti newspaper *Al-Qabas*. As relations worsened, the Saudi press led the charge against Al-Jazeera, citing it as one of the region's biggest headaches. Following a meeting between the Qatari and Israeli Foreign Ministers in Paris, diplomatic relations between Qatar and Saudi Arabia were nearly terminated.

The Saudi daily newspaper *Al-Watan* published a string of damning articles about Qatar and Al-Jazeera. An article entitled 'Al-Jazeera Channel and Gangrene' vividly described Saudi sentiments towards the network:

Gangrene is an illness that affects human beings, especially those who are suffering from diabetes. Gangrene starts at the body limbs when the victim is infected with a wound in the finger, leg or hand. When this lethal disease invades any organ of the human body, the cure is no doubt, amputation or severance for fear that the disease may deteriorate and spread to other parts of the body. The outcome is ineluctably death. The human body symbolizes here the 'Gulf Cooperation Council' [GCC] and the gangrene is regrettably the Qatari 'Al-Jazeera' channel. This malicious gang that made up what is called 'Al-Jazeera' is working intensively with all means and ways to destabilize GCC countries, by producing artificial, self-styled and malicious programmes . . . In an attempt from our part to cure this gangrene and the chronic headache caused by this channel to our Qatari brothers, we suggest a remedy similar to the one used to cure gangrene, which is amputation or severance prior to the spreading of the disease to other organs of the body.

Another article accused the Qataris of being like Saddam Hussein, who also sought to divide the Gulf countries from one another. Ironically, Al-Jazeera had fallen out with the Iraqis too, who decided to ban the network's Baghdad correspondent from working for ten days because he had used some expressions that displeased the Ministry of Information.

The Saudi press tried to start a whispering campaign alleging that Al-Jazeera was shedding viewers because it had become boring. The newspaper *Al-Jazirah* wrote:

Limited faces and few personalities . . . Repeated and reiterated slogans and issues . . . This is the current state of 'Al-Jazeera' satellite channel lately. There is nothing new in what the channel has been broadcasting for some time. During this period, it lost many and many of its viewers who had seen a good omen in the launch of this channel, as a distinguished media platform. But it did not take long for its viewers to progressively desert it, since they

started finding out about the intentions and the objectives
of this channel. Since those who believe in the orienta-
tions of this channel are a minority – thank God – in the
Arab world, among them a limited number of our Saudi
citizens – naturally – those in charge of 'Al-Jazeera' have
no alternative but to rotate these faces and names by hosting them in successive chat shows . . . The only thing that
changes is the female presenter.

Besides Bahrain, Kuwait and Saudi Arabia, Jordan also crossed
swords with Al-Jazeera over *The Opposite Direction*. 'This station
has exceeded all professional and moral values in dealing with
many national issues,' the Jordanian Minister of Information was
quoted as saying in a Jordanian newspaper. 'Jazeera intentionally
means to harm Jordan and its pan-Arab stances sometimes directly
and at times indirectly,' he declared shortly before revoking
Al-Jazeera's licence and annulling the accreditation of its journalists, effectively closing the office. The source of the dispute
this time had been a Palestinian university professor from the
US who had accused the former King of Jordan and his father
of having a pro-Israeli stance and the current King of working
for the CIA.

Al-Jazeera defended the freedom of its guests to say whatever they liked and asserted that what they said was not the
opinion of the station. This excuse did not impress the Jordanian
authorities, which set the state news agency and associated newspapers on Al-Jazeera like a pack of dogs.

'Once again Al-Jazeera satellite channel resumes its suspicious
role and crosses all red lines violating all professional and ethical
values in dealing with many pan-Arab issues,' said one editorial
in the newspaper *Al Ra'y*. Qatar had Zionist links, Al-Jazeera
was its tool and the Emir had turned his country into a giant
American aircraft carrier. 'The time has come for officials of
Al-Jazeera and those who finance it to review their march and
assess their work,' said another paper. 'Al-Jazeera's main goal is
to create disturbance among the Arabs and provoke sedition for

purposes known only to those in charge of the channel and those who plan [programmes] for them.'

Zionist paranoia was rampant; conspiracy theories were rife. One Jordanian paper asserted that 'fifty Qataris, who have been carefully chosen, have been receiving training courses for more than two weeks under the supervision of Israeli security agencies'. These secret agents, it was hypothesized in a second paper, were being distributed around the Arab world, where they would carry out the dark orders of the Israeli-American alliance. Arab governments would be toppled; a new world order would be set in motion.

International free speech and media groups, like Reporters sans Frontières, condemned the closure of Al-Jazeera's bureau in Jordan. But the bureau remained closed and shortly afterwards Jordan recalled its ambassador from Doha. As the Al-Jazeera journalists left the country amid acrimony, Jordanian airport officials seized their remaining videos, suspecting they had been made since their accreditation had been annulled. Upon inspection it turned out that the recordings, which were of the twelfth Arab volleyball championships, had been stopped the moment accreditation was withdrawn. Jordanian security duly returned them.

As time passed, some small efforts were made by Jordan to mend fences with Qatar, but relations were not resumed. The chairman and editor of two weekly Jordanian newspapers were arrested after they published pictures of the Qatari Emir and his Foreign Minister dressed as belly-dancers. Under the front-page banner headline 'Qatar . . . nest of spies', a photomontage showed the two in mini-skirts, the Emir singing into a microphone. The journalists were charged with 'undermining relations with a foreign country, contempt against the Qatari head of state and his Foreign Minister, as well as propagating false information'.

Although Al-Jazeera was driving Qatar into regional isolation, it seemed most Qataris remained proud of Al-Jazeera. A poll in a Qatari newspaper, in which a grand total of 342 people participated, found 107 thought Al-Jazeera should be closed down, while 235 thought it should stay open. Throughout these disputes the people of all the countries that had fallen out with Qatar continued to watch the station as hungrily as they always had done. Nothing could be done to stop them.

Confusingly, at the same time as Al-Jazeera was making enemies in the Arab world for its supposed Zionism, the American and Israeli press were criticizing it as a platform for terror. Neoconservatives and Likudniks in the White House, as well as Sharon's administration, regarded Al-Jazeera as just another facet of the Arab media war machine, along with Hezbollah's Al-Manar channel, Palestinian hate radio and Arab government-sanctioned propaganda newspapers.

America and Israel, taken aback by recent displays of Al-Jazeera's influence on the region during Afghanistan and the raid on Jenin, had resolved to invest seriously in their own media programmes before the next crisis came along. Congress approved $245 million for cultural and media projects in the Middle East. A $30-million chunk of this money was to be spent on a new Middle East radio network, which would bring the voice of freedom to the Middle East, just as the Voice of America had been broadcast in Germany during the Second World War. The news station, Radio Sawa, which means 'Radio Together', was to be broadcast from powerful FM and AM radio stations, as well as in digital audio from three different satellites, twenty-four hours a day. Slick with Arab and American pop hits, Radio Sawa was aimed at the under-twenty-fives. Every half-hour there were to be five-minute news segments.

The station, which was advertised with thirty-second promotional spots on Al-Jazeera, received a mixed reception. In more liberal Arab countries, like Qatar, it was a reasonable success, but in Jordan, which has a high Palestinian population, less so. Al-Jazeera's editor-in-chief, Ibrahim Hilal, scoffed at the new station. 'American taxpayers are wasting their money on Radio Sawa,' he said. 'Arabs understand that it is a tool of the US government.'

Undaunted, its founder, Los Angeles radio mogul Norman J. Pattiz, began work on a new twenty-four-hour Arabic-language satellite television network, also to be broadcast in the Middle East. This new TV network was explicitly planned to rival Al-Jazeera. The federal agency behind the Voice of America summoned top entertainment executives from all the major Hollywood studios to a private luncheon at the Museum of Television and Radio in Beverly Hills to discuss the new network's content.

To be a commercial as well as a political success was never going to be easy. The Saudis, who dominated the crowded Middle East advertising market, were antipathetic towards all prospective competitors, including the Americans. CNN had already been scared off starting an Arabic-language channel of its own when it realized it would be challenging the formidable will of the House of Saud for advertising revenue. If the American government started an Arabic-language channel, its pockets would need to be at least as deep as the Emir of Qatar's and there was some doubt that the US taxpayer would have the staying power. Some argued that the $170 million spent on starting up these projects would be better spent on Arab cultural exchange or public health programmes. 'I don't know what advantage we gain by primarily playing pop music to the Arab world,' said the President of the Voice of America journalists' guild about Radio Sawa. 'You may gain a larger audience of teenagers. That's like feeding candy to kids. But I don't think we are following the mission given us by the VOA charter of representing America in a comprehensive way to the rest of the world.'

The Israel Broadcasting Authority had its own media offensive planned. On one of the same satellites Al-Jazeera used, it began broadcasting its own Arabic-English satellite channel receivable throughout Europe and the Middle East. News and current affairs heavy, the new channel also featured plenty of old uncensored Egyptian movies from the fifties and sixties. Eight hours each day would be in Arabic. This was not propaganda, Israeli Minister without Portfolio Ra'anan Cohen emphasized, just high-quality news broadcasting.

Al-Jazeera's West Bank bureau chief, Walid al-Omary, gave the new station short shrift: 'We are not in competition with the Israelis for the Israeli Arabs. They have lost that battle. Most of them now prefer to watch Al-Jazeera than to see Israeli TV, because Al-Jazeera has more credibility and more relevance to their situation. Even the ordinary Israelis have started watching Al-Jazeera now. Many times they have asked me why there is no translation in Hebrew. Sometimes at the checkpoints the Israeli soldiers tell me, "You are the perfect station, you do a great job", but more often they tell me, "You are fascists, you are anti-Semites."'

Ambitious as these new plans were, it would be a few years before anyone could tell for sure if America and Israel's two-pronged media offensive would bear any fruit. In the meantime there was nothing that could be done about the volleys of abuse coming from the television, the Internet and the mosque, except endure them.

One clear sign that the media war was being lost was the swelling grass-roots campaign to boycott American goods in the Middle East. In Lebanon, an empty Kentucky Fried Chicken restaurant was blown up in the middle of the night. Sheikh al-Qaradawi displayed a flashing banner on his website demanding, 'Boycott America from Pepsi cans to Boeing.' McDonald's franchises across the Arab world struggled to stress that they were locally owned and run, but sales plummeted. Lebanese McDonald's sent off sixty thousand text messages denying an Internet rumour that profits from each sale went to Israel. Most consumer goods with a link to America reported a 20–30 per cent drop in income.

Pitifully, despite there being some three hundred million Arabs, together they accounted for less than 3 per cent of America's total exports and the real business America did with the Arab world, like weapons, technology and airplanes, was never under threat. Nevertheless, for many individuals and small groups who owned franchises on American products, this was a disaster.

The boycott proceeded together with more fund-raising TV appeals, or telethons. These were anything but symbolic. Appeals on several Arab news channels, but not Al-Jazeera, helped raise millions of dollars for food, medicine and supplies for Palestine. A government-sponsored telethon in Saudi Arabia raised more than $85 million. Jordan's Ministry of Health claimed donations had led to the accumulation of ten thousand tons of medicine, blankets and tents, as well as thousands of litres of blood. Seventy Red Crescent trucks were filled with supplies and the contents were wrapped in fine tissue paper adorned with flowers.

In June 2002, after Yosri Fouda's *Top Secret* investigation into the black hole of Guantánamo Bay had been aired on Al-Jazeera, he received a mysterious phone call in his office in London. A mysterious man, identifying himself simply as Abu Bakr, invited him to fly to Karachi, where Al-Qaeda, he was assured, had something genuinely 'Top Secret' awaiting him. Fouda's gut told him at once that this lead was genuine.

'It was very instinctive,' he told me in his office, throwing his long, thin hands around as he spoke. 'When you are in the business for long enough you smell something, but you don't know what it is and I smelt that there was something at the other end waiting for me. What it was I didn't know. I was trying to resist flattering myself with the idea that it might be bin Laden himself, but then I thought maybe Al-Qaeda just wanted to hand something over. I thought perhaps I might just be coming back with some tapes.'

Working on a hunch, Fouda jumped on a plane to Pakistan. 'I did not tell anyone what I was doing, even my boss. Luckily, I went to Pakistan shortly before this to do another programme I was doing about Guantánamo Bay, walking in the footsteps of those guys who crossed over from Afghanistan to Pakistan. So I told my boss I was trying to investigate a part two.'

Before Fouda left London, Abu Bakr had given him very specific instructions on how to behave, in a series of irregular phone calls. He was told to wear Pakistani clothes, fly on a

particular plane, book into a certain hotel – then cancel at the
last minute and check into a different one. Each call would tell
him how to make the next rendezvous point. Abu Bakr was
taking no chances Fouda might be followed.

After a few days of this kind of clandestine activity, Fouda
eventually came face to face with Abu Bakr in his hotel room
in Karachi. He could tell at once he was a dirt-poor Pakistani
working man. Abu Bakr told him the time had come to go to
the rendezvous, but first Fouda had to put on a blindfold and
get in the boot of the car. Then he was taken on a ride through
the backstreets of Karachi. As Fouda told me his tale, from the
window of his office I could see the Houses of Parliament just
over the river. He looked knife-edge sharp in suit and tie, because
he had an appointment on *Richard and Judy* later that afternoon.
It was hard to imagine him trussed up in the back of a cab in
Pakistan.

After a disorienting journey the car eventually bumped to a
halt somewhere in Karachi's sprawl. Abu Bakr led Fouda inside
a house, where, when the blindfold was removed, he found
himself face to face with two men he recognized at once from
his past research into Al-Qaeda: Ramzi bin al-Shaibh and Khaled
al-Sheikh Muhammad. Both men were known Al-Qaeda
associates and former room-mates of suspected chief 9/11
hijacker Muhammad Atta. Each had a $5-million bounty on his
head, courtesy of the American government.

'Do you recognize us now?' Sheikh Muhammad asked him
jokingly. 'If you don't know who we are yet, you can rest assured
that you will know when the intelligence dogs start to knock
on your door,' added Ramzi with a smile.

The pair said that they had much to tell Fouda about how
9/11 had been perpetrated, but before the interview went ahead,
he had to agree to certain conditions. One of these was that he
would use the recording equipment they had there and, after it
was done, he would leave empty-handed. A copy of the interview would be forwarded to him later. Fouda agreed. 'When I
calculated all the risk I knew they were going to be more

concerned about their own safety and if they were, then I was safe,' he told me. 'In our business you take what you call calculated risks. It is up to you in the end to decide how far you can go with a certain story and how you calculate that risk. Calculating each risk will necessarily be a completely different process from one person to another, but you have to remember in the end it is you who might end up paying for it.'

Before Fouda's interview, it had been thought that Ramzi and Sheikh Muhammad had only peripheral roles in 9/11. Now Fouda was finding out that they had, in fact, masterminded the whole operation. 'Five minutes into the interview I was thinking, how am I going to present the fact that they actually did it, are they going to like it or not, and what is this actually going to mean for my life? And then five minutes later I realized I was in a win-win situation. The Americans wanted a damning piece of evidence, these guys wanted to take the credit for it, and then there was me wanting to get a scoop. So everybody was happy,' observed Fouda, laughing. I could think of no one more likely to emerge from that house alive than him. Peering into those inscrutable, obsidian eyes, I could tell without a doubt that this guy had balls of steel.

Fouda stayed with the fugitives for two days and nights, living on simple street food brought to the door of what seemed to be an otherwise empty building. The windows were barred. As the three men talked, many important details about 9/11 came to light for the first time.

At first Fouda was naturally dubious that the pair were telling the truth, but as they started talking he soon became convinced. 'Until they started telling me about specific details, the kind of detail you could go back and check out, until they started to do this, I was in the middle,' he said, weighing his hands like evenly balanced scales.

'As a journalist you have to doubt everything and suspect it. But if they tell you about specific things that happen on a certain date at a certain time, specific emails and phone calls on a certain date, I knew I could check that out.'

Ramzi confessed to being the coordinator of the attacks. He was supposed to have been the twentieth hijacker on what he called the 'Holy Tuesday Operation', but had not been able to acquire an American visa. Since 9/11 he had become the 'information coordinator' of Al-Qaeda, responsible in part for its high media profile. He had a collection of five mobile phones and several laptops to which he constantly referred as they spoke and it was clear he was proud of his technical know-how.

Flight 93, which crashed in a field in Pennsylvania, had been intended to strike Washington's Capitol building. Nuclear targets had been considered, then dismissed as potentially too apocalyptic, 'for the moment', said Sheikh Muhammad, 'and I mean for the moment.'

'I was stunned because I had studied these guys and when I met them face to face they told me these things I could not believe,' Fouda recounted. 'After one or two surprises I just ceased to be surprised any more. It was surprise, surprise, surprise . . . And it was not like they were bluffing because they were telling me specifically the sort of thing you can go back and check, the day, the hour, that email I sent and so on . . .'

The conversations were filmed so that the wanted men's faces and voices were deliberately obscured: shots of the back of the head, the foot, a glimpse of a beard. Besides speaking about 9/11, Fouda learned much about Al-Qaeda's operational strategy. Ramzi gave unspecific warnings about future Al-Qaeda attacks at the heart of America. Sheikh Muhammad boasted that Al-Qaeda had a 'department of martyrs' still full of volunteers. He gave Fouda a gruesome video of the execution of *Wall Street Journal* reporter Daniel Pearl and asked him to air it. Fouda did not ask whether the Sheikh had been one of those responsible for killing him.

As agreed, the interviews were shot on Al-Qaeda equipment and Fouda did not get a tape. When the time came for him to leave, Abu Bakr turned up to drive him back to his hotel, as stealthily as before. 'After I did the interview I came back. The deal was that they would keep the tapes and then provide me with copies later,' said Fouda. Back at the hotel, Fouda decided it would be the right thing to give Abu Bakr some money for the effort and expense he had incurred setting up the meeting.

'The guy who was the go-between, he used to call me from the street making international calls and he was such a poor guy, I mean it was quite obvious that he did not have money to wash or to eat. As I was leaving I left him $200 and I said this is for the international phone calls. He did not want it but I was really insistent and so he reluctantly accepted it. Later he came back and gave me it back and said, "This was such a mistake. When Khaled al-Sheikh Muhammad found out, he pushed me against the wall"', said Fouda, clenching a hand around his throat as if being throttled, '"and he said, how could you accept something like this from him?"'

Back in the hotel, Fouda heard nothing for days. He had no way of contacting Ramzi and Sheikh Muhammad directly, so he was at a loss what to do next. 'Immediately after the interview everybody went their own way. It was very difficult to pass a message either from me to them or from them to me,' he said. He began to fear the whole escapade may have been a waste of time.

Then he received a call from an unknown man asking for $1 million in exchange for the tapes. The interview, it turned out, had fallen into the wrong hands. Only later did he discover what had happened.

'This was the fault of the intermediary Ramzi and Sheikh Muhammad were not after my money. Ramzi was furious. Abu Bakr told me later he was afraid that the Pakistanis would find the tapes at his place, so he left them with some of his friends and those friends started asking for money. He immediately started to panic and cry, and he said to me, "You think that I am lying!" And I said, "No, I don't think you are lying." I knew – I knew – that neither Khaled nor Ramzi were involved in this and I knew that sooner or later Khaled and Ramzi would find out about this and that would be bad.'

Fouda received successive calls for cash in exchange for the tapes. As he consistently refused, the asking price dropped. There are occasions when it is right to pay contacts, Fouda told me, but in this case it was out of the question.

'The rule is that we don't pay people. But in fact it's common practice in our business to pay someone like a consultant or someone, if this is the main way they make their living and the sum is very minimal. I have paid some people before. But it depends who you are paying and for what purpose. The question is, irrespective of your willingness to pay someone or how much you are paying them, is this going to be used to highlight or discredit a certain kind of agenda? If it is, then you don't pay.'

There was another reason Fouda refused to pay apart from the risk of compromising his journalistic integrity. 'If you see that the money that you are paying is going some place or another,' he gave me a knowing wink, 'than that is quite another thing. That is why it was completely out of the question that I pay anybody out of Al-Qaeda. Actually they contributed to the production if you look at it – indirectly – because they kept me for two nights, otherwise I would have stayed in a hotel, and they fed me when I was with them. But it was completely out of the question that I would pay them. I completely refused.'

Since Fouda refused to pay, he never received the videos. Fortunately, Ramzi was so determined to claim his title as 9/11 mastermind, he had another copy. 'When eventually, after two months, Ramzi found out about this, he tried to do something. Luckily he had kept an audio version, which he sent me. And he sent me a message apologizing for what had happened.'

Now back in London, Fouda received a forty-five-minute audio CD of his interview with Ramzi. With no video, it was clearly second best, but it remained an important scoop never-theless. Most importantly, there was plenty of new detail about 9/11. Fouda got straight to work editing the interview for the *Top Secret* special, which was scheduled to air on the first anniversary of the attacks.

'I always cut my programmes here in London,' Fouda said. 'I did not send them via the uplink to Doha, so no one in Doha knew what was on them before they were aired. My boss was a bit upset with me because I hadn't told him, but he later understood and said, "Yeah, if I was you I would not have said either."'

As 11 September 2002 approached, it became clear that other elements in Al-Qaeda had no intention of letting the anniversary slip by uncelebrated. Al-Jazeera received several other videos and faxes, including a video with new footage of the 9/11 hijackers planning the attacks, some new footage of Osama bin Laden and a faxed statement from the ousted Taliban leader Mullah Muhammad Omar vowing to fight on in Afghanistan.

Yosri Fouda's documentary was shown in two halves over two weeks. The day after the second programme was shown, Pakistani Special Forces descended on the Karachi hideout and after an intense three-hour gun battle, Ramzi bin al-Shaibh was arrested. Half a dozen of his Yemeni guards were taken too, but several other suspects, including possibly Sheikh Muhammad, got away. Ramzi was promptly handed over to the Americans, who whisked him out of the country and away to some unknown secure location.

For the first time, it seemed, Al-Qaeda had burned its fingers playing with the media. When Fouda found out, he knew at once it was his death sentence.

It was in the middle of the night. I had been working five months non-stop, travelling from Karachi, to Florida to Germany, Cairo, Beirut, everywhere in the world. It was the very first night and I had finished working ten minutes before the show was supposed to be on air. I went back to my hotel in Doha, thinking the next morning I would be reclining on the beach. Then in the morning the night editor rings me up and says, 'Why don't you grab a shower and come here and join us?' And I said, 'Why? What's happened?' and he said, 'Ramzi bin al-Shaibh has been arrested and everybody has been calling us wondering when you are going to turn in bin Laden.' And I said, 'Shit!'

To the world, it looked like Yosri Fouda had tipped off the Pakistani authorities as to the whereabouts of Ramzi's lair. Messages on 'jihad online', a website known for its close links with Al-Qaeda made the link straight away, pointing out that Ramzi's arrest had taken place 'a few days after he appeared in an interview with Yosri Fouda, the host of Al-Jazeera's *Top Secret* talk show, in which he admitted that he was responsible for the logistic and financial aspects of the two raids on New York and Washington'. The knives were out for Fouda. 'A kind of treachery', was the verdict on the same Al-Qaeda website. Accusations were flying that Al-Jazeera was in cahoots with the CIA or the Bundesnachrichtendienst, Germany's secret service. Germany had a warrant out for Ramzi's arrest too. 'If the report is true, it shows that brother Ramzi fell into their hands due to some sort of betrayal. Therefore, all brothers must be careful,' avowed the website.

'I always anticipated that the period after the programme was going to be more difficult than the period in between the interview and releasing it, or even the time I actually spent there with them,' Fouda told me matter-of-factly, his unblinking eyes peering deep inside my own. 'I tried to think of all the repercussions that might happen when the show went out. I have to say I did not anticipate the scenario that the day afterwards he was going to be captured.'

Fearing for his life, Fouda decided to stay in the safety of Doha while he tried to clear his name. He was afraid to go anywhere, least of all back to Pakistan. 'Not now. Not while I'm being called a pig and a traitor,' he said at the time.

He vehemently denied that he had been a catalyst for the arrests. He thought his best defence would be to lay out all the facts of his investigation, however banal, and this would show, he hoped, that he had done nothing dishonourable.

'Although I did not like it because it was irrelevant to the story, I was forced to talk about certain things that I did not want to talk about, like when exactly I got the visa and when I first arrived in the country. I just had to set the record straight and talk about facts one, two, three, four.'

Chief editor Ibrahim Hilal helped pour scorn on the idea that Al-Jazeera had conspired with the Americans in the arrest. 'Now we're accused of being an American tool. It's just as crazy as Al-Jazeera being a tool of Al-Qaeda. I don't think they needed Al-Jazeera to know that he was in Karachi. Everyone knew it.'

'I can't blame people for thinking what they do,' said Fouda at the time. 'I myself tried to think if there could be some link. But why would the intelligence apparatus wait for all this time to act?' He had met the fugitives in June, but the arrests happened the day after the show was aired in September. It looked like the security services may have been holding off until the documentary had been broadcast.

No way, Fouda told me sneeringly. 'I would love to believe that American intelligence people knew about this beforehand. I would love to, but I don't think they did. You have these stories, about the FBI sitting there in black vans at a distance listening to what was going on and stuff like that . . . but you don't take a risk with a guy like this. If you looked at the FBI's website one day before my programme went out, you would not have seen that Khaled al-Sheikh Muhammad was the head of the Al-Qaeda military committee and the guy behind 9/11. All you would have seen is that he was implicated in the 1993 bombing and had a loose link to Al-Qaeda. He only had $5 million on his head.'

While Fouda had been filming some location shots in Florida near the flight schools in which the 9/11 hijackers had been trained, his producer did receive one enquiring call from the FBI, but it was not connected to the case. 'Once the FBI guy found someone American talking to him – the producer was born in Milwaukee, Wisconsin – he did not call again,' Al-Jazeera's Washington bureau chief told me.

So how did the security services find Ramzi's hideout? Fouda rejects the possibility that American intelligence agents might have tailed him and instead puts it down to a lucky break:

I think it was utter coincidence. Some people like to make up stories, saying that I was taped or that my phone was bugged, but I don't think that was the case. Neither Ramzi nor Khaled ever called me, it was always that guy Abu Bakr and it was always from a payphone in the street and never for more than twenty seconds. He would get the message across and that would be it. I think those guys later on, after the interview, made mistakes. The longer you are on the run, the more you tend to get complacent.

The Pakistani Interior Minister at the time went on the record as saying they had got some information from the neighbours who lived in that bit of Karachi, reporting some Arab-looking guys. So they sent about twenty para-troopers and to his surprise one of them turned out to be Ramzi bin al-Shaibh. He went on record as saying if he had known one of them was going to be Ramzi bin al-Shaibh, he would have sent half his army.

Fouda's explanation is not very plausible. More likely what happened was that in the days preceding the airing of the interview, the US National Security Agency's computer used an audio clip of Ramzi's voice taken from the trailer for the show and matched it with an intercepted telephone call. The NSA computer based in Fort Meade, which sieves millions of phone calls each day, can pinpoint a phone anywhere in the world with one short call. Then Pakistani intelligence were quickly tipped off.

If Fouda did inadvertently play some small part in Ramzi's arrest, the twentieth hijacker committed some brazen mistakes of his own. Every call Ramzi placed or email he sent contributed to his chance of being caught. Holing up for a prolonged period of time in one location with another wanted man doubled his chances of being grassed up for the reward money. Inviting a famous, foreign journalist to the hideout was obviously a big risk, and turned out to be his third and final mistake.

'They knew that as terrorists anything they decided to talk about, anything they said at all, would help. Their way of thinking, their way of speaking, their way of doing something, anything, would help people catch them,' Fouda assured me. As an investigative journalist who made knowing people his business, I believed him.

So why, I wondered, did they stick their heads above the parapet?

'Why did they do such a thing? Why did they take the trouble, risking their own lives coming out of their hideout and inviting a journalist all the way from London?' asked Fouda rhetorically, throwing up his hands.

> You can find many reasons for this. First of all, Al-Qaeda was very much on the run and they wanted to lift morale and send a strong message to the Americans that they could still function: that they could come out of their hideouts, bring someone all the way from London, give them an interview and then go back again. That in itself, is a message. And then there was the psychological part. Don't ignore this! If you do something spectacular, if you go underground for three years and then do something spectacular like 9/11, maybe one day you would like to tell the world about it. And that is the reason. And yes, I do believe in the end it led to their capture.

When the *Top Secret* documentary was first broadcast it passed the Western media by completely. After Ramzi was arrested the programme was revisited in great detail. The American press was awash with questions about Yosri Fouda, his report, his methods and his ethics. Some said Al-Jazeera was playing into the hands of the terrorists by helping Al-Qaeda celebrate the anniversary of 9/11. Fouda defended the show's timing, claiming editorial requirements meant that the documentary was not ready before then. What was undeniable was that he had kept the interview secret, when he could have tipped off the authorities.

'You get all sorts of people saying how could you keep that information to yourself for such a long time? And I say to them, "Fuck off! Why don't you try and do it?" I put my life on the line to come back with this information and now perhaps we can all learn something from it. When I decided to keep this information to myself for a month or two it was not because I wanted to hide something. It was because I wanted to get everything right and then deliver it. It was all to do with the past anyway, not the future.'

Jihad Ballout made the same point with regard to Taysir Alluni following his interview with bin Laden. 'There was no way Taysir knew where bin Laden was, but that is not at all to infer that if he knew he would tell if he did. Nine-eleven has taken away the sacred right of all journalists to safeguard their sources or information,' he told me.

'The situation would be quite different if I had information about an imminent attack on a civilian target,' said Fouda. 'Then I would have sought out somebody to tell, but other than that I am not prepared to do somebody else's job.' At the time, Fouda denied he would ever testify as a witness against Ramzi in an American court, or officially identify him, even if he were issued with a legal summons. 'I am a journalist and no one has the right to force me to testify or even reveal the identity of any of my sources,' he said.

Whatever the truth about how the Americans found Ramzi bin al-Shaibh, it did not spell the end of the romance between Al-Jazeera and Al-Qaeda. A few days later Al-Qaeda exonerated Fouda of any involvement in Ramzi's arrest.

'Out of the keenness to reveal the truth and put an end to tales and rumours, the press office of Al-Qaeda organization wishes to inform everybody that Al-Jazeera TV channel and Yosri Fouda – presenter of the *Top Secret* programme – have nothing to do with the recent incidents in Karachi, and that what happened was the result of God's will and wisdom.' The message was circulated around all the militant Islamic websites.

In an interview with the London-based newspaper *Al-Sharq*

al-Awsat a short time afterwards, Fouda thanked God for this acquittal. He told me later that he believed he had been acquitted simply because he had behaved honourably:

> When you agree to a certain deal, you have to be honourable, even if you think of them as bastards or terrorists. If you give your word you have to stick with it. When they said to me no cameras, we'll send the tapes afterwards, no talking about our means of communication and so on, I thought, it does not really make any difference: what I am really interested in is the details surrounding 9/11. I could have said no. This is why they took the trouble of issuing the statement when my life was threatened. They issued the statement clearing my name and that of Al-Jazeera and saying that we acted properly and that I stuck by my word.

So in the end everything turned out all right for Yosri Fouda and Al-Jazeera. Making contact with Al-Qaeda had been an opportunity the fearless sleuth had seized with both hands. The kind of access he had enjoyed to the inner echelons of Al-Qaeda remained something Western news journalists could still only dream of. It was not long before Al-Qaeda started sending more tapes and faxes to Al-Jazeera, showing that its trust in the network remained intact. The network even released a CD-ROM about the relationship between Al-Qaeda and the events of 9/11. Entitled *A Day that Shook the World*, the documentary contained much, but not all, of its unreleased footage.

In fact, this episode seemed to elevate Al-Jazeera to preferred-network status for other extremist groups too. In the following months it received exclusive tapes from the renegade Afghan warlord Gulbuddin Hekmatyar, as well as from the Chechen rebels who seized seven hundred hostages in a Moscow theatre. A month later more news came from bin Laden himself, the first hard evidence that he had survived the bombing in Afghanistan.

*

That autumn the prospect of an American-led war against Iraq began to materialize. This promised great problems and opportunity, for both Al-Jazeera and Qatar. In September US High Command began moving its headquarters from Florida to As-Saliyah, the smaller of the two military airbases in Qatar's pancake-flat desert. The other, Al-Udeid, had giant hangars for jumbo transport aircraft, bomb-proof underground bunkers, eight miles of roads and the longest runway in the region. One hundred and twenty fighter jets could be parked on its eighteen-acre airplane parking lot. US troops had been arriving there in increasing numbers throughout the past year, but it could house ten thousand in total. Al-Jazeera was the first news network invited to look around the base, even before it had been officially opened.

As war brewed, the relationship between America and Qatar grew closer. Qatar's Emir, who had reportedly sealed his deal with America 'on a handshake', was rapidly coming to terms with the reality that he had positioned his tiny country in the front line in the War on Terror. In Al-Jazeera's studios, only twenty miles from Al-Udeid, network executives were beginning to make their own preparations for war.

Saudi Arabia, America's bitter and broken-hearted former lover, finally decided to withdraw its ambassador from Doha. It was the first time such a severe step had been taken against a fellow Gulf Cooperation Council country. The other countries in the region all sided with Saudi Arabia against Qatar. At a meeting in Muscat, Ministers of Information from across the region accused Al-Jazeera of 'insulting and defaming' all of them. If Al-Jazeera did not tone down its coverage, they warned, they would call for an official Arab boycott by advertisers, journalists and all government officials. When the Qataris held a GCC meeting in Doha the only head of state who showed up was from Oman. The other four countries all boycotted it in protest against Al-Jazeera.

In the run-up to war Kuwait also shut down Al-Jazeera's bureau, citing the network's 'lack of professionalism and neutrality'. The move was expected, because the Kuwaitis had shown increasing displeasure at the growing Al-Jazeera operation in Baghdad in preparation for war. Derisory remarks about Al-Jazeera in the Kuwaiti press had grown more frequent and staff found themselves subjected to ever more harassment by the Kuwaiti security services. Following the closure, a Kuwaiti court convicted *The Opposite Direction* of insulting the Kuwaiti people and ordered the network to pay a 'symbolic' compensatory fine of approximately $15,000.

As Al-Jazeera passed its sixth birthday, there were distinctly mixed views about who was thought to be 'behind' it. It was popularly held in the Arab world that Al-Jazeera was a pawn of the CIA, the American press regularly decried the station as a mouthpiece for terror, the Israelis complained about its alleged pro-Palestinian bias, while the Kuwaitis had shut Al Jazeera's bureau for supporting Saddam Hussein.

In the first few days of January twenty members of the Palestinian Mukhabarat raided the Al-Jazeera bureau in Gaza at two o'clock in the morning and arrested the correspondent, for 'inflicting damage to the interests and reputation of the Palestinian people and their struggle'. They claimed that Al-Jazeera had been wittingly disseminating information received from Mossad. The correspondent was questioned for eighteen hours about, among other things, his source within the Al-Aqsa Martyrs Brigades, which he ultimately refused to divulge. A month later the director of Al-Jazeera's Ramallah bureau had a lucky escape when someone planted a bomb in his car.

Despite the political fallout, Arabs were still glued to Al-Jazeera. The network was now estimated to have on average forty million viewers – more than CNN. In fact, the only news network with more viewers was the national Chinese state-controlled television station. A Gallup poll taken at the end of the year showed that the people in countries where Al-Jazeera had been shut down, like Saudi Arabia, Jordan and Kuwait, still chose Al-Jazeera as their first source of news. According to the poll, 54 per cent of Kuwait's residents and 51 per cent of Jordan's described Al-Jazeera's news coverage as objective. By comparison, only 19 per cent of Kuwaitis felt the same about state-run Kuwaiti news.

At the close of 2002 financial and diplomatic pressures on the station were accumulating as never before. Bureaux in six countries were now closed down and over four hundred official letters of complaint had been received. Ongoing Saudi pressure on potential advertisers meant that Al-Jazeera, which had expected to be in the black by 2001, was running a $30-million annual loss. Its marketing director estimated that if it were not for Saudi Arabia, the network would be taking twice the advertising revenue. A substantial undisclosed sum from the Japanese television network NHK for Al-Jazeera output went some way towards rebalancing the accounts, but once again it was the Emir's munificence that kept the station broadcasting.

7

Countdown to War

As war in Iraq loomed, the world's media scurried to have their full resources in place for the kick-off. A flurry of new regional satellite news channels, from Algeria, Saudi, Lebanon, Dubai and Iran, were all rushing to be ready on time. The greatest potential rival to Al-Jazeera from this gang of tyros was a channel called Al-Arabiya. Launched with some fanfare in February, Al-Arabiya was broadcast from glittering Dubai. Its format was very similar to Al-Jazeera's: Arabic news interspersed with sport, weather, business news, commentaries and panel discussions, and after two weeks of broadcasting just twelve hours a day, it stepped up to become a twenty-four-hour operation.

The $200-million start-up fund for Al-Arabiya had come from a conglomerate of Saudi, Lebanese and Kuwaiti businessmen. The new network's parent company was the Middle East Broadcasting Centre, which was owned by a brother-in-law of Saudi Arabia's sickly King Fahd. MBC was so closely linked to the King it was sometimes said it should be called 'My Broadcasting Station'. There was little doubt the House of Saud had Al-Jazeera squarely in its sights. It had long been clear to the Saudis that cancelling the BBC Arabic project had been a costly mistake which had helped spawn Al-Jazeera. Now, by spending more money than Qatar, they hoped to outspend and so eventually outrun Al-Jazeera. Few things would afford the

Saudis more pleasure than cutting both Al-Jazeera and the spit of land upon which it sat down to size and one way of doing this would be to draw the Arab world's attention to Qatar's pivotal role as host to the American forces.

Besides more cash, the other major advantage Al-Arabiya had over Al-Jazeera was access to all the countries in the region from which Al-Jazeera had been barred – Jordan, Kuwait, Saudi Arabia and Syria – prompting Baghdad's most famous blogger, Salam Pax, to suggest Al-Jazeera should change its motto to 'Al-Jazeera: The only Arab news network with no offices in the Arab world'. Kuwait in particular was expected to be an important news source during the coming war and the bureau there remained closed. From the start, Al-Arabiya was able to profit from MBC's well-established network of thirty-one bureaux around the world. MBC had been a pioneer in the early days of the Arab satellite movement and had once been the most popular Arab news channel, before it was eclipsed by Al-Jazeera.

Al-Arabiya's backers had spared no expense in trying to win viewers from Al-Jazeera. With such a small pool of television news talent in the Arab world from which to choose, the channel was obliged to poach some of its five hundred staff from other organizations and fifteen Al-Jazeera journalists were offered jobs at the new channel, at two or three times their previous salary. Five said yes. George Kirdahi, heart-throb host and icon of the Arabic version of *Who Wants to Be a Millionaire?*, was headhunted to become the host of a flagship political talk show on Al-Arabiya. Like Al-Jazeera, the new channel drew its staff from across the Arab world.

The director-general of Al-Arabiya was a former Jordanian Minister of Information. Its chief editor was a BBC veteran who had worked for Al-Jazeera until 2001 and from the outset he was keen to stress that despite Al-Jazeera's obvious popularity there was room for another major Arabic news channel. Although Al-Arabiya was going to have the same freedom as Al-Jazeera, he insisted, it was to be less sensationalist in how it handled current affairs. 'In the United Kingdom, there is the *Guardian* and there is the *Mirror*,' he said, without mentioning Al-Jazeera directly. 'Both newspapers are very different and yet both achieve massive sales. We're our own network with our own character.'

The American administration and many Arab governments all had their fingers crossed that Al-Arabiya would be a raging success and so eclipse Al-Jazeera. Everyone who disliked Al-Jazeera lined up eagerly to do interviews on Al-Arabiya to give the channel the strongest possible start. President Bashar al-Assad of Syria and US Secretary of State Colin Powell were two of the first. Powell was so keen to lend Al-Arabiya his backing that he gave his interview three days before the channel was even launched, something quite unheard of.

Al-Arabiya executives painted a picture of Al-Jazeera's talk shows as 'childish', while their channel, it was implied, was somehow going to be more 'mature'. These high-sounding claims turned out to be worthless. Within two months Al-Arabiya had shown itself to be more or less a carbon copy of Al-Jazeera, with its talk shows proving just as divisive. Al-Arabiya stopped saying that Al-Jazeera was childish and started saying that it was accurately reflecting the level of debate in the Arab world. The influence of its Saudi backers was in evidence and Al-Arabiya soon acquired a reputation for only shyly tackling topics close to the heart of the Saudi regime, like women's rights and issues surrounding militant Islam. Nevertheless Al-Arabiya established itself as a popular news channel, second only to Al-Jazeera.

Despite the new regional competition, Al-Jazeera was bullish about its prospects in the forthcoming war. Even though CNN had five times more employees than Al-Jazeera worldwide, there was great international expectation, especially in the West, that Al-Jazeera would be the channel to watch. Al-Jazeera's Arabic-language website was receiving between ten and thirteen million hits daily, of which about 45 per cent came from within the US and Europe.

In the run-up to the war the BBC approached Al-Jazeera to cut a news-gathering deal. It wanted access to some of

Al-Jazeera's facilities, notably its uplink in Kabul. In exchange, the BBC was offering help in training staff and in building the new Al-Jazeera English-language website. Within Al-Jazeera, the overture was regarded as a mark of respect: until the advent of Al-Jazeera the BBC had been regarded with an unparalleled reverence in the Middle East. Deeper links with every major Western network were always welcomed as another possible way of making inroads into the coveted English-language news market.

This deal done, a month later Al-Jazeera and the BBC agreed on a second, much bigger deal. Al-Jazeera bought a thousand hours of BBC current affairs, wildlife, history and science documentaries to run on the new Arabic-language documentary channel that it was preparing. It was anticipated that the new channel, Al-Jazeera Documentary, would be launched at the same time as Al-Jazeera's English-language channel. To encourage more of these mutually beneficial agreements, the British Council arranged a journalist exchange programme between the two news organizations. Trainees from each company would spend some time working in each other's facilities, in London or Doha.

Britain's ITN also struck a lucrative deal with Al-Jazeera in the weeks before the war. Unlike the BBC, ITN was after Al-Jazeera's back catalogue, not its facilities. A five-year agreement was signed giving ITN the rights to license Al-Jazeera's footage to customers worldwide. At once ITN began heavily plugging Al-Jazeera's archive footage from within Iraq around the world.

The BBC and ITN were not the only ones with their eye on Al-Jazeera's resources at this crucial juncture. A few days before the war began Muftah al-Suwaidan, the executive director of Al-Jazeera's London bureau, received a call from BT (British Telecommunications), who told him that the Ministry of Defence had called asking for its help accessing Al-Jazeera's internal feed. This was the line Al-Jazeera used to send both video and audio material unseen between London and Doha.

BT receives an annual subscription from Al-Jazeera to keep this line open 365 days a year.

'I said to BT, "No! you are not allowed. If you give them our feed I will take you to court,"' Al-Suwaidan told me. 'I really don't know what they were after, but I told BT, that if the MoD call again, ask them to call me!' The Ministry of Defence did call again and, as instructed, BT refused to let them access Al-Jazeera's internal feed and directed them to Al-Suwaidan instead. 'They called me again and said, "We are really interested to see your programme. We just want to see the Al-Jazeera channel,"' recalled Al-Suwaidan. 'So I gave them the telephone number for subscriptions at Sky and told them they could pay.'

Al-Jazeera's managers in Doha were determined to perform well in the forthcoming war. Apart from anything else, the network urgently needed more revenue from selling footage. Its executives were nurturing hopes that Al-Jazeera might become the preferred conduit of information for Iraqi officials, placing the network in the same kind of exclusive position it had enjoyed in Afghanistan.

In recent months the station had invested heavily in Iraq. General manager Muhammad Jasim al-Ali had been shuttling back and forth, tinkering with its plans for coverage. He had met the quixotic Iraqi Minister of Information, Muhammad Said al-Sahaf, who was soon to become famous for the most barefaced lies in the history of warfare and, together with Dr Faisal al-Qasim, presenter of *The Opposite Direction*, he had even met Saddam Hussein. They were hoping to conduct an interview, but as it turned out, things did not quite go as they wanted.

Knowing that this was probably to be Saddam's final television interview, the two men were determined to make the most of the opportunity. Faisal al-Qasim had prepared his questions well in advance and the pair felt ready for whatever audience the dictator decided to grant them. But when the interview finally came around, Saddam was uncooperative. While Al-Qasim asked questions, the dictator kept behaving erratically, joking around, despite the fact that war was by now staring him in the face. 'Why don't you ask me any questions about women?' Saddam kept demanding, unhelpfully, 'What about women?'

Al-Qasim did his best to ignore him and keep the interview on an even keel. After all, war was only days away. 'Beautiful women!' Saddam kept roaring. Then turning to Muhammad Jasim al-Ali, who was standing nearby, Saddam interrupted again. 'Do you smoke?' the tyrant asked him. 'I smoke little cigars,' said Al-Ali. 'What about you? You smoke?' the tyrant asked Al-Qasim, forcefully. 'No,' replied Al-Qasim, who by now could feel his agenda slipping quickly away from him. 'You should smoke,' advised the tyrant. Then turning back to Al-Ali, he thundered, 'Why the hell do you only smoke little cigars? If you are going to do something, do it properly! Do the big things! I used not to smoke, when I was in prison. That was because they would throw the cigarettes we got under the mat behind the door and I wouldn't smoke those because it was humiliating.' Al-Qasim and Al-Ali nodded politely in agreement.

'If you want to smoke, smoke a hubble-bubble, or a big cigar,' the dictator continued. 'Here, have one of mine,' he said, proffering a box of Cohibas which had been sitting on the table in front of him. 'I've still got that cigar,' Faisal al-Qasim told me. 'One day I'll auction it on the Internet for $10,000!'

Al-Jazeera had strong links with Iraq, and it now determined to capitalize on these, so as to capture the best footage. The network first opened a bureau in Baghdad in 1997 and this had remained open ever since. Two of the three correspondents there, bureau chief Faisal al-Yasery and correspondent Diyar al-Omary, were Iraqis. The third man was a Jordanian Palestinian named Majed Abdul Hadi, who had been in Baghdad four months before the start of the war.

Al-Yasery had a particularly important connection with the Iraqi regime: he had once headed Iraqi television. He was the reason why Al-Jazeera was the only international news agency with permission to operate an uplink from Iraq. Nevertheless, operating under the oppressive Ba'ath Party was far from easy and concessions had to be made to placate the regime. Saddam Hussein was fastidious about the use of the correct titles for him and his men and any deviation from this would spell summary closure. The Iraqi Kurdistan region had to be referred to as 'Northern Iraq', for example, which angered the Kurds so much that in the weeks before the war citizens in the Kurdish city of Sulaymaniyah formed a petition against Al-Jazeera urging the network to stick up for them more against the Iraqi regime and to start by calling their land by their preferred name, 'Kurdistan'.

In the run-up to war the number of staff Al-Jazeera had in Iraq was hugely increased from three to more than thirty. Eight teams, each comprising a correspondent, a cameraman, plus supporting drivers and technicians, were deployed there. The network had far more journalists in Iraq than any other news organization. Two new journalists were sent to Baghdad, bringing the total there to five: Taysir Alluni, the Syrian who had covered the Afghan war; and the Palestinian Maher Abdullah, another veteran Al-Jazeera correspondent, who was best known as the presenter of *Religion and Life*, opposite Sheikh al-Qaradawi.

Two Al-Jazeera journalists were stationed in the southern city of Basra, a Syrian and an Algerian; the second had been the Kandahar correspondent after the fall of the Taliban. The Al-Jazeera correspondent in the northern city of Mosul was also a former Kandahar correspondent, who had been one of Al-Jazeera's team in Iraq during Operation Desert Fox in 1998. The correspondent in the autonomous Kurdish zone was a Jordanian Palestinian called Waddah Khanfar, who, after the war, became the Baghdad bureau chief and in October 2003, Al-Jazeera's director-general.

Besides saturating Iraq with journalists, Al-Jazeera also had correspondents at the Pentagon, the White House, the Department of State and in New York, at the UN. The head of Al-Jazeera's US operations was Hafez al-Mirazi, who had spent thirteen years working with the Voice of America. Ten Al-Jazeera staff were stationed at the As-Saliyah base, headed by the smouldering Lebanese Omar al-Issawi, who was soon to become something of a pin-up in the West, while four more correspondents covered events from London.

With such a deep local knowledge of Iraq, the network hoped better to access local information that could rival Western networks. Network executives hoped that Al-Jazeera's credibility might even draw news tips from ordinary Iraqi civilians. Covering the war in Afghanistan had in some ways proved an important rehearsal for the network: in some ways it was a country more perilous and inaccessible than Iraq. To avoid being demolished by the Americans again, great pains were taken to communicate the coordinates of all the network's bureaux, in Basra, Baghdad and Mosul, to Coalition Central Command as well as the names, addresses and coordinates of hotels where correspondents were staying, and the code Al-Jazeera was using for its signal on the satellite transponder was handed over.

The US government, meanwhile, was making its own media preparations for the war. At Coalition Central Command, at the As-Saliyah military base on the edge of Doha, US top brass splashed out $200,000 on a space-age set from which they could deliver their daily war briefings and an A-list Hollywood set designer was enlisted to dress the set to make it look as majestic as possible, so it might shock and awe Iraqis into submission. State-of-the-art plasma screen and television projection technology used to display maps, graphics and videos of action was shipped from Chicago to make the Pentagon look its imperial best.

The coalition media offensive was unfolding in other, more covert ways too. Top Iraqi military officials all had to have their telephone numbers changed, after finding that whenever they picked up the receiver to make a call, rather than hear a dial tone, they heard a man's voice in Arabic instructing them, 'Don't use chemical weapons!', 'Don't obey commands to attack civilian areas!' and 'Don't offer resistance!' The Iraqi ISP mail server was disconnected for three days after an email was sent out at midnight to all users urging them in Arabic not to resist the coalition in the event of an attack, nor to support Saddam's army, but instead to come forward with information about weapons caches. An email address where information could be sent was listed. The server was shut down fifteen minutes after the message went out, by which time it had already been widely downloaded.

Other coalition media developments were also underway. Following the moderate success of Norman Pattiz's Radio Sawa, the Middle East Television Network, or Al-Hurra, was now being planned. Al-Hurra, which means 'the free one', would draw on America's media experience in the Cold War and aim to spread freedom and democracy around the world. Congress earmarked a 'supplementary' $30 million for the project, which meant that, although it was federally funded, the money would not come out of the Department of State's regular annual budget. Al-Hurra would not be ready in time for the war, but it would be running soon after and it was hoped it would redress the balance of influence in the region in America's favour.

Meanwhile, the US advertising campaign in the Middle East had run into problems. In January, following a chilly reception across the Muslim world, Charlotte Beers's high-profile 'Shared Values' television campaign had been abandoned. The advertisements, which featured cheerful Muslims living in the US testifying to the tolerance characteristic of life in America, had been banned from several state television networks by Arab governments. Some private television stations had run them briefly, but after frosty feedback they were pulled, officials fearing that they might be doing more harm than good. Al-Jazeera had not been a platform for these ads, because the Department of State considered that, at $10,000 a minute for a prime-time slot, it was just too expensive. This was still considerably cheaper than advertising in America – a slot half that length on prime-time NBC cost about $400,000.

The Pentagon had decided on a new way of handling the media in the forthcoming conflict, called 'embedding'. Or rather, it was not new, but a throwback to how the media had been handled by the US in the Second World War when 'accredited' journalists wearing military uniforms had eaten with the troops in their mess halls and with officers in their clubs. The idea was the brainchild of Assistant Defense Secretary Victoria Clarke.

This time more than five hundred international reporters, photographers and television crew were to be 'embedded' in coalition military units as they participated in the assault on Iraq. Once again they would eat, sleep and travel with their military units, for free, as long as they obeyed certain ground rules set out in advance. This was a reversal of the Pentagon's media policy in every war since Vietnam, when media 'body counts' had damaged its faith in the press for a generation. Many in the military had held the press responsible for the crescendo of public disquiet over that war and in Grenada and Panama active measures had been taken to keep the media at bay. As recently as Afghanistan, media access had also been tightly controlled.

Now hundreds of journalists were to have a front-line view of life as embedded correspondents with the American military. More than three-quarters of them were American. The remaining slots were given to journalists from foreign and international news organizations. Al-Jazeera was promised six 'embed' slots, a lot compared with most other news organizations and an indicator of the new gravity with which the network was regarded in the Pentagon. Unfortunately, the network could take only two of the six slots on offer because the others were with military units in Kuwait and Bahrain – both countries from which Al-Jazeera had been banned and both still in no mood for forgiving: Kuwait had even tried, unsuccessfully, to make all networks pledge not to share any pictures with Al-Jazeera during the war. In the end, one Al-Jazeera reporter and one cameraman were embedded with the US Marines. The reporter, whose name was Amr al-Kahky, was the network's former Baghdad correspondent. Later a second reporter and cameraman were sneaked into southern Iraq through Kuwait, despite the embargo.

Al-Jazeera was not embedded in any British units. Rather than being a deliberate boycott, this was because the Ministry of

Defence had been wrong-footed by this American-inspired media initiative. Although the first British war correspondent had reported the Crimean War in the 1850s – when his accounts of the horrific conditions in which the nation's soldiers were fighting and the incompetence of its commanders contributed to the resignation of the government – Britain had little recent experience of embedding journalists. There had been a few British embedded reporters in the first Gulf war and a couple of war correspondents during the Falklands war in 1982, but nothing of the magnitude that the American administration had in mind now. Eventually 157 journalists were embedded with British forces.

During the build-up to war in Iraq the lengthy embedding process was made lengthier by the diplomatic charades that were playing out on the world stage. The MoD had to keep up a pretence that the war might never happen, so although soldiers could be seen to be preparing, the British government was reluctant to start giving masses of journalists training in pre-deployment, chemical weapons, fire-fighting and sea survival. Embeds also needed to be issued with, and trained to use, sophisticated equipment, including protective NBC suits and masks. When, in January 2003, it finally became diplomatically acceptable to be seen training journalists, the MoD barely had enough time to organize British journalists, let alone ones from Arab networks.

Consequently, the MoD decided on a policy of embedding only British nationals. One exception was made for an American, but, assuming that staff at Al-Jazeera would probably not be British, the MoD did not offer the network any embed places at all. Every member of the Al-Jazeera London bureau does, in fact, have a British passport, but because until the Iraq war the MoD had absolutely no relationship with Al-Jazeera or any of the other Arab networks, besides spying on them, unsurprisingly it was completely ignorant of how they worked. So, at the start of the war, with one exception, every journalist embedded with a British unit was a British national from a British media organization or news agency.

The basic rules for all embedded journalists were that they

could not report about ongoing missions, unless cleared to do so by their local commander; nor report the specific results of completed or future missions; nor report any stories that violated 'operational security' or specified numbers of troops, aircraft or ships; nor could they travel in their own vehicles. The Ministry of Defence was operating the 'green book' system, adhering to a set of rules for correspondents operating within British military forces. All embedded journalists also signed an agreement stipulating that they could be expelled by the military at any time.

There was no doubt that this new policy was going to change dramatically what the public saw and heard on the news, but media commentators were divided as to exactly what the effect would be. Critics were concerned that the media's total dependence on the military meant that they could be deterred from filing an unflattering story and that jeopardizing 'operational security' might be something over which two reasonable people could disagree. It was clear that networks were under pressure to cooperate with the military to keep their journalists embedded, without which collaboration they would not have competitive pictures. It was debatable too whether a journalist facing the same hardships as the troops he or she was living with twenty-four hours a day could remain critical and objective.

In addition to this completely new media environment, technology had also changed since the Afghan conflict. Videophones, which had transmitted the hopelessly grainy images of the Kabul bombing, were now virtually a thing of the past. Modern computer technology had advanced to the extent that news teams could edit footage in the field on laptops, to the same standard as if they were in a studio.

As it did on every network, Al-Jazeera's news in the weeks before the war grew heavy with debate about the rights and wrongs of this pre-emptive war. The majority of Arab guests and callers featured on Al-Jazeera were against the war. Despite the American media offensive, most Arabs were horrified by a US administration that seemed to be salivating at the prospect of a unilateral invasion of a Muslim country for its own sinister reasons. Many people saw the war in religious terms – a Christian crusade which should be met by jihad. Such opinions, voiced loud and often on Al-Jazeera, fuelled suspicions in the West that the station was a terrorist fifth column or a megaphone for those whose sole objective was to subvert the war effort.

In the light of Al-Jazeera's influence during the Afghan conflict, the coalition had finally come to understand that, like it or not, the network could foster anti-American sentiment and weaken the political stability of other Muslim countries in the coming weeks. Al-Jazeera had long-standing links with Baghdad and if the American administration were foolish enough to scorn rather than woo Al-Jazeera, then it might play into the hands of Saddam Hussein.

So, as part of a new policy of engagement, key protagonists from the Bush administration appeared on Al-Jazeera to present the case for war. US National Security Adviser Condoleezza Rice, Secretary of State Colin Powell and, uncharacteristically, Defense Secretary Donald Rumsfeld all gave lengthy interviews. It was Rumsfeld's second appearance on Al-Jazeera in two years. Tony Blair turned the network down, choosing to set out his case for war on MTV instead. Never out of the limelight long, bin Laden mailed a sixteen-minute audio-tape to Al-Jazeera, the first in three months, which the network promptly aired, in keeping with its guiding principle 'The opinion . . . and the other opinion'.

Once again it seemed mysteriously that Washington had known about the tape in advance. For once US officials did not quibble that the tape might not be genuine, suggesting either that they already had had time to run tests on it or that it suited their strategic objectives to have bin Laden speak up at this crucial time. Colin Powell told a Senate panel early on the day of the transmission, hours before it had been aired, that the tape Al-Jazeera was going to broadcast later that day was evidence of bin Laden's 'partnership with Iraq'. Staff at Al-Jazeera were bemused as to how Powell could have heard the tape in advance: they had aired it within hours of receiving it.

Since Coalition Central Command and Al-Jazeera's studios were only a twenty-minute drive apart, military staff tried to foster personal relationships with the network. Every news network was assigned a special media liaison officer and Al-Jazeera's was a young lieutenant – soon to become vaguely famous for his leading role in the Al-Jazeera docu-movie *Control Room* – who normally ran the Pentagon's liaison office in Hollywood. He attended a spring barbecue, together with American top brass, at the Doha home of Al-Jazeera's head of news gathering, Omar Bec Merhebi.

It was clear even before the war had started that Al-Jazeera had a different perspective on events to either other Arab or Western broadcasters. The Arab state television networks were struggling to present a dignified and unified rejection of the war by Arab governments on behalf of their peoples. Al-Jazeera's news reports and commentary exposed the true contradictions that had riven the region in the lead-up to war. Not only could most Arab governments not sum up the political will to condemn the war, in most cases they were covertly going to considerable lengths to support it.

In the weeks before the war two meetings of Arab leaders, both televised on Al-Jazeera, ended in a slanging match. On 1 March at an Arab League summit at Sharm el Sheikh, a quarrel broke out between Saudi Arabia's Crown Prince Abdullah and Libya's Colonel Qadhafi over the American military presence in Kuwait.

Qadhafi had made a speech criticizing the King of Saudi Arabia for permitting the American military to use his territory during the first Gulf war. Now, as war drew near once again, Saudi Arabia, politically opposed to the war, had responded to American pressure and quietly closed a number of airports near the Iraqi border to civilian aircraft so that they could be used by the US military.

'King Fahd told me that his country was threatened, and that he would cooperate with the Devil to protect it,' Qadhafi told the Arab League. Since the Saudi King has the sacred Muslim duty of protecting the shrines at Mecca and Medina, this remark was regarded as deeply offensive. 'Saudi Arabia is a Muslim country and not an agent of colonialism like you and others,' snapped back Crown Prince Abdullah, the *de facto* ruler of Saudi Arabia. He was referring to rumours that the Libyan leader had been brought to power in 1969 with help from the CIA.

Then, pointing and wagging his finger at Qadhafi, the prince let forth a torrent of meaty Bedouin insults. 'You! Who exactly brought you to power?' he cried. 'Don't talk about matters that you fail to prove. Your lies are behind you, while your grave lies in front of you.' A bewildered-looking Qadhafi stammered, 'By God, I don't know how I am going to answer this man . . .', at which point the television feed that Egyptian television was using to transmit the summit live around the world was abruptly cut off. Libya then immediately recalled its ambassador from Saudi Arabia and reconfirmed plans to withdraw from the Arab League. Thousands of demonstrators took to the streets of Tripoli to protest at Crown Prince Abdullah's comments and riot police had to use tear gas to prevent them breaking into the Saudi Embassy.

Four days later, at a meeting of the heads of state and representatives from the Organization of the Islamic Conference (OIC) in Doha, in a five star hotel just down the road from Coalition Central Command, a violent argument broke out between the Iraqi and the Kuwaiti representatives. Delegates were supposed to be finding a unified position on the impending crisis in Iraq when the Kuwaiti official interrupted the speech of the second-in-command of Iraq's Revolutionary Command Council, with the immortal line, 'Shut up, you dog.' The Iraqi delegate then shouted back at the Kuwaiti, calling him a 'traitor'. 'Shut up, you minion, you [American] agent, you monkey! You are addressing Iraq,' said the Iraqi, before grievously insulting the Kuwaiti official's moustache – a serious insult between Bedouin men – at which point a general fracas broke out and the ensuing comments became inaudible, though one Kuwaiti minister could be seen shouting and waving the little Kuwaiti flag he had on his desk.

The Arab state networks played down these blatant ruptures between Arab countries. Even newcomer Al-Arabiya, sensitive to its Saudi financiers, ran muted reports. Al-Jazeera, by contrast, was vocal in criticizing the bickering between the Arab leaders. Commentators analysed how Egypt and Saudi Arabia had been marginalized by the United States at the expense of the smaller Gulf countries, who had been shameless in capitalizing at their discomfiture. Now not one of these Gulf countries could bring itself wholeheartedly to condemn the war in Iraq or even America's new pre-emptive strategy that was helping to bring it about. The position of the Arab rulers, it was argued time and again, was contradictory, hypocritical and completely subject to their individual relationships with America.

Al-Jazeera also demonstrated its independence of the political mainstream in the Arab world and its resilience to political coercion, when, within days of being granted permission to reopen its bureau in Amman, the network carried some reports that were politically embarrassing to Jordan. On 17 March, following an official visit from King Abdullah II of Jordan, the Emir of Qatar had decided to commute the death sentence of a Jordanian journalist held on espionage charges. In return the Jordanians agreed to reopen the Amman bureau and four days later it was business as usual. Much to the embarrassment of the Jordanian government, one of the first reports the bureau submitted revealed just how much money they stood to make out of the war on Iraq.

Before the war it was evident that Al-Jazeera was as out of step with the climate of news on American as on Arab networks. While Al-Jazeera, like many international networks, was deeply sceptical of the White House's case for war, American networks wolfed it down uncritically. And while Al-Jazeera emphasized the possible humanitarian cost of the war and worried about its legality, American networks concentrated on exactly how and when the military might dislodge Saddam Hussein.

In retrospect, the absence of any weapons of mass destruction has made it abundantly clear that the American media failed to interrogate its administration adequately over its case for war, but in truth the flaws were not only visible in hindsight. For months leading up to the war, all the mainstream American media failed in its duty to interrogate politicians thoroughly.

For example, when Jim Lehrer interviewed Donald Rumsfeld in September 2002, six months before the war started, he did not challenge the Defense Secretary on his several inaccuracies. In an episode of *NewsHour with Jim Lehrer*, a leading American television show, Rumsfeld repeatedly stated that the United Nations weapons inspectors had been expelled from Iraq. 'We have seen the situation with Iraq where they have violated some sixteen UN resolutions and finally threw the inspectors out . . . We have gone through . . . four years where they threw the inspectors out and there's been no one there,' he asserted. But, as Rumsfeld knew well, and as Lehrer should have known, in December 1998 the UN inspectors were withdrawn by UNSCOM (United Nations Special Commission) so that America could start bombing.

In the same show Rumsfeld also spoke of 'the nexus between weapons of mass destruction, terrorist states, and terrorist networks' and referred to Iraq's plans for 'invading Saudi Arabia, which they were ready to do'. Presumably this referred to Pentagon claims that in September 1990 Iraq had been massing hundreds of thousands of troops along the Saudi border in preparation for an invasion. But the Florida newspaper the *St Petersburg Times* had subsequently published satellite pictures which showed no military build-up and the Pentagon claims had been embarrassingly and comprehensively discredited. So, while publicly laying the foundations for war, Rumsfeld had supplied a succession of misleading statements, statements which the host had a duty to question. Instead Lehrer was distinctly accommodating, giving the Defense Secretary a massage rather than a pummelling.

On 5 February 2003 Secretary of State Colin Powell travelled to New York to present his case for war to the United Nations. In preparation for his arrival the tapestry of Pablo Picasso's anti-war tableau *Guernica*, which has hung outside the UN Security

Council chamber since 1985, was quietly covered up. Instead of the tapestry, which features the civilians of the small Basque village of Guernica in northern Spain being blown to bits by German bombs during the Spanish Civil War, Secretary Powell spoke against a baby-blue banner with the UN logo imprinted on it.

Presenting his case for war, Powell asserted that Iraq had acquired mobile biological weapons labs and supplied evidence suggesting that Iraq had ties to Al-Qaeda. Using a combination of intercepted tapes, satellite photos, videos and complex technical diagrams, he described Iraq's 'policy of evasion and deception'.

'Every statement I make today is backed up by sources, solid sources,' he avowed. 'These are not assertions. What we are giving you are facts and conclusions based on solid intelligence . . .

'Saddam Hussein is determined to get his hands on a nuclear bomb,' he said. 'He is so determined that he has made repeated covert attempts to acquire high-specification aluminum tubes from eleven countries, even after inspections resumed.' He went on to allege that a Palestinian terrorist specializing in poisons headed an Iraq-based Al-Qaeda terrorist ring.

When the speech was over, CNN anchor Paula Zahn turned to former Department of State spokesman James Rubin for his opinion on Powell's case for war. 'You've got to understand that most Americans watching this were either probably laughing out loud or got sick to their stomach,' she said. 'Which was it for you?'

'Well, really, both,' Rubin replied. The American people 'will believe everything they saw', he confirmed. 'They have no reason to doubt any of [Powell's] sources, any of the references to human sources, any of the pictures, or any of the intercepts.'

The next day the American newspapers warmly endorsed Powell's case for war. Iraqi protestations that there were no weapons of mass destruction were assumed to be lies. 'If you believe that, you are probably a Swedish weapons inspector,' sneered the *Wall Street Journal*. The *New York Times*, more sceptical of the case for war than some, ran no fewer than three front-page articles raving about Powell's 'nearly encyclopedic catalogue that reached further than many had expected'. It marvelled at his 'intelligence breakthrough' that 'set forth the first evidence of what he said was a well developed cell of Al-Qaeda operating out of Baghdad'. When one *New York Times* journalist, Judith Miller, was later quizzed about her apparently uncritical acceptance of the White House case for war, she declared that, as an investigative reporter specializing in intelligence, 'my job isn't to assess the government's information and be an independent intelligence analyst myself. My job is to tell readers of the *New York Times* what the government thought about Iraq's arsenal.'

There was, however, a great deal of debate on Al-Jazeera over the veracity of Powell's claims. In the Arab media, the issue of Iraq's weapons of mass destruction had always been connected to the issue of Israel's nuclear weapons. For many commentators the central question, whether Saddam had them or not, prompted a further question: what about Israel? But as the clock leading to war wound down, most Americans were now convinced of what Colin Powell called the 'sinister nexus' between Iraq and Al-Qaeda – although this remained completely unproven. Even before the war started, Arab and American viewers had almost diametrically opposed perspectives on the war.

In the final hours before the war began President Bush made a speech calling on all journalists and foreign nationals to leave Baghdad 'for their own safety'. For twenty-four hours networks across the world hovered in a news limbo, while the world waited for the now inevitable storm. Diplomats, weapons inspectors and the last remaining foreign-aid workers left overland across the desert for Jordan by car.

These final travellers making the last journey out of Iraq included China's last reporter and with him went the Chinese eye-view on the war for hundreds of millions of his compatriots. For fear of an accidental death, like in 1999 when American bombing had killed three in the Chinese Embassy in Belgrade, the Chinese government had ruled that no Chinese reporters were allowed to stay in Iraq. Of the three thousand foreign reporters who visited the country during the course of the war, not one of them was Chinese. The Chinese government, which had aligned itself with America's War on Terror, foresaw that an accidental killing of a Chinese reporter could provoke an outbreak of anti-Americanism, which could then seamlessly lead into anti-government sentiment. But in accordance with the two-thousand-year-old wisdom of Sun Tzu, who, in *The Art of War*, declared 'in war nothing is too deceitful', one heroic Chinese reporter tried to stay behind in secret. He was found and escorted out of the country by the Chinese Ambassador himself, in his own car, to make sure he could not sneak back in.

Although CNN had famously remained in Baghdad during the first Gulf war, this time all the networks knew the stakes were higher. Firstly, it was no secret that the US was planning 'regime change', which made it more likely that foreign journalists might become hostages to a desperate Iraqi regime or fall prey to an angry Baghdad mob. Secondly, this time Baghdad was the primary American target, making it a much more dangerous place to be.

ABC and NBC news teams had already left Baghdad. Fox News had been kicked out in February in retaliation for an Iraqi journalist's expulsion from America. Of the major American networks in Baghdad, only CBS and CNN were left, and they were assessing their position by the hour. At the last minute, CBS left too.

When the Iraqis threw out CNN, two days after the war started, it was more of a body blow to viewers in China than those in any other country. Since there were no Chinese reporters in Iraq, on the first day of the war the Chinese government had ordered that the five most popular news channels be replaced with round-the-clock CNN, with simultaneous translation.

Al-Jazeera remained in Baghdad. 'At the end of the day,' said media relations manager Jihad Ballout, 'I don't know how you would be able to do your job if you were not there on the scene.' Al-Jazeera's resolution to stay was a major factor in the American television networks' decision to leave. All the big American players had sharing agreements with Al-Jazeera and now they were banking on the network, as well as on free-lancers, for their footage from within Baghdad.

8

Iraq

In the early morning of 19 March 2003, Iraq time, the tension in newsrooms across the world was palpable as the curtain rose on the war. The first the West knew of it was the thud of detonating bombs and the crack of retaliatory anti-aircraft fire, audible from CNN's still cameras that had been left stationed at strategic points around Baghdad. There were not many other good pictures of the bombing in Baghdad, but the Pentagon's new media policy meant that from the very start viewers were spared the same format of windy pundits and animated maps that networks had concocted to cover Afghanistan. Extraordinary action shots of F-18 Hornets taking off in streams of red and orange from the deck of aircraft carrier USS *Constellation* and US tank columns rolling across the Kuwaiti border awed anchors and analysts alike. American networks picked up Al-Jazeera's feeds from within Baghdad almost immediately. Viewers were taken aback by the juxtaposition of the jingoistic coverage and the calligraphic Arabic logo, but it was something they were going to get used to. Iraqi TV ran an old movie followed by a programme about heartburn.

All the news networks, plus many governmental websites, were swamped by unprecedented levels of Internet traffic, as people everywhere tried to uncover the latest news and pictures from Baghdad. Websites took three or four times longer than usual to load up under the heavy weight of hits. Al-Jazeera's website, the Downing Street website and the Coalition Central Command website saw the heaviest traffic. Such was the strain, the Al-Jazeera site almost came to a grinding halt, working only intermittently. Yahoo and MSNBC reported a 40 per cent increase in interest in the Internet's top fifteen news sites.

During the first days of the war, while Western networks travelled to Washington, Downing Street and the House of Commons, Al-Jazeera focused on the war's reception in the Middle East. The network's usual live and recorded programming schedule was suspended in favour of rolling twenty-four-hour news. Only one special report was aired, investigating links between US oil companies and key members of the Bush administration.

In the opening days of the war Al-Jazeera adopted the tagline 'War on Iraq' as its slogan for its war coverage. Coincidentally, this was the same tagline the BBC used, except, of course, the BBC's slogan was in English. Among the other Arab networks, Abu Dhabi TV, by contrast, opted for the more neutral 'In the Line of Fire', while Al-Arabiya chose 'The Third Gulf War'. (In the Arab world the first Gulf war was the Iran–Iraq war and the liberation of Kuwait was the second.) Choosing this more neutral-sounding tagline cost Al-Arabiya dearly: the network's Kuwaiti backers pulled a quarter of their funding, unhappy that the network was not using the slogan 'The Liberation of Iraq'.

Reporting the war was different for Arab networks than it was for Western ones, not least because most of them, including Al-Jazeera, had Iraqis on the staff who personally knew the places being bombed. It was evident from the very start that Al-Jazeera rejected the legitimacy of the invasion. This stance had been implicit in its reports before the war, but once the bombing began, it became explicit. The network contested the coalition's strategy and motives in the way it edited and juxtaposed its pictures, as well as in its terminology. Initially Al-Jazeera was alone among the major news networks in using the term 'invasion forces' to describe what not only the British and American media, but also media in non-aligned countries like France and Germany, called the 'coalition forces'. Then other Arab news channels began using the term too. Never once in the twenty-one days of conflict did Al-Jazeera acknowledge that invading Iraq had anything to do with democratization. For Al-Jazeera this was not about liberation: it was a colonial conflict.

From the first to the last day of the war, Al-Jazeera would end its news bulletins with the anchor saying, 'We leave you now with live pictures from Baghdad.' Then coverage would cut to a camera overlooking the city, all commentary would cease and the tagline 'Baghdad is burning' would appear on the screen. For a few minutes viewers would just watch the flames and smoke rise up from the city. Showing Baghdad like this, to underline that the city itself was a casualty of war, was a hugely powerful emotional statement. Baghdad was one of the great historic centres of the Muslim world until it was ransacked by the Mongol hordes, and now it was being attacked again, this time by an American-led coalition. No commentary was necessary and the symbolism ran deep for Arab viewers. Occasionally news would even be interrupted to bring viewers live pictures, without commentary, of the city on fire.

One of the first consequences of the war was a wave of protests around the Middle East and Al-Jazeera gave these solid coverage. In Yemen an estimated thirty thousand protesters took to the streets after Friday prayers, ten thousand Palestinians marched in Gaza and in Sudan a police station was set on fire. America was obliged to close several embassies in the Gulf. In the centre of Cairo a few thousand anti-war protesters hurled stones and debris at police while chanting slogans against America and Arab leaders whom they regarded as complicit in the war. Al-Jazeera covered the demonstrations at length as they descended into a bloody riot, even though banners denouncing Qatar as an American puppet were clearly visible in the crowd.

The network's wide deployment across Iraq lent its reports a panoramic effect. Each reporter filed reports that reflected the events of the area he was in, whether the stories were political, humanitarian or military. Often viewers were taken on a rotation through four correspondents, reporting live from four different locations in Iraq simultaneously – Baghdad, Mosul, Basra and the Kurdish zone in northern Iraq. This gave Al-Jazeera an overview of events in Iraq unequalled by any other station. Never did one event or correspondent dominate the news for long. The emphasis was on a polyphony of views from all over the world, to reinforce the complexity of this war.

Al-Jazeera's wide deployment also meant that the network was in a good position to cross-check all the reports it received with correspondents in other parts of the world. All the information the channel received, whether it came from Coalition Central Command or from the Iraqi Ministry of Information, was treated with equal scepticism. Much to the coalition's chagrin, for the first part of the war information coming from the Iraqi Minister of Information, Muhammad Said al-Sahaf, and information coming from the coalition spokesman, Brigadier General Vincent K. Brooks, in the daily news conferences at the As-Saliyah base, was treated as equally unreliable. Coalition press conferences were also given twice daily at Coalition Naval Command in Bahrain. These sessions, which normally consisted of a brief slide show followed by a question-and-answer session, were always carried live on Al-Jazeera, as were announcements and speeches by coalition commanders around the world, from Ari Fleischer, Defense Secretary Rumsfeld and President Bush, as well as Tony Blair and Foreign Secretary Jack Straw in Britain. Al-Jazeera also televised live all the press conferences given by the Iraqi Minister of Information, as well as irregular broadcasts by other Iraqi ministers, including the Prime Minister, the Foreign Minister and the Ministers of Commerce and Interior, and intermittent announcements by Saddam Hussein.

Besides spokesmen from the two sides in the war, Al-Jazeera also featured plenty of miscellaneous commentators, from the Shiite President of the Islamic Cultural Center in Los Angeles, who proclaimed himself neutral, to Ahmad Chalabi, one of the most important and hawkish of the dissident Iraqis who supported the invasion. Critics on one side were meticulously balanced with critics on the other. Commentary on the war on Al-Jazeera was holistic: Ba'athists, neoconservatives, anti-war Europeans, Kurdish and Arab nationalists, there was an impressive display of diversity and so no one clear message. Various military strategists appeared, but the principal military expert in residence was Egypt's retired Major-General Muhammad Ali Bilal, commander of Egyptian forces in the 1990–91 Gulf war, who made frequent appearances from the start of April.

Over the following days, both sides in the war unsurprisingly began pushing out a lot of propaganda. News from Iraq, confused at the best of times, seemed on occasion to suggest two different wars were taking place at once. One of the coalition's initial objectives was the deep-water port of Umm Qasr, in the extreme south of Iraq, and although the town had a population of just six thousand, it took four days to capture. Such apparent difficulty for the coalition sparked the first fears of a tougher-than-expected resistance and a prolonged campaign.

Reports about how the battle for Umm Qasr was going varied wildly. While CNN was reporting that the town had been secured, Al-Jazeera was still reporting fighting. The MoD announced that Umm Qasr was 'secure' three times over three days, before it fell. When an explanation was later demanded of Britain's Minister of Defence, Geoff Hoon, in the House of Commons, he blamed imprecise language: the coalition had not clearly differentiated between the port of Umm Qasr and the town itself, which shares the same name. 'Umm Qasr is a town similar to Southampton,' he said, meaning the port and the town were in separate places. 'He's either never been to Southampton, or he's never been to Umm Qasr,' reflected one British squaddie on patrol in Umm Qasr. 'There's no beer, no prostitutes, and people are shooting at us. It's more like Portsmouth.'

The coalition's plan was to storm up the centre of Iraq towards Baghdad, ignoring the towns and cities along the way. But air raids had left Basra, Iraq's second-largest city, with neither electricity nor water and Al-Jazeera, which had the only news team inside the city, was transmitting urgent reports of a deteriorating humanitarian situation. Thanks in part to Al-Jazeera, international pressure was brought to bear on coalition commanders to do something about the situation immediately. The coalition's plan was changed and saving Basra became an immediate priority for the British troops.

For a few days it looked like capturing Basra and resolving the humanitarian situation was going to be a tough objective indeed. After all, Umm Qasr, a much smaller town, had taken four days to capture. British troops encircled Basra, forcing Iraqi irregular forces to hole up among the civilian population. The Iraqi forces were a mix of the Ba'ath Party security services, the Fedayeen Saddam and regular troops from the 51st Division. Many of them had disposed of their uniforms and dressed in civilian clothes, apparently in preparation for house-to-house fighting. British commanders were faced with the difficult choice of sending in ground troops, which would most likely have resulted in politically unacceptable numbers of casualties, or bombarding the city, either by air or by artillery, inflicting a great deal of collateral damage on civilians. It was a stand-off.

Then a mysterious rumour arose which seemed to be just what the coalition had been waiting for: a popular uprising was taking place on the streets of Basra. Word had it that the oppressed Shia were rising up against the regime. British military spokesman Group Captain Alan Lockwood told a Qatar news conference: 'The Shia population attempted to attack the ruling party. The ruling party responded by firing mortars at the crowd that was advancing.' The MoD described the scenes of civilian casualties in Basra as so 'horrific' that British officers had to be forcibly restrained from rushing in to try to stop the carnage. This is 'just the sort of encouraging indication we have been looking for', said Major-General Peter Wall, the deputy to the commander of Britain's forces. On hearing the rumour British forces took this as their cue to unleash a full-scale artillery assault on Basra, while American and British warplanes dropped one-thousand-pound satellite-guided bombs on selected targets, among them the Ba'ath Party headquarters in the centre of the city.

Most of the British and American networks and printed press carried the rumour of the Shia uprising as if it were a fact. 'Don't look now, but the Shiites have hit the fan!' snorted Fox News anchor Neil Cavuto. The story might, in time, have turned into a self-fulfilling prophecy had not Al-Jazeera been in Basra to report the truth of the situation. Once the bombing had stopped, the Al-Jazeera correspondent in the city reported an eerie calm on the streets, no uprising, no disturbances. Pictures were broadcast of a deserted city centre and quiet streets. 'The streets of Basra are very calm and there are no indications of violence or riots,' Al-Jazeera's Basra correspondent told the anchor in Doha. 'There are no signs of the reported uprising. All we can hear are distant explosions in the south east, and we believe fighting is going on there.'

Over the next few days Basra remained under siege and Al-Jazeera fed the outside world with plenty more exclusives about conditions inside the city. The news team visited the dilap-idated Al-Jumhuriyah Hospital, where Iraqi civilians lay wounded and dying. Among bloodstained bodies strewn across a tiled floor, a medical worker pulled back a blanket to reveal a child with the back of its head blown off. 'It's a huge mass of civilians,' one angry woman told the camera. 'It was a massacre.'

On 23 March the Al-Jazeera team in Basra directly contra-dicted a second coalition claim. The American spokesman at Coalition Central Command announced that the head of the Iraqi 51st Division in Basra had given himself up. Al-Jazeera tracked down the officer in question and interviewed him live.

During the siege of Basra four American missiles hit the Sheraton Hotel, which the Al-Jazeera team were using as their headquarters, in one night. Two of them exploded. The Pentagon had been informed beforehand that Al-Jazeera was using the facil-ity and its team were the only guests staying in the hotel at the

time. No one from Al-Jazeera was hurt. There was no investigation and no official explanation was forthcoming.

Discrediting fake coalition reports was a natural consequence
of Al-Jazeera's policy of scepticism towards all parties, including the coalition, combined with the channel's panoramic
deployment. A third similar incident happened at the beginning
of April, when Brigadier General Brooks announced at a daily
press briefing at Coalition Central Command that the Grand
Ayatollah Ali al-Sistani, a key Shia leader based in Najaf, had
issued a fatwa 'instructing the population to remain calm and
not to interfere with coalition actions'. Al-Sistani's office immediately sent Al-Jazeera a statement denying that he had done any
such thing, which the network immediately broadcast,
completely contradicting what Brooks had just said.

The only occasion on which Al-Jazeera reported unsubstantiated information from the coalition as fact was near the end
of the war, when the American army was nearly at Baghdad
and there was absolutely no means of cross-checking details.
Even then the anchor would qualify the information by saying
that the coalition was the exclusive source for this report. For
example, during the battle for Baghdad airport, on the outskirts
of the city, there were no journalists present and Al-Jazeera, like
everybody else, had no choice but to report exactly what it was
told by Coalition Central Command. By this stage in the war
the Iraqi Minister of Information, who told countless lies about
downed US airplanes, the number of civilian and coalition
casualties and the humanitarian situation in Iraqi towns, had
been so discredited that Al-Jazeera merely mentioned in passing
his claims that the Republican Guard had retaken the airport.

A study by Professor Justin Lewis of the University of Cardiff
into how the four major British television networks – BBC,
ITN, Sky News and Channel 4 – reported the war found that
49 per cent of unsubstantiated statements issued by the British
government during the war were reported as fact. Only 17 per
cent were qualified as being based solely on uncorroborated
government reports.

Consequently, several incidents reported on British television turned out to be quite wrong, including the Basra uprising, the fall of Umm Qasr and the alleged firing of a scud missile from southern Iraq into Kuwait. Professor Lewis's report found 89 per cent of references to WMD on the British television networks assumed they existed, while only 11 per cent expressed reservations.

When a marine commander in Qatar was asked about the Iraqis' claims to have captured US troops he dismissed them as 'Iraqi lies'. Al-Jazeera, it emerged, had learned of the capture of the men and women of the ambushed 507th Maintenance Company not just before other news media, but before the Pentagon itself. Seven minutes of footage from an Iraqi TV tape were run, showing five recently captured American servicemen and women. The terrified captives were interviewed the Pentagon called it 'interrogated' – while one more seriously wounded man lay slumped on a stretcher.

Even more controversially, later the same day Al-Jazeera screened pictures of several dead American and then British servicemen, some of whom appeared to have been executed with a shot in the head. After an early battle at Nasariya, Al-Jazeera broadcast a thirty-second video of exuberant Iraqis celebrating over the corpses of two dead British soldiers. Their bloodied bodies, still in desert uniform, lay on their backs in a dusty road, next to what appeared to be an overturned British Army Land Rover.

The Doha anchor apologized for the 'horrific' pictures, explaining that 'it is in the interests of objectivity that we bring them to you'. The Pentagon and the MoD were livid. An MoD spokesman wasted no time in condemning the footage, declaring, 'We deplore the decision by Al-Jazeera to broadcast such material and call upon them to desist immediately.'

Following the screening of the US prisoners, Australia's Department of Defence declared that Al-Jazeera's failure to pixelate the faces of captives infringed the Geneva Conventions. In a press conference, carried by Al-Jazeera, Defense Secretary Donald Rumsfeld and General Richard Myers, chairman of the Joint Chiefs of Staff, singled out the channel for criticism. 'It's a violation of the Geneva Convention for the Iraqis to be showing prisoners of war in a humiliating manner,' Rumsfeld told CNN's Wolf Blitzer. Tony Blair concurred, speaking of Al-Jazeera's 'flagrant violation' of the Geneva Conventions. Article 13 of the Conventions stipulates that 'prisoners of war must at all times be protected against insults and public curiosity'.

This emotional debate blew up out of all proportion. Leaving aside the facts that the last time Rumsfeld had mentioned the Geneva Conventions in public had been to deny their provisions to the prisoners in Guantánamo Bay, that Al-Jazeera was a non-state actor that had never signed the Geneva Conventions and that all the Western networks showed pictures of Iraqis being taken prisoner live both before and after this incident, experts disagreed on the contemporary relevance of these rules of war.

Laid down in 1949, when there was no such thing as international television news networks, the principle in question, that prisoners of war should not be subjected to public curiosity, was supposed to prevent a confrontation between prisoners of war and a hostile crowd. There is little doubt that these prisoners' privacy had to some extent been violated. But it is a moot point whether being broadcast worldwide on satellite television is analogous to the scenario imagined in 1949 of being heckled and harassed by an angry mob. Arguably, they were being televised for propaganda purposes, not for public curiosity.

The US Department of Defense issued a statement requesting that news organizations 'not air or publish recognizable images or audio recordings that identify POWs'. It said the request was 'out of respect for the families and consistent with the principles of the Geneva Conventions'. The MoD was less concerned about the footage of the prisoners than about the soldiers' corpses. Since Al-Jazeera was available in Britain, either as part of a package with Sky or free-to-air from the Hotbird satellite, it was theoretically possible that the soldiers' families could learn of the deaths of their relatives first by spotting them on Al-Jazeera. There followed what the MoD later termed 'a full and frank exchange' with Al-Jazeera, marking the low point of the network's relationship with the coalition.

'I received two calls, one from the Pentagon, and one from the White House,' Al-Jazeera's Washington bureau chief, Hafez al-Mirazi, told me. 'The Pentagon was very clear that they wanted us to stop playing the tape until they notified the families of the POWs. I conveyed that to Al-Jazeera's editor-in-chief and manager.' These two executives then decided to accede to the Pentagon's request not to show the pictures for eight hours while the families were informed.

'Al-Jazeera stopped playing the tape to accommodate what we perceived to be a humanitarian request,' said the Washington bureau chief, 'although maybe editorially speaking we were not convinced that the interests of four or five families to know first were more important than the agony of 250,000 families guessing whether it was their kids or not. But at some point you have to decide whether to accommodate such a request, even if you are not broadcasting to American families whatsoever – which we were not. But we did.' Other stations, meanwhile, did not.

Although it held off screening the footage, Al-Jazeera did not accept that it had done anything wrong and the network then ran the footage of the dead US soldiers two days in a row. The images were also available on the Al-Jazeera website. The video of the captured US prisoners was linked to the site as well, which prompted a flood of Web visitors from America. Al-Jazeera spokesman Jihad Ballout argued, at the time and later to me, that showing coalition losses was an essential part of depicting the war accurately. He readily acknowledged that there were different ideas about what constituted acceptable standards of decency, but he claimed that nothing went on Al-Jazeera unless it was newsworthy. Failing to show these images would be a dereliction of the network's duty to present the war as comprehensively as it could. 'It is newsworthy. Whatever your view is, you have to agree with me. It is newsworthy. It is indicative of the way that the conflict is taking shape. Would it be better to deceive people?' he said. He pointed out that Al-Jazeera had run an interview with a mother of one of the prisoners immediately after the POWs had been shown, which, he argued, balanced the dehumanizing aspect of showing the captives.

As regards the pictures of the corpses, Ballout pointed out that when Al-Jazeera had shown dead Palestinians, Afghans and Iraqis during Operation Desert Fox, the US had not objected. During the first Gulf war many Iraqi soldiers had been shown burned to a crisp in bombed-out vehicles on the road out of Kuwait. 'Look who's talking about international law and regulations,' said Ballout. 'We didn't make the pictures – the pictures are there. It's a facet of the war. Our duty is to show the war from all angles. Truth is sometimes unpleasant and gruesome, and I feel distressed when people ask me to dress it up.' When the coalition got fed up with arguing, the two parties agreed to disagree. The matter was put down as a professional difference in opinion and no long-term sanctions against the network were taken. The American liaison officer attached to Al-Jazeera's team in Doha diplomatically ruled that the real blame lay with Saddam's regime. Despite the disagreement Washington officials continued to appear on Al-Jazeera.

Britain's Sky News also incurred the fury of the Ministry of Defence when it ran the same footage of the dead British soldiers. From the MoD's point of view, Sky had acted even more irresponsibly than Al-Jazeera, because executives there should have known better about what constituted acceptable standards of decency in Britain and there was a much higher chance that relatives of the dead men could identify their loved ones by watching Sky, rather than Al-Jazeera. Sky argued that it had pixelated the faces, but the MoD insisted that families would still be able to recognize a close relative. The BBC finally ran the footage on 1 June, in an episode of *Correspondent* which caused a second public outcry.

All the American news anchors decried the images as 'horrifying' and 'disgusting' and issued constant reminders that war crimes against coalition prisoners would be prosecuted. CBS was also the only American network to air the video of the captured POWs at any length; NBC issued a short clip. Moments after CBS aired the tape, as the network went to a commercial break Pentagon spokeswoman Victoria Clarke called to insist that the network obscure the soldiers' faces, which it duly did before running the footage again.

The American press had not always been so sensitive. In 1993 CNN had broadcast pictures of dead US troops being dragged through the streets of Mogadishu by Somali militia, but now all the Western news networks had tightened their editorial policy, especially with regard to showing images of the dead. Al-Jazeera, in stark contrast, daily showed mutilated and bloodstained corpses, children with their brains blown out and adults missing limbs. It would be wrong to think such strong pictures had any less impact in the Arab world than they had in the West. Arabs were horrified at what they saw on Al-Jazeera and there were calls in the Arab press not to let children watch television unsupervised for fear of psychological scarring.

Such even-handed presentation of the two sides, combined with a much more explicit editorial policy, provoked suspicion in the West. Why, wondered the American press, did Al-Jazeera anchors refer to Saddam Hussein as 'President' and not as a 'dictator'? And what about calling coalition troops 'invasion forces'? Al-Jazeera correspondents in Iraq never seemed to spell out the horrors of Saddam's regime in every report the way the Western press did, and on one occasion the network spent two hours showing Baghdadis searching in vain for a pair of downed American pilots in the River Tigris, which looked perhaps a little too vitriolic, although the BBC showed the same images. One Al-Jazeera report featured an old Iraqi peasant with an apocryphal tale about shooting down an Apache helicopter near Karbala with a hunting rifle. The incident smelt strongly of Iraqi propaganda trying to shame the local tribesmen into resisting the advancing coalition.

'If you have people like Al-Jazeera pounding people in the

region with things which are not true then it is not easy,' said Rumsfeld. 'We know it has a pattern of playing propaganda over and over again.' What angered the coalition commanders most about Al-Jazeera was its early adoption of the term 'resistance' to describe the Iraqi forces. The term was first wholeheartedly adopted on the third day of the war, after coalition spokesmen repeatedly assured the press that the towns of Nasariya and Umm Qasr had fallen, when they had not. After American troops became tangled in fierce gun battles while taking Najaf, the term 'resistance' began to be heard more frequently, often in connection with another word the coalition did not like: 'Vietnam'. Al-Jazeera was not the only major news network that used this kind of terminology, but it was the first. Al-Arabiya, Abu Dhabi and others soon began to evince the same kind of scepticism and as the war wore on Al-Jazeera seemed less radical. After a week of fighting, even the Western press started to feel gloomy about how things were going. On 24 March the *New York Times* ran a typically downbeat article:

> Optimistic statements in Washington may have created expectations that this war would be swift and relatively casualty-free. Certainly, allied forces have covered considerable ground and thrust deep into Iraq. But now that the military has raced toward central Iraq, American forces are girding for real battle . . . And now there are dangers to the rear too. American forces have been attacked by the fedayeen, militia that are under the command of Saddam Hussein's son Uday, which have begun attacks in the south to harass and try to slow the advancing American troops and supply columns . . . There was no disguising the fact that the attacks by the fedayeen were a setback and a surprise.

The American administration was so disgruntled at this spread of downbeat rhetoric at this point in the war that it dispatched the slick Department of State spokesman Dr Nabil Khouri to pay a visit to Al-Jazeera's chairman in Doha. Khouri told Al-Jazeera executives that the network's reports were not just encouraging the use of a lot of unhelpful terminology, but were actually glamorizing the Iraqi position. Every opportunity, he said, was being taken to portray the advancing allies as beleaguered and the Iraqis favourably.

'The first few days in the war several channels – I am talking about three or four days into the war – were really blowing out of all proportion the resistance offered by Saddam's regime, the troops, who were resisting in various parts of the country,' Khouri told me. 'The talk show hosts were almost exuberant.' I could sense the steely, bureaucratic toughness of a Department of State official behind his cool explanation. Khouri, a middle-aged Arab-American, a Maronite Christian I guessed by his name, has salt-and-pepper hair, a neatly trimmed goatee and an effortless charm. He has a PhD in political science and spent ten years as an academic before joining the Department of State. His impeccable manners and slow, measured way of speaking do little to conceal a forceful intellect and the love of a good argument.

'The nuance of the title "resistance" has a very positive connotation in Arabic,' he assured me. He was referring to Palestine. 'Not everybody who grabs a gun and shoots at the coalition forces in Iraq really qualifies as resistance. There is no such thing as a unified resistance movement in the country. Unless you know who these people are, all you can say is that they are an assailant, an armed person. Objectivity dictates that you think before you use a certain term.'

This is a pretty thin argument: it is common sense that people shooting at invading troops can reasonably be termed 'resistance'. Certainly Tony Blair seemed to think so: at a press conference in Brussels on the third day of the war he said, 'I should warn that our forces will face resistance, and that the campaign necessarily will not achieve all of its objectives overnight. It's important to emphasize that.' A few days later he reaffirmed that coalition forces could expect to meet 'resistance all the way to the end of this campaign'.

Khouri told me that he thought Al-Jazeera had fallen into the old trap the Arab media always fell into, of jumping to conclusions and telling the viewer what the network thought they wanted to hear. It was just like when Sawt al-Arab radio told the Egyptians they were winning the Arab-Israeli war in 1967. 'If I am an Arab viewer I need the media to give me the facts and not wishful thinking, and I need them to give me good sound military analysis . . . The majority were just expressing political views, ideological views, things that they thought the Arab masses would like to hear. But not good sound analysis,' he said.

The kind of good sound analysis the coalition was looking for was the kind which suppressed all possible narratives about the war except for one question, which was to be echoed over and over again: how is the war going militarily? This was the only conversation the coalition wanted to have, because with such overwhelming military might, there was never any doubt it would have military victory. By doggedly dealing with this one aspect of the war, the coalition – and most of the Western media – did not stop to address other, trickier questions, like: what will happen when the war is over? Was it just? Where are the WMD? Are we now safer then we were? What are the economic and humanitarian consequences for Iraqis?

The coalition managed to keep the media under control by tightly managing the day-to-day briefings at Coalition Central Command and by keeping tight control over the flow of infor-mation from embedded journalists. The vast majority of embed-ded journalists were American and as a result every US network usually had a generous supply of exciting action footage. None of the Arab journalists embedded with coalition units found themselves in front-line fighting units, only in units with command and support roles.

Life for Al-Jazeera's embeds with the US Marines was not easy. Amr al-Kahky, the Al-Jazeera correspondent embedded with the Marines, told later how he was harshly discriminated against. While all embedded journalists suffered some problems, like having no independent transport and not being able to stop to take photographs, US soldiers told Al-Kahky and his cameraman at once that they regarded Al-Jazeera as an enemy news station and all its staff as a threat. Security was persistently cited as the reason why the team could not say or do certain things, which made their work impossible. The military understood that even withholding information for a couple of hours was often enough to make all the difference to journalists and the soldiers were particularly wary about letting the pair speak to local Iraqis. Members of the anti-Saddam Free Iraqi Forces travelling with the unit accused the pair of being operatives for Saddam's regime and threatened to kill them. When Al-Kahky reported this, he was told there was nothing that could be done about it. It was suggested Al-Jazeera file no more reports. Al-Kahky took the hint.

Al-Jazeera's embedded experience was better at least than that of the Al-Arabiya team. They were embedded with the US 101st Airborne Division and also found their commander made their job impossible. Eventually they decided to discharge themselves, but had not gone far when they were captured by Iraqi tribesmen. They spent a week as guests of a local tribal chieftain before being released and were found later, rather bedraggled, by British troops, as they made their way back to Kuwait.

In the daily briefings at Coalition Central Command it appeared as if all the news organizations had equal access to information, but their experiences varied. When one Chinese journalist asked a question, Brigadier General Brooks began his reply by saying that he thought this was a good question. His off-hand comment was front-page news in China: 'Brooks Says Chinese Ask Good Questions,' bellowed Beijing newspapers. If the Al-Jazeera correspondent stuck up his hand, he received an answer just like anyone else, but the American military's top priority was always the American media and when the conferences were over, American media officials would prioritize American journalists over foreign ones. Away from the cameras, when Al-Jazeera asked a question it was often rejected on security grounds. Sometimes coalition spokesmen held smaller press briefings behind closed doors, to which Al-Jazeera was never invited. When the Al-Jazeera team asked why, a US officer told them that they were 'a station that has a reputation'. If there was an opportunity for a limited number of journalists to visit additional facilities – an aircraft carrier, for example – American news teams invariably were chosen in preference to Arab journalists.

Although Britain and America were presented as having identical media strategies, away from the cameras the MoD had quite a different philosophy regarding the press. It believed that the interests of the coalition were better served by constructive engagement with all journalists, no matter where they were from. British media relations operators in Doha and Bahrain saw it as their job to give the press a strategic overview of the war, so that sense could be made of the rather dislocated reports coming from the embeds. One British media officer I spoke with compared his role to holding up the box of the jigsaw so that journalists doing the puzzle could see how all the pieces fitted together. A closer relationship with the press afforded British media officers the opportunity to impress some of their own messages on to the news. Their principal message was that the war was targeting Saddam's regime, not the Iraqi people or Islam. Pains were taken to stress that a similar coalition had once come to the aid of the Muslims in Bosnia. As the British spokesman, Group Captain Alan Lockwood sometimes appeared on Al-Jazeera twice a day, by the end of the war he had become very friendly with the network's staff. He and other British officers often had breakfast with Al-Jazeera staff in Doha.

Luckily for the coalition, much of the British and American media was happy to go along with the coalition's overarching narrative about Iraq's liberation. American television networks were particularly patriotic and markedly pro-war. They were happy to abide by the will of the coalition press office, giving disproportionate importance to trivial developments, like the deck of cards featuring the fifty-five most wanted Iraqis, the 'rescue' of Private Jessica Lynch and the pulling down of the statue, at the expense of more important events, especially the broader international context.

Things that did not conveniently fit into the victory narrative were omitted. The Iraqis themselves were reduced almost to an abstraction. If civilian casualties were shown at all, they were portrayed only in the context of receiving medical treatment from the advancing coalition troops. In the lexicon of the Pentagon, and then in the loyal American media, body bags became 'human remains pouches' and coffins became 'transfer tubes'. American dead arriving home did so in the early hours of the morning at a small military airport in Delaware. President Bush did not attend a single ceremony for the dead, either during or after the war.

Starting the day after the invasion of Iraq the American national media watchdog Fairness and Accuracy in Reporting (FAIR) began monitoring the flagship US nightly news shows on the five major American networks – ABC, CBS, NBC, CNN and Fox News – as well as on PBS (Public Broadcasting Service). The study lasted throughout the three weeks of the war. Together these six networks total approximately the same number of viewers as Al-Jazeera. FAIR's survey found that, of the 1617 sources who spoke about the war on the six networks, 71 per cent supported the attack on Iraq while just 3 per cent opposed it. Yet at the same time polls by Gallup, CBS and USA Today found that about 30 per cent of the American population opposed the war. Not one of the five major American networks interviewed a spokesman from any of the various anti-war organizations, but all featured pro-war voices at length.

The most popular American nightly news show, NBC's, has about eleven million viewers. Less than a month before the bombing began, NBC's chief foreign affairs correspondent, Andrea Mitchell, was commenting on the report of the chief UN weapons inspector, Hans Blix, in which he said he had found no conclusive evidence of Saddam's weapons of mass destruction. 'For the US, it's a nightmare scenario,' she told viewers. 'If Iraq destroys the missiles, it will be much harder to get support for military action.'

FAIR's survey also found that 68 per cent of those who appeared on the major American news shows during the war were former or current members of the US government and two-thirds of them were military. In other words American news coverage of the war was saturated with military experts and crisp government spokesmen. Contrary to what might have been expected, FAIR's research did not find that Fox News was an outlier in the study and CBS, which featured just one voice opposed to the war, emerged as the most pro-war channel. That voice was Michael Moore's anti-war tirade at the Oscars.

With the Western networks endorsing the war so assertively, second-hand reports in the Western press about what Al-Jazeera had said or done made the network look conspicuously pro-Saddam. It was true it was enjoying exceptional access in Iraq. Besides press conferences, Al-Jazeera's reporters were being taken to see hospitals full of civilian casualties, bombed bridges and roads, plus any other evidence of civilian casualties or collateral damage the Iraqi Ministry of Information could rustle up. But for many Americans, whether serving in Iraq or watching at home, it was the images Al-Jazeera had shown of the POWs that confirmed beyond doubt that Al-Jazeera must indeed be the propaganda wing of the sinister nexus that surely existed between Al-Qaeda and Iraq. A grass-roots movement against the network began, spearheaded as usual by the tabloid press.

'Al-Jazeera is the great enabler of Arab hatred and self-deception. It propagates the views of Osama bin Laden. It cheer-leads for Palestinian suicide bombers. It has become Saddam's voice . . . Iraqi journalists and their Arab press colleagues are basically civil servants carrying out editorial orders of dictators. Al-Jazeera "journalists" produce propaganda by choice . . . Meanwhile, real journalists are dying in Iraq,' ran one editorial in the *New York Daily News*.

At the start of the war the English-language version of Al-Jazeera's website was launched: http://english.aljazeera.net. Edited by a former BBC journalist, this at first restricted its content to Iraq, offering eyewitness accounts of coalition bombing as well as photos, and later the controversial pictures of the dead coalition soldiers. It had been up and running less than twenty-four hours before concerted, anonymous attacks by hackers began, as well as on Al-Jazeera's much more popular Arabic-language website. Al-Jazeera's online chief editor said he thought those responsible had to be an organization, rather than a lone hacker, because they were using an exceptionally powerful computer.

The attacks took various forms: at one point hackers managed to replace the news with a message that read 'Hacked by Patriot, Freedom Cyber Force Militia' beneath a patriotic American logo. Later this was replaced with a stars-and-stripes map logo bearing the slogan 'Let Freedom Ring'. Sometimes hackers redirected surfers to porn sites or just blitzed the site with so much data that it became so congested as to be useless. At one point the domain name was hijacked and the whole site was redirected to another server, so visitors just received an error message. These attacks ran for weeks and occasionally staff were unable to update information for days at a time. Eventually Al Jazeera began offering text-message news updates to mobile-phone users instead. Broadcast in English and in Arabic, these were available in 130 countries. 'Cyber terrorism', the usual term to describe this kind of electronic attack, was not applied in the Western press to the attacks on Al-Jazeera.

There were other vigilante-style attacks against Al-Jazeera, as well as against companies perceived as affiliated to the station. Qatar Airways endured a spate of bomb scares. Americans identified as having business links with Al-Jazeera were criticized. American billionaire media tycoon Stanley Hubbard was attacked in the American press for selling studio space in Washington to Al-Jazeera. 'That'd be, hello!, the same Al-Jazeera that runs Osama bin Laden's weekly "Death to the American infidels!"

videos. The same Al-Jazeera pumping gross distortions, half-truths and outright lies about this country into coffeehouses all over the Middle East,' said a Minnesota newspaper.

AOL and Yahoo! both pulled their advertising campaigns on the Al-Jazeera website. In early April a company called Akamai Technologies, which provided content-delivery services for the new Al-Jazeera English-language website pulled out of its contract without explanation. Al-Jazeera pointed to the fact that the CEO of Akamai Technologies sat on a panel that supplied computer advice to the White House and that the FBI was another of Akamai's clients.

DataPipe, the US-based company which hosted the Al-Jazeera website, announced that it no longer wanted to work with the network. DataPipe's other clients had been lobbying to expel Al-Jazeera since they had begun incurring collateral damage from the repeated hacking attempts. Because American web-hosting companies were refusing to host the network's websites, Al-Jazeera moved its Internet hosting operation to France. In an interview with a Qatari newspaper the chief editor of Al-Jazeera Online blamed lobbyists in the US, who he said were trying to deny Al-Jazeera all manner of important support facilities.

Meanwhile, the Al-Jazeera team covering the war at Coalition Central Command in Doha found their equipment vandalized, including power cables cut and cameras broken. They suspected American journalists were responsible. BBC staff helped repair their equipment by supplying spare parts.

The Al-Jazeera team in Washington ran into unexpected problems when trying to sublease seventeen thousand square feet of office space from an American television production company. An agreement had been struck before the war started to put Al-Jazeera on the lease. The network had been operating from the property for some time, as a client but not a tenant. Only when war broke out did the landlord start to make things difficult for the station. He refused, for example, to allow telecom technicians access to the building's telephone exchange, so Al-Jazeera's office could not be wired up with a high-speed

Internet service. Staff had to maintain contact with Doha via a dial-up service, which caused severe disruption.

The landlord said he was uneasy about leasing the property to a company that was 'a target for people who do not understand or do not agree with its business principles and philosophies of those of its ownership'. Some of the tenants, he claimed, were worried about sharing a building with Al-Jazeera. The irony was, besides the Republic of China having an office in the same building, America's Associated Press television network was also operating out of there, and one of its syndicates was Hezbollah's Al-Manar television. The first guest Al-Jazeera received was Condoleezza Rice. Nevertheless, the landlord had a problem specifically with Al-Jazeera and a court case ensued. The network eventually had to move to a new building, where it needed to rebuild all its studios at a cost of millions of dollars. As they say in Arabic, 'Business is cowardly.'

Al-Jazeera's New York bureau had similar problems when trying to secure office space in Manhattan. A suitable space was located and the network told the landlord it was happy with it and was interested in renting it. At first it was not necessary to make clear to the landlord that his client was going to be Al-Jazeera. Talks progressed to a very advanced level and it looked like the deal was about to be closed. Then, completely out of the blue, the landlord changed his mind. 'We couldn't possibly think of any other reason except that we were Al-Jazeera,' shrugged the channel's New York correspondent.

In an unprecedented step the New York Stock Exchange (NYSE) withdrew credentials from the two Al-Jazeera journalists who had worked there since the channel's inception in 1996. The pair had primarily been responsible for banking and financial advice as well as live, daily market commentary, and had nothing directly to do with the war. Initially the NYSE said their sudden expulsion, which came without warning or any kind of notification, was part of an attempt to make space on the crowded floor, but no other journalists were expelled. An NYSE spokesman later cited security concerns as the reason, as well as a desire to accommodate only networks that aired 'responsible business coverage', although he did not mention Al-Jazeera by name. After the two Al-Jazeera journalists had been kicked out of the NYSE, they applied to broadcast from the Nasdaq, but were turned down there too.

The expulsions, which came at the height of the row over the POWs, served to deflect attention from the controversial appointment by Dick Grasso, head of the NYSE, of a Wall Street banker to the NYSE's board. There were allegations that Grasso's new appointment conflicted with various financial interests of his – and in September 2003 it emerged the NYSE had been a carnival of corruption at this time.

The NYSE's move against Al-Jazeera was such a blatant attack on freedom of expression that it even prompted a brief backlash of sympathy. The president of the Society of Professional Journalists castigated the NYSE and urged it to reconsider: 'A decision to deny Al-Jazeera reporters credentials does nothing to support our country's image as a place where the free exchange of ideas and information serves as the foundation for everything America does,' he said.

James Carey, a professor of journalism at Columbia University, called the move 'a colossally stupid thing to do'. Many American and all the British papers, as well as plenty of media advocacy groups, piled in on Al-Jazeera's behalf. The *New York Times* sprang to its defence, insisting in an entire editorial that 'if our hope for the Arab world is, as the Bush administration never ceases to remind us, for it to enjoy a free, democratic life, Al-Jazeera is the kind of television station we should encourage'.

When Baghdad fell, an Al-Jazeera team went to Dearborn, Michigan, to cover the Iraqi–American reaction. This suburb of Detroit has one of the largest Iraqi Shiite communities outside Iraq. The two-man team was filming a street parade celebrating Saddam Hussein's demise, when they were set upon as supporters of the dictator. Police had to rescue them from a mob of about fifteen hundred angry Shiite demonstrators.

Al-Jazeera did not face problems during the invasion of Iraq in any of its European bureaux. Life in London, Paris, Moscow and Berlin was tranquil compared with the rigours of reporting from the United States. On the contrary, its staff were smothered with messages of respect and support whenever they were recognized. Often when staff from the London bureau were out filming, as soon as people realized that they were from Al-Jazeera they would go up to them to shake their hands. The team would be thanked for speaking up against the war and there were many enquiries about the forthcoming English-language channel. People would say how much they had enjoyed the English-language website and how sorry they were that it had been shut down. Just as in the Middle East, Londoners spontaneously offered assistance of all kinds and often gave tips about stories.

Besides encountering problems operating within America, Al-Jazeera also came under pressure from the coalition inside Iraq. Whether the channel was deliberately targeted or there was just a generally aggressive coalition policy towards un-embedded journalists, is not clear. Before the fall of Basra, besides the Al Jazeera headquarters being hit by missiles, the team was almost blown up a second time by British tank fire as they filmed the Iraqi authorities distributing food. After the siege of Basra a cameraman was detained and questioned for more than twelve hours, his camera and equipment seized, as he was leaving the town. On another occasion British soldiers stormed the network's Basra bureau and beat up the security guard.

After the fall of Baghdad an Al-Jazeera jeep was riddled with bullets by US soldiers at a checkpoint. The vehicle, which was clearly marked as press, had been travelling between the capital and the airport and had already been waved through the checkpoint by the soldier on duty when the shooting occurred. The passengers were all unhurt, but the jeep was badly damaged. Al-Jazeera regarded the shooting as deliberate and took it as a warning.

The worst incident occurred on 8 April, in the last days of

the war. An Al-Jazeera news crew were on the roof of the downtown Baghdad bureau, preparing a live broadcast about the arrival of the Americans in the city, when an US A10 'tank killer' aircraft unexpectedly fired two missiles in their direction. These struck the pavement in front of the office and the generator nearby, blasting windows and doors out into the street. An Al-Jazeera correspondent and producer, Tareq Ayyoub, was seriously injured by shrapnel from the blast. As flames and smoke belched out of the building, Abu Dhabi TV captured Taysir Alluni, the Al-Jazeera correspondent who had made his name in Afghanistan, bundling Ayyoub into an Abu Dhabi TV car with help from staff of the rival Arab network. Ayyoub's chest was covered in blood. He was rushed to hospital but his wounds proved too severe and he died a short time later.

The moment Al-Jazeera announced that one of its correspondents had been hurt, Ayyoub's wife called the network asking what had happened to her husband. She guessed it was him, although no one had mentioned his name.

Tareq Ayyoub was one of two correspondents sent to Baghdad from Jordan near the end of the war to relieve those who had been in the capital for months. At just thirty-five, the Jordanian national, who was married with a one-year-old daughter, was the youngest Al-Jazeera correspondent in Iraq. He had been in Baghdad less than a week when he was killed.

Ayyoub was a rising star at Al-Jazeera, well liked by all the staff, and the network was grief-stricken. A statement from Doha immediately denounced his death as a 'tragic act'. 'Al-Jazeera . . . believes that the real victim is journalism and professional integrity,' the statement read. 'Al-Jazeera reiterates its commitment to continue in its pursuit of professional, comprehensive and balanced journalism.'

The bureau the Americans had attacked had been in a villa in a residential neighbourhood. There was no doubt they knew exactly where it was because on 24 February Al-Jazeera's managing director had written a letter to Victoria Clarke, the US Assistant Secretary of Defense for Public Affairs in Washington, listing the address and map coordinates of the Baghdad bureau – Lat: 33.19/29.08, Lon: 44.24/03.63 – and warning her that civilian journalists would be working in the building. The missiles struck the exact coordinates the network had given the US military more than a month earlier.

The next day Al-Jazeera ran a tape of Ayyoub reporting from the same roof the night before. Watching Ayyoub sitting cheerfully among a pile of sandbags, staff in Doha were dazed; some were crying, others stood around thunderstruck. There was fury at America. Another Al-Jazeera correspondent in Baghdad, Majed Abdul Hadi, branded the death a crime. 'I will not be objective about this because we have been dragged into this conflict,' he emotionally declared live on Al-Jazeera. 'We were targeted because the Americans don't want the world to see the crimes they are committing against the Iraqi people.' Al Jazeera's correspondent in Mosul reported that Iraqis were refusing to be interviewed in the network's office in the town because they took it for granted that Al-Jazeera was now a US target.

Reports about Ayyoub's death in the West were overshadowed by a separate attack on the Palestine Hotel which happened less than three hours later on the same day. Two other journalists, a Spaniard working for Telecinco and a Ukrainian working for Reuters, were killed when an American tank fired a shell into the hotel, a location also well known for housing journalists, who broadcast daily reports from there. Coalition Central Command claimed that this too was an accident. They initially claimed that the tank was returning fire, although later, after many eyewitnesses contradicted this account, the story was quietly dropped. At the time the US military spokesman, Brigadier General Vincent K. Brooks, said the military had not known journalists were staying there.

European stations' evening news reports paid emotional tributes to their journalist colleagues who had died in the Palestine Hotel, while Ayyoub was reduced to a footnote if he was mentioned at all. When news of the death broke across the Arab world, however, there was outcry. Ayyoub became a 'martyr' and his death a deliberate assassination. The Arab press accused the coalition of stopping at nothing to muzzle Al-Jazeera so as to cover its atrocities. In the Occupied Territories dozens of Palestinian journalists staged a sit-down protest outside the offices of the International Red Cross and the Committee to Protect Journalists in New York wrote an open letter to the Defense Secretary Rumsfeld to remind him that he had an obligation to protect all journalists, that the attack had contravened the Geneva Conventions and that there should be an immediate enquiry.

Tareq Ayyoub's distraught widow made an emotional appearance via telephone on Al-Jazeera. She was both overcome with grief and furious. 'My message to you is that from hatred grows more hatred,' she said. 'My husband died trying to reveal the truth to the world. Please do not try to conceal it, not for the sake of American policy, not for the sake of British policy.'

Al-Jazeera's managing director wrote again to Victoria Clarke asking why the office had been targeted – when he had notified her previously about the exact location of the bureau and warned her of the presence of journalists. In her reply Clarke did not answer his questions, but offered condolences to Tareq Ayyoub's family, explaining, 'War by its very nature is tragic and sad . . .'

Coalition Central Command claimed that 'significant enemy fire' had been issuing from near the Al-Jazeera bureau and that the attack had been an act of self-defence. Taysir Alluni, speaking on Al-Jazeera, was dismissive of the military's argument. 'This is a flimsy pretext. The bombing was aimed at a certain balcony. It could not have been a mistake. The excuse that they suspected that a sniper was there is unacceptable. We assume that the goggles used by planes, tanks and other weapons have advanced to such a level that even small inscriptions or even faces can be recognized. The excuse that a cameraman is taken for a sniper is a flimsy one. A state of deep anger and wrath prevails here regarding those who fired the missile.'

During an emotional news conference held over Tareq Ayyoub's death, Al-Jazeera's chairman, Sheikh Hamad bin Thamir Al Thani, contradicted the Pentagon's claims that shooting had issued from the bureau before the attack. He declared that although he did not know whether the attack had been deliberate or not, he recalled how the Kabul bureau had also been targeted two years previously by the US military. The conference, which was held at night, on a lawn outside the Doha office, was well attended by the tearful Al-Jazeera staff. Prayers were said in memory of their dead colleague and a video of his work, set to music, was shown.

'The majority of the press corps was still present in Doha covering As-Saliyah and they all, of course, came and covered it,' recalled Jihad Ballout. 'I counted on my fingers there were seventy six separate cameras, still cameras and video cameras. We got a lot of sympathy. I recall a representative of a Canadian television news organization, who I don't want to name, actually had tears in her eyes when she was posing questions to me. I was on the podium and she was sitting down in her chair. She almost choked. We had a lot of support.'

Dr Nabil Khouri, the US Department of State spokesman, was in Doha the day Tareq Ayyoub was killed, and said: 'I was in Doha on 8 April and both incidents the Palestine Hotel and the Al-Jazeera offices, were hit on the same day. I went on the air very quickly.' His verdict was that the attack had been a legitimate response to fire: 'I and my other colleagues from the State Department got a verbal response as to what happened. It involved returning fire from near the villa, which was occupied by Al-Jazeera.'

Khouri told me he thought the attack on the Palestine Hotel and the air attack on Al-Jazeera were responses to the same area of Iraqi resistance: 'If you want to think of it in military terms, it was practically the same front from the Al-Jazeera office to the Palestine Hotel, it was a stretch of one mile maybe . . . that whole sector of Baghdad was firing at American troops as they were coming across the bridge. The Al-Jazeera office was right between where the American troops were and what is behind that office.'

Several months later an independent inquiry into the attack on the Palestine Hotel by the media watchdog Reporters sans Frontières came to quite a different conclusion. The attack had been 'an act of criminal negligence' by the US military, its report said. It was 'criminal that information about the presence of so many journalists at the hotel was not communicated by the military hierarchy to the tank units that arrived on the Al-Jumhuriya Bridge on the morning of 8 April'.

The report also accused the American authorities of lying at the highest level to cover up the killings:

> Supposed legitimate self-defence in response to shooting from the hotel – the excuse offered right from the begin-ning and re-stated at the highest level of the US govern-ment – was pushed in an effort to dominate the media and political discourse. This first version of events became the official version and was a lie by the authorities . . . By focusing debate on technical military problems, the US government ignores the key to the tragedy – that the soldiers in the field were never told that a large number of journalists were in the Palestine Hotel. If they had known they would never have fired . . . The US govern-ment must bear some of the responsibility. Its top leaders have regularly made statements about the status of war reporters in Iraq that have undermined all media security considerations and set the scene for the tragedy that occurred.

Khouri told me that he had seen 'a fairly detailed report on the Palestine Hotel incident', but, he explained, 'I did not see a specific report about the Al-Jazeera incident but it was the same day – it was practically the same few hours.' He never saw a report because there was not one. On 14 October 2003 Reporters sans Frontières wrote to the Pentagon asking to see the results of the promised investigation into the attack on Al-Jazeera, which it was obliged to release under the Freedom of Information Act. So did the Committee to Protect Journalists.

'We followed up the case very closely,' Joel Campagna from the CPJ told me one wet spring morning, almost exactly a year later, in his office in New York. He explained:

To date six of the twenty-four journalists killed in Iraq have been killed by US fire. We found out about six months after the attack, when we queried the Pentagon, that no investigation had ever been launched into that incident. That was the only case where a journalist was killed by US fire and an investigation was not launched.

We were certainly troubled when we learned that, in fact, no investigation had been conducted into the Al-Jazeera incident. I don't have any evidence that there is a way to connect the dots to suggest that the station had been singled out for fire. However, one has to ask the question, how were two news bureaux, one in Afghanistan, one in Iraq, hit by US missiles, in one instance killing a journalist? How did that happen on two separate occasions and why, to date, has there not been an adequate explanation? I think that Al-Jazeera, as well as other press freedom organizations are right to ask that question. Answers need to be provided. There is a lot more that needs to be known.

Without an investigation, no one was ever held responsible for Tareq Ayyoub's death and his widow never received the justice or the answers to her questions she sought and deserved. A life-size cardboard photograph of him wearing a battered helmet and an oversize blue bullet-proof jacket stands in the corner of the Al-Jazeera newsroom in Doha to this day.

Al-Jazeera's Jihad Ballout told me that he thought the attack on the Baghdad bureau was part of the coalition's effort to control the flow of information on the battlefield. Pulling on a cigarette, he said cynically:

> When you are at war you would like to utilize all elements at your disposal for your war effort. Americans are no different to anyone else. Americans certainly would have loved to be in control of the process of channelling information out of the theatre of action. They could not do that with Al-Jazeera there. If I was a military leader I would have been distressed.
>
> When their cameraman was shot dead later on, the Pentagon sent a communication to Reuters. Secretary Colin Powell sent a letter to the Spanish Ministry of Foreign Affairs about the Spanish cameraman who died. Al-Jazeera has never received any official apology, word or anything – there has not been an investigation either – into the bombing of our Baghdad office. I think the investigation is long overdue and I think it is in the interest of America and American values for this investigation to be conducted, not only for Al-Jazeera and Tareq Ayyoub's family – who are entitled to an explanation – but because it is detrimental for America and for what America stands for in terms of democracy and freedom of expression, not to tell the world what happened then.

After Ayyoub was killed Al-Jazeera's management decided to pull all its reporters out of Iraq. Al-Jazeera and Abu Dhabi TV both appealed to the coalition commanders to rescue their staff who remained in Saddam-controlled Iraq, either in Baghdad or Mosul.

Besides its problems with the coalition during the war, Al-Jazeera also ran into difficulties with the Iraqi regime. Reporting in Iraq had never been easy. All the networks operating there were obliged to have an 'escort': a Ba'ath Party flunkey, courtesy of the Ministry of Information, whose job it was to keep an eye on them. Most of these minders were fairly surly types, some carried guns and all had a penchant for passing names of offenders on to the Ministry of Information for blacklisting.

The first signs of trouble came before the war had even started. All foreign journalists had to stay at one of two big hotels in Baghdad, the Al-Mansur and the Al-Rashid. All the foreign TV networks except Abu Dhabi TV and Al-Jazeera had been obliged by the regime to lease offices in the Iraqi Ministry of Information. When the bombing began the Iraqis instructed these two networks that this special arrangement was now over and they had to move into the Ministry.

This presented something of a dilemma for the network as the Pentagon had expressly warned Al-Jazeera that the Ministry of Information was a bombing target and so was the Al-Rashid. The US Department of Defense had told the Baghdad bureau that it was not 'going to change its military plans to protect journalists'. Operating from inside a known Pentagon bombing target naturally put all the Al-Jazeera staff under considerable pressure. A report by the network about just how much pressure journalists in Baghdad were facing infuriated Iraq's Minister of Information. He barged into the Al-Jazeera bureau in Baghdad brandishing a rifle and warned the staff that he would not tolerate this kind of defeatism.

The Minister threatened the Al Jazeera staff in Baghdad several times during the war. He warned that unless their reports improved he would close the bureau down, and more than once Iraqi police overran the office. Network executives in Doha were acutely aware that their correspondents and crews in Baghdad, Basra and Mosul were effectively hostages to the regime. Negative reports about events in Iraq ran the risk of provoking a punishing response. As a result interviews with Iraqis during the war steered clear of topics like Saddam's human rights abuses, because both interviewer and interviewee had no choice but to self-censor.

After the war was over Al-Jazeera rebroadcast several bulletins that had been censored at the time for fear of upsetting the regime and jeopardizing the safety of other journalists in Iraq.

One report featured an interview with an Iraqi citizen in Nasariya, in which the man said that Saddam's regime should bear the responsibility for what had befallen Iraq. The second report was about Ba'athists menacing Iraqi tribal chiefs who did not put up a show of resistance to the coalition troops.

Al-Jazeera was not the only network in Iraq that had to watch what it said about the regime. Before the war several Western news agencies had their staff detained and tortured, but never dared make the news public for fear of jeopardizing the safety of other correspondents in Iraq. During the war Al-Arabiya had one of its two uplinks confiscated without explanation and Abu Dhabi TV was forced to stop transmitting at gunpoint.

The Iraqi Minister of Information cultivated a particular loathing for Amr al-Kahky, the Al-Jazeera correspondent embedded with the US Marines, and Waddah Khanfar, Al-Jazeera's correspondent in the autonomous Kurdish zone. Al-Kahky, reporting before being silenced by his embed unit, had displeased the regime with his frank reporting about the fall and subsequent coalition occupation of Umm Qasr, while at the same time the Ministry of Information was trying to pretend the resistance was still going on.

Waddah Khanfar incurred the Minister's wrath early in the war when he ran a series of emotional reports from the autonomous Kurdish region in Iraq. One report told the pitiful story of an Iraqi Kurdish villager and his family who had suffered terribly under Saddam's regime. A second report featured Khanfar interviewing Kurdish families fleeing from their villages for the surrounding countryside. The villagers were scared that Saddam was going to gas them again. 'The cold won't kill us, but the chemical weapons will,' one told Khanfar.

Kurdish issues had also been discussed on *The Opposite Direction*. Saddam's treatment of the Kurds had been condemned so vigorously that Faisal al-Qasim liked to joke that there was probably an epidemic of Iraqi Kurdish families calling their sons Faisal in his honour.

Reports on Al-Jazeera about the terrible things Saddam had

done to his own people hit the regime particularly hard, by undermining its support in the wider Arab world. Iraq's Minister of Information vowed to Al-Jazeera's Baghdad correspondent, Majed Abdul Hadi, that if he ever caught Waddah Khanfar and Amr al-Kahky he would have them hanged. He tried to intimidate the Baghdad bureau into persuading Doha to change its editorial policy to favour Saddam and he threatened Hadi that if there was no improvement he would cut off his arms.

Halfway through the war the Iraqis banned two of the network's correspondents in Baghdad from reporting altogether. There was no clear reason why. Al-Jazeera later said the issue had simply been money. The Iraqis demanded frequent bribes from all foreign news organizations and usually these were just paid, but this time, after some disagreement, Taysir Alluni was instructed to leave the country.

In protest, the network announced it was going to cease filing live reports from Iraq, restricting its activities to pre-recorded material plus reports from international agencies only. An Al-Jazeera spokesman insisted that it was not up to the Iraqis to dictate who could and who could not work in Iraq. A few days later the Iraqis rescinded the decision and reporting continued as normal.

Despite all the allegations of bias that issued from both sides during the invasion of Iraq, the simple truth is that Al-Jazeera did not favour anyone in the war. Like most Arabs, it opposed Saddam's regime and opposed the invasion. Al-Jazeera strived to show that this war was not simply about freedom from tyranny, like the liberation of France in 1944, but a complicated conflict that provoked many differing opinions around the world. It also tried to show that, despite all the electronic military wizardry and political promises, war had a human cost and the people who suffered most in the end were ordinary Iraqi civilians.

Al-Jazeera neither exaggerated the power of resistance nor downplayed the strength of the advancing coalition force. Contrary to what the US Department of State claimed, the network reported Iraqi resistance only where it existed and it balanced these reports with details of coalition successes, like the ease with which British forces finally entered Basra and the absence of resistance when American troops arrived in towns and villages in southern Iraq. Every time a town or city fell to the coalition, Al-Jazeera reported it at once. When the long-anticipated 'Battle of Baghdad' never materialized after American troops had finally arrived in the capital, Al-Jazeera was as taken aback as everybody else. It also went to great lengths to translate many speeches, interviews and announcements into Arabic, so that coalition commanders could be heard at length, unedited and in their own words.

When the statue of Saddam Hussein was toppled in Fardus Square, Al-Jazeera veteran Maher Abdullah was there to give a blow-by-blow account. He did not deny that the Iraqis present in the square were ecstatic at the statue coming down, but he noted that the pictures of the crowd trampling on the fallen dictator's image would be received with ambivalence around the rest of the Arab world. Many Arabs, including some in Al-Jazeera's headquarters in Doha, felt a relief tinged with bitterness. While they were happy to see Saddam go, they felt humiliated at the speed at which the Americans had taken this supposedly powerful Arab country. 'Iraq and the Arab world were now entering a new and unknown era which could turn out to be either better or worse,' Abdullah prophesied. 'Let's hope,' he added, 'that Iraqis find democracy and independence.' Provocatively, he pointed out that many Arabs probably fantasized about pulling down statues of dictators in their own squares.

On 11 April Al-Jazeera stopped counting the days since the war began, implicitly declaring hostilities over. The network's heavy investment had paid off: it had been the most popular news channel in the Arab world. Viewership had increased by about 10 per cent, peaking at fifty million. Many new viewers came from Indonesia, the world's most populous Muslim country, where local channel TV7 began to broadcast Al-Jazeera's signal at the start of the war, but a remarkable four million Europeans had subscribed to Al-Jazeera in the first week of the war, doubling the number of European subscribers.

The search engine Lycos reported that 'Al-Jazeera' had become its most popular search term; three times more so than the next most popular item. This was a direct result of Americans, denied pictures of the dead and captured soldiers by their own networks, turning to the channel. In fact, Americans had now been so exposed to Al-Jazeera and its journalists during the war that a fervent underground interest in the network had been sparked. Flattering articles began to appear in the American press, in addition to the derogatory ones. Al-Jazeera's correspondent at Coalition Central Command, Omar al-Issawi, had particularly caught the public imagination, perhaps because he was the only Al-Jazeera correspondent Americans had actually seen speak each day, when he asked questions at the daily briefings. The international press observed that even Brigadier General Brooks always addressed him as 'Omar'.

'As the war has progressed, however, Al-Issawi has become something of a celebrity, emerging as one of the more eloquent and coolheaded commentators,' ruled the *New Yorker*, in a veritable pin-up piece which continued:

> Al-Issawi has a taut, lean build and the cautious air of a man who has weathered many controversies and covered many wars. Thirty-six years old, he is a Lebanese citizen who was born and raised in Kuwait and educated at colleges in Iowa and Virginia. He speaks in a determined, formal Sidney Poitier kind of English, his voice low and soft and mellowed by Marlboros. He wears desert khakis, suede boots, and an impressively pocketed correspondent's jacket, and often carries a stainless-steel thermos filled with viscous Turkish coffee. He collects silk textiles and fine kilims on his frequent travels as a foreign correspondent and likes to rocket around Doha in his new BMW M3, listening to heavy metal.

While other networks had sustained losses through deferred or cancelled advertising campaigns – Sky News and Fox both dropped all advertising as soon as the war started – Al-Jazeera, which made so little money from advertising anyway, was in a better position. Instead the network made a tidy profit selling footage. Twice its correspondents had found themselves in exclusive positions for a prolonged duration: once in Basra at the start of the war, and once in Mosul at the end. In Mosul it was Al-Jazeera alone which reported how the Iraqi army had melted away, leaving only foreign *jihadis* to defend the city, and later, how the city had descended into abject chaos as looters emptied banks, the university and other public buildings of everything right down to their carpets.

All the major Western channels had used Al-Jazeera's feed from Baghdad, Basra or Mosul at one time or another. 'Our success is a factor of our people's networking in Iraq, and their ability to anticipate events through contacts on the ground,' said Jihad Ballout.

'Who Covered the War Best? Try Al-Jazeera,' ran a headline in *Newsday* magazine. 'Throughout the war in Iraq, Al-Jazeera has been accused, both by US and Mideast officials, of being a propaganda tool. But continued attacks on the Arab satellite network, most dramatically exemplified by the recent US bombing of a newsroom in Baghdad that killed a correspondent, show that Al-Jazeera's approach to covering the war – both critical and multidimensional, with an ideological commitment to democracy, openness and pluralism – has seriously threatened the political projects of the world's most powerful,' raved the article.

An Arab survey covering several countries, carried out by the UAE's University of Sharjah, found Al-Jazeera the most credible out of all the Arab news channels during the war, followed by Abu Dhabi TV, with Al-Arabiya third. Al-Jazeera.net was rated as the most credible online news source. A week into the war the London-based free speech organization Index on Censorship gave Al-Jazeera an award for accuracy. Even the MoD conceded that it had been satisfied with how Al-Jazeera had presented the war, with the significant exception of the footage of the dead soldiers.

In Afghanistan Al-Jazeera had been popular because it was the only network there. During the invasion of Iraq Al-Jazeera was watched through choice. It had broken the hegemony of the Western networks and, for the first time in hundreds of years, reversed the flow of information, historically from West to East.

A month after the war the two Al-Jazeera reporters were allowed back into the New York Stock Exchange and a man from California turned himself over to the FBI as the hacker who attacked Al-Jazeera's website. A deal was struck with an American non-profit educational organization to transmit limited Al-Jazeera broadcasts via cable in the US for the first time, so half an hour of news became available every morning to American Arabic speakers.

9

Aftermath

After more than three decades of Saddam Hussein's stranglehold on the media, one of the first consequences of the dictator's demise was a rampant proliferation of the press in Iraq. Within weeks of the fall of the regime, hundreds of newspapers were being published, Internet cafés had sprung up in all the major cities and in a two-mile stretch in Baghdad there were more than fifty shops selling satellite receivers. Iraqis were spending their life savings to be able to tune in to satellite channels from across the world: entertainment was popular, but news was the priority.

Among the plethora of new voices jostling to be heard in Iraq was the coalition itself. *Commando Solo*, the US Air Force cargo plane which had been specially modified to become a flying radio and TV station, was back in business, circling above Iraq transmitting television and radio several hours each day. It had last seen action broadcasting to the Taliban; now it was pumping out news on frequencies formerly used by Saddam's regime.

Even though Al-Jazeera and Al-Arabiya were the two most popular channels in Iraq, Iraqis had reservations about both. The Shia, in particular, thought that Al-Jazeera had been too generous to Saddam's regime in the years before the war and over-critical of the Arab countries who allied themselves with the

American-led coalition. They objected to the network's description of the American troops as 'invaders' and believed that too much credence had been given to Saddam's Minister of Information during the war. Both networks were seen to be too quick to report coalition shortcomings after the war was over and to give too much time to pro-Saddam voices.

When Al-Arabiya ran a live report on the Friday following the end of the war, after prayers outside a mosque inside Baghdad, a crowd of Iraqis set upon the correspondent, intent not on hurting him but on taking the opportunity to send messages to loved ones outside Iraq letting them know that they were safe. Although there was no official Al-Jazeera position on the occupation, the network's talk shows were rife with debate about the reasons behind Iraq's rapid defeat and what shape the new Iraq might take. An episode of the talk show *Behind the Events* a few days after the war ended, with Robert Menard, the head of Paris-based Reporters sans Frontières, Amr al-Kahky, the Al-Jazeera correspondent who had been embedded with the US Marines, and Majed Abdul Hadi, one of the network's Baghdad correspondents, reflected inconclusively on the merits of the new occupation.

Al-Jazeera's correspondents in Iraq were shuttled around so that those who had been in Iraq for months were replaced with fresh faces. The London office was bolstered with half a dozen new staff, bringing the total to twenty, including one former award-winning journalist from the BBC: Afshin Rattansi, who had won a Sony award for international journalism in 2002 for his work on the Radio 4 programme *Today*. He now became Yosri Fouda's associate producer, working on his *Top Secret* investigative series. A new method of distributing Al-Jazeera's news was also inaugurated. Al-Jazeera.net teamed up with a Dubai-based telecommunications company to offer news to paying subscribers via mobile phones. It was the first time such an operation – between website and handset – had been tried on such a scale in Arabic.

The comprehensive network of correspondents and freelancers Al-Jazeera had put in place at the start of the war continued to deliver outstanding results. Often the network reported stories several hours ahead of rival Western networks. Al-Jazeera continued to enjoy especially good access in the areas considered the most dangerous – and the most newsworthy. In the aftermath of the war former Saddam strongholds like Mosul, Fallujah and Tikrit were rich seams of stories and from the very first days after the war was officially declared over Al-Jazeera began carrying exclusive reports about violent confrontations between Iraqis and US troops.

Life for the Al-Jazeera news crews in Iraq, as for everyone else, was not easy. The lack of security was a day-to-day concern. Often staff were threatened or attacked by angry crowds of demonstrators. 'The truth is that there is growing indignation,' reported Baghdad correspondent Waddah Khanfar, after one demonstration ended in violence. 'This began by the talk about water and electricity shortages and job-related issues. The talk then shifted to the issue of dissolving the institutions and the failure to pay salaries.'

As Iraq was engulfed by a scorching summer, the news became saturated with reports about Iraqis angry at the lack of water and power, the coalition's disbanding of the Iraqi army and the tough security measures taken by the occupying troops. Intermittent reports arrived of unarmed Iraqis shot dead by edgy American soldiers, at checkpoints, demonstrations or during house searches, and there was criticism throughout the Arab media that the Americans, short of linguists and ignorant about local customs and Islam, were proving culturally insensitive. House searches and the treatment of Muslim women were of particular concern. Al-Jazeera's talk shows continued to debate the legitimacy of the occupation. *The Opposite Direction* considered provocative questions like 'Is America a benevolent power?' and 'Can the United States be resisted?' Often guests and callers strongly disapproved of the occupation and some even called for revolt. This was evidently not the peaceful, grateful reception the coalition had hoped for. American soldiers were still dying every day.

At the start of May the Emir of Qatar visited Washington. He was the first Arab leader to do so since the war had ended. President Bush made great show of thanking this staunch coalition ally. 'Mr Emir, you made promises to the United States and you kept them,' he said. 'We are proud to say you are a friend. We appreciate your silent support. The Emir also presents a strong example to be followed in that area of the world. He is a reformist and has set a new constitution that allows women to vote. He has appointed a woman in the post of a minister. He is a strong leader, who believes in the importance of education and that an educated people have a better chance to achieve their dreams.' For his part, the Emir reconfirmed his allegiance to Washington and spoke of the many bonds that tied their two countries ever closer. Then he was invited to the Oval Office for a photo opportunity and lunch with the President.

As a more permanent solution to Iraq's media needs, in the aftermath of the war the Coalition Provisional Authority (CPA) set about establishing an Iraqi news network. This, to be called the Iraqi Media Network (IMN), would replace Saddam's defunct Ministry of Information. Costing $6 million a month, IMN was the most expensive media project the US government had ever embarked upon and there were high hopes that it would be not just a news and entertainment channel but a national forum in which Iraqis from all ethnic groups could engage in constructive dialogue. There was talk of open discussions, debates and credible, balanced news, which would allow Sunni, Shia and Kurd to come together and hear one another's point of view. In the long term the coalition envisaged the IMN one day becoming a national television service, like the BBC: independent but publicly funded. In the short term it was no secret that the new network was intended to lure Iraqis away from the siren call of Al-Jazeera, which helped train the staff.

Before Saddam fell, Iraq had eighteen television stations, various government radio stations and a national newspaper with a circulation of sixty thousand, run by the dictator's delinquent son Uday. The IMN was the first and most important step in replacing the old set-up, with two radio stations, a newspaper and a single TV channel. American contractors furnished the IMN with powerful AM and FM radio and television transmitters which could reach about two-thirds of Iraqi homes. Most, but not all, the regional offices of Saddam's old TV network now came under the IMN umbrella. Some offices, in former Saddam strongholds, were not interested in serving the coalition. On 13 May the IMN went on air for the first time.

The director of the IMN was a highly respected journalist, a former Iraqi exile named Ahmad Rikabi. While in exile Rikabi had made his name as the voice of the US-funded Radio Free Iraq, before he was headhunted by the American administration to head this vital new venture. Iraqis were expectant that America, so famous for its media, as well as its Bill of Rights and First Amendment, would have little problem in constructing an exciting, liberal news network in Iraq. But no sooner had the IMN started broadcasting than it ran into problems. The first and biggest was that Iraqi reporters, who had never had the opportunity in the past, were too quick to embrace the democratic principle of responsible criticism of those in charge, which in this case meant the Coalition Provisional Authority. The CPA, which had no credible experience in running a television station, was unhappy about this development. Its members had not just spent all this money setting up a news network only to see it start criticizing them. They wanted to keep the IMN simply as a platform for important official announcements, with managed news and limited questioning.

But there were other problems too. Programme planning was a shambles. Rather than encourage a local television production industry, the CPA bought Arabic programmes from Lebanon or Saudi Arabia. The European and American movies that ran on the channel were from Uday Hussein's personal video collection, looted from his mansion and broadcast illegally, without attention to copyright law. One children's cartoon which ran for twenty-six episodes, originally in Japanese but dubbed into Arabic, was about the aftermath of an apocalyptic world war, fought with massively destructive magnetic weapons, far more deadly than today's nuclear weapons. During the course of the war most of the planet is destroyed, the continents are blasted apart and sink beneath the sea. There are only a handful of survivors, most of whom are children and the hero of the story is a young boy called Adnan who foils the invaders' plans to capture the lethal magnetic weapons and rule the world, though sadly his adoptive grandfather is killed by the invaders along the way. This was an interesting choice of children's programming given the circumstances.

Staff at the new network had to brave daily threats as 'collaborators' and despite the fact that the IMN was so expensive a project, the reporters were earning just $30 a week. When they tried to bargain collectively for higher wages – they went on strike twice – they were told that if they were not happy they should leave. Many left voluntarily to join news agencies that paid a living wage. Owing to the lack of funding, basic equipment, including camera batteries, tripods and editing equipment, was in short supply. Rikabi's request for a $500 satellite dish to pick up the Reuters news feed was turned down as too expensive.

Unsurprisingly, the IMN made a poor first impression on Iraqis. When they saw that anti-coalition protests carried on Al-Jazeera and other Arab news networks were ignored on the IMN in favour of American public affairs programming, news conferences and CPA photo opportunities, they naturally assumed the station was simply the mouthpiece of the coalition. After thirty-five years of practice, they knew propaganda when they saw it.

After two months Rikabi walked out and the network was left floundering. He had grown tired of constantly struggling with the coalition authorities, trying to make the IMN something more than a mouthpiece for their propaganda. For weeks he had complained that, without more investment from the Pentagon to make programmes and equip and train staff, they were wasting their time trying to compete with Al-Jazeera and Al-Arabiya. But what finally pushed Rikabi to go was his belief that the CPA had compromised his authority, making his position no longer viable. He was angry that even though he was supposed to be the station manager, the CPA reserved the final say as to how the station was run. When it consistently rehired staff he had let go, either for being incompetent or because they were former members of the Ba'ath Party, he decided to quit.

'Saddam Hussein is doing better at marketing himself, through Al-Jazeera and Al-Arabiya Gulf channels . . .' said Rikabi as he left. 'The United States needs to listen to Iraqis more, and not just in the media sector.' There was not enough effort to enlist local staff, he added, and money was being thoughtlessly invested in the wrong place.

The fact was, the administration in Iraq could not make up its mind whether the IMN was an independent news channel or a coalition mouthpiece and so the channel wound up being neither. An independent report into Iraq's media by the BBC World Service Trust found that most Iraqis saw the IMN as 'the mouthpiece of the CPA'.

An American television producer drafted in as an adviser to the coalition's media enterprise later echoed Rikabi's complaints about the new network. 'Its role was envisioned to be an information conduit, and not just rubber-stamp flacking for the CPA,' he explained. 'Through a combination of incompetence and indifference, the CPA has destroyed the fragile credibility of the IMN. Once diminished, credibility is hard to restore . . .' he wrote in a television industry publication a few weeks after he left Baghdad. 'The stakes are high and getting higher every day. President George W. Bush has spoken of "engaging in the battle of ideas in the Arab world". But in Iraq we have already lost the first round by failing to establish credible media, let alone influencing the rest of the Arab world.'

When Rikabi walked out, so did many of the Iraqi staff, leaving the IMN, launched with such fanfare just a few months earlier, looking decidedly moribund. A multi-billion-dollar San Diego-based defence contractor called Science Applications International Corp. (SAIC), which already had operations in Iraq ranging from building infrastructure to running businesses, was called in to relaunch the station. Although SAIC, which itself was overseen by the US Department of Defense's Office of Psychological Operations, had zero experience in media development, it charged the Pentagon $100 million in operating costs while it learned. It was a bit like asking the BBC to start intercepting ballistic missiles. Although SAIC paid executives up to $273 an hour and enlisted a security service made up of former members of the US special-forces unit Delta Force, charging $1000 per day for each man, Iraqi reporters were kept on Saddam's $120-a-month pay scale. Some were earning as little as $60 a month — not enough even to buy respectable clothes to appear on screen. When they demanded a clothing allowance, they were granted $150, but only for clothes for above the waist.

Under SAIC's guiding hand, the network was put to work as a platform for important announcements, like when curfews were imposed. A taped message from America's Proconsul in Iraq, Paul Bremer, was run every Thursday and Friday at 7 p.m, dubbed into Arabic, which to many Iraqis sounded coldly reminiscent of Saddam's era. The broadcast frequencies and many of the staff were the same as under Saddam; even the singers who had sung his praises on the old Iraqi television network were commandeered to sing odes to Iraq's liberation. Rikabi's successor lasted only a few weeks before being replaced with a former CNN executive editor.

A Department of State survey in mid-October 2003 found that the IMN was watched in 59 per cent of Iraqi homes that did not have satellite dishes. In homes that had satellite dishes this figure dropped to 12 per cent. Where there was a satellite dish, Al-Jazeera and Al-Arabiya, which were almost equally popular, were watched instead. About a third of Iraqi homes had satellite dishes. The Department talked these figures up as an improvement, but anecdotal evidence suggests that while viewers soaked up the entertainment they switched off the news. In Iraq's post-war media free-for-all there were plenty of alternatives.

'Iraqis use it mainly for entertainment, to follow football matches, Egyptian serials, Arabic music video clips, and late night movies but NEVER for their daily news,' was the verdict of one Iraqi blogger, 'Zeyad', writing in the 'Healing Iraq' blog (http://healingiraq.blogspot.com). 'They prefer Al-Jazeera or Al-Arabiya for that, largely due to the apparent professional style of these stations.'

Despite denials by the coalition, further surveys indicated that the IMN was one big flop with Iraqis. Its ignominious downward spiral culminated in demonstrations in the Shia holy cities of Najaf and Karbala in November, demanding the channel cease broadcasting altogether. At this point the Pentagon, facing reality, began talking about handing the channel's management over to someone else. The $100-million, two-year contract drew dozens of bidders, most of them PR companies or engineering or defence contractors.

Before the handover of the IMN to its new management, Pentagon officials paid the station a visit to review SAIC's work. They discovered that SAIC had been paid for work it had never finished and that several containers of valuable gear had been sitting unloaded. Worse still, there were inexplicable discrepancies between expensive transmitting equipment for which SAIC had charged the Pentagon and the actual equipment present in the field. SAIC, which had manipulated its close links to the US Department of Defense to secure the job in the first place, stood accused of profiteering and a Pentagon audit agency was sent in to conduct a proper inventory. In March 2004 a report by the US Department of Defense Inspector General concluded there were major problems in 22 of the 24 contracts the military had awarded in Iraq – eight of which were with SAIC.

It emerged that amongst other things, SAIC's media manager had insisted that an H2 Hummer and Ford C350 pickup truck be bought and airlifted to Iraq from the United States. Although this request was initially refused by the military contractor, by later resubmitting the same request to a different office within the Department of Defense, SAIC had managed to get what it wanted. The Inspector General could not ascertain the exact amount this had cost, but one invoice for 'Office and Vehicle' was uncovered totalling approximately $381,000. 'DOD [Department of Defense] cannot be assured that it was either provided the best contracting solution or paid fair and reasonable prices for the goods and services purchased,' ruled the Inspector General's report.

On another occasion SAIC appointed a member of staff enlisted on a media contract to head its garbage disposal operations in Iraq. An email to the contracting officer about the garbage assignment warned, 'Sit down before you read this attachment! I'm still in shock that "Management" believes this is okay. I'm not sure what to do . . . besides cry.'

SAIC denied it had done anything wrong. A fresh start was urgently needed, so a smart New York advertising company called J. Walter Thompson was brought in for some emergency rebranding. It recommended a renewed publicity campaign for the IMN and a relaunch under a new name: Al-Iraqiyah TV. SAIC paid J. Walter Thompson $890,000 for its advice. The new-look Al-Iraqiyah would now finally offer the kind of 'quality programming that we hope will attract the average Iraqi citizen's attention to what's going on in their own country, and that will compete with Al Jazeera and Al Arabiya and other stations,' said General Richard Myers, chairman of the Joint Chiefs of Staff. He hoped in vain.

Al-Iraqiyah TV changed its programming so regularly – three times in a month – that it had no chance of shoring up any loyal viewership. Eight months after it had been established, it had successfully squandered millions of dollars forging an unshakeable reputation for tiresome propaganda, stage-managed news and mediocre entertainment programmes. The network's website ran intermittently and the poor staff still lived under the shadow of constant death threats for collaborating. One on-air presenter and her family had to be relocated for their own safety.

A second Department of State poll a few months later suggested that about one in ten Iraqis now watched the IMN, compared with two out of three who watched either Al-Jazeera or Al-Arabiya. The President of Internews Network, an international non-profit organization that supports and develops open media worldwide, said he thought Al-Iraqiyah 'the worst mess I have ever seen in my life'. Iraqis must have been puzzled at how America had managed to make such a dog's breakfast out of something even a deranged sadist like Uday Hussein had managed to run relatively smoothly.

Soon after the war ended Al-Jazeera broadcast a report alleging that American troops had arrested the President of the US-appointed Iraqi National Congress, Dr Ahmad Chalabi, for embezzlement. The Iraqi dissident, who had been instrumental in helping America make its case for war, had been sentenced *in absentia* in Jordan to twenty-two years' hard labour for massive bank fraud. At the end of the war Chalabi, an MIT-trained mathematician, returned to his homeland, as America's first choice for President of the new Iraq. He had been in exile for forty-five years. Shortly after the story of his arrest had been broadcast on Al-Jazeera, Coalition Central Command in Doha issued a report denying it.

A short time later Chalabi himself appeared on Al-Jazeera's rival, Abu Dhabi TV, to ridicule Al-Jazeera's reports of his arrest. He went on to claim that he had uncovered material that would seriously incriminate the station. 'Al-Jazeera is completely infiltrated by Iraqi intelligence,' he said live on Abu Dhabi TV. 'We got the information from the files of Iraqi intelligence.'

Chalabi was in a good position to start slinging mud around. He had powerful backers through whom he had managed to position himself as the power behind the vacant Iraqi throne. Although the *casus belli* with which he had provided the Pentagon turned out to be utterly fallacious, he remained well beloved of war architects Vice President Dick Cheney, Deputy Defense Secretary Paul Wolfowitz and neoconservative theoretician

Richard Perle. An adviser to the Pentagon and a consummate Washington insider, Perle chaired the Defense Policy Board until he resigned from this position in February 2004. The American Defense Intelligence Agency kept Chalabi on a stipend of $340,000 a month. He had also recently been appointed head of the de-Ba'athification commission by the Iraqi National Congress, giving him exclusive access to several dozen tons of documents and files seized from Saddam Hussein's secret security apparatus. This, above all, put him in a panoptic position of power.

Chalabi decided to share his intelligence on Al-Jazeera exclusively with Rupert Murdoch's *Sunday Times*. The article was entitled 'How Saddam's Agents Targeted Al Jazeera'. Slightly strangely, however, according to the newspaper, the files pertaining to Al-Jazeera that Chalabi possessed had not come from the tons of Saddam's secret files he had been given by the Americans, but from a bonfire in Baghdad. A close aide to Chalabi, whose job it was to track down former members of the regime, said he had stumbled across the remnants of the bonfire of documents – and, by extraordinary coincidence, among the few unburned files he had been able to rescue was some scandalous inside information about Al-Jazeera. Realizing their significance, the aide had handed the files on Al-Jazeera straight to his boss, Chalabi, who then decided to give exclusive access to the *Sunday Times*. The files covered the period from August 1999 to November 2002, a very substantial stretch of Al-Jazeera's history, from before the intifada until the lead-up to the war in Iraq.

The *Sunday Times* journalist who read the documents was only allowed to do so under the close watch of an armed guard. Her article revealed that three of Al-Jazeera's staff had been on the payroll of Saddam's Mukhabarat: their mission, to secure favourable coverage about Iraq on Al-Jazeera. Two Al-Jazeera cameramen were identified as Iraqi agents, as well as a third, unnamed employee, identified only as someone involved in 'international relations'. This mysterious third man, who was clearly not an anchor, journalist or an employee of significant editorial influence, was code-named 'Jazeera 2'.

The files showed that Jazeera 2 had pleased his Iraqi handlers by passing them two letters the network had received from Osama bin Laden. An Iraqi Embassy official in Qatar had written, '[Jazeera 2] has a distinguished stand in the cooperation with us, continuously providing us with the information we request. I made him aware of the appreciation of his efforts. He has been presented with a set of gold jewellery for his wife.' The two cameramen had, according to the documents, been less useful, only managing to pass on some information about the views of other Al-Jazeera staff, as well as some footage of the Iraqi army in the first Gulf war.

The documents boasted that during this time Al-Jazeera had been an 'instrument' of Iraqi intelligence that could 'foil' American aggression. In October 1999, so the documents claimed, the Iraqi agents in Al-Jazeera had successfully exerted their influence to stop the broadcast of a tape showing Saddam's gas attack on the Kurds at Halabja. A document headed 'Presidency of the Republic, Mukhabarat Service' concerned Muhammad Jasim al-Ali, and although it was never suggested that Al-Jazeera's general manager was an Iraqi agent, it seemed he had been a target of Iraqi intelligence. Another document described a meeting with him.

Al-Jazeera issued a statement denying it had been working on behalf of any foreign intelligence organization. Network executives acknowledged that they had been subject to many conflicting pressures while working in Iraq, but rejected accusations that they had been influenced by anyone. Jazeera 2's employment, the station said, had been 'terminated some time ago'.

A few weeks later Muhammad Jasim al-Ali left Al-Jazeera. The network said that the general manager's move was unconnected to the allegations in the *Sunday Times*. A Qatari who had served Al-Jazeera for eight years, Al-Ali had originally been seconded from Qatar television and the network explained that the board of directors had decided that the time had come for him to go back to his original job. He would continue to serve on Al-Jazeera's board of directors. A week later Adnan al-Sharif, a British national of Palestinian descent, became the network's acting general manager. He had started at the BBC in 1989 as a current affairs and news producer and a presenter on the BBC World Service's Arabic-language radio programmes. Together with Sami Haddad and Jamil Azar, Al-Sharif had been one of the founders of Al-Jazeera and, before returning to work at the BBC again for a few years, he had been one of the station's original anchors.

This episode seemed to many Arabs and analysts alike to be a crude attempt at a smear campaign by Chalabi, a man with the motive, the means and the temperament to carry it out. Chalabi hated Al-Jazeera, just as he hated anything that questioned his return to rule Iraq. This hatred arose mainly from the fact that he had been appointed to the Iraqi Governing Council, the governing body that had been created by the Americans to rule the country. Since the Americans had hand-picked each member of the Council, ordinary Arabs regarded every one of them with suspicion. The Councillors, including Chalabi, were often spoken of on Al-Jazeera, as well as on other Arabic channels, as American lackeys – and Chalabi wanted revenge. His choice of newspaper too – a Murdoch backed paper known for its support for the war – seemed like a decision calculated to ensure a sympathetic hearing for the case against Al-Jazeera. Interestingly, Chalabi's access to secret files had already afforded him similar evidence which he used to attack two other key anti-war voices besides Al-Jazeera: President Jacques Chirac and George Galloway MP.

Subsequently, many more of Chalabi's intelligence sources, the foundation of the Bush administration's case for war in Iraq, turned out to be false. The defectors and scientists he supplied, touting tales of weapons of mass destruction, turned out to be a well-organized group of fabricators. As a deception, it was well orchestrated: Chalabi even managed to make his 'evidence' of Saddam's WMD available to several other intelligence services, which he knew the CIA would contact when trying to verify his stories.

'Anyone who can get the US to invade Iraq must be a very clever politician,' said one former US Ambassador after a visit to Iraq. 'As for the people his INC coached in London to disinform the US intelligence community about Saddam's non-existent weapons of mass destruction, you've got to hand it to the guy. Don't blame him. Blame the Pentagon for not seeing through him.'

Chalabi fell from favour with the American administration as his stories unravelled. Sensibly enough, not entirely trusting him, the *Sunday Times* couched its accusations in journalistic disclaimers. 'The files apparently reveal . . .', 'the documents claim . . .', 'the files appear to confirm suspicions . . .'. Facts are 'alleged', 'purported' and 'apparent'. Not all the documents seen by the paper were even incriminating and the Iraqis complain about Al-Jazeera's unfavourable coverage too. The grandiose claim that the network was an 'instrument' of Iraq in the war certainly seems to be the talk of a junior intelligence officer struggling to impress his boss. As for Saddam's regime preventing Al-Jazeera airing footage of Halabja, the network, in fact, aired several programmes about Saddam gassing the Kurds right up to the very start of the war. Nevertheless, whether or not Al-Jazeera had been penetrated by Iraqi intelligence, this was a major embarrassment for Al-Jazeera.

Publicly the network was stoical about the revelations. 'You can never guarantee that any person working in a newsroom cannot be an intelligence agent,' said Al-Jazeera's editor-in-chief. None of the three members of Al-Jazeera's staff who were incriminated by Chalabi and the *Sunday Times* was in a position to influence the editorial process or the output of the station. Since they all appear to have been Iraqis, they could all have been subject to pressure from Saddam's nefarious Mukhabarat to do what they were told but there was no evidence that they were. Nevertheless, privately Chalabi's exposé rattled the network more than the response given at the time by its management might suggest and prompted an internal review which led to structural changes to try and ensure such a thing could never happen again.

However, the coincidences surrounding how this evidence supposedly came to light, and the fact that other voices critical of the American-led invasion of Iraq have also been similarly smeared, raise as many questions about the methods of Ahmad Chalabi as they do about Al-Jazeera. The fact is that Al-Jazeera's coverage of the war upset the regime so much that the station's staff were repeatedly threatened and bureaux were closed down. The agents could not have been having too much effect.

In the spring of 2003, after vicious bombings in Saudi Arabia and Morocco, both attributed to the Al-Qaeda terror franchise, Al-Jazeera received another taped message. This time it was purportedly from Dr Ayman al-Zawahiri, head of the Egyptian Islamic Jihad group, Al-Qaeda's chief ideologue and Osama bin Laden's right-hand man. The audio-tape castigated a number of Arab countries allied to the coalition and called on Muslims to rise up and attack Western embassies and commercial interests.

'O Muslims, muster your resolve and attack the embassies of America, England, Australia and Norway, their interests, their companies and their employees . . . Set the ground ablaze under their feet . . . Kick these criminals out of your homelands,' said the voice. 'Do not allow the United States, Britain, Australia, Norway and other crusaders – the murderers of your Iraqi brothers – to live in your countries and enjoy their wealth and spread corruption.'

At first the coalition expressed doubt that the recording, which was heavily edited and only about four minutes long, was authentic. The voice was Egyptian, like Al-Zawahiri's, but it sounded too young. Al Jazeera would not say how it had come by the tape, but once it had been accepted that the voice probably was Zawahiri's, the coalition came down hard.

'The text of the tape is disgraceful,' raged US Department of State spokesman Richard Boucher. 'We have to ask: why would a television channel air this kind of repeated threats and statements calling on people to commit horrible crimes against innocent people? Airing this tape is an irresponsible act.'

'We think it was unfortunate that Al-Jazeera ran the tape,' Colin Powell told reporters. 'All it does is heighten tension throughout the region to allow this kind of terrorist to have access to the airwaves. In any event, it has heightened tension throughout the world and it spreads more hatred throughout the world,' he fumed. 'I wish they had made a different editorial judgement.' The American administration, he confirmed, had made its displeasure known to the Qatari government. Al-Jazeera aired the criticism of its coverage by both Powell and Boucher.

Following the airing of this tape on Al-Jazeera, Paul Bremer, as the US-appointed civilian administrator of Iraq, drew up a regulatory framework for the country's rapidly expanding media landscape. A new civilian authority responsible for monitoring all the media in Iraq was founded and a new media commissioner was ordained to regulate journalists' activities through a system of punitive fines. Anything which might be deemed to incite violence was now expressly forbidden, as were promoting 'ethnic and religious hatred' and circulating false information 'calculated to promote opposition' to the occupation authority. These new guidelines immediately put publishers and journalists under pressure to start exercising self-censorship.

Al-Jazeera broadcast several more tapes in the summer of 2003 which the coalition viewed as inflammatory. One video broadcast by the network came from a mysterious group that called itself the Muslim Fighters of the Victorious Sect. This group, of whom no one had ever heard before, claimed to be responsible for several attacks against US interests. To prove this, it enclosed a hazy video of a bomb detonating under a US military vehicle. The tape came with a message – a warning to Iraqis not to cooperate with the US forces 'for their own safety'.

A few days later Al-Jazeera received and broadcast a second tape from a different group, the People's Resistance for the Liberation of Iraq. The tape appealed to engineers, explosives experts and other professionals who sought revenge against the Americans to come to Iraq to fight against them. 'Come to a country that does not have a government, but has an angry

Mujahadeen people, who desperately need you.' Al-Jazeera also received several other hand-delivered tapes from Iraqi groups showing attacks on coalition troops, which it did not run.

The day after Bremer announced a bounty of $25 million on Saddam's head, Al-Jazeera's newsroom in Doha received an anonymous call from inside Iraq offering a message from the fallen dictator. A tape recording of Saddam speaking was then played down the phone. Because of the way the tape was transmitted, the quality was extremely poor and although the message ran for some thirty minutes, large chunks were inaudible. Only about fifteen minutes were eventually played to air.

It was not the first message from the ousted dictator: a letter had already been published in the London-based Arab newspaper *Al Quds Al Arabi* and a tape had been given to the *Sydney Morning Herald*, but it was the first time Saddam's voice had been heard on a TV network since the fall of his regime. The message was aired several times, with a little more added each time.

'I am in Iraq and with a comrade,' said the voice. 'I tell you that I miss you, miss you, oh beloved people, even though I am among you and in your ranks . . . I bring you the glad tidings . . . that the cells and brigades of jihad and sacrifice have been formed on a large scale, comprising male and female mujahadeen, and launched their honourable battle against the enemy . . . What will come in the days ahead will, God willing and with His help, be tough on the infidel invaders and honourable for the believers.' The voice went on to call on regular Iraqis to shelter and assist the resistance fighters.

Since it was widely held at this time that the Iraqi resistance responsible for the daily attacks on American soldiers were acting out of a die-hard loyalty to the deposed tyrant, a broadcast of his voice was exactly what the authorities in Iraq did not want.

'I say this to the Arab media: stop advising the Iraqis to fight the Americans,' said one Sunni member of the Iraqi Governing Council. 'These media are threatening us from the first day of the war until now,' echoed a Shiite cleric, also on the Council. 'Come see the mass graves,' he added. Ahmad Chalabi, now

Acting President of the Iraqi Governing Council, concurred.
'There are many sides, including some officials in the Arab
countries and some Arab satellite channels, who encourage action
against the current Iraqi status quo and who incite terrorism.'

These messages that Al-Jazeera was receiving from Saddam
and other nebulous Iraqi groups were beginning to make the
network look rather suspicious. Rumours began circulating that
Al-Jazeera had more connections to the insurgents than it was
letting on. Network executives, sensitive now after the espionage
allegations, moved quickly in an attempt to stamp them out.
'Airing the audio-tape in no way means that we are siding with
Saddam or with the former regime,' chief editor Ibrahim Hilal
told AFP. 'We are a media outlet whose job is to inform . . .
and if we receive more tapes we will broadcast them.'

The coalition did not believe him. There were rumblings
among American commanders that Al-Jazeera did not just have
videos of old attacks against coalition troops, but had advance
knowledge too. As the insurgency persisted, suspicions about
Al-Jazeera grew and jittery American media officers became
increasingly guarded about the information they shared with the
Arab press. Al-Jazeera's journalists in Iraq suddenly found themselves subjected to a litany of arrests, beatings, threats, equipment confiscations and general harassment at the hands of
American troops.

In one incident in Ramadi, a flashpoint town about 65 miles
west of Baghdad which marks one corner of the so-called 'Sunni
Triangle', two Al-Jazeera cameramen were apprehended by US
troops after they came close to witnessing an explosion that
killed seven Iraqi police recruits. The American troops thought
the journalists were suspiciously close to the blast, as if they had
been tipped off in advance. The pair were hooded and cuffed
and then, according to an Al-Jazeera spokesman, 'roughed up'.
After a couple of hours of interrogation the soldiers drove the
pair into the desert and dropped them off, leaving them to find
their own way back to town.

In a separate incident American troops fired at an Al-Jazeera camera crew who were trying to fix up some lights at night. 'As they were testing their camera lights, some American soldiers in the vicinity fired warning shots towards them,' said a network spokesman. 'In a situation as tense as it is in Baghdad, one can understand that everybody is edgy. They probably confused the camera lights as some kind of signals being given,' he added.

A few weeks later the same correspondent, with three other Al-Jazeera employees, was arrested again, this time by Iraqi police. He had been filming anti-coalition protests. The correspondent was charged with 'inciting violence', and after a few hours all four were released. The Iraqi police who made the arrest said they had been acting at the request of the American forces in the area.

Al-Jazeera journalists in Iraq were beginning to feel that all this harassment was revealing a pattern. The coalition, they sensed, was trying to convey a message. Although they had no legal justification to take action against Al-Jazeera, they were behaving in a threatening way, in the hope that Al-Jazeera might water down its reporting. Meanwhile, other Western news channels, reporting the same news, went unpenalized.

As Al-Jazeera's senior correspondent in Iraq pointed out scathingly:

A short while ago, we saw a report, which was not filed by Al-Jazeera correspondents in Ramadi or Fallujah, but by the British Reuters news agency or the US ABCN. The report conveys the feelings of Fallujah people who were shown carrying arms. Had this report been from the Al-Jazeera correspondent it would have been regarded as incitement. He would have been arrested and called to account. Such reports by US and other agencies would be regarded as a professional journalistic coverage.

There was an explosion in Ramadi yesterday. Everybody heard it. The Al-Jazeera correspondent was not there and the explosion was not reported. Have the explosions stopped after the arrest of Al-Jazeera correspondent in

Ramadi? A short while ago, we heard gunshots in Baghdad. Would the shooting stop if there were no cameras?

Despite Al-Jazeera's protestations that its journalists were simply doing their job, there was no let-up in the tide of arrests. A few weeks later Al-Jazeera's correspondent in Mosul and his driver were arrested as they filmed Iraqis shooting at American troops. The correspondent immediately declared a hunger strike. He was released the next day but his tape was confiscated.

Al-Jazeera's relationship with the US administration took another blow when, during an interview on Fox News, Deputy Defense Secretary Paul Wolfowitz lashed out at the network. He blamed it for the escalation in violence against American troops in Iraq. American soldiers were dying every day and the enemy was elusive. He accused Al-Jazeera of 'false reporting and very biased reporting that has the effect of inciting violence against our troops'.

Both Al-Jazeera and Al-Arabiya, he said, were 'endangering the lives of American troops, and, you know, they have a way, when they want to cover somebody favourably, including Saddam Hussein in the old days, of slanting the news incredibly. Well, a little bit of honesty would help and the lack of – and ending this incitement would be what we'd like to see. The minute they get something that they can use to spread hatred and violence in Iraq, they're broadcasting it around.' Wolfowitz added that the US administration was speaking with the Qatari government about Al-Jazeera. 'We're talking to the owners of those stations and asking for some balance in their coverage.'

He singled out one particular report by Al-Jazeera for criticism. The station, he said, had broadcast the arrest of a certain anti-American imam, when, in fact, no such arrest had ever occurred. 'Al-Jazeera ran a totally false report that American troops had gone and detained one of the key imams in this holy city of Najaf, Muqtada al-Sadr. It was a false report but they were out broadcasting it instantly.'

Both Al-Arabiya and Al-Jazeera staunchly defended themselves against Wolfowitz's accusations. 'It's obvious Al-Jazeera is on the carpet and the victim of slander,' said the network's Baghdad correspondent. 'It's simple: the US forces want the media to be in their service. That is unacceptable, even in the Third World. Any self-respecting media refuses to submit to the wish of the government and even less so when this government is an occupier.'

'The problem is that Western media were not expecting to find large Arab competitors who found success thanks to their respect of the truth, something that doesn't please some people,' the network's acting manager, Adnan al-Sharif, told AFP. The problem, he said, was Al-Jazeera's habit of broadcasting 'news without first trying to ask the Americans'.

Regarding the report about the imam's arrest, Al-Jazeera insisted that it had never said that an arrest had occurred: it had simply reported claims to that effect. Wolfowitz had evidently heard a 'mistranslation'. The Arabic for 'cordoning off' had been translated into English as if the house was under siege.

'Al-Jazeera never stated at any time that Muqtada al-Sadr was detained,' explained the Baghdad bureau chief, Waddah Khanfar. 'Our correspondent, Yasser Abu Hilala . . . stated he had received phone calls from Muqtada al-Sadr's secretary and two of his top deputies saying the imam's house was surrounded by US forces after he called for the formation of an Islamic army. The phone calls were not only made to our offices but to all the offices of Al-Sadr's followers in Baghdad, resulting in a massive demonstration in front of the Republic Palace within forty-five minutes, which we reported, along with the *New York Times*, CNN and others.'

The next day Khanfar wrote a letter to Paul Bremer, claiming that the network had been subjected to an ongoing campaign of harassment by the American forces. He said that his staff and offices had been 'subject to strafing by gunfire, death threats, confiscation of news material, and multiple detentions and arrests, all carried out by US soldiers'.

Khanfar also pointed out to the Proconsul that it was unreasonable to suggest that Al-Jazeera had favoured Saddam Hussein

during the war when both he and another of Al-Jazeera's senior
Baghdad correspondents had been expelled from Baghdad by
the regime for their reporting; the Ministry of Information had
twice shut down Al-Jazeera's office; and the network's staff had
been threatened and assaulted by the Iraqi Minister of
Information because of their unfavourable reports.

Bremer had little sympathy for Al-Jazeera. 'I know that a
number of news channels, including Al-Jazeera, want to portray
the disruptive acts of the remnants of Saddamists as resistance,'
he said in an interview with an Iraqi Kurdish newspaper, 'but
what they are referring to is not resistance; it is, however, a
resistance against the freedom which has been realized for the
Iraqi people and also against the efforts being made by the
coalition to rebuild a sustainable economy.'

This laying of blame on Al-Jazeera for the resistance was a
sign of Washington's growing disorientation in Iraq. Expecting
to be treated as liberators, Americans were being killed and they
could not understand why. The Bush administration's outbursts
against Al-Jazeera went hand in hand with attacks on other
spectral enemies, including Ba'ath Party loyalists, Saddam
Hussein's inner circle, local bandits, Iranian agents, Al-Qaeda,
Syrians, other anti-American *jihadis* and angry Sunnis. Everyone
was blamed except the Iraqi resistance.

Al-Jazeera's sickly relationship with the American administration
was beginning to fester in the summer sun. Senior US officials,
among them Rumsfeld and Cheney, had developed a habit of
dropping off-the-cuff remarks denigrating all the media coverage in Iraq. Jihad Ballout, Al-Jazeera's media spokesman, was
kept very busy with television and newspaper interviews, defending the network's reputation. 'I was interviewed in Atlanta in
the wake of Rumsfeld's attacks on Al-Jazeera, when he said our
coverage was inciting violence against our troops,' he recalled.
'It was a grave, grave allegation that we had really to refute. I
had a representative from the Pentagon debating the issue with
me. He kept repeating the same statement: "Al-Jazeera has an

angle." I responded, saying, "Yes, we have an agenda." Our agenda is to enhance the revolution in the Arab media and to bring it up to standards with the Western media. It is so simple, that people tend, I think there is an expression in English, "They can't see the woods for the trees."'

Al-Jazeera's London bureau recalled a frostiness coming out of Downing Street that summer. Tony Blair never missed a chance to make a pointed remark about Al-Jazeera during his monthly press conferences. The bureau's chief, Mostefa Souag, recalled:

I remember I asked the Prime Minister a question about Iraq. A very usual kind of question actually, related to something published in the British media and he went, 'Oh! Al-Jazeera! All right!' Then, rather than answer my question, he gave us a lecture about how Al-Jazeera should be asking the people in Iraq what they thought, rather than just talking about them, while Al-Jazeera had been doing exactly that kind of work, more than anybody else on any other channel. We had hours of people in the street talking into our microphones, but he did not even know about it.

He had some kind of prejudice and we felt that. It happened with a few other ministers too, and after it happened we talked to their press officers or to them directly and quite often they felt a little bit embarrassed because they realized these reactions were based on something wrong: ignorance, or misconception or misunderstanding, not on factual accounts.

Even though the coalition took every opportunity to bludgeon and besmear Al-Jazeera, the bulk of the world's press spoke out in defence of the network. Arab newspapers and television channels decried the United States. In chorus they all asked the same question of the coalition: how could the interim authorities claim to be instigating democratic values in Iraq while at the same time they were intimidating and arresting journalists?

'The escalation of Iraqi resistance operations is not an outcome of incitement by Al-Jazeera satellite channel TV or other Arab media,' asserted one Qatari newspaper's website. 'It is rather a logical outcome of the acts of violence which many US military units commit when they break into homes and arrest people. It can also be attributed to the US political failure to quickly establish a democratic government.' The vast majority of Arabs, including Iraqis, shared this opinion.

'It has become a customary practice of the US to make false accusations and try to find a scapegoat whenever its policy fails and it comes under mounting external and internal pressure,' said the English-language newspaper *Gulf News*. 'It is obvious that the US is determined to silence the freedom of expression of outspoken Iraqis and the Arab media as resistance attacks against its occupation troops in Iraq gain momentum and their casualty toll mounts every day. By making such silly accusations, the US is, in fact, confirming its inability to understand the Iraqi people and admit its faulty policy and behaviour. What does America expect of the people who have been promised freedom but are suppressed almost daily?'

International press freedom organizations also rallied to Al-Jazeera's defence, saying they deplored the attitude of US troops towards journalists in Iraq. 'While feelings of frustration are understandable, the US military must not displace these thoughts on to journalists carrying out their professional work,' said the secretary-general of the International Federation of Journalists.

It was not only Al-Jazeera's reporters who found themselves subject to harassment by the coalition. Two journalists from Iranian television were arrested and detained for unspecified 'security violations' without any evidence being provided by the coalition. Their belongings were later taken from the hotel where they were staying and the pair were then sent to a military detention camp near Baghdad airport. A Japanese journalist from Nippon Television Network was arrested and beaten up by American soldiers after he filmed a raid on a house in Baghdad by American troops in which several Iraqi civilians were killed;

four Turkish journalists were detained and had their photographs digitally erased by US troops. Under Bremer's new media rules, American troops continued to raid newspaper offices in Baghdad deemed to be propagating hate or spreading false information and at least two newspapers and one radio station were shut down. On 18 August a Reuters cameraman was shot dead by American troops, bringing the total number of journalists killed to eighteen. American soldiers had killed at least four.

Despite the furore, Al-Jazeera's editorial style was not compromised. The network aired more audio messages from Saddam Hussein and read out a letter he had sent it. This did nothing to endear the network to Iraq's administration and at the end of August Al-Jazeera found its staff detained for a third time. A bomb had gone off in the flashpoint town of Ramadi, injuring several American soldiers and destroying two vehicles. Al-Jazeera correspondent Hamid Hadid was interviewing witnesses when American reinforcements arrived. They arrested the Al-Jazeera crew and confiscated their equipment, but ignored reporters from other networks who were present at the scene.

'Why did the US forces pick on you in particular?' the Doha anchor asked Hadid after he had been released. 'We put this question to Captain Warfell, commander of the force in the area,' Hadid replied. 'We told him: we are not the only ones in the area. There are other channels also covering the incident. Why did you pick on us? The only answer we received from him was, you either remain silent or we will take further action against you.' The soldiers threatened to shoot Hadid or any other Al-Jazeera correspondent if they caught them in Ramadi again.

In another incident one of Al-Jazeera's Baghdad correspondents was covering the aftermath of a bomb explosion in the capital's Al-Ghazzaliyah district, when another bomb exploded nearby. American soldiers arrived, arrested the correspondent and took her to Baghdad airport, where they interrogated her and held her overnight. Her arrest had been so sudden she had not even been allowed time to collect her microphone and glasses, which she left on the ground where she had been preparing to deliver her report. Like most of the others, she was not charged with any offence.

Al-Arabiya, welcomed before the war by Colin Powell as the reasonable voice of the Arab media, had come to be regarded by the coalition as even more troublesome than Al-Jazeera. When Al-Arabiya aired footage of masked men, who claimed to be from an unknown resistance group, threatening to kill members of the Iraqi Governing Council, the American administration was furious.

'We find Al-Arabiya's decision to air the remarks of these masked terrorists to be irresponsible in the extreme,' said a Department of State spokesman. 'We have to question why an organization claiming to be a legitimate news service would effectively provide this conduit for terrorists to communicate plans, tactics and incitement to murder and to attempt to disrupt the peaceful aspirations of the Iraqi people.' Al-Arabiya replied, somewhat weakly, that the footage might help prevent terror attacks. After this incident the Governing Council announced that in future it would sue stations which incited violence.

A new chapter in Al-Jazeera's turbulent history opened on 5 September, when one of the network's most famous reporters, Taysir Alluni, was arrested by police in Spain and charged with being a member of Al-Qaeda. The first he knew of the charges against him were when eight plain-clothed Spanish police arrived at the door of his family's home at Alfacar, four miles outside Granada, with an arrest-and-search warrant.

Alluni was taken to Spain's Soto del Real maximum-security prison, where he was interrogated by the judge who had ordered his arrest, Judge Baltasar Garzón. One of the country's most senior judges, Garzón was a magistrate at Madrid's national court. He has a reputation for tackling Basque terrorists and is well known in Spain for indicting the former Chilean dictator General Augusto Pinochet.

Taysir Alluni was chief of Al-Jazeera's bureau in Kabul during the war in Afghanistan. He had interviewed Al-Qaeda members and Taliban officials, scooped an interview with Osama bin Laden and nearly been killed when American missiles destroyed the Kabul bureau. After the Afghan war he had been one of Al-Jazeera's eight correspondents in Iraq during the war and when his friend Tareq Ayyoub had been killed by the American missile strike on the Baghdad bureau, he had been a vocal critic of America. He was originally from Syria, but had fled in 1980 when the Syrian army began killing students thought to be associated with the Muslim Brotherhood, a militant Islamist group suspected of trying to overthrow the secular government. Some of the other alleged Al-Qaeda members arrested at the same time as Alluni were also Syrian immigrants who had gone to Spain for the same reason at the same time. Alluni had become a Spanish national and had returned to Spain from Doha to collect his PhD when he was arrested.

In the days immediately following Alluni's arrest, there was rampant speculation as to what the charges might be. It was widely held that he might have unwittingly passed messages and money to Al-Qaeda operatives. But when, on 12 September, Garzón published a document that laid out the case against Alluni, as well as eleven other men arrested since November 2001, it emerged that the charges against him were far more serious.

The twenty-three-page court document suggested that Alluni did not just naively give money to the wrong guy. It alleged that the journalist 'performed acts of support, finance, supervision and coordination, characteristic of a qualified militant in that criminal organization'. If the charges were right, Alluni was deeply involved in Islamic terrorism, having become a member of a Spanish-based Al-Qaeda cell — a cell believed to be instrumental in planning 9/11 — several years before Al-Jazeera sent him to Afghanistan to run its Kabul bureau.

The case against Alluni included evidence of telephone conversations with known Al-Qaeda operatives dating back to the mid-nineties. He had been under constant surveillance, it emerged, since at least early 2000. Bugged telephone recordings showed he was in frequent contact with Imad Eddin Barakat Yarkas, alias Abu Dahdah, the suspected ringleader of Al-Qaeda's eight-man Spanish cell. Abu Dahdah was arrested in November 2001. Judge Garzón was overseeing his case also.

In 2000 and 2001 Alluni made several trips back to Spain from Afghanistan, during which undercover police in Granada shadowed Alluni to a number of clandestine meetings with Abu Dahdah and his alleged Al-Qaeda accomplices. One meeting in particular was regarded as highly suspicious: in Granada in July 2001, Alluni was supposed to have met a Syrian-born German called Mamoun Darkazanli, who was under investigation by Spanish and German police for his suspected ties to the Hamburg Al-Qaeda cell. Darkazanli was thought to be bin Laden's financier in Europe. In December 2001 Spanish police circulated an internal report expressing suspicion about why Alluni had been allowed access to bin Laden if he was not a member of Al-Qaeda.

Shortly after the meeting between Darkazanli and Alluni, lead 9/11 hijacker Muhammad Atta met Ramzi bin al-Shaibh, the 9/11 mastermind who had once been interviewed by Al-Jazeera's Yosri Fouda, in north-eastern Spain. Although they could not prove it, Spanish police were sure there was a link between Alluni's meeting with Darkazanli and the subsequent meeting between Ramzi bin al-Shaibh and Atta. If a link could be found, it would prove what the Spanish police suspected, that the Madrid Al-Qaeda cell had been instrumental in providing support for the 9/11 hijackers in the run-up to the attacks.

The charges also alleged that when Alluni was working as a translator for the Spanish news agency Efe, he provided money and support to Muhammad Baiah, also known as Abu Khaled. Abu Khaled, a suspected Al-Qaeda courier who was wanted by Turkish police, had stayed at Alluni's house in January 1998 and prosecutors allege that Alluni had allowed him to use his address and phone number fraudulently to apply for Spanish residency.

It was alleged that Abu Khaled's job was to funnel funds between Spain and Afghanistan for Al-Qaeda. Alluni, it was alleged, had carried funds for Al-Qaeda too. When he became Al-Jazeera's Kabul correspondent in 2000, ringleader Abu Dahdah supposedly gave him money to take to Afghanistan. Five wire-tapped phone calls in the indictment suggest Abu Dahdah was using Alluni to send money to Abu Khaled in Afghanistan. Worse still, Alluni was charged with recruiting young Muslims in Granada to become terrorists. Finally, court documents also alleged that Alluni's wife was the sister-in-law of Muhammad Haydar Zammar, a Syrian-born German in custody in Syria on suspicion of recruiting the 9/11 hijackers. Zammar was thought to be an intimate part of the support structure that helped the hijackers in the lead-up to the attacks.

At first Judge Garzón told the police there was insufficient evidence to support the allegations, but after six days of questioning, the maximum permitted under Spanish law, Alluni was charged with a list of terrorism-related offences, including being a 'prominent' member of Al-Qaeda. It was the second anniversary of 9/11 and on the same day Garzón issued charges against thirty-five other terror suspects, including Osama bin Laden. The charges against Alluni alleged, in effect, that Al-Qaeda had penetrated Al-Jazeera at the highest level.

Alluni admitted that he had carried some money, no more than $1000, from Spain to friends in Turkey and Afghanistan, on about five or six separate occasions, but he contested the accusation that it had been for Al-Qaeda. All the money that had passed through his hands, he said, was from Syrian nationals living in exile to other Syrians and it was being given out of a sense of solidarity, not for terrorism. Some of the money had been for a wedding.

Alluni admitted that he knew Abu Dahdah as well as some of the other Al-Qaeda suspects and that they had visited his home and he had helped them with their Spanish paperwork. But he claimed that – like taking money abroad as a gift or inviting foreign guests into your home – this normal Arab practice was now being taken out of its cultural context and was being presented as something suspicious. 'We are Muslim and our religion requires us to give a certain amount of money per year, a *zakat*, to the poor,' he said. (The Koran stipulates that Muslims must give a *zakat*, a portion of their annual income, to charity.) 'People from the community in Spain viewed the Afghans as very needy.'

Poor command of Arabic by the Spanish police had, Alluni said, contributed to the muddle. As regards bin Laden, he was just doing his job as a journalist. 'The accusations that I was helping finance Al-Qaeda are ridiculous,' Alluni said. 'Mr bin Laden is a multimillionaire, why would he need these small sums?' Besides, he pointed out, he had not been the only journalist to interview the terrorist chief. *Time* magazine, Britain's *Independent* newspaper, ABC News and CNN had all interviewed him in recent years.

The Arab media were quick to depict Alluni as an Arab Vaclav Havel. Within days there was a demonstration on his behalf outside the Spanish Embassy in Pakistan. Arab human rights organizations and journalists' federations condemned the arrest and called on the Spanish authorities to release him. Al-Jazeera anchors wore Alluni's face on badges with 'Free Taysir' printed on them as they delivered the news, and his face behind bars was shown during commercial breaks.

Al-Jazeera executives sprang to Alluni's defence with a high-profile campaign. Chief editor Ibrahim Hilal insisted that Alluni was being persecuted because he refused to cooperate when Western intelligence agencies asked him to become an inform-ant. Alluni's lawyer said his client was a victim of Western bias. Al-Jazeera chairman Sheikh Hamad bin Thamir Al Thani called the arrest a 'grave injustice' and urged the Spanish Prime Minister to intercede on Alluni's behalf. 'That a journalist has sources inside an underground organization is a cause for pride, not infamy and persecution,' he said.

This was 'only another link in a chain of pressures and perse-cutions against Al-Jazeera to try to influence its professional stance,' declared Jihad Ballout. 'For us, Alluni is an excellent journalist,' he added. 'We know nothing about his political ideas . . . that's something you will have to ask him,' he said. 'The arrest is all the more strange since over two months of holidays in Spain, Alluni interviewed several political leaders, including Prime Minister José Maria Aznar, and took part in several political meetings.'

It did not make sense, Ballout pointed out when I spoke about the case with him in Doha, that Alluni's meeting with bin Laden was regarded as so portentous when it had been Al-Jazeera's correspondent in Islamabad who had been invited to the marriage between bin Laden's son and Al-Zawahiri's daughter. That same correspondent had met bin Laden several times, yet he was not being charged.

'If a Westerner gets an interview with bin Laden, it's a scoop,' said Maher Abdullah, the host of Al-Jazeera's talk show *Religion and Life*. 'If it's an Arab, he becomes an associate. It's very racist, actually . . . It's going to make us very popular in the Arab world . . . It shows Spain and the liberal democracies are just as hypocritical about freedom of speech, and of journalists, as the countries in the Third World are. Maybe it will hurt us in the States, but in Europe, no.'

In an interview on Al-Jazeera, Alluni's wife, Fatima, pointed out that there had never been any problems between her husband and the Spanish authorities before. In fact, the Spanish Ambassador in Qatar had recently complimented Alluni on his balanced reporting. Interviewed by Al-Jazeera, she said:

I would like to say that when we were in Doha before the war on Iraq, the Spanish Ambassador summoned us along with all the Spaniards living in Doha to brief us on the war circumstances and the precautions that should be taken by the Spaniards living in an Arab state threatened to be struck by Saddam.

Taysir told the ambassador and another person from the embassy about the Spanish press reports. They told Taysir that he was useful for them and that his work and coverage of Afghanistan was excellent and neutral. They asked him whether he was going to Baghdad. He said what the press was saying differed from what they were saying. They told him that he should not care for what the press was saying, that he was welcome, and that there was nothing against him at all.

If her husband had had something to hide, Fatima Alluni said, he would never have come back to Spain.

The International Federation of Journalists described the arrest as 'the continuation of a concerted campaign against Arab media in general, and Al-Jazeera in particular. We think this arrest has more to do with political interests than criminal interests . . . Intimidating the messenger is no answer to the crisis of terrorism'.

Sections of the Spanish press were critical of Judge Garzón's decision to press charges against Alluni. An article and a cartoon appeared in the centre-right Spanish daily newspaper *El Mundo* questioning whether he had gone too far. A satirical cartoon depicted the judge as 'superstar Garzón', wearing only a toga, attempting to try Darth Vader.

After forty-eight days in jail Alluni was released on bail of six thousand euros, on health grounds. The fifty-six-year-old had recently undergone a serious heart operation. Under the conditions of the bail agreement the journalist could not leave the country without the permission of the court and had to check into a Spanish police station once a week.

Throughout the trial Al-Jazeera's Jihad Ballout was confident that Alluni would eventually be vindicated. 'There is a school of thought that Taysir Alluni's arrest has something to do with his contacts, with his journalistic activities and with his beliefs,' explained Ballout diplomatically. 'You have to remember that Taysir Alluni was in Afghanistan and he single-handedly told the world what happened and some people were unhappy about this. Taysir Alluni was one of our main correspondents in Iraq during the war.'

Ballout believes that the arrest may have been a way of interrogating Alluni about his contacts in Al-Qaeda. 'According to Taysir himself, when Taysir was first questioned almost all the questions were about his contacts,' Ballout told me. 'Who does he know? What exactly did bin Laden look like when you met him? Was his left hand injured? Was he walking properly? Was he using his stick? What kind of a stick? The first session had nothing to do with allegations against him. It was principally about the years he spent in Afghanistan.'

Ballout finds it telling that when Alluni stood before the judge seventy-two hours after he was first arrested, there was not enough evidence to charge him.

He stood before the investigative judge and because of lack of evidence – and this is a unique event in the history of Spanish law – he did not dismiss the case, but gave the authorities three more days to come up with a more solid case against Taysir.

If these guys had solid evidence, because he had been under surveillance for such a long time, you would have thought they would have a very tight case against him. This indicates to me, as it would to any observer, that they had no real case at that point.

Because of that, everybody including his lawyers and all the observers were expecting Taysir to be released. But what changed things 360 degrees was what they called 'information files' – one would assume these files were intelligence files – received from various countries including America and Israel.

Ballout refused to be drawn on the significance of this inter- vention by foreign intelligence services, saying only, 'The real issue is that the only way the judge could be comfortable in prolonging his arrest was in the light of files that were obtained from intelligence agencies in different countries. Perhaps that will tell you that the Spanish authorities in themselves did not have a solid case against him.'

The terrorist attacks in Madrid in March 2004 dramatically hardened the mood of the Spanish judges towards all the Al-Qaeda suspects. In December that year Alluni was rearrested and his health quickly deteriorated. Spanish judges said they deemed it necessary as they feared Alluni was liable to skip bail and flee the country. The Spanish Attorney-General ruled that should Alluni be found guilty, he deserved to serve no less than nine to twenty-five years in jail, a suggestion which horrified the broad coalition of human rights and media freedom groups who had by now united in Alluni's defence.

The beleaguered journalist spent the final months before his trial languishing in a maximum-security jail, together with some of Spain's most notorious gangsters and Basque separatists. Alluni spent 119 days in solitary confinement. As his heath worsened, calls grew for his bailed release on humanitarian grounds, but he was not let out until March 2005, just days before his trial began. Three factors brought about Alluni's release from prison: the involvement of the Qatari and Spanish governments; the appeals from Islamic and international organisations; and the International Solidarity Campaign to Free Alluni launched by Al-Jazeera. Arriving back home in Granada at three o'clock in the morning after a five-hour journey from jail, during which he was strapped to a metal chair in the back of a police van, Alluni was immediately placed under mandatory house arrest. It was clear the Spanish police were taking no chances.

As the trial drew near, a symposium of more than a hundred Spanish, European and Arab intellectuals and media professionals gathered to condemn Alluni's arrest and call for his immediate release. The symposium included representatives from Human Rights Watch, the International Federation of Journalists, Amnesty International, envoys from the Jordanian, Palestinian and Moroccan Journalists' Unions, and also cadres from various TV stations and newspapers.

Finally, in May the trial began. The Al-Jazeera correspondent denied the charges against him, but spoke at length about his meeting with Osama bin Laden. He told how he was blindfolded and taken to meet the terrorist mastermind by armed men, just days after the 9/11 attacks. 'I was taken out of the car, they removed the blindfold and there was bin Laden. He welcomed me and said that he was sorry for the inconvenience,' Alluni told the court. His defence team called on the judge to play the recordings of the bugged phone conversations, from which most of the prosecuting evidence had been drawn.

Alluni's lawyer pointed out that bin Laden could hardly have been said to have favoured Al-Jazeera over other news channels, since it had been the only channel present in Afghanistan at the time. Furthermore, he added, it had not even been Al-Jazeera who had aired the interview. It had been CNN, who had got hold of the tape through unknown circumstances, angering the Qatari network.

In his concluding remarks, the Spanish state prosecutor stated that although he remained unsure of the real nature of Alluni's links with Al-Qaeda, he had no doubt that when Alluni interviewed bin Laden, he was in fact 'interviewing his boss.'

At the end of September 2005 Alluni was sentenced to seven years in jail for collaborating with Al-Qaeda. This was in addition to the two years he had already spent under arrest. It had been a scoop too far. The court found that Alluni had been working for Al-Qaeda in exchange for interview access to its leaders, and that regardless of the journalistic material he may have produced as a result of this deal, the time had come for him to face the consequences of associating with terrorists. 'Journalistic truth, like all other truths, cannot be obtained at any price,' the 450-page judgment read. 'Taysir Alluni committed the wrongdoing of collaborating with a terrorist group and, for that, he must now pay.'

Abu Dahdah meanwhile, whose bugged telephone conversations with Alluni had provided vital evidence in the case, was sentenced to twenty-seven years in jail for commanding an Al-Qaeda cell and for collaborating with the 9/11 hijackers. The court did not agree with Alluni's claims that his relationship with Abu Dahdah was simply a way of accessing a secret and dangerous terrorist organisation. 'Taysir Alluni did not belong to the group led by Barakat [alias Abu Dahdah]. He possibly felt superior to it . . . but he collaborated with it,' the judgment read. They dismissed the argument that he had handled money out of an Islamic sense of duty. 'Taysir helped them, not out of that sense of helping which forms part of the favours that all good Muslims should do for their fellows, but in order to obtain . . . exclusive information on Al-Qaeda and the Taliban regime,' the judges ruled.

Mamoun Darkazanli, however, walked free after Germany's highest court ruled his European arrest-warrant invalid. His lawyers argued successfully that he could not be extradited to Spain, since the German constitution prohibits the extradition of German citizens. German Justice Minister Brigitte Zypries regretted the ruling, called it 'a blow for the government in its efforts and fight against terrorism'.

Al-Jazeera completely rejected Alluni's guilty verdict. So did most of the rest of the press in the Arab world, where the case had widely been viewed from the very start as political rather than criminal. The arrest was assumed to have been made at the behest of the Americans. The international press freedom organisations also rejected the verdict. 'It sets a dangerous precedent, particularly for anyone who seeks to interview bin Laden in the future,' said a spokesman from Reporters sans Frontières. 'Journalists have always investigated terrorist groups. It's part of our job.'

It is notable that although Alluni was found guilty of giving the Syrians $4500 in cash, the court failed to prove that he knew that they were members of Al-Qaeda. Being a Syrian himself, Alluni may have passed on the money to his compatriots innocently. There is certainly nothing unusual about handling cash in Afghanistan, since at this time there were not any cash machines, functioning banks or means to wire money throughout the whole country.

It seems strange too that so much emphasis was placed on Alluni's interview with bin Laden, since many journalists have interviewed him and never before has it been regarded as criminal. At one point the judge even said it was suspicious that Al-Jazeera had sent Alluni to Afghanistan. As a journalist, Alluni clearly had a professional reason to travel to Afghanistan and interview bin Laden, and the judge's assertion that Alluni was interviewing his boss does not seem to fit with the questions Alluni asked at the time. Despite being in an environment of intimidation, Alluni asked amongst other things why Al-Qaeda kills civilians. This is not a soft or easy question.

Al-Jazeera appealed against the verdict, but in June 2006 Spain's Supreme Court upheld the ruling. Personally, although I do not know whether Taysir Alluni collaborated with Al-Qaeda or not, I was surprised he was found guilty. I did not think the evidence convicted him beyond reasonable doubt and nothing he did seemed to merit seven years in prison (plus two years waiting for trial).

The verdict must be seen in the context of a continued campaign against Al-Jazeera around the world. The American administration, in particular, has confessed to having deliberately targeted Alluni in the past. US missiles blew up the Kabul bureau where he was working in 2001. There was certainly enormous political pressure to see one of Al-Jazeera's star reporters go behind bars – Alluni was stingily critical of American foreign policy, a devout Muslim, a charismatic emblem of the channel, and his reports of civilian casualties in Afghanistan had seriously undermined the coalition's case for the War on Terror.

Whatever Alluni did or did not do the verdict is undoubtedly a blow against journalism, particularly Arab journalism. Listing the bin Laden interview on the charge sheet is a strike against freedom of expression and is reminiscent of the worst days of the Franco dictatorship or McCarthyism in America. The fact that Alluni conducted the first interview with bin Laden after 9/11 should be grounds for praise, not persecution. By comparison the Western journalists who have met with bin Laden have had no doubts raised about their motives.

Meanwhile, Alluni remains a salaried member of the network's editorial team, even from behind bars. Al-Jazeera continues to pay his lawyer's fees and all related expenses.

Once again mounting pressure on Al-Jazeera seemed to make no impact on its reporting. On the same day that Alluni was charged, another video showing bin Laden and Al-Zawahiri was aired. This one was almost surreal in its seeming innocence, as the pair wandered in pretty woodland, carrying walking sticks and AK-47s as they plotted more terror attacks. An audio-tape featuring just Al-Zawahiri also ran on Al-Jazeera, calling on Iraqis to resist the occupation. 'Rely on God and devour the Americans, like lions devour their prey,' Al-Zawahiri said. 'Bury them in the Iraqi graveyard.' Both tapes, which were of markedly higher quality than in the past, received saturation coverage on Western networks. As usual, Al-Jazeera would not divulge how it had obtained the tapes. Two days later the network broadcast a long extract from the same video, of one of the 9/11 hijackers reading his will and exhorting Muslims to fight America.

Throughout the summer Al-Jazeera had suffered increased harassment from the authorities in Iraq, including threats, attacks and imprisonment. It had failed to make any impression on its reporting. Finally, at the end of September, firm action was taken. Ostensibly, it was the Iraqi Governing Council who took the decision to punish both Al-Jazeera and Al-Arabiya, although it was popularly believed, rightly or wrongly, that the real decision to move had been taken by the Americans. 'We believe that these two channels have played a leading role in sowing sectarian and racial sedition in Iraq,' said a spokesman for the Governing Council. 'They also advocate political violence and killing GC [Governing Council] members and coalition troops. They also promote the aides of Saddam and air pictures of masked men threatening to kill the GC members. They also employ some of the former regime's henchmen,' he said. The spokesman produced a list of rules that the two networks had violated as he spoke. 'We will not let them broadcast footage of US soldiers being ripped apart,' he added.

Later that day, in an interview on Al-Jazeera, another Governing Council spokesman also accused Al-Jazeera of broadcasting hidden messages to militants. 'Some of the messages of terrorists broadcast by Al-Jazeera and Al-Arabiya were actually coded messages to carry out certain operations,' he claimed, but he did not provide any evidence of this.

The Governing Council had initially intended to expel both the channels, but this was moderated at the last moment. Instead both Al-Jazeera and Al-Arabiya were told they could not cover any official activities in Iraq for two weeks and if the networks did not change their editorial policy, it was made clear, fines or expulsion would follow. In an attempt to show that the Governing Council could act independently of the coalition, Proconsul Bremer implausibly claimed he knew nothing about the ban before the Governing Council imposed it, but the heavy hand of the CPA was clearly visible to Iraqis. The ban, which served further to diminish credibility for the Governing Council, which many Iraqis already viewed as an illegitimate gang of sycophants, was a watershed for the media in post-war Iraq. The move undermined the Council's calls for democracy, which cannot exist without a free press, and its stated independence from the US administration. Many Arab observers stated that they could now see that life under the coalition was similar in spirit, if not in practice, to life under Saddam Hussein.

Al-Jazeera staff were unimpressed by the moves against them, but they had no choice but to comply. Baghdad bureau chief Waddah Khanfar, for example, said in an interview with Doha:

> Our viewers should know how the private and Arab news media are being treated. The Iraqi Governing Council's statement today included a host of unsubstantiated ideas. The statement speaks about abstaining from incitement to violence against individuals and groups and incitement to violence against the ruling authorities and its officials. I do not know what they mean by this. They did not accuse us of any specific incident. There is no defined legal

framework within which one can discuss these matters. These are just a group of general ideas that could become a sword brandished at our necks that might scare us at times and scare those working in other fields too. This will result in conveying half the truth.

'This decision is without any doubt a blow to press freedom,' said Reporters sans Frontières in a statement. 'When media such as Al-Jazeera and Al-Arabiya give a voice to extremist political parties calling for violent and armed acts, they themselves are not guilty of inciting violence.'

At the same time as the Governing Council issued the ban on the two networks, a new set of rules for all the media was announced, 'in order to allow them to continue working in Iraq'. The media also had a responsibility, the Governing Council's security chief said, to hand over information about 'any violent action that aims to breed disorder and fear'.

'Will the journalist become an informer?' demanded Waddah Khanfar scornfully. 'If he gets any information, should he rush to inform the authorities? Where is the law that protects the sources of information of the journalists? We know the laws that are exercised in free countries. What about democracy in this field?'

As winter approached, unsubstantiated accusations against Al-Jazeera continued to issue forth from the halls of Washington and on the streets of Baghdad, where American soldiers continued to harass and arrest Al-Jazeera's staff. So relentless was the pressure on Al-Jazeera that, for the first time in its history, some viewers thought they could see signs that it was buckling under the pressure and toning down its reports of resistance in Iraq to placate America. Articles appeared in the Kuwaiti and Saudi press claiming that evidence had been uncovered proving that the American administration had decided to silence the network once and for all. A story began in a quality Kuwaiti newspaper, quoting an unnamed, Gulf-based US diplomat, who claimed Congress had instructed President Bush to put 'all possible pressure' on the Qatari government to shut Al-Jazeera down for good.

The article stated that a number of meetings had taken place over the summer at the headquarters of the Security Intelligence Committee of the House of Representatives attended by key members of Congress, the Pentagon, the Department of State, the FBI and the CIA. According to the piece, during the meetings, which concerned 'US-Qatari relations in light of the role Al-Jazeera has played in inciting anti-US sentiment', representatives discussed the problem of Al-Jazeera's flagrant promotion of terrorist groups, including Al-Qaeda. It was agreed that the network deliberately set out to harm American interests both at home and abroad, especially in Iraq and Afghanistan, and that something had to be done.

The purpose of these meetings, the paper quoted the diplomat as saying, was to establish how America could pressure the Qataris into cracking down on Al-Jazeera to make it change its editorial policy. Various possible sanctions were postulated, including cutting off US economic support to Qatar, moving the Al-Udeid airbase elsewhere or annulling the fifty-year US-Qatar defence treaty, leaving Qatar at the mercy of its neighbours. On the second anniversary of September 11, the American diplomat was quoted as saying, the committee unanimously decided to advise the President to instruct the Qataris to close down Al-Jazeera altogether and, if that proved impossible, Al-Jazeera should at least be forced to replace its current staff with journalists who were 'moderate and neutral'.

This poorly substantiated story was almost certainly apocryphal. For a start, the exciting-sounding 'Security Intelligence Committee of the House of Representatives', where the decision to shut down Al-Jazeera was supposedly reached, does not exist. Secondly, the idea that America could force Qatar to close Al-Jazeera by threatening to withdraw its economic support is fanciful – Qatar is massively wealthy and does not receive economic support from America or anyone else. Nevertheless, the story was repeated and distributed via email and in the press, with the result that shock waves rocketed through the Arab media and into Al-Jazeera's newsrooms.

The rumour that America had finally managed to exert its influence on Al-Jazeera by squeezing the Qataris rippled through the Arab world and for a couple of months everything that happened to the network was seen in this light. Shortly after the article appeared, Al-Jazeera took down from its website two satirical cartoons about the American occupation in Iraq, an action that was widely cited as 'proof' that Al-Jazeera had been tamed by America. One of the cartoons showed the Twin Towers exploding then being replaced by two giant gas pumps rising out of the ground. The second cartoon, captioned 'Green card soldiers', showed young Latino men waiting in an immigration line being turned into soldiers heading for Iraq.

When the British journalist Yvonne Ridley, one of Al-Jazeera's most anti-American reporters, well known for her speeches vilifying George Bush, was fired, again this was widely assumed to be at the instigation of the CIA. Ridley had become a high-profile figure in the Muslim world after being captured by the Taliban while trying to sneak into Afghanistan in disguise. She had been working as a journalist for the *Sunday Express* at the time. She later converted to Islam. She claimed subsequently in her book that the CIA had been responsible for her imprisonment by deliberately leaking false documents to the Taliban that framed her as a Mossad spy.

After converting to Islam, Ridley became the senior editor of the Al-Jazeera English-language website, where she was well known for her anti-American bent. Her last article before she was fired was about American soldiers abusing Iraqi women and children while conducting house-to-house searches. She sent a photograph of a seven-year-old Iraqi girl in plastic hand restraints to the US military in Florida for comment. She was warned by the military not to publish the photo, but she did so. When she was dismissed a short time later, her supporters immediately pointed to America as the reason.

When Al-Jazeera shuffled its management around, again this

was taken as a sure sign of America's influence at work. Waddah Khanfar, formerly the Baghdad bureau chief, replaced Adnan al-Sharif, who had been acting managing director. Khanfar, a Jordanian of Palestinian origin, had been Al-Jazeera's correspondent first in Africa, then, during the war in Afghanistan, he had been its man in New Delhi, India. His posting to New Delhi was more important than it looked at first glance: during the Afghan war Al-Jazeera had no correspondent in Northern Alliance-held territories in Afghanistan, but obviously needed to have a relationship with them, since they were one of the belligerents. There was a heavy Northern Alliance presence in India, because India had supported the Alliance against the Taliban long before 9/11, so Khanfar cultivated an important relationship with Alliance members there, without which Al-Jazeera would have been exclusively dependent on their sharing agreement with CNN for access to that side of the war.

At the end of the Afghan war, Taysir Alluni left Kabul and Khanfar became Al-Jazeera's new Kabul bureau chief. During the war in Iraq Khanfar had been Al-Jazeera's correspondent in Kurdistan and had been a major irritant to the Iraqi regime. When the war was over, he became the chief of the Baghdad bureau. Conspiracy theorists took note of the comment by Al-Jazeera's chief editor, that he hoped Khanfar's appointment would fortify the relationship between the network and the American authorities in Iraq.

In November, on Al-Jazeera's seventh birthday, there were even more changes among the senior management. 'We have a new manager and new board of directors and certain reorganizations,' Jihad Ballout told AFP. The appointments, he said, were made on the orders of the Emir, to 'enhance the station's capabilities and ensure the standards of professionalism'.

The role of Sheikh Hamad bin Thamir Al Thani as chairman, and those of his deputy and the heads of finance and administrative affairs, remained unchanged. A Lebanese was appointed to the board of directors – the first time a non-Qatari had held the post. Muhammad Jasim al-Ali, Al-Jazeera's general manager, who had been mentioned in Chalabi's spy allegations earlier in the year, left the channel. 'The changes are normal, just like any organization, and it does not indicate a shift in editorial policy. On the contrary, everything is being geared towards maintaining Al-Jazeera's initial ethos of "The opinion and the other opinion",' Ballout said.

At the same time Al-Jazeera launched its sports channel. This meant the regular Al-Jazeera news channel no longer covered sport, which made more room for news and current affairs programming.

These administrative changes provoked rampant speculation that Al-Jazeera had now been utterly beguiled by the CIA. The evidence to support this is pretty thin. The acid test, of course, would have been whether the news coming out of Iraq had softened towards America – and there was scant evidence of that. Al-Jazeera was undoubtedly under massive pressure to tone down its reporting, but it did not. As if to prove this, in October another bin Laden audio-tape was broadcast. This was an important development, as the tape was obviously recent and carried detailed information about what Al-Qaeda was planning to do in the medium term. The tape contained a serious, strategic, political statement, which spoke specifically about recent events in Iraq, internal Palestinian politics and the Iraqi Governing Council. It showed that bin Laden was not just still alive, but actively following world events while planning his next move. It also showed that any influence America might have had over Al-Jazeera had dissipated as quickly as it appeared.

Before long the American administration was once again blaming Al-Jazeera for inciting resistance in Iraq with what it alleged was inaccurate and downright deceitful reporting. 'At the present time, two of the most popular stations, Al-Arabiya and Al-Jazeera, are, you know, just violently anti-coalition, and were pro-Saddam Hussein in the case of Al-Jazeera in such an obvious way,' Rumsfeld said during a speech at the Pentagon in November.

Three days after Rumsfeld's outburst twenty Iraqi policemen burst into Al-Arabiya's Baghdad bureau and seized transmitting equipment and satellite phones. The network was being closed down on the orders of the Iraqi Governing Council for broadcasting another tape featuring the voice of Saddam.

Rumsfeld then claimed that both Al-Arabiya and Al-Jazeera had links to the Iraqi resistance and that both channels knew in advance of attacks on coalition troops. 'They've called Al-Jazeera to come and watch them do it, and Al-Arabiya. Come and see us, watch us when we – here's what we're going to do,' Rumsfeld told a news briefing at the Pentagon. Asked if American troops had any evidence that these channels were cooperating with the resistance, he replied, 'The answer is yes, I've seen scraps of information over a sustained period of time that need to be looked at in a responsible, orderly way . . . I opined, accurately, that from time to time, each of those stations have found themselves in close proximity to things that were happening to coalition forces, before the event happened, and during the event.' But the Defense Secretary supplied no evidence to support his accusations. Never had either of the news channels captured an attack on the coalition 'live'.

Around the same time that Rumsfeld was making these accusations, an Al-Jazeera cameraman was arrested by American troops after a roadside bomb attack against an American military convoy near the Iraqi town of Baquba. The cameraman, Salah Hassan, was taken for interrogation to a police station, where soldiers repeatedly accused him of having advance knowledge of attacks on coalition troops. Hassan told the soldiers that if they checked his tapes they would be able to tell that he had not arrived on the scene until some thirty minutes after the attack happened.

The soldiers did not believe him and Hassan was driven from the police station in Baquba to the large American military base at Baghdad airport and locked in a bathroom for two days. Then he was hooded and bound and flown to Tikrit, where he spent a further two days in another bathroom, before being driven south in a convoy of trucks, with a group of other prisoners, to the jail whose name, although notorious under Saddam

Hussein, was before long to achieve international infamy under the Americans: Abu Ghraib. Although the management had changed, as Hassan was about to find out, torture was still standard policy at America's principal military detention centre in Iraq.

When Hassan arrived at Abu Ghraib he was still hooded and bound. American soldiers stripped him naked and sang 'Happy Birthday' to him, then beat and tortured him. Addressed only as 'Jazeera', 'boy' or 'bitch,' he was made to stand outside for eleven hours at a time, in the cold November night air. Then he was dressed in a dirty red jumpsuit covered in someone else's fresh vomit, before being interrogated by two American civilians. They repeated the allegations made when he was arrested, that he had prior knowledge of terrorist attacks. Hassan told them to check his tapes, which would show that he had not arrived until afterwards. After he had been interrogated Hassan was locked in a tiny isolation cell, where he listened to the wailing of old women and a mentally disabled teenage girl down the corridor.

Al-Jazeera, meanwhile, hired a top Iraqi lawyer to try to get Hassan out. The lawyer managed to force the case into Iraq's newly established Federal Supreme Court, set up to try war criminals. Hassan's case was the first the court ever heard. When he was tried in front of members of the Governing Council, all the charges against him were dropped for lack of evidence. Hopes that he might then be freed, however, were dashed when, after the verdict, Hassan was taken back to Abu Ghraib. There he was subjected to another round of torture lasting three days, before being taken to the edge of Baghdad and unceremoni-ously dumped, still wearing the vomit-strewn jumpsuit. He had been incarcerated for more than a month.

Hassan was one of two Al-Jazeera staff who served time inside Abu Ghraib that November – the other Al-Jazeera employee, a cameraman named Suhaib al-Samarrai, was in Abu Ghraib for more than two months. Few in the West believed their stories at the time, probably because they were Arabs, perhaps because they worked for Al-Jazeera.

In recent months there has been no respite in the harassment of Al-Jazeera's reporters in Iraq, nor any end to the anti-Al-Jazeera rhetoric issuing out of Washington. In January 2004 Al-Jazeera was banned again from covering 'official events' in Iraq by the interim authorities. The ban lasted a month. Since then Donald Rumsfeld has described Al-Jazeera as 'consistently lying' and 'working in concert with terrorists'. He has declared Al-Jazeera to be 'violently anti-coalition' and has accused the network of causing 'great damage and harm in Iraq by continuously broadcasting wrong and inaccurate information, impairing what the coalition forces are trying to achieve in Iraq'. National Security Adviser Condoleezza Rice has accused Al-Jazeera of 'purely inaccurate' reporting and of presenting a biased account of developments in the Middle East. Colin Powell has called Al-Jazeera 'horrible' and 'slanted', and Department of State spokesman Richard Boucher has said Al-Jazeera has 'established a very clear pattern of false and inflammatory reporting' and has been 'using it to try to inflame the situation'.

Little by way of solid evidence has been produced to substantiate these allegations. The Coalition Provisional Authority did say it had compiled a 'list of false and misleading reports' by Al-Jazeera, but the list was never made public, since it was said to contain 'sensitive information'.

By April 2004, twenty-one Al-Jazeera journalists had been held and released by American troops in Iraq. So, when Qatar's foreign minister, Sheikh Hamad bin Jasim bin Jabr Al Thani, paid a visit to Washington, unsurprisingly Colin Powell once again took the opportunity to have what he termed 'intense and candid' discussions about Al-Jazeera's output with him. Besides being Qatar's foreign minister, Sheikh Hamad is also a major shareholder in Al-Jazeera. Powell lodged an official complaint, telling reporters at the Department of State that the channel's coverage was spoiling America's relationship with Qatar. Al-Jazeera, he made clear, was part of the problem, rather than part of the solution in Iraq.

A few days later Sheikh Hamad told reporters in Washington

that having listened to the Secretary Powell's concerns, as well as those of Defense Secretary Rumsfeld and Vice President Cheney, he would ask that Al-Jazeera's output be reviewed. 'We will take this concern back to Al-Jazeera and they have to review it because we need Al-Jazeera to be professional and we don't want anybody to send lies or to send wrong information,' he told press at the White House. At the same time he stressed he was not a spokesman for Al-Jazeera and that the Qatari government was not responsible for its output.

One of the things US officials were particularly angry about was Al-Jazeera's allegations about prisoner abuse in Iraq, which they said were inflaming Iraqi passions against the occupation. Only a few days later, pictures published in the *New Yorker* magazine revealed that what had happened to the two Al-Jazeera employees in Abu Ghraib had, in fact, happened to many others at the hands of American troops. An episode of *The Opposite Direction* went on to ask the question whether torture in Arab jails was not far worse than that which had been uncovered at Abu Ghraib. Eighty-six per cent of respondents agreed that torture in Arab jails was worse.

Three months after Sheikh Hamad bin Jasim bin Jabr Al Thani's promise to Colin Powell that Al-Jazeera would be reviewed, the network issued a new 'code of ethics', the first for an Arab news station. The code committed the network to drawing a line between news and commentary, to avoid 'the trap of propaganda and speculation', and always to strive to keep key values, like transparency, honesty and balance, in focus. It was intended as an internal document, not a press release, but it was seized on by the world's press, discussed, and to a great extent, praised.

Al-Jazeera was keen to point out that it had been adhering to these values since it had begun broadcasting, eight years previously, but since the company had grown substantially since then – to include more than seventy correspondents in twenty-three bureaux on five continents – the time had come to formalize these rules. At the same time that Al-Jazeera announced its new code, it set up an internal department to monitor its own output, to measure how it was living up to the principles it had set itself.

Meanwhile in Iraq, despite working under tremendous pressure, with staff beaten, shot at, bombed, threatened, intimidated and their equipment confiscated, Al-Jazeera continued to capture breaking news. It did not cease broadcasting tapes from Al-Qaeda, nor from the Iraqi insurgents, including dozens of videotapes of hostages taken in Iraq. The network received and aired many tapes, showing violent executions, including several decapitations, though contrary to what some have said, the network never broadcast the actual moment of death. Nor did the network shy away from screening hard-hitting reports depicting the coalition as heavy-handed in its handling of the occupation. Pictures have shown American soldiers arresting and blindfolding people, evicting women and children from their homes and demolishing buildings. In Falluja Al-Jazeera reported American snipers shooting at women and children, reports denied by the Americans, but corroborated by other international observers in the city. Al-Jazeera's relationship with the American administration has deteriorated to a new low.

These reports have come at a high price. On 21 May 2004 during a shoot-out between American troops and Iraqi militia men, another Al Jazeera journalist was killed. Rashid Hamid Wali, an assistant cameraman, was peering over the roof of his hotel in Karbala to look down into the street, where he had heard US armour start moving, when he was shot in the left eye. The bullet passed out of the back of his head and he died instantly. He had been working in Iraq for just over a year and had six children, the eldest of whom was just sixteen. It was not clear who fired the shot.

Following the handover of sovereignty in Iraq to a new government headed by Prime Minister Iyad Allawi, Al-Jazeera was once again heavily criticized for threatening the security of the country. Eventually, on 7 August 2004, to loud cries of outrage from around the world, armed policemen forcibly closed down the Al-Jazeera bureau in Baghdad and banned the network from operating in Iraq for one month. The Iraqi interior ministry asked the lawyer representing Al-Jazeera to sign an order agreeing to change its reporting policy in Iraq, which he refused to do.

How could the interim Iraqi government claim to be representing press freedom and the rights of journalists in a liberated Iraq, when the Arab world's most prestigious news agency was being repeatedly harassed and banned? shrieked international news organizations in unison, including the Iraqi Union of Journalists, Reporters sans Frontières and the International Federation of Journalists. A broad selection of the Western press condemned Allawi's decision too.

Ironically, when Allawi banned Al-Jazeera for its alleged pro-resistance stance in Iraq, Iraqis claiming to represent the resistance were simultaneously threatening the network for being too pro-American. They had also warned in the days just prior to the ban, that if Al-Jazeera continued with its pro-American coverage, they would target employees at the Baghdad bureau.

While Al-Jazeera was under pressure from both sides in Iraq, there was no let-up in the problems the network's correspondents faced in other parts of the world. In Palestine, callers identifying themselves as Palestinian Authority security men and Fatah activists warned Al-Jazeera staff that they should stop covering the intra-Palestinian fighting and anti-corruption protests against Arafat's Palestinian Authority in the Gaza strip, or face the consequences. Yasser Arafat was struggling to retain control of Gaza when demonstrations had broken out against an appointment of one of his close relatives as his security chief.

Following Al-Jazeera's coverage of the atrocities committed in the Darfur region of Sudan, the network's bureau chief in Khartoum was arrested and charged with defaming the state, false reporting and customs violations, effectively shutting the bureau down. He was fined and served seventeen days in prison. The head of Al-Jazeera's Moscow bureau was denied a visa to go to Latvia, to report on its accession to the European Union, for no apparent reason. The authorities froze Al-Jazeera's operations in Algeria indefinitely, after a discussion criticized the

President's national reconciliation programme. The plan involved a partial amnesty for several thousand Muslim extremists in an attempt to end Algeria's long-running civil war.

In the UK, Al-Jazeera drew widespread condemnation when it aired a video from one of the four suicide attackers behind the devastating London bombings of 7 July. In the message, Yorkshireman Mohammad Sidique Khan declared he was 'a soldier' inspired by Osama bin Laden. In a second message on the same tape, Al-Qaeda's Ayman al-Zawahiri claimed responsibility for the blasts.

There was also no sign of a let-up in Al-Jazeera's steady expansion. A one-woman bureau opened in Hong Kong, the bureau in Turkey expanded considerably and a new Nordic bureau opened in Oslo. The Al-Jazeera website was shortlisted for a prestigious Webby award and, in July 2004, Al-Jazeera announced plans for a possible floatation on the stock market in Doha. The board of directors commissioned a feasibility study by external consultants, to see whether a transfer of ownership might help Al-Jazeera turn a profit – something it was still yet to do.

In November 2005 a shocking scoop by the British tabloid newspaper, the *Daily Mirror*, threw new light on the attacks and harassment Al-Jazeera had suffered in the past at the hands of the American administration. According to the newspaper, on 16 April 2004, President Bush suggested to Prime Minister Blair that it might be a good idea to bomb Al-Jazeera headquarters in Qatar.

There were suggestions that this may have been meant as a joke but, while Blair's office declined all comment, the White House reacted angrily. Significantly, however, it did not quite deny the existence of the memo altogether. 'We are not interested in dignifying something so outlandish and inconceivable with a response,' declared White House spokesman Scott McClellan. But for Al-Jazeera, an American plan to bomb them again was far from inconceivable.

The comment was allegedly made in April 2004, when Al-

Jazeera was the only international news organization within Fallujah. At the time, American troops were laying siege to the city, which has a population of about 300,000 people. Correspondent Ahmed Mansour and two cameramen were inside, transmitting about 30 to 50 minutes of exclusive live footage each day. This included graphic pictures of dead women and children, totally contradicting what the world was hearing from the US military spokesmen at the same time. The tension between Al-Jazeera and the American administration was at a peak.

While the American media were reporting that Iraqi civilians were being allowed to leave because there was a ceasefire, Al-Jazeera was reporting that US airplanes were still relentlessly bombing them. Most controversially of all, Al-Jazeera repeatedly alleged that American helicopters and snipers were firing on ambulances, civilians and civilian vehicles – something independently corroborated by other sources, including Dar Al Salam Arabic radio, Knight Ridder, New Standard, UPI, Al-Arabiya and others – but strenuously denied by the US military.

At the time, US officials publicly and vigorously attacked Al-Jazeera. Among them were Vice President Dick Cheney and Pentagon chief Donald Rumsfeld, who accused the network's correspondents of aiding rebels. The following August, Al-Jazeera was banned from Iraq.

On hearing the news of the memo, Al-Jazeera's managing director Waddah Khanfar promptly flew to London at once to lodge his complaint in person. Unfortunately for him, Tony Blair was in the Caribbean at the time, giving Her Majesty's government the perfect excuse to refuse Khanfar an audience with the Prime Minister.

News soon followed that two civil servants were to be prosecuted over the leak of the document: David Keogh, who worked at the Cabinet Office, and Leo O'Connor, a researcher for Labour MP Tony Clarke. The British government were desperate that all further details of this damaging story be suppressed but rather than try and sue the *Mirror* for breach of confidence, which would doubtless have evoked a cast-iron public-interest defence, they decided to invoke the recently updated Official Secrets Act.

Section 3 of the Official Secrets Act, or OSA, states that a crown servant is guilty of a criminal offence if he or she makes a damaging disclosure relating to international relations without lawful authority, where they came by that information because of their position in government. Under Section 5 of the act, a person who receives such information from such a person is guilty of a criminal offence if he or she then discloses it knowing it is protected under the OSA.

After the prosecution had been announced, the government fell silent. Only the Attorney General Lord Goldsmith spoke to threaten the rest of the British media that should they reveal the memo's content further, they could expect to be charged using the OSA. Despite international offers to publish the memo in full, from publications ranging from *Spectator* magazine to the Blairwatch UK blog, few further details from the memo have appeared. Meanwhile, the court case against the two civil servants has begun. David Keogh and Leo O'Connor have been charged under the OSA with passing and receiving secret documents and both have pleaded not guilty. The opening session of the trial was held behind closed doors. Foreign Secretary Jack Straw requested that the whole proceedings be tried *in camera*.

One other clue to the contents of the memo comes from a request under the Freedom of Information Act, made by British blogger Steve Wood. Wood asked the Cabinet Office for more details of the conversation between Bush and Blair about bombing Al-Jazeera. While refusing to reveal details, the Cabinet Office did confirm that they do hold information relevant to the request. Given the very specific nature of the question, this is the first official confirmation that a memo of such a conversation actually exists, contradicting statements by the Prime Minister's official spokesman in January 2006 when Al-Jazeera made a similar request. Then Blair's spokesman had replied that to the best of his knowledge there had been no conversation between Bush and Blair about bombing Al-Jazeera in Qatar.

The four-page memo was written by Britain's Ambassador in Washington, Sir David Manning, and classified 'Top Secret'. Such a classification, in a wartime situation, would not have been undertaken lightly. It means publishing the memo in full would do serious damage to Britain's public interest. Presumably it contains information that, had it been fully leaked, would be very damaging – why the Green Zone in Iraq is so vulnerable for example, or details of how to differentiate between friendly and enemy vehicles in Iraq. Possibly there is more frank information about the US assault on Fallujah. British Generals were known to be concerned about heavy-handed US tactics during the siege.

Publishing this kind of information would also be a legal risk. Under the OSA, if the document is considered to be a threat to national security, civil servants and security personnel have no public interest defence, although the media may well do. Information about who exactly has seen the memo has been confused further because while some of the protagonists in the story claim to have actually seen the original memo, others seem only to have seen a praece.

It is possible that the document was over-classified to protect politicians' embarrassment, but this is unlikely. 'Top Secret' documents tend to be so for a reason. It would certainly not be 'Top Secret' to save Bush from embarrassment as that is not in the British national interest. In fact Tony Blair comes out of this rather well, as the moderating force who uses his influence to rein in the bloodthirsty President.

It seems unlikely, however, that what Bush said was a joke. A one-liner would not have made the record. Nor is it likely to be an off-the-cuff remark. Bush would not have suggested bombing Al-Jazeera to Blair unless he had already cleared this as a viable solution with his own people.

There is a chance the memo will make its way into the public domain, in full, soon. In the era of information, it is hard to keep things suppressed for long, especially as the Internet under-mines traditional concepts about responsibility for publication. Al-Jazeera certainly intends to get to the bottom of this, together with help from British law firm Finers Stephens Innocent LLP.

Downing Street has been stalling. They did not respond to Al-Jazeera's Freedom of Information Act request within the twenty-working-day period defined under the law. Nevertheless, the network remains optimistic that the contents of the memo will be disclosed sooner or later and, when it is, they expect that some incidents in Al-Jazeera's troubled history may be cast in a new light. 'The lawyers are optimistic the memo will even-tually be revealed, it's rather a question of when. It is not really expected the memo will come out during the upcoming trial,' said a network spokeswoman.

Perhaps the only thing that has become clearer since this murky story emerged is that dropping a bomb on Al-Jazeera would be no less incendiary than dropping a bomb on Qatar's mammoth North Field gas reserves. If Arab hearts and minds are the secret to the War on Terror then America could consider such an act the end of its campaign.

10

Free Speech and the Domino Effect

In the West it has become an article of faith that a freer Arab media heralds social and political change in the Middle East. Optimists theorize that satellite TV will sweep away traditional Arab obstacles to progress and dissolve seemingly intractable problems and that an 'Islamic Glasnost' will ensue. One Jordanian politician I met, who has written extensively about human rights and the freedom of the press, told me he thought Al-Jazeera was the first step towards an Arab version of the European Union. 'Of course Al-Jazeera is bringing democracy,' he told me. 'Before we had been ignorant about how Arabs lived in other countries; now Jordanians know and care about events on the other side of the world.'

But to believe that satellite television is automatically going to make Arab societies democratic is to presume that the current state of affairs in the Arab world results from an information deficiency, which is not true. Except in the most authoritarian Arab countries, the news has long been available to the determined via the radio, and that never brought about much democracy. In Algeria the press has gone so far as to threaten to sue the President, but no one would say that Algeria's military dictatorship is very democratic.

Many Arabs I met told me that the explosion of new media in the Middle East is simply tranquillizing them. With so much talk about Al-Jazeera, it is easy to forget that the most popular shows on Arab television are Egyptian and Lebanese soap operas and films, as well as imported Western game shows. *Who Wants to Be a Millionaire?* is one of the biggest hits of recent years, presented by a debonair Lebanese sex symbol. His catchphrase is 'Jawaab nihaa'i?', or 'Is that your final answer?' I found locals glued to WWF wrestling in several Jordanian cafés I visited. Stony-faced old men sat around staring impassively, as steroid-pumped American men in plastic pants heaved each other around the ring and beat their chests.

In the gloomiest analysis, some assert that the information revolution might actually be bolstering oppressive Arab regimes' control over their people: the public vents its anger on Al-Jazeera's talk shows, while real power remains entrenched in the hands of the regime. As Dr Mamoun Fandi, a respected Arab writer and professor at the US government's National Defense University in Washington DC, put it:

> I am very concerned about the mushrooming of satellite television in the Arab world where the media becomes the arena for politics rather than actual politics. This is sort of living vicariously through the media. That is not actual living. This is vicarious politics, this is virtual politics.
>
> Governments in the Arab world are encouraging that trend whereby the media becomes a substitute for real politics . . . You allow people to participate in harmless politics, politics that does not lead to any serious political change. So everybody is happy. The Arabs are happy that they see themselves on television the same way that as a child I was very happy to discover the Polaroid. Snap, yes, I do exist.

Fandi has a point: if someone in Egypt or Saudi Arabia watching Al-Jazeera changes their mind about a certain issue there is still no political mechanism in place for them to do anything about it. They cannot go out and vote in an election or join a political party, so the impact of Al-Jazeera on the viewer is not automatically translated into the process of democratic change, the way it might be in the West. This is an important point, but it is not Al-Jazeera's fault and does not mean that the channel has no impact on the democratic process at all. A free press is an important piece of the jigsaw.

Power in the Arab world remains concentrated in the hands of the same individuals and small elite groups who have handled matters of state for decades. Until January 2006 when Hamas won in Palestine, not one leader of an Arab nation was fairly and freely elected; indeed, no other region in the world – not even sub-Saharan Africa – has such a poor record. Most Arab governments still regard the media as a handy tool for packaging and falsifying information for their public. By evoking emergency state laws they can shut down dissenting newspapers and arrest journalists as they like. Arab press unions, like Arab opposition political parties, are prevented from growing strong. 'The media,' wrote the Arab poet Ahmad Matar, 'is a means of torture.'

In recent years there have been signs of change in the media in the Middle East. Where before Arab governments controlled the information flow, today Arab satellite dishes can access about fifty major Arabic-language channels and many more from Europe and America. Many of these new TV stations are simply Arabic versions of successful Western channels. The other Arab satellite news channels which have sprung up in recent years, like Abu Dhabi TV and Al-Arabiya, are clear imitations of Al-Jazeera. Other, established channels, like the LBC (Lebanese Broadcasting Corporation), Future, MBC, ART, Orbit, ANN and many state television news channels, have changed their style to be more like Al-Jazeera.

The Internet has begun to seep slowly through calcified Arab societies. It has taken longer to grip the Arab world than almost anywhere else. In 2002 the United Nations and the Arab Fund for Economic and Social Development produced jointly *The Arab Human Development Report 2002*. Written by Arabs for Arabs, this revealed in painstaking detail how slowly modernization had come to the Arab world. It showed that Arab countries still had the world's lowest level of information connectivity, meaning that the percentage of people with access to a computer was lower than in any other region in the world. There are only eighteen computers per thousand people in the region; the global average is seventy-eight per thousand.

This is changing. When I went to Jordan I found hundreds of cyber cafés and the Internet is now a mandatory subject for children aged from six to sixteen in the country's schools. The university town of Irbid applied for a place in *The Guinness Book of Records* for having the most Internet cafés in the world in one street: over five hundred in just over half a mile. Even in my run-down hotel there was a computer with creaky Internet access monopolized by one old Bedouin with a wispy white beard.

In the West, when new technology develops, governments diligently collect data through the telecommunications industry before responding with regulatory laws. Appointed experts monitor progress and fine-tune the legislation, and gradually policy develops. In the Arab world media policy is based on whether the ruler thinks the new technology will weaken his grip on power or not.

Since satellite transmission comes from space and cannot be blocked for any practical length of time, Arab governments have had no choice but to accommodate. This decision was not reached painlessly. When satellite television first arrived and the number of satellite dishes in Arab countries started to mushroom, many Arab governments, including Qatar's, instinctively banned the import and sale of dishes, but the information floodgates could not be closed. A satellite dish costs just $100 and once you have one you can receive dozens of channels, including Al-Jazeera, free-to-air. For another $5 you can buy a black-market decoder that allows you to receive hundreds more channels free.

In Al-Jazeera's early years Arab rulers vengefully punished the station whenever they disapproved of the reporting – when Arafat closed down the Ramallah bureau over the incident with the shoe, for example, or when the Egyptians deported Faisal al-Qasim's brother Magd. Then the realization slowly dawned that Al-Jazeera was not going away and, more importantly, there might be a way to make some political capital out of this new phenomenon. Cynics might argue that this was a process of damage limitation rather than a genuine desire for progress: satellite television was accommodated because it was unstoppable, while the Internet, which can be more easily controlled, continued to be subject to widespread bans.

In 2000 a new trend towards liberalizing the media in the Middle East began to become apparent. Egypt, Bahrain, Dubai, Jordan and Yemen all tried to attract Arab and Western media – first satellite television channels, then newspapers – by providing various financial incentives, like tax exemptions and lower production costs. In spring 2000 President Mubarak opened a 'media free zone' near Cairo, which he hoped would attract foreign TV stations. Since many Arab satellite channels were based in European capitals, where production costs are relatively high, he was confident Egypt could offer a cheap alternative. Prospective customers included the Saudi-owned MBC and Syrian-owned ANN, both based in London, and the Saudi-owned Orbit Television, based in Rome. Al-Jazeera, still happily entrenched in Doha, was not expected to move its headquarters, but an Al-Jazeera bureau did open in Cairo in May 2000, transmitting via an Egyptian satellite.

As part of the deal the Egyptian government promised that companies in the media free zone would not be subject to Egypt's usual rigorous censorship laws, but media companies were wary that the government might change its mind later on, after they had installed themselves. Transmissions were still being monitored and the Egyptians wanted all the new companies to abide by a 'code of honour', which sounded suspiciously like censorship under another name.

In an attempt to display its new tolerance, at the same time as the media free zone opened, Egypt gave its state news channel an Al-Jazeera-style makeover. Out went dreary soaps and tacky cabaret acts; in came political talk shows with edgy names. Egyptians were surprised to find themselves watching programmes called *In Depth*, *Breakthrough* and the heavily censored *Without Censorship*. But it was not long before everyone realized it was the same old propaganda rehashed by the Ministry of Information, only in an Al-Jazeera-style format. Ironically, the transformation of the Egyptian media to look more like Al-Jazeera came at the height of Egypt's feud with the network.

In February 2000 King Abdullah II hosted a media conference in Amman, in which he unveiled a newly tolerant media environment for foreign news companies working in Jordan. There was to be no more state censorship, he ruled. The King's Minister of Information told emotional delegates he hoped he would be Jordan's last such minister. 'A ministry of information means censorship,' he declared. Excited journalists from twenty-eight countries gathered to discuss free speech in the Arab media. Qatar was held up as the paragon of virtue; Syria ignored its invitation altogether. It was regarded as quite remarkable that the conference, organized by the liberal International Press Institute, was being held in an Arab country at all. Ironically and much to Jordan's embarrassment, one of the first channels attracted by the new tax breaks was one of the most extreme religious channels around: a Salafi channel called Al-Majid. Salafism is a particularly puritanical strain of Islam.

With the start of the second intifada in the autumn of 2000, Arabs everywhere began to follow the news with renewed vigour. This was food for thought for Arab governments, who, seeing the spell Al-Jazeera cast over its growing audience, decided to accelerate the liberalization process. In 2001 Dubai hosted the first annual Arab Media Forum. The government, eager to become the regional information technology hub, rolled out the red carpet to lucky hacks flown first-class from across the Arab world to spend the night at the glitzy $1500-a-night Bourj al-Arab waterfront hotel. Prizes worth $310,000 were handed out, mainly to Palestinian journalists covering the intifada.

Ironically, the star of the show, Al-Jazeera, boycotted the event when it discovered it had been excluded from several prize categories because of the political fallout from a recent episode of *The Opposite Direction*.

After 9/11 this liberalizing trend was halted and in some cases reversed. New anti-terror legislation, ostensibly aimed at terrorists, instead attacked the press and restricted civil liberties opportunistically. The language of the new laws was deliberately indistinct so that authorities had wide latitude as to whom they could take to court. In Jordan on 9 October, jail terms of up to three years for slandering the monarchy were reintroduced. In Morocco Article 41 of the sinister new press act prescribed three to five years' imprisonment for 'any attack on Islam, the monarchy or territorial integrity'. The traditional contempt which Arab governments had for press freedom quickly resurfaced, a stance epitomized in Zimbabwean President Robert Mugabe's pithy comment, 'You report, we deport.'

In the past few years there have been signs of a cautious shift back towards media liberalization. It has been two steps forward, one step back. Some countries, notably Qatar, Bahrain, Jordan and Morocco, have moved faster than others, but even in Saudi Arabia, where journalists still rigorously censor their own work, frank discussions about the 9/11 attackers have helped broach previously taboo issues. Dissidents have been allowed to speak publicly without going to jail and Saudi state television has considerably loosened up. Now Saudi TV features programmes with Al-Jazeera-like names, like *An Event and a Dialogue* and *With the Events*. These even have women presenters.

The war in Iraq accelerated the process of media liberalization. Under pressure to show some democratic credentials, Egypt and Saudi Arabia both made great show of tinkering with their state press apparatus. In February 2004 the President of Egypt announced that prison sentences for press offences were henceforth abolished, although to date the people's assembly has not ratified this decision. There has also been a steady expansion in the number of privately owned media outlets, ending the Egyptian government's forty-year monopoly on the press.

The Saudis established the Saudi Journalists Association. Plans for this had been in the works since 2001, but after Saddam got the chop, its formation was suddenly hastened. It has not, it might be added, done much. When a long list of high-profile Saudi journalists were suspended by the government for no good reason, the Saudi Journalists Association sat back and did nothing.

Today the number of complaints the Qataris receive about Al-Jazeera programmes in the Middle East has dwindled to a trickle. During the station's early years, in 1997 and 1998, the long-suffering Qatari Foreign Minister said he feared setting foot outside the country because he always got such an earful about Al-Jazeera. GCC summits, he once confessed, were a particular headache. Now there is a certain attitude of resignation towards Al-Jazeera: most recent complaints have been American or African, not Arab.

'The Arab political and security status quo have realized that banning us does not do the trick – they cannot intimidate the media any more,' Al-Jazeera's press spokesman Jihad Ballout told me, not without pride.

'The reactions of governments to Al-Jazeera went through three phases in my opinion,' said Yosri Fouda, counting them off on his fingers. 'The first phase was utter shock: trying to politically interfere with Qatar itself, withdrawing ambassadors from Doha, trying to persuade the Emir of Qatar to wise up and all the rest of it. When that did not work, it went into phase two, which was smear campaigns in their own media, while arresting and hassling our journalists, and closing down our bureaux around the world. When this didn't work they went into phase three – which is "OK, since we can't beat them, why don't we try to not exactly join them, but provide our people with something that looks like Al-Jazeera."'

As a result Arab governments launched new channels in imitation of Al-Jazeera – but for all the wrong reasons. 'I would love to think that when Abu Dhabi TV was launched the people behind it believed in something and I would love to think the same about Al-Arabiya, but I tend more to think that they were both launched in the hope of rendering Al-Jazeera insignificant. But it has worked out positively as far as the Arabs are concerned. The more variety, the more choice there is, the better for them,' said Fouda.

Arabs now have more choice when they switch on their television than anyone thought possible ten years ago. Al-Jazeera has been truly iconoclastic. The tedious opening bulletins or stories about the nation's king or president making fatuous speeches are now a fading memory; in its place Arabs have live news coverage. There is a new regional standard in accurate reporting. Al-Jazeera let the Arab public speak and be heard, by giving over a large proportion of its live shows to taking calls, emails and faxes. It gave Israelis a voice, whereas previously few Arabs had ever heard one speak. It helped the Arab advertising market coalesce and expand. It accustomed Arabs to a standard form of Arabic speech and led to a growing sense of regional integration. It set a new standard of excellence in translation and is used as a benchmark by professional translators all over the world. The network's Arabic-language website is an exceptional resource, which includes pages and pages of programme transcripts stretching back years. The *Top Secret* show founded the tradition of investigative reporting in the Arab world. *The Opposite Direction* has broken every taboo and done great things for women's rights. Perhaps most important of all but hardest to quantify, Al-Jazeera significantly expanded the parameters of debate within families.

Politically, Al-Jazeera made Arab leaders more accountable for the way they behave. One example of this was in February 2000, when the station interviewed the former bodyguard of the Lebanese Phalangist leader Elie Hobeika. The bodyguard, Roger Hatem, also known as 'Cobra', had written a book about Hobeika's connection to the Sabra and Shatila massacres in Lebanon and about numerous political assassinations in which, he alleged, Hobeika had been involved. Within days the reclusive Hobeika appeared on a rival channel to refute the allegations. Al-Jazeera made him account for his actions.

'This is our biggest contribution to change life in the Arab world,' Al-Jazeera's West Bank bureau chief, Walid al-Omary, told me. 'It is very important. I think we can say Al-Jazeera is broadening the Arab perspective, Before us no one was saying anything about Arab leaders or Arab corruption or about the Arab situation even. These were sensitive issues. Now I believe that the Arab world is moving towards huge changes, more democratic changes. In the last few years people can watch foreign television stations. The information revolution is here, the Internet too. People can start asking their leadership, "Why are we in this situation?"'

Arab leaders have even begun to obey some of the basic rules of appearing on television, like looking smart and keeping speeches brief. These tendencies are not yet universal: Libyan officials still tend to drone on for hours and up to his death Yasser Arafat seemed neither to find time to have a shave or put on a suit. But junior government officials and press officers, Al-Jazeera's Amman bureau chief, Musa Ajloni, told me, are gradually beginning to understand the importance of working the press. Even the Israelis, historically much more adept at working the media than the Arabs, have been taught some valuable lessons by Al-Jazeera. 'The Israelis have become much more proactive in handling Al-Jazeera,' said Al-Omary. 'They have become much more aggressive at sending us press releases to try and get interviews and to draw our attention to certain things.'

Despite these advances, there is still plenty of room for progress in how Middle Eastern countries deal with the media. Human rights organizations still keep a steady tally of journalists in the Middle East who are tortured to death by bullying dictators or puritanical mullahs. Real power has not been relinquished and regimes could clamp down hard again at any moment. Al-Jazeera is still denied a bureau in Syria, Algeria and Saudi Arabia, and these countries continue to do all they can to stop it broadcasting. If they could find a way to prevent Al-Jazeera's satellite transmissions, they would.

Not one Arab satellite channel, including Al-Jazeera, could survive without political and financial support either from an Arab government or from a wealthy member of the Arab elite who has close ties to its government. With so many new satellite channels flowering in the Middle East, an international Arab regulatory body is now needed to organize the new channels and protect them from their paymasters. Since satellites are transnational, more international cooperation will be required. There is already a suitable international body in place, the International Federation of Journalists, but Arab journalists do not make much use of it, regarding it as a Western, not a truly international, organization. Currently the IFJ has just four Arab affiliates out of a possible seventeen.

Although access can be made hard by uncooperative regimes, still Al-Jazeera insists that no stories are off limits. If it seems that some sensitive topics have been skipped, issues like defence spending, or profiles of Arab leaders and influential Arab families, this is only because of a lack of resources, never for political reasons. Covering these kinds of topics in the Arab world is particularly hard, because there is not the same massive library of pictures available that we have in the West. You cannot, for example, make a documentary on the playboy lifestyle of a Saudi prince the way you can report on a top footballer in the West, because there will be almost no pictures available of him or his family or friends. But issues that cannot be explicitly covered for a lack of pictures are at least discussed in programmes like *The Opposite Direction*.

In future, all the Arab satellite channels, including Al-Jazeera, need to make more and import less of their programming. Too many Arab channels buy in drama, documentaries and entertainment programmes that tackle important social, health and educational issues in a non-Arabic context. Al-Jazeera depends heavily on old British and American documentaries to fill its schedule and it also depends heavily on a single religious scholar for too many of its religious opinions: Sheikh Yusuf al-Qaradawi.

I decided to visit the Middle East to try to find out what Arabs really thought about Al-Jazeera. I wanted to choose one Arab country in which to pursue a more in-depth exploration of public opinion, somewhere relatively middle-of-the-road, not too front-line in the War on Terror and small enough to allow me to meet a representative slice of society. Initially I had been planning to visit a family in Dubai to review opinions about Al-Jazeera. 'Dubai? That'll be nice. They'll give you a good insight into Al-Jazeera,' said Jihad Ballout when I mentioned my plans to him. When I told him later my plans had changed and I had decided to go to Jordan instead, the network's media relations manager sounded concerned. 'Jordan? Why do you want to ask people in Jordan about Al-Jazeera?' he said. 'They are so political.'

With this comment in mind, a few days later I found myself in the bosom of a Jordanian family in Amman. The father, a respected publisher and something of a patriarch in the community, had kindly agreed to let me speak with him and his family about Al-Jazeera and about the Arab media more generally. His family was educated, urbane and unlike most people living in Jordan, really Jordanian rather than Palestinian-Jordanian. One of his daughters had been educated at Glasgow University.

The whole family had assembled to welcome me on the day of my arrival for lunch: mother and father, daughters, cousins and the son, who had just returned from the Hajj in Mecca. There were eight of us in all, seated around the dining table, in the centre of which sat a huge mound of steaming rice on a round metal tray. Great hunks of lamb stuck out like icebergs. As we tucked into the feast we exchanged pleasantries, skirting around the reason for my visit. I spoke Arabic with some of the family and English with others. Some of them spoke much better English than I did Arabic. Then, when we had almost finished eating, the father addressed me sternly, peering over his spectacles. 'So tell us why you have come here and what it is you want to know!' he demanded.

There was silence as I outlined my project. I had come to Jordan, I explained, to find out what people thought about Al-Jazeera. Many people in the West, I said, have heard of Al-Jazeera, but are suspicious of it. They associate it with Osama bin Laden or blame it for deliberately inciting resistance in Iraq. I had come to Jordan to try to find out whether Jordanians watched Al-Jazeera, what they thought of its reports and whether they thought it had a positive or negative effect on Jordan's relationship with the West.

Hardly had I finished my little speech when animated streams of comment burst forth from everyone in the family. Dad, kids, cousins, everyone had something urgent to say about Al-Jazeera. Maybe Ballout had been right, I reflected: perhaps Jordanians are more political than other Arabs.

This is what they told me: when Al-Jazeera first appeared it had been 'like oxygen to a drowning man'. No one could believe the shows it had on. Some said they had never expected to see something like this in their lives, but when it came they were so happy that they had been watching Al-Jazeera ever since. They watched other channels too, MBC, Al-Arabiya, Abu Dhabi TV: for them the news was made up of many different sources, but Al-Jazeera was certainly the first and remained one of the most important.

Their opinion of Al-Jazeera had changed in the past few months. It had become clear, they said, that around October 2003 America and Israel had finally managed to exert pressure on Al-Jazeera. Where before the station had been a ferocious watchdog of all that was going on in the Middle East, now it offered only tepid criticism of American and Israeli outrages.

In Jordan, I was quickly learning, the heat from the Palestinian conflict is more keenly felt than in other parts of the Arab world. Most Jordanians are actually displaced Palestinians. So it was perhaps unsurprising that, for this family, considering Al-Jazeera led seamlessly to considering how the network had covered recent events in the ongoing Palestinian intifada. That day an American-made F-16 Israeli bomber fired a missile into a car in

Gaza, missing its intended target but killing a twelve-year-old boy on his way to school. We talked about that.

Everyone in the family, but especially the women, wanted to know why Al-Jazeera did not openly condemn the attack and call for resistance. It was a war crime, a murder, a breach of domestic and international law. Why would they skirt around these issues? By refusing to condemn Israel's aggression and occupation, Al-Jazeera was failing the Palestinians. While the network's news turned a blind eye to the Palestinians' suffering its talk shows were deliberately sowing discord between Arab nations, undermining any chance of a concerted Arab response.

Instead, Al-Jazeera covered Israeli casualties and aired long, unedited interviews and speeches by Israeli spokesmen. 'You can tell from the way the host asked the questions they are against the Palestinians; Al-Jazeera has a clever way of slanting the news,' said one of the cousins.

'It's the piper who calls the tune,' the father told me cryptically. 'What do you mean by that?' I asked, puzzled. 'Ask yourself who funds Jazeera – and then think about their policy,' he replied. 'He means, it's an American-backed ploy to sow dissent between the Arab nations,' explained his daughter matter-of-factly. President Bush was the first serving US President to visit Qatar after the invasion of Iraq. US investments in Qatar have jumped from $300 million to $30 billion in the past decade.

This all seemed very strange to me. In the West Al-Jazeera is usually regarded as hopelessly biased against America and yet here I was being told that Al-Jazeera is undermining Arab unity and subverting the Palestinian cause. I explained this paradox to my family. 'Some people in the West think Al-Jazeera is against Israel and America . . .' I ventured. This the family found laughable. 'Faisal al-Qasim [the presenter of *The Opposite Direction*] pretends to take a tough anti-American stance,' a cousin told me. 'It tricks people into thinking they are watching an anti-American channel, when, deep down, Al-Jazeera is dividing Arab society so as to keep Arabs subjugated.'

Although most of the family still watched Al-Jazeera regularly, they all suspected that the channel was a Zionist-American trick. The main evidence for this was that Al-Jazeera could clearly be doing more to help the Palestinian cause than it was. It was not, in other words, like Al-Manar, the Hezbollah channel, which actively campaigns on behalf of the intifada every day. 'I don't like the way Al-Jazeera shows dead bodies,' piped up the son. 'When people are killed there is no reason to show them on TV. They should let the dead have some dignity.'

What I had heard over lunch puzzled me. Did everyone in Amman think like this or had I just stumbled across one family with zany ideas? Back in my hotel I met the head of the Jordanian Writers Association. I told her that I was looking to speak with writers, journalists and politicians about Al-Jazeera. She asked me what kind of questions I wanted to ask them, so I explained it was nothing too taxing, just whether they watched Al-Jazeera, what they thought about it, that kind of thing. No problem, she assured me. 'We all know what we think of Al-Jazeera here in Jordan,' she said as she turned to leave. 'America is behind it, simple as that,' she added with a wink and a smile.

Over the next two weeks I met politicians, newspaper editors, journalists, writers, academics, a hospital manager, Jordanian staff at the British and American embassies, as well as plenty of ordinary working men, in the souk and in coffee shops. Most people watched Al-Jazeera regularly, usually in concert with other channels, but none believed the network's news could be taken at face value. Every single one had an elaborate theory about who they thought was the real power behind the station. My Jordanian family, who had surprised me at the start with their suspicions of a Zionist conspiracy, turned out to have the most moderate views about Al-Jazeera in town.

Most Jordanians I met thought Al-Jazeera was an American-Zionist plot. The argument is more emotional than rational and goes something like this: Al-Jazeera is sponsored by America, as part of a strategy to divide and rule the Arabs and so aid the Israeli oppression of the Palestinians. You can tell this because

Al-Jazeera is too sophisticated a channel for the Arabs to have set up on their own, so the Israelis must be behind it. Its talk shows hypnotize the masses, ready for brainwashing. The fact that it is so widely available and free is in itself suspicious.

If ever Al-Jazeera once told the truth about events in Palestine, since the invasion of Iraq there have been clear signs that it has buckled to American pressure. It has changed its staff and watered down its terminology to placate Donald Rumsfeld. Martyrs have been downgraded to guerrilla fighters; Israeli outrages are now dressed up as legitimate military action.

Al-Jazeera's presenters target the countries most antagonistic to America's neoconservative agenda. Jordan is regularly picked on because Jordanians identify closely with the Palestinians and because, unlike Saudi Arabia, Syria or Qatar, for example, it is a soft target. In the past exiled Hamas leaders have been sheltered in Qatar, compelling evidence that Qatar has a mysterious stake in disrupting the Palestinian leadership.

Al-Jazeera's talk-show hosts were regarded with particular suspicion. In the Middle East no one comes without baggage and even before they open their mouths Al-Jazeera reporters are judged on their name or nationality. Most Arabs I spoke with were aware of which country each journalist came from and they assumed that reporters would never be as critical of their own countries as they would be of others. Dr Faisal al-Qasim, for example, is a Syrian and I often heard that this was why *The Opposite Direction* went easier on Syria than on other countries.

Qatar, it was assumed, was never criticized, because its relationship with America could scarcely be closer. Sheikh Hamad bin Khalifa Al Thani was seen to be completely dependent on America for his wealth, his security and his throne.

This discombobulated stream of fears and allegations usually leads smoothly into tales of other woes. The Arabs are the most oppressed people on earth, their leaders all corrupt and useless sycophants; none of the Gulf Arabs understand or care about Palestine because they lead a life of luxury supported by America; they are kept wealthy because only the poor revolt; American imperialism is no different from the European colonialism of yesteryear; all the Arab leaders owe their power to America and live in fear of being deposed like Saddam Hussein, and so on.

Interwoven into this web of fear were even more pernicious conspiracy theories. Even well-educated leaders of society – editors, journalists and politicians, for example – believed that no Jews died in the Twin Towers because they were tipped off in advance. Most people I spoke with told me that Mossad and the CIA hijacked the planes in the first place, to give the Bush administration's Likudniks and neoconservatives *carte blanche* to restructure the Arab world. Jews had been arrested for the attacks in Washington, I was assured, but had then been quietly released. American soldiers in Iraq were systematically raping Iraqi virgins.

This depressing string of fantasies, coherent in no meaningful way, is a sad indictment of contemporary Arab society. Since there was no logic to these fears, there was no reasoning either. Because Al-Jazeera presents a plurality of opinions, it was easy to see 'proof' everywhere for one theory or another. If I pointed out that the Bush administration was one of Al-Jazeera's most vocal critics, this was cited as proof that I had been suckered into believing exactly what they wanted me to believe. Being banned from reporting in Iraq was all part of the act, because if Al-Jazeera were revealed as the fifth columnist it really was, everyone would immediately turn it off. Nothing could shake the suspicion that although Al-Jazeera might not be Al-Hurra it was run on the same principle. While the Arab public was glued to their sets they were being fed hidden messages and indoctrinated with American values.

How exactly this propaganda was being transmitted, or what exactly the message was, was never clear. Free of the burden of logic, people would swear that Al-Jazeera was a platform on which anybody could say anything about anyone and then in the same breath tell me Al-Jazeera was an Israeli puppet whose sole aim was to subjugate the Arabs. 'When you are losing all the battles, it is very easy to start believing in conspiracy theories and saying everything is the fault of Mossad and the CIA,' Walid al-Omary had warned me in Ramallah. Having been deceived so many times in the past, from the Balfour Declaration to Iraq's non-existent weapons of mass destruction, Arabs have learned to trust nobody. Now, it seemed, when assessing the world around them, rational analysis was submerged in emotions. Bush's announcement that the War on Terror was a 'crusade' and the Undersecretary of Defense's declaration that it was really a clash with 'Satan' had not done much to help either.

Although many of the Jordanian concerns I heard about Al-Jazeera were undoubtedly paranoid ramblings, some of the issues raised were reasonable. What effect do the backgrounds of Al-Jazeera's presenters have on the news? And what exactly is the nature of Al-Jazeera's relationship with the Qatari government? And with America? Most importantly of all, is Al-Jazeera biased, and if so, who to and how much?

When Al-Jazeera first appeared its presenters were regarded as very anti-establishment and by regional standards this was true enough. Many of them are exiles, which is not in itself surprising – the Arab world is full of exiles – but to be professional journalists meant that they had to suppress their national identities completely, otherwise the news would have unworkable bias. This made them better journalists, but it also made them suspicious. How could anyone be sure that they had really surrendered their national allegiances? And if they were not secretly representing their own nation, maybe they were espousing a secret pan-Arab message? Pan-Arabism is a political movement in the Middle East that holds that all Arab countries should unify.

About a third of Al-Jazeera's staff come from the aborted BBC Arabic-language news operation. One of the things about the channel's staff that distinguishes them from some other news outfits is the pride they take in Al-Jazeera. They know they are making history and they wear their complaints like a badge of honour. The network is small enough to possess a sense almost of family loyalty and morale is very high. I met couples who had met and married through their work at Al-Jazeera. The staff are closer to one another than in other news organizations, perhaps because they are thrown together in Qatar as expatriates, but also because they are given more individual responsibility than in other organizations. Each reporter is an individual news cell, often writing, shooting and editing his own work, and staff can easily move laterally to different departments, trying their hand at new things and forging new connections. Most of them are bilingual and the standard of translation, in particular, is first class. Even when the ordinary journalists – not the studio translators – are translating from English or Hebrew or any other language into Arabic, they tend to be extremely fluent.

Many of Al-Jazeera's journalists have worked for oppressive and bureaucratic Arab state television stations. I often heard them say they never expected to work for a news organization like this in their lifetime. Trying to coerce dyed-in-the-wool hacks like these, who have spent decades fighting the system, into following a party line would be like trying to herd cats. Several of the staff told me sincerely and independently of one another that if they sensed any pressure to censor their work they would resign at once.

'Nationality is a problem for all journalists,' Al-Jazeera's London bureau chief, Mostefa Souag, who is Algerian, told me. 'Reporting something personal or painful, you have to learn how to deal with these kinds of things. No one can claim to be completely neutral – you would be robotic, not completely human – but every good reporter gets to the point where they can distinguish between personal feelings and objective reality. If it is too much to do, then he has to tell his editor or producer, I am sorry, I cannot do this.' There have been occasions in the past, he said, when he had handed over reporting events in Algeria to another reporter, because it had been too emotional for him.

'Bear in mind that 80 per cent of the staff at Al-Jazeera, if not more, are educated in the West, have practised in the West, most of them have dual nationalities, they have lived in the West, they are exposed to Western cultures,' said Jihad Ballout.

'But still the stigma of being an Arab initially obscured their better judgement in the West. The simple answer is that these guys are young professionals trying to impose their stamp and will on the Arab media. And they love their job. They are trying to do their job as well as possible. Why does there have to be an angle?'

The exact nature of Al-Jazeera's relationship with Qatar certainly merits examination. Al-Jazeera should by now be making enough from advertising to cover its costs, but in 2003 the BBC reported that the channel had to be bailed out by the Emir, again, to the tune of $29.5 million. Although Al Jazeera makes more from advertising than either of its two big rivals, Abu Dhabi TV and Al-Arabiya, and although its advertising revenue doubled between 2003 and 2004, it still seems unable to make enough to cover its rising costs. It refuses to disclose exact figures for its revenue or spending, but it has an operating budget of about $40 million a year and in 2002 it took only about a fifth of this in advertising.

Besides advertising, Al-Jazeera has sharing agreements with other broadcasters and makes money selling footage. Fox pays $10,000 a month to use Al-Jazeera's feed and paid more during the Iraq war. But the simple fact is that a combination of continued Saudi pressure on regional Arab advertisers not to work with Al-Jazeera and an Arab advertising market that is no way near big enough to sustain all the new channels means Al-Jazeera is still heavily dependent on the Emir.

Al-Jazeera started life on a loan of five hundred million Qatari riyals ($137 million) from the Emir and he has since shelled out several consecutive loans, probably amounting to tens of millions more dollars. Exactly how many of these millions are government money and how many are his personal millions is not clear. At least two of his dynastic relatives are on the board of directors. This kind of money is small change to a man as rich as the Emir and for the impact it has had on Qatar's stature in the region, the network is cheap at the price. Certainly he never expected his investment to bear such abundant fruit in terms of regional power and prestige. But this relationship raises important questions about Al-Jazeera's editorial independence.

Al-Jazeera makes no secret of its connection to Qatar. 'Al-Jazeera depends on grants from the State of Qatar. If it was not for the Qatari government Al-Jazeera would not exist,' Ballout told me frankly. The network's stated position is that although it takes Qatari money, this has no impact whatsoever on its editorial policy.

In the Arab world it is widely held that the only channel whose motives are truly transparent is Al-Manar, Hezbollah's propaganda channel. The idea that the Emir of Qatar would pay money to support a station without having a say in how it was run is almost unthinkable and certainly no foreign government treats Al-Jazeera as if this were the case. When any other country, from America to Bahrain, takes umbrage at Al-Jazeera, their diplomats approach the Qatari government first and the station's management second, if at all. There is a deeply held belief at the governmental level that the Qataris are the real power behind Al-Jazeera.

'Sheikh Hamad Al Thani used to be the Deputy Minister of Information, then he became the chairman of Al-Jazeera,' observed Egyptian Professor Mamoun Fandi. 'He is the same guy with a different title. Does that mean they abolished the Ministry of Information? This is the same guy! What we have is the idea that if you give it a different name somehow it is a different animal. Well, it's not. Most of us are so gullible to say the "independent Al-Jazeera". Come on! Get serious!'

'I wonder if you would say the same thing about the BBC or if you would say the same thing about NPR [National Public Radio] in the States?' retorted Ballout when I put this to him. 'On the contrary, if you want to apply this formula, then the BBC is in a much more awkward situation because not only does it get money in terms of direct grants from the government, it also takes money from the taxpayers, through the licence fee. If a government subsidizes a media it does not automatically mean it is under the beck and call of that government.'

In establishing Al-Jazeera, it seems that the Qatari government has taken a wily decision: that intermittent attacks against it on Al-Jazeera are a price worth paying for the international prestige brought by the station. The government is savvy enough to know hosting a massive American airbase in its heartland is never going to be wildly popular, but it is better that any criticism be aired in public. Such a sensible resolution is very unusual in the Gulf, but Qataris are thicker-skinned than their neighbours, perhaps because a history of trade has conditioned them to dealing with the wider world – unlike the House of Saud, for example, which hails from the landlocked isolation of the inland desert.

As a result news on Al-Jazeera detrimental to Qatar is not edited and talk shows have not shied away from topics that are critical of the Emir's policies. One episode of *The Opposite Direction* discussed specifically whether it was right or wrong to host the American airbase at Al-Udeid, a very controversial issue for the Qataris. At the height of the intifada and in the run-up the war in Iraq, when all America's allies were being hounded in the Arab world, public demonstrations, politicians, guests and callers frequently abused Qatar on Al-Jazeera. During the war Al-Jazeera interviewed a variety of experts, most of whom were critical of the Qatari role in hosting the American military presence. On the station's seventh birthday a whole episode of the show *Without Borders* was dedicated to criticizing Al-Jazeera and a Saudi journalist staunchly opposed to Al-Jazeera was invited on to do the job properly. He claimed then that Al-Jazeera was a puppet of the Qatari government.

When followers of the deposed Sheikh Khalifa bin Hamad Al Thani attempted a coup against Qatar's new Emir in 1996, the conspirators were caught and put on trial. The trial's full proceedings were televised live on Al-Jazeera – a first in the Arab world. The defence counsel alleged that the defendants had been subjected to torture and a spokesman from a human rights organization attacked the Qatari criminal justice system. Al-Jazeera covered it.

More recently the Qatari Foreign Minister was interviewed at length on Al-Jazeera by veteran Al-Jazeera journalist Ahmad Mansur during two episodes of *Without Borders*. He was given a grilling by both Mansur and the public, who called in to put questions to him. Nothing was edited and the calls were live. Criticism of Qatar happens quite often. When America attacked Afghanistan one of the first American casualties was an airman from the Al-Udeid airbase. Hafez al-Mirazi, the Washington bureau chief, went straight on air, saying, 'Contrary to what we all hear from Qatari officials that there is no involvement in the war effort in Afghanistan, the first casualty came from Al-Udeid, Qatar . . .'

Notably, Al-Jazeera is not the only media outlet based in Qatar to have been shown tolerance by the government. In June 1999 Qatari state newspapers published a selection of citizens' views on the Al Thani family's financial appropriations, a taboo topic even in the most liberal Arab countries and something that would certainly not have gone ahead without a nod from the Emir himself.

Al-Jazeera criticizes its backers at least as severely as MBC covers the Saudi royal family, the Lebanese Broadcasting Corporation scrutinizes its various investors or Fox News investigates Rupert Murdoch. Of course, the network could always be doing more to investigate Qatar. It has been suggested that Al-Jazeera should 'prove' its independence by interviewing the deposed Emir, who now lives in Switzerland. But this fails to account for the fact that Qatar is such a tiny country with a minute population, at least half of whom are under eighteen and maybe a third of whom are members of the royal family. Although such an exercise might temporarily satisfy the station's critics, it would certainly not serve its audience: Qatar is not Egypt or Saudi Arabia.

But since Qatar is such a small country it is impossible to believe that there is no relationship at all between Al-Jazeera and the Qatari government. Even though the Emir does not phone up the chief editor every day and tell him what he wants at the top of the news, there is probably an informal connection of some kind, although this has a negligible effect on Al-Jazeera's editorial policy. Certainly most reporters I met in Al-Jazeera's bureaux in the countries I visited seemed to be oblivious to any connection with Qatar at all. But would, for example, the London bureau need to tip off Doha if they were planning to interview a hot Saudi dissident, so they could let Qatar's Foreign Ministry know in advance?

'No!' the London bureau chief, Mostefa Souag, told me emphatically. 'We don't ask for clearance. We ask for Doha's editorial needs. For a start you don't bring a Saudi dissident on the show just because he is a Saudi dissident. It has to be connected to a story. But if the Saudis announce something important or there is something in Saudi Arabia that is news, as part of our policy "The opinion and the other opinion", we would bring someone else on to express the other point of view. We don't need someone to tell us, "You can do that." As long as we are balanced we know we are doing the right thing.'

'Very often in Arab countries the rule is that you don't touch your government,' added the London bureau's executive director, Muftah al-Suwaidan. 'Qataris have never had a problem with Al-Jazeera doing anything. For example, the military base in Qatar was a very big thing. In any other Arab country, like Egypt or Saudi, you would not be able to talk about this. Al-Jazeera had the first big report about it: they interviewed officials, asking, "Why did you do this?" Qatar is a small country and there is not much news going on. When there is something newsworthy we do it.'

It is remarkable that this understanding between Al-Jazeera and the Qataris has lasted. It is a testament to the progressive vision and tolerance of the Emir. 'There is nothing extraordinary about our Emir,' the Qatari Ambassador in London told me, shrugging nonchalantly. 'He is just a human, like you or I are human. He just knows it is better to lead now, rather than sit back and do nothing and then sometime later be forced to move, and then no matter what he does it will be too little too late.' Whether in the future the Qataris can resist temptation to dabble in the editorial process remains to be seen. What is clear is that as long as the channel remains in Qatar and receives financial support from the Emir it will be subject to suspicion. But there can be no doubt that any price viewers pay as a result of Al-Jazeera being stationed in Qatar, by way of under-reporting local Qatari events, is far outweighed by the benefits.

Al-Jazeera's history is peppered with accusations that it is biased. In the Middle East I was told time and again that it targeted the Arabs. In the West it is repeatedly alleged that Al-Jazeera spreads hate against Israel and America. The station claims that it is just doing its job. 'Al-Jazeera is a news organization. Al-Jazeera does not deal in politics,' the network's spokesmen have reiterated countless times. 'Accusations of bias are all rubbish. What we are trying to do is disseminate news as accurately as we can, as comprehensively as we can, full stop.' But no one, it seems, believes this.

The US Department of State, along with Defense Secretary Rumsfeld and Deputy Defense Secretary Wolfowitz, has been among the most persistent critics of Al-Jazeera. 'A lot of what they do is inciteful and not edited with any sense of balance,' one well-placed source in the Department told me. Specifically, the American administration has objected to certain terms used by Al-Jazeera, like 'resistance', 'martyr', 'occupation' and the 'so-called War on Terror'. Officials have said there are too many anti-American voices on Al-Jazeera's talk shows and that the network shows pictures of American troops humiliating Iraqis, for example by shouting at them or searching their houses. This has all been calculated, it is alleged, for political effect.

'Al-Jazeera is the eight-hundred-pound gorilla of the Arab media and the Qataris are using it to do a kabuki dance,' a high-level Department of State spokesman told me. 'The Qataris have opened their arms to the United States, but that is not a popular thing to do. So they use Al-Jazeera to be anti-American so that people can see they are not in bed with the United States – they are doing one thing but meaning another.'

In the view of another senior American government official:

Al-Jazeera is a political entity – definitely not balanced – and they definitely have an agenda. They are very responsible for a lot of the things that happen [in Iraq] because they almost give permission in a way. In some cases they were showing up ahead of time before some horrendous things were happening. After you show people things, bloody attacks, and then your commentary overlays the video, and then you have young people watching that so they go out and commit acts of terrorism – you have to say you have some responsibility. There doesn't seem to be any ethical guidelines and no monitor, no self-monitor, in terms of what are you going to show. It's vivid Technicolor.

Not only does the US government hold that Al-Jazeera slants its inflammatory news: it manipulates its talk shows too. The same senior government official told me, 'We have had people go on Al-Jazeera as a panellist and the topic is never what it is supposed to be, or a person would make a statement and then they will have somebody else on to refute it and then the other one doesn't have a chance to come back. I don't think, in terms of responsible journalism, that is responsible.'

'The news they get about Iraq is so completely biased that it is ridiculous,' said Molly McKew, Fellow at the American Enterprise Institute for Public Policy Research (AEI). One of America's largest and most respected 'think tanks', the AEI is a non-partisan, non-profit organization based in Washington and is known to exercise considerable influence on the Bush administration. Scholars from the AEI frequently testify before congressional committees and are consulted by the government on a broad range of issues, including foreign policy. Ronald Reagan once said that '[no think tank] had been more influential than the American Enterprise Institute'.

'Every newscast starts with the Israeli–Palestinian conflict and, "Oh, here are how many Palestinians died today,"' said McKew. She went on:

We watched Al-Jazeera when we were in Iraq and you just saw the same loop footage over and over again of wounded Palestinian children in the hospital or people in the street over and over again. It is the same stuff over and over again with overlaid stories of whatever they feel like talking about that day – just that sort of overexposure of war and violence – I don't think it's very responsible.

Al-Jazeera tends to focus on the Palestinian conflict as the source of all their problems which AEI in general will tell you is complete crap. There are so many problems the Arab world faces, so saying that all their problems are to do with founding of the state of Israel is just absolutely ridiculous.

There was about thirty days when Al-Jazeera was banned from being in Baghdad or at least taping in Baghdad because it had become very apparent that they were paying the cameraman to get gory, nasty pictures of American soldiers being wounded or attacked.

They were definitely getting tips and then not doing anything about it. Getting a tip about a protest or something is one thing, getting a tip about people being bombed or killed is entirely different. There have definitely been cases in Iraq where they have been directly related to attacks against American soldiers and against the American-trained Iraqi police force.

I am not sure how the financial exchange occurs. I think there is probably payment both ways, but there is definitely interest in getting Al-Jazeera to places where there are attacks to get the footage out on the news.

McKew believes that Al-Jazeera, besides collaborating with the resistance in Iraq, generally slanted its news against the American occupation. 'They do have a very anti-American foreign policy agenda and they are very against the Iraq war . . . You will never see any positive news about Iraq on Al-Jazeera. There is no news of government or state building or reconstruction building or new health systems or anything. It is all just bombs and attacks and protests and Shiites rioting in the west and south and really no other news in Iraq. They make it look like America is an occupying force and that the people of Iraq are in need of liberation from us when, in fact, when you ask most Iraqis that is not the case.'

Nor was it just Al-Jazeera's news that she did not like:

Some of our scholars participate in the talk shows. For the most part they speak in English. They ask attack-based questions or they say the interview is going to be about American policy in Iraq and then it's 'Oh! But the Jews are in charge of this' and then they just get mad and leave. It's that kind of thing.

It is the incessant focus on foreign policy and on American action in the world and not on domestic policy in any of the Arab countries. It is external: 'How has America screwed us today? Well, let's see today they passed a bill on this . . .' It is never about 'Here's what we could do to improve our own economic situation' or anything like that. It is the lack of domestic understanding or self-introspective understanding that really skews everything that they are talking about towards bizarre radical topics and not actual coverage of issues that people need to know about in the Arab world.

McKew believes that Al-Jazeera is like this partly because of its close ties to an extremist religious agenda. 'The more radical interpretation of radical Islam is what Al-Jazeera latches on to most vehemently in their portrayal of everyday events on the news and in their interpretation of policy. This scares people and it scares me,' she said.

Like the Jordanians, she thought the financial relationship that Al-Jazeera had with the Qataris deserved inspection:

> Their sources of funding come for a reason and it is not just, 'Here, run a news network.' It is, 'You are going to go out, you're going to broadcast this, and this is the issue you are going to be working on.'
>
> I have been told their financing is not always on the books and not necessarily 'unsuspect', I guess is the right way to say it. I think a lot of people wonder where their money is coming from and exactly who is funding them and for what purpose. The money that comes to fund their network often comes with a political agenda, regardless of where it comes from. Often their money comes from sources that we would view as radical or extremist.

But Al-Jazeera, I pointed out, is funded by Qatar, which is America's prime ally in the Gulf. 'We have many allies, we don't like all of them,' retorted McKew. 'Funding is one of the things we would look at more closely if we were to go after Al-Jazeera, but trying to leave the Emir of Qatar out of it would probably be something we would be interested in doing in the short term, if only for the sake of not pissing off yet another ally in the Middle East.'

Al-Jazeera does not present the news from a completely objective point of view – that would be impossible – but during the war in Iraq its tone was notably sympathetic to the Iraqis and hostile towards the Americans. Similarly, in Afghanistan, the Taliban were often presented as the noble underdog and America as the vengeful colonial aggressor. There are other trends in the network's coverage: a general cynicism about Arab regimes allied to America is detectable. Although Al-Jazeera has employees from various religions, including Jews, it is clearly sympathetic towards the Palestinians and their geopolitical goals. It is obvious the channel did not agree with the way the coalition set about deposing Saddam Hussein. Since the war ended Al-Jazeera has been critical of the coalition's mishandling of the occupation in Iraq.

But Al-Jazeera has never supported violence against America. Not once have its correspondents praised the attacks or called for more. No evidence has ever been put forward that Al-Jazeera knew beforehand about any attack on the coalition. Its journalists capture the best footage of the struggle in Iraq because they speak the language, know the country and have saturated it. 'Any local station in any place will have regional news that they can dominate,' the Washington bureau chief explained. 'Just like Doha cannot call me up and demand why the CNN guy got something before me from the Pentagon or why the *Washington Post* got the leaked story – because in America they are always going to leak it to an American source.' As for the Department of State's theory that Al-Jazeera collaborates with the Qataris for political effect, the Al-Jazeera journalists with whom I spoke around the world found the idea simply bemusing. They rarely think of Al-Jazeera even as a Qatari network – they shoot and edit packages in the field, uplink them and they are broadcast a few hours later. They do not stop to think for even a second about the nationality of their station or its financier.

Terminology is a perennially sticky issue for editors and journalists everywhere. Was it an 'invasion' or a 'liberation'? Did Basra 'fall' or was it 'occupied'? Although the Department of State objects to the term 'resistance' to describe the insurgents in Iraq, Tony Blair uses it too and, ironically, the US fought hard to have its actions in Iraq awarded the status 'occupation' by the UN. After the handover of power in June 2004, and after a wrenching internal debate within Al-Jazeera, the term 'occupation' ceased to be used on the news, though it was still used occasionally on the website. 'Martyr' is a more complicated term, because it is not a word we would normally use in English in this context. The Arabic word, *shaheed*, is rich in history and has implications of sacrificing oneself for a worthy cause. Al-

Jazeera uses it to describe the dead in Palestine: most controversially, to refer to suicide bombers. Al-Jazeera reporters used
to say 'martyr' to describe Iraqis killed in the war, but a few
months after the war ended they ceased using the word, except
in reported speech. This change in terminology was cited as
proof by Jordanians I met that Al-Jazeera had watered down its
coverage to placate America.

According to the Koran, the title of martyr is conferred only
by God: it is not an earthly doing. Muslims are supposed to pray
to God that He might make the deceased a martyr. When news-
men use the term, its original context has already been somewhat distorted: they are not literally inviting their audience to
petition God.

Calling the Palestinian dead 'martyrs' did not begin on
Al-Jazeera and it is not used with the intention of romanticiz-
ing the conflict. The word is used throughout the Arab media
to refer to anyone who dies fighting for Palestine. The only time
you do not hear it being used in the Arab world is on American-
backed Arabic-language radio and television news channels like
Radio Sawa and Al-Hurra, which have adopted phrases like
'guerrilla fighter' and 'suicide bomber' instead. To most Arabs,
calling someone who dies fighting for Palestine anything other
than a 'martyr' is strange and disrespectful, but it is not a neutral
term.

Al-Jazeera's West Bank bureau chief, Walid al-Omary,
explained to me why he uses the word. 'Many times people ask
us, why do you use the term "martyr"?, for example. What are
we supposed to use? Those people lost their lives because they
are fighting for their freedom and many of the Palestinian people
were killed – more than 90 per cent of them during this intifada
– were civilians. They are not armed. They were killed in demonstrations or they were killed by the Israelis because they threw
stones, or sometimes they are killed because the Israelis want to
kill one activist and they demolish a whole building. What are
we supposed to call these people?'

'We use "so-called" to describe the war on terror, but we are not the only one – Reuters doesn't use the word "terrorist" at all,' observed Washington bureau chief Hafez al-Mirazi. 'I use "resistance" and I use "anti-American" for people who object to the US occupation. In US news conferences sometimes US officials use the word "resistance" anyway. And then there are our friends at Al-Hurra who say, "No! We have our own political dictionary. Resistance in Arabic means something else!" This is baloney and maybe someone could explain to me then what "occupation" is in Arabic? If the American officials use the word "occupation", why don't their press?'

This kind of terminology accurately reflects how Arabs perceive events, although several times Arabs reminded me that whether a reporter used the word *shaheed* or not did not really make a huge difference to them: what is more important is that civilians are dying and mosques are being bombed. Besides, although these terms may reflect an ideology at odds with the West, the American press has a terminology of its own which is equally charged. For example, although the West Bank and Gaza are occupied by Israel in contravention of the Geneva Conventions, and the UN Security Council, which includes America, has repeatedly demanded Israel's withdrawal and the removal of all the settlements, a study in 2001 by the American national media watchdog Fairness and Accuracy in Reporting (FAIR) found that 90 per cent of American network television news reporting on the situation in the Occupied Territories failed to mention the words 'occupied' or 'occupation' or any other variant of the word. The *New York Times* omitted the term from two-thirds of its news reports on the subject. Instead the West Bank and Gaza are described as 'contested' or 'disputed' or often simply as 'Israel'.

This is not an isolated example. The American press describes Israeli assassinations of political activists as 'targeted killings', the Israeli military becomes the 'security forces' and Israeli settlements, all illegal under international law, become innocuous-sounding 'neighbourhoods'. American stations frequently talk about a 'period of calm' when no Israelis, but dozens of

Palestinians, are killed, and when in 2000 Amnesty International put out a damning report on Israel's gross violations of human rights in the Occupied Territories, most American papers, including the *New York Times*, totally ignored it.

FAIR concluded that reports in the American press on the conflict between the Israelis and Palestinians were grossly misrepresented in favour of Israel. The Palestinians were overwhelmingly represented as the aggressors, typically characterized as hateful without reason, with no explanation offered as to what their grievances were.

Al-Jazeera operates the same stringent editorial processes as the Western media in covering the same events and ends up with a different product. This is because there are deep cultural differences between the people making the editorial choices and, like any commercial station, Al-Jazeera is pitching itself at its viewership. Bias is a natural consequence of the commercial process. Al-Jazeera treats its audience exactly as the mainstream cable networks and FM radio stations in the US treat their domestic audience. It caters to public opinion because in spite its royal subsidies, it wants to get audience share and it wants to sell advertising.

Any bias in no way invalidates the network's news. Journalists around the world treat Al-Jazeera with the same respect they treat news from any other major international news network. Al-Jazeera has sharing agreements with CNN, ABC, NBC, Fox News, the BBC, the Japanese NHK and the German ZDF, who all regularly use its footage and reports.

In fact, Al-Jazeera is probably less biased than any of the mainstream American news networks. Knowing it is scrutinized more rigorously than any other news station, Al-Jazeera is fastidious in presenting both sides of the story. Only the BBC tries harder to be neutral, although as the Hutton Inquiry revealed in 2004, even the BBC gets it wrong sometimes. Certainly compared with most other Arab news stations, Al-Jazeera remains a model of professionalism and objectivity. Unlike most other Arab news channels, it has never, for example, held a telethon to raise money for Palestine.

Although Al-Jazeera stands accused by the US Department of State of misinforming Arabs with its one-sided approach to every issue, it is ironic that the network has, in fact, done more to educate Arabs about the machinations of democracy than any other broadcaster. After 9/11 Al-Jazeera started a weekly talk show called *From Washington*, broadcast from Washington and hosted by the network's Egyptian-American local bureau chief, Hafez al-Mirazi. He has interviewed many serving members of the current American administration on the show, as well as a variety of other politicians, Republican and Democrat.

In January 2004, at the start of the US primary elections, Al-Jazeera started another weekly show, *US Presidential Race*, which, like *From Washington*, was also broadcast from the Washington bureau. *US Presidential Race* was strictly about the forthcoming American elections and it covered most of the primaries in the major states. It continued through the November elections and beyond, up until the President's inauguration.

The programme took great pains to explain to Arab viewers the American political and electoral process, how delegates are chosen, how the modern primary election system originated and so on. Al-Jazeera reporters travelled around America, visiting Arab communities in various states. They went to places where Arabs would gather and they interviewed people, asking them what they thought of the elections, what were the key issues, who they were going to vote for and why. The discussions were hosted by a mediator in the studio in Washington. By the time the election arrived, Arab viewers had an opportunity to follow the democratic process every step of the way.

'I often say to people,' Al-Mirazi told me, 'maybe we should put an ad in US newspapers saying, "Let's admit it, we were not balanced in covering the crisis since 9/11" – and put a picture of bin Laden and Bush and under bin Laden put, "A total of five hours, all the tapes together" and then under Bush put, "More than five hundred hours of live broadcasts in addition to all the reports". Sometimes when all the American networks are not carrying Bush, Al-Jazeera is carrying him. Two times we did that.' In the run-up to the war, when Colin Powell made a speech at the Center for Strategic and International Studies in Washington, Al-Jazeera was the only television network to cover his speech live and in its entirety.

Al-Jazeera's London bureau has a similar focus on British politics. Three weekly programmes come live from London, besides which Al-Jazeera gives extensive coverage to the nation's news, politics, opposition activities and goings-on in parliament. Another weekly programme comes live out of Brussels, covering European political affairs.

'I think that if you look at the totality of Jazeera's coverage you will see that their coverage is quite fair,' said Rami Khouri. 'They give you Bush or Bremer live when they have a news conference and they translate simultaneously and they don't interfere. They give you a variety of views from within the region and from around the world. I watch these stations regularly and I think that Al-Jazeera is very, very professional and broadcasts a wide range of opinions. So I think the accusations are not very credible.' Khouri is well placed to make this judgement. Besides being executive editor of Lebanon's *Daily Star* newspaper, he is a bilingual media expert, an internationally syndicated political columnist and a member of the Brookings Institute Task Force on 'US Policies Towards the Islamic World'.

Most bilingual media observers agree with Khouri. 'It provides the one window through which we breathe,' Cairo-born novelist and Booker Prize nominee Ahdaf Soueif said of Al-Jazeera. 'Al-Jazeera has an agenda, but that's not inherently bad,' I was told by Dr Jon B. Alterman, director of the Middle East Program at the Center for Strategic and International Studies. He had previously been on the Policy Planning Staff at the Department of State, an International Affairs Fellow at the Council on Foreign Relations and a Special Assistant to the Assistant Secretary of State for Near Eastern Affairs. 'I think Al-Jazeera sometimes goes for the cheap and easy instead of the hard and good, because it's always easiest to have the bad guys and the good guys go at each other. But you only have to watch someone like Al-Hurra or ANN to realize how skilled Al-Jazeera is at what they do.'

Besides, said Alterman, who has made over a hundred appearances on CNN, American networks have agendas too. 'I got a call from one American network, they did the pre-interview, they said they were going to send a car and do everything and they called back half an hour later saying, "I just have one more question for you, were you for or against the liberation of Iraq?" Is this a litmus test? What was the point of the question? I never had that with Al-Jazeera.'

In January 2002, following viewers' complaints about the one-sided nature of Fox News's coverage of the events following 9/11 and during the Afghanistan conflict, Britain's communications regulator, the Independent Television Commission (since replaced by Ofcom) wrote a four-page letter of complaint to the channel. Problems included the ubiquitous fluttering of the American flag, the anchors' 'Old Glory' lapel badges, using the pronoun 'we' interchangeably to describe Fox News and the American military and reporter Geraldo Rivera in Afghanistan brandishing a gun. Despite claiming to be 'fair and balanced', Fox News, as it appears in America, could never be broadcast from within Britain, since it would contravene the television regulator's rules on 'due impartiality'. It can, however, still be received by satellite from overseas.

Fox News commentator Bill O'Reilly was advocating the breach of international law when he announced shortly after 9/11, 'The US should bomb the Afghan infrastructure to rubble – the airport, the power plants, their water facilities, the roads . . . The Afghans are responsible for the Taliban. We should not target civilians, but if they don't rise up against this criminal government, they starve, period.' Besides being inhumane, his suggestion contravened the protocol additional to the Geneva Conventions, 1977, Article 54 (2), which stipulates, 'It is prohibited to attack or destroy . . . objects indispensable to the survival

of the civilian population, such as . . . drinking water instal-
lations and supplies of irrigation works.'

Fox was not the only news outlet with radical ideas. CNN
discussed housing Arab-Americans in concentration camps,
Newsweek wondered whether torture would 'jump-start the
stalled investigation into the greatest crime in American history'
and the *New York Post* decided the best response to 9/11 'should
be as simple as it is swift – kill the bastards . . . A gunshot
between the eyes, blow them to smithereens, poison them if
you have to . . . As for cities or countries that host these worms,
bomb them into basketball courts.' Yet the White House saw fit
only to complain about Al-Jazeera. There were no European
complaints about the channel, though, nor was it the subject of
any investigation either by Britain's Independent Television
Commssion or the Conseil Supérieur de l'Audiovisuel in France,
where it is registered as a broadcaster.

British viewers were not the only ones complaining about
Fox's style. 'Have you seen Fox News?' Muftah al-Suwaidan, executive director of Al-Jazeera's London bureau, asked me, utterly
astonished. 'I wouldn't like to even compare or use them as a
point of reference. It is so pro-Israeli and anti-Muslim. The way
they tell the news – they make a joke about Arabic culture, about
our leaders, everything. I was in the States when the Israelis took
the West Bank and Gaza. Fox was so biased. I was so angry.'

Al-Jazeera's New York correspondent, Abdul Rahim Foukara,
said:

When I look at the American media from an emotional
point of view, as an Arab living in America, it's obviously
very upsetting, in the same way I would imagine it would
be for an American perhaps watching Al-Jazeera or Al-
Arabiya or any other Arab channel. But when I look at
American news – and American media owners make no
bones about it – they're almost willing to acknowledge that
they're running a business rather than news. So when you
look at it through those eyes, I'm not saying it's justified,

but you understand why it is the way it is. When it's anti-Arab you know that television is out there to make money, and anti-Arab sentiment becomes a commodity just like any other commodity that you sell.

Fox News is biased, agreed US Department of State spokesman Dr Nabil Khouri, but that is not the point. 'I would prefer to watch Al-Jazeera any time rather than Fox,' he said.

I don't like the style of that station and I would not want you to use them as a model, but why do we criticize Al-Jazeera and not criticize Fox? Well, how many Arabs watch Fox? I am concerned about US-Arab relations. We have a serious problem with Arab public opinion. Fox does not matter one bit when it comes to our conflict with the Arab world. Al-Jazeera does.

A lot of surveys and analysis has shown that public opinion in the Arab world right now is shaped to a large extent – and I am talking about 75–80 per cent – by these channels. That is a huge responsibility to have particularly in a time of war, in a time of crisis, in a time where very fundamental issues are being decided upon in Iraq and where public opinion could cause certain conflicts to erupt into violence or could cause a more moderate approach to those conflicts.

To Americans Al-Jazeera seems especially biased. This is because the popular American media has not reported particularly comprehensively about foreign affairs for years. For a decade American news has been steadily turning into entertainment. Somewhere between the trial of OJ Simpson and Janet Jackson's nipple, analytical news reporting in America was replaced with celebrity journalists providing sound bites and prejudice, to be recycled later as news. Given this dearth of quality foreign news, it is no surprise that second-hand reports from Al-Jazeera about rising levels of hatred for America in the Middle East seem made up.

For ten years American warplanes and the Ba'athist regime exchanged fire over Iraq every single day, although this went virtually unreported. After 9/11 the American media, like the American security services, was surprised to wake up to find unprecedented levels of hatred for American foreign policy around the world. None of the American networks was prepared for the ensuing War on Terror, so Al-Jazeera scooped the invasion of Afghanistan and for a few weeks became news agency to the world.

After 9/11 all America's big domestic television networks agreed to the White House demand to censor their news in the name of patriotism. Never have the major news organizations been less critical of an American government. So swept up were they on a tide of patriotism that they failed to question the case for war put to them by President Bush, Donald Rumsfeld and, above all, Colin Powell. Delivering his ultimatum to Saddam Hussein on the eve of the invasion of Iraq, President Bush told America there was 'no doubt that the Iraqi regime continues to possess and conceal some of the most lethal weapons ever devised'.

As late as August 2003, 69 per cent of Americans believed Saddam Hussein was 'personally involved' in 9/11, according to a poll by the *Washington Post*. Eighty-two per cent believed he had 'provided assistance to Osama bin Laden'. Fifty-seven per cent of Americans, in a CNN/USA Today Gallup poll, said the war on terrorism and the invasion of Iraq were the 'same war'. Nobody in any other part of the world thought like this.

'Many stories stenographically reported the incumbent administration's perspectives on WMD, giving too little critical examination of the way officials framed the events, issues, threats and policy options,' concluded a study by the Center for International and Security Studies at Maryland (CISSM) and the University of Maryland, a year after the war was declared over.

The holes in the case for war are visible not just with the benefit of hindsight. If the American press had been doing its job, analysing the compelling evidence against the White House's case for war put forward by the UN weapons inspectors Hans Blix and Muhammad El Baradei, instead of repeatedly interviewing patriotic pundits, they might not have got it all so wrong. Barely two years after 9/11, watchdog journalism in America was found asleep in its kennel – again.

Today, despite all that has happened, it is still not uncommon for the quality American press, for example the *New York Times*, to muddle up terms like 'Muslim', 'Arab' and 'Persian' on the front page. After years of neglect the American media seems to have forgotten how to report foreign affairs. Complex foreign disputes are judged on the same vapid values that are used to judge domestic ones. Historical context is routinely discarded and complicated situations are reduced to a childlike simplicity. The War on Terror becomes a battle of Good versus Evil, and Saddam Hussein and Osama bin Laden are reduced to 'evil-doers' to be defeated by a 'crusade'. The American media rigorously self-censors for fear of being labelled unpatriotic or, worse still, anti-Semitic.

In this intellectual climate, devoid of history, analysis or intelligent comment, the American public naturally has no idea about riddles like Iraq or Palestine and so it is no wonder that Al-Jazeera looks like the bearer of bad news. Compared with what is seen and heard in the sanitized American media, Al-Jazeera's reports of civilian casualties in Afghanistan or the suffering and hatred in Palestine seem not just incomprehensible – they seem fictitious. After all, the American press, which routinely ignores Muslim casualties, has not covered it.

This notwithstanding, it is probably true that Al-Jazeera propagates hate. In the main this is a product of the talk shows, not the network's news. Although Al-Jazeera's journalists try hard to be balanced, most guests and callers do not. Unquestionably, many of the voices heard on Al-Jazeera are deeply illiberal and often express strong anti-Western or anti-Semitic sentiment and the Islamist slogan 'Islam is the solution' is frequently heard.

Whether Al-Jazeera must take responsibility for the opinions of its bigoted guests is not an easy question to answer. 'What do you do with these people, ignore them?' said London bureau chief Mostefa Souag, throwing up his hands. 'Just present the people who have the pro-American message? You cannot do that and be objective and claim to have integrity. You have to present both points of view. If you see a programme with only one side represented without the other, you can call Al-Jazeera and accuse them of supporting or encouraging one side.'

Although Al-Jazeera deliberately solicits polemical guests, it always balances their points of view with opinions from the other side. 'We do have programmes where people come out very strongly with opinions against America – but in the same programme we have people who come very strongly with opinions the other way. In many ways we are a mirror, just showing,' said Muftah al-Suwaidan, executive director of the London bureau.

It is important to remember that Al-Jazeera did not manufacture these opinions. Its talk shows are empty vessels where anything can be said and heard, and in an oppressive region, this is why they are so popular. Free speech is not an unalloyed advance. It may seem paradoxical that when Arabs finally have a chance to express themselves freely they express illiberal views, but people are often more conservative than their governments. Americans often point out that Israel is the only democracy in the Middle East, which is just as well for them, because if Iraq, Egypt, Saudi Arabia, Qatar and many other Arab countries had truly democratic elections, the people would choose governments far more militant than the ones they have now. They would close down airbases, kick out American contractors and declare war on Israel. This is the sad truth, but it is true despite Al-Jazeera.

The Arab world is not the only place where the public is more militant than the government. When BBC Radio 4 asked listeners to the *Today* programme what new law they would like to see introduced, the majority wanted the right to kill an intruder in their home. Closing down Al-Jazeera would not address the roots of narrow-mindedness any more than closing down Radio 4: it would simply be shooting the messenger. The good news is that since the opinions expressed on Al-Jazeera are honestly held at least, if the Arab world saw a reason to feel more positive about American policy then we could confidently expect to see a reflection of that in future on Al-Jazeera's talk shows.

But it is not only Al-Jazeera's talk shows that spread hate. Its truthful reports from the West Bank and Gaza have probably made peace and reconciliation between Palestinians and Israelis more elusive too. By graphically showing Palestinian suffering, Al-Jazeera may well have contributed to a hardening of the Arab position against Israel, not least among the Israeli Arab community. The difference in scale between the Arab responses to the first and second intifadas, which came before and after the advent of satellite news, is evidence for this.

Israeli Arabs have long been in a strange position. Regarded as a security risk by their own country, they have lived on the margins of society. This is partly because their country does not want them, they are not obligated to serve in the Israel Defense Forces, but partly through their own choosing: often they identify more with the Palestinians anyway. Caught between the obligations of the law of the land on one hand and their sense of duty to help their kin on the other, they have faced the unenviable challenge of trying to be loyal to both sides at once. As Arabs outside the Occupied Territories have stirred to support the Palestinians, their sense of isolation has deepened. Where before there was a tendency to abstain from the troubles in the Occupied Territories, there has been a growing trend for militancy and in recent years several suicide bombers have been drawn from the ranks of the Israeli-Arab community. There has been a corresponding rise in the calls from within the rest of Israeli society for the nullification of Israeli-Arab citizenship and expulsion from the country.

Network spokesman Jihad Ballout disputes that Al-Jazeera manufactures militancy:

> Our job is to disseminate facts and it is up to people how they see the facts for themselves. Some people might say if a Palestinian has seen the heavy-handedness with which the Israelis are dealing with the intifada, he will think twice

before he goes and joins a demonstration. Some people will say, 'No! The Palestinians are more aggravated and they want to fight more.' This is not for us to determine. What we should determine is what is newsworthy, what is factual, what is relevant and give it to people. So I really take issue with this description of incitement. The people of Palestine do not need Al-Jazeera to let them know what their rights are and what they should do against occupiers. We did not create the situation.

At least, thanks to Al-Jazeera, Palestinians in the Occupied Territories no longer depend on rumours for their news. 'It is not easy in the Arab world now, even in Israel, to tell people the truth. It is very easy to speak about emotions, to be more sensational and less factual,' Walid al-Omary told me in his office in Ramallah. 'It is not enough to be honest. First you must be honest, but then you must investigate everything. You need a lot of courage to tell the people the truth.' Al-Jazeera has helped quench the culture of conspiracy among the Palestinians; occasionally, as in Jenin, this has even been of advantage to the Israelis.

Whether Al-Jazeera's footage will continue to galvanize support for Palestine in future remains to be seen. Human nature tends to become inured to horrible pictures. Maybe the motivational effect the initial intifada pictures had on the Arab world in the winter of 2000 will not be repeated.

When I was in Jordan I wanted to find out how Al-Jazeera's coverage of events in Iraq had been received. I wanted to know whether it was, as is so often alleged, inflammatory. Jordan, I soon learned, has close links with Iraq. One night the President of the Jordanian Writers Union and her friends took me to a nightclub just outside Amman, near the airport. It was March and there was nearly a foot of snow on the ground. Ignorantly anticipating winter sunshine, I had packed flip-flops for the trip, and I sat shivering in these and a thin, long-sleeved T-shirt as her four-wheel-drive Mercedes churned through the snow.

The nightclub she took me too doubled as a restaurant. The centrepiece was a very loud band playing the timeless hits of legendary Arab songbird Umm Kalthoum on a synthesizer, drums and a funky slap bass. The main act that night was a singer called Mr Ali, but when we turned up, at about ten o'clock, the cavernous club was still empty, save for six eager waiters looking very smart in racing-green waistcoats.

Dinner was ordered and I braced myself for Mr Ali. I knew from previous visits to Arab nightclubs that this might last a while. He did not show up until well after we had eaten, when the waiters brought us water pipes and coffee. A tanned crooner in a brown suit, he looked like he might have been more at home on a cruise ship than in a snowbound nightclub.

Cheesy is not a word in the Arab songwriter's handbook and after a couple of bottles of decidedly ropy rosé, fed up with Mr Ali losing his love to the night, I was ready to leave. But the hits kept coming and I was duty-bound to stay with my friends. Midnight came and went, 1 a.m., 1.30, until finally, at 2 a.m., I could stifle my yawns no longer. Just as I was getting ready to go a pair of Iraqis who had been dining at a table nearby jumped up and started dancing. First the two men slung their arms around each other's shoulders and kicked out their feet. Then, as one clapped along to Mr Ali, the other spun and swayed around him, like a flamenco dancer. He twirled his prayer beads, then whirled his handkerchief above his head as he stomped his feet in a sombre traditional Iraqi dance.

Speaking to the pair afterwards, I learned that Jordanians and Iraqis share strong tribal links. Many Jordanians have family or businesses in Iraq and the American-led attack on Iraq, they said, felt like an attack on Jordan itself. Iraqis, they told me, recognized Jordanian songs the way an American might recognize a British one.

America, they said, had broken international law invading Iraq. They did not believe that the war was for democracy, but for some nefarious purpose, which probably had something to do with oil. No one expected troops to be leaving any time soon. They hated Bush and his cabal, but there was some sympathy for the American GIs, who were sitting ducks in Iraq. 'No one deserves to die aged twenty, miles from home,' one of the men told me.

There has been much soul-searching in Washington about why America is so unpopular in the Middle East. Often-cited reasons are that Arabs misunderstand America's real intentions, Arabs hate American freedom or there is some toxic quality inherent in Islam. Some even believe that Arabs can never like America as long as Israel exists. But none of these is the correct diagnosis of the problem and consequently all the solutions offered have been misconceived and disastrously executed. Meanwhile, America's unpopularity has escalated to the point where today it is a serious threat to the region's stability and American national security.

Arabs do not resent America's freedom and wealth. Spend a few minutes chatting to people in any souk or coffee shop in the Arab world and you will find that most people love American culture, have an encyclopedic knowledge of American TV and movies and harbour dreams of living in America. The Iraqis I spoke with in Jordan were happily puffing away on American cigarettes. Arabs lust after the idea of becoming part of America. Young Arabs in Yemen would ask me all the time how they could get a coveted green card and they spoke with fondness of friends and relatives already living in the States. Even members of the Palestinian Authority send their children to America to be educated, invest their money there and, if they can, visit on holiday.

Nor is America's unpopularity due to some inherent problem within Islam, even if a tiny fraction of fanatical Muslims, like Osama bin Laden, would have us believe otherwise. The Christian Arabs I met in Jordan feel exactly the same way about America as Muslim ones. Nor is Arab antipathy to America born of some immovable objection to the existence of Israel, which is just as well, because if it were there would be no hope for peace. Israel has the right and the weapons to defend itself to the bitter end. Fortunately, every Arab government, including the Palestinian Authority, has now recognized Israel's right to exist.

The new American-backed Arabic-language media programme operates on the principle that the rift between Arabs and the West is fundamentally the result of a giant misunderstanding, an information deficit, which can be rectified by careful explanation of the West's good intentions. Tony Blair has spoken of a 'gulf of misunderstanding' between East and West. Once Arabs can be made to see what the West is really on about, the problem will be solved.

'One of the biggest problems in the Middle East comes from an incredible lack of information,' said Molly McKew, Fellow of the AEI.

> Most people don't know what is going on in their own countries and in the Middle East. Misunderstanding and misinformation is a big part of why Arabs are the way they are in the Arab world and I think that it has to do with focusing on specific issues again and again and again. When all you see is Americans attacking Iraqis or Afghanis, then yes, you are going to hate America. And if you have no idea what America actually is or what is going on here or what we do in the rest of the world or aid programmes or any of that stuff or that most Arab countries receive absurd amounts of foreign aid that they just don't know about, then yeah, you are going to have a bad opinion of the United States and you are going to hate our foreign policy . . .

During the Cold War, programmes to communicate US policy abroad, like scholarships to help foreign students study in America, international broadcasting initiatives and information outlets in US embassies, were all major priorities. Since the eighties the amount of money available to fund public diplomacy programmes has dropped, in real terms, by more than 50 per cent. More recently, in response to the rising tide of anti-Americanism, Congress, the Department of State and the White House have all stepped up spending on peddling America to the Middle East. Since 9/11 the Voice of America and the BBC have increased programming to the Middle East and Central Asia, and several new radio and television stations have been launched. A billion dollars has already been spent, yet still that does not seem to be enough and some well-meaning senators are campaigning for even more. 'The aggregate amount that we devote to communicating the American vision to the rest of the world, about $1.2 billion, is less than half of what some individual American companies, such as the Ford Motor Co. or PepsiCo Inc., spend on advertising each year,' Senator Richard Lugar lamented in March 2003. A billion dollars spent on public diplomacy is about the same as what Britain or France spends on public diplomacy, or about 0.25 per cent of the US military budget, for the same period. Only about $25 million of this billion is spent on programmes that actually impact on Arabs in their home countries.

Polls show us that despite America's renewed efforts this campaign has been bewilderingly ineffectual. A report commissioned by the US Congress published in October 2003, drafted by thirteen experts and overseen by a former US Ambassador to Syria and Israel, found anti-American sentiment in the Arab world had reached what it called 'shocking levels'. The document, entitled *Changing Minds, Winning Peace*, advised, 'We call, in this report, for a dramatic transformation in public diplomacy, in the way the United States communicates its values and policies to enhance our national security. That transformation requires an immediate end to the absurd and dangerous underfunding of public diplomacy in a time of peril.' If 'America does not define itself' to the Muslim world, the report's author warned, 'the extremists will do it for us'.

In response to these alarm bells, in spring 2003 the American government launched its most adventurous media project since the launch of the Voice of America in 1942. It was called the Middle East Television Network, or Al-Hurra. Al-Hurra was to be the new American Arabic-language satellite service. The chairman of the Broadcasting Board of Governors (BBG) described it to the Senate Foreign Relations Committee as 'the most important public-diplomacy initiative of our time'. 'Al-Jazeera should not go unanswered in the Middle East,' he added. President Bush said it would cut through the 'hateful propaganda that fills the airwaves in the Muslim world'. It was launched in January at a cost of more than $100 million to US taxpayers. The money came out of the $74.7 billion the Bush administration had earmarked to spend on the war and on home-land security, and would keep it going for the first year. The blueprint for Al-Hurra's programming suggested it would look something like a hybrid between CNN and the Discovery Channel, and the BBG, which oversees all American govern-ment civilian broadcasting, including the Voice of America, would command the new channel.

Al-Hurra, staffed by a strange mix of American media exec-utives and established Arab journalists, would be receivable by satellite in twenty-two Middle Eastern countries as well as terres-trially in Iraq. It was to be based in Springfield, Virginia, but would share news bureaux across the Arab world with Associated Press. The director of the new channel was a Lebanese called Muwaffaq Harb, who had been the former Washington bureau chief for a major Arabic daily newspaper.

'We're contending with a media environment that includes hate speak in radio and TV,' said media mogul Norman J. Pattiz, founder of both Radio Sawa and Al-Hurra. Pattiz is a member of the BBG, along with Colin Powell, leaving the channel open from the very start to high-level accusations of being nothing more than a shameless exercise in propaganda by the US Department of State.

Pattiz and Harb both insisted Al-Hurra was absolutely not a propaganda outlet and had complete editorial independence. 'We don't do propaganda,' Pattiz insisted. 'We're going to put out a product that will be superior to what they can get in the region. Our product will be sampled because of who we are. The challenge is to make sure that the product is good when we go on the air, not because of who we are but because of the way information is presented.'

It was a controversial decision to back Al-Hurra instead of the Voice of America, which had spent decades building a credible reputation, and a lot of people in Washington were wondering why all this money was being invested in a tyro. But, in fact, it was the same project: Al-Hurra was just the Voice of America under a different name. The Voice of America's Arabic service closed down when Al-Hurra started and a source at the Sudanese Embassy in London told me that he knew five Sudanese employed for that service who now work for Al-Hurra.

The Al-Hurra headquarters were to be in Virginia, not Washington, where the Voice of America is based, and, just like the Voice of America, neither Al-Hurra nor Radio Sawa can legally broadcast inside America. This is due to the 1948 Smith–Mundt Act, designed to prevent state-funded stations competing with regular commercial stations, which rules that information by these kinds of broadcasters 'shall not be disseminated within the United States'.

Al-Hurra launched with much fanfare and an exclusive interview from President Bush, recorded a week in advance. It was met with a resounding hostility in the Arab press, including on Al-Jazeera. 'I predict that if Al-Hurra television does offer Arabs and Muslims a better understanding of American society and values, its main impact will be to heighten Arab anger and irritation with US policy in the Middle East because the gap between American values and American foreign policy conduct will become even more obvious to newly enlightened Middle Easterners,' prophesied Rami Khouri. 'Al-Hurra, like the US government's Radio Sawa and *Hi* magazine before it, will be an entertaining, expensive, and irrelevant hoax. Where do they get this stuff from? Why do they keep insulting us like this?'

Rejected in the Middle East, Al-Hurra was also immediately stabbed in the back. 'It has a chance of turning out to be one of this country's most ill-conceived and wasteful experiments ever in public diplomacy,' blasted the *Washington Post*. 'No one seems to have asked three critical questions: What precisely is the market niche for this station? What will its programmatic content be? And is this the most effective and efficient way to spend a new, large pot of public diplomacy money?'

Critics pointed out that it was superfluous to launch a second, very expensive Middle East TV Network, when Al-Iraqiyah, the disastrous SAIC-run TV network in Iraq, was already broadcasting. 'Everyone tells me they have separate missions, but I can't get it through my thick skull what the difference is,' said Mark Helmke, a senior adviser to Senator Lugar. 'And I'm not sure the average Iraqi will see the difference either.'

Anecdotal reports soon after the channel started suggested that although Arabs enjoyed some of the documentaries, they discarded the news out of hand. I visited Washington two months after the launch, where I met a spokesman from the Department of State to talk about the new channel and I visited Al-Hurra's Washington bureau, which remains in the Voice of America building, where Radio Sawa is too.

The spokesman took pains to dissociate the Department of State from Al-Hurra. I was constantly reminded that the new station was a 'supplementary', which meant that it is federally, not publicly, funded by Congress. No money comes out of the Department of State's budget for the channel and Al-Hurra employees are not employees of the Department of State, I was told emphatically.

The idea was that Al-Hurra would follow the success of Radio Sawa, which had come out with huge market shares in some countries – 70 per cent in Morocco, according to Nielsen polls. The big question though, was were these channels 'moving the needle', as they say in the Department of State, in terms of diminishing levels of anti-American sentiment?

'In the Middle East it is impossible to tell if one station moves

the needle. Every Arab you ever meet has a view of America
that comes from a myriad of sources. It comes from the bill-
board selling Coke, it comes from watching *Dallas*, it comes
from reading magazines, I mean, they are bombarded with
images! How we could measure the effect of one radio station
would be nearly an impossible task,' I was told by the Department
of State, although this logic seems to fly in the face of the
American administration's constant criticism of Al-Jazeera, which
holds the station single-handedly responsible for inciting
violence.

When the Department of State officials I met who worked
at Al-Hurra told me they were journalists, it was patently ridiculous – they were clearly not – and indeed they are wrong even
to pretend to be. Al-Hurra staff are not even allowed to question
the US administration, only to repeat policy internationally.
When Radio Marti, a similar US-backed media venture, also
under the direction of America's Broadcasting Board of
Governors, started questioning the Clinton administration about
its Cuba policy, the director of the US information agency issued
a memo to the then head of America's Cuba Broadcasting
reminding him that 'the employees of Radio Marti are employees of the US government'. Al-Hurra, like Radio Marti, is, in
short, a mouthpiece for the regime.

The day I visited Al-Hurra I also stopped by the Radio Sawa
offices, the other big American-backed media initiative. The
offices looked pretty moribund, the mood decidedly sombre.
This might be because they are always sombre – it must be
tough working at a place where you know most of the Arab
world reviles you as a propagandist and collaborator – but it
might also have been because the day I visited the station was
in the process of being moved out of the Voice of America
building, down the road to Virginia, to serve under the same
banner as Al-Hurra. This too would be understandably demor-
alizing: while before staff at Radio Sawa had been part of the
Department of State, where employees have career security and
fat pensions, now, at the whisk of a pen, they were being

consigned to the same uncertain future as employees at Al-Hurra.

The staff at Al-Hurra told me they were angry at being subverted by powers within Washington itself, but they understood why. When the Department of State first decided to set up a new Arabic-language TV station, fierce bidding ensued from a number of well-connected applicants for the whopping $100-million start-up fund. Most people thought that the best way to spread America's message would be to make programmes one at a time, then give them away to Arab channels for free. Most Arab satellite television stations import about two-thirds of their output, so this should have been easy enough. Al-Hurra argued, successfully as it turned out, that if you let the Arabs control the distribution, they could sandwich programmes between negative reports and ruin the message by showing it out of context. Production and distribution both needed to be controlled, otherwise, Al-Hurra warned, the same thing could happen to the new channel as happened to the joint BBC-Orbit Arabic project, when the Saudis, who had been the distributors, had switched the signal off whenever they did not like what was on. Congress agreed and Al-Hurra got the cash.

According to sources within Al-Hurra, some of those individuals and companies who were passed over in the bidding process became bitter at missing out on the millions and that is when things got ugly. Now, the staff complained, Al-Hurra was facing attacks on two fronts: total rejection in the Middle East and a rearguard assault from within Washington.

The network began by running a series of travelogues, featuring young women travelling in the Middle East. The idea was to reach out to the female Arab audience, a demographic Al-Hurra staff have said they feel is neglected. They know this is true, they told me, because they conducted extensive market research before the channel was launched. But many of Al-Hurra's travelogues aimed at women are in English with Arabic subtitles. The US government's own figures show that 53 per cent of the female population in Egypt, and more than

75 per cent of the female population of Iraq, is illiterate. Their research could not have been very extensive.

When I saw Muwaffaq Harb, Al-Hurra's director, at a conference in Cambridge, England, some of these points were put to him. 'We do not promote US foreign policy, we explain it. There is a difference,' he argued, looking edgy in a sharp suit. When pushed on what exactly he meant by this, he became very defensive and walked out while the discussion was still going on. Sadly, Al-Hurra is just another ill-conceived Washington media stunt, leading nowhere.

In July 2004 nearly half of the Voice of America's thousand-strong staff signed a petition addressed to Congress, protesting against what they called the 'piece-by-piece' dismemberment of their sixty-two-year-old service. The petition took issue with an array of recent decisions made by the Broadcasting Board of Governors, but cited in particular the Board's decision to close the VOA Arabic service in favour of fanciful new projects which had, according to the petition, 'no editorial accountability' and were 'killing VOA'.

Their grievances were bolstered by the results of a survey conducted by Professor Shibley Telhami, Arab media and policy expert at the Brookings Institute. A poll of 3,300 Arabs in Morocco, Egypt, Jordan, Lebanon, the United Arab Emirates and Saudi Arabia found none cited Al-Hurra as their first-choice television news station and only 3.8 per cent of respondents cited it as their second choice. Al-Jazeera was found to be the most popular news channel.

Arabs I spoke with across the Middle East told me the US media offensive has, if anything, made them more distrustful of America. Arab media staff attached to the British Embassy in Amman told me that the American media campaign in Jordan is seen as splashy and expensive, heavy on slogans and glitz but light on sustainability and long-term impact. Local partners and methods are ignored and Jordanian employees are never trusted to do a proper job. It is extraordinary that America, traditionally so gifted at advertising and so rich in resources, has managed to put together a public diplomacy campaign that is neither public nor diplomatic.

Rather than upset the locals with culturally insensitive media projects and waste money on multi-million-dollar television stations run by defence contractors with close links to the White House, the American administration would have done better to try to deliver its message through trusted outlets – like Al-Jazeera. At first American officials hesitated over doing interviews on Al-Jazeera because they calculated that it might reward a station with a reputation for militancy or that it might be seen as stooping to compete with Osama bin Laden. These fears were misguided, and they fail to take account of the fact that by 9/11 Al-Jazeera had already become the *de facto* platform for announcing new policy initiatives in the Middle East, for regional leaders from Libya to Israel. These leaders did not choose Al-Jazeera for their policy announcements because they appreciated everything they saw and heard on the channel, but simply because they wanted to borrow the network's credibility and reach its wide audience.

If, instead of savaging Al-Jazeera for its allegedly biased reporting, the Department of State had engaged with the network positively, it would have sent a clear message to the Arab world that it was serious about freedom of the press and serious about freedom of expression. However, the US administration sent a different message: freedom of expression is important for Americans, but not for Arabs – just as civil rights for Arabs are not important the way they are for Americans. 'If I was a strategist in the Bush administration I would advise him strongly to communicate with the Arab world through the media that is best viewed in Arab opinion, and that is Al-Jazeera,' said Jihad Ballout.

Al-Jazeera's chief news editor, Ibrahim Hilal, spoke for many Arabs when he said, 'I find it strange that the United States has this rage against Al-Jazeera. American officials are attacking us for exercising the principles that we have learned from their own country.'

Stubbornly boycotting Al-Jazeera was counterproductive, leaving America's position unexplained and undefended. Trying to censor Al-Jazeera only increased its popularity, just as, when the British government replaced the voice of Sinn Fein leader Gerry Adams with an Irish-accented actor in the eighties, they only drew attention to what he was saying. Pressuring the Qataris to 'tone down' the station was deeply hypocritical and outraged even the most pro-American Arabs.

'This is sad, because if the US would like to promote independent media they should keep the channels open with the station,' said Washington bureau chief Hafez al-Mirazi. 'Even if they think that a government might have influence on it, they should not encourage this kind of influence and should try first to solve it through the executives or the heads of the station. But that is not the case and they don't make a secret out of it.'

When Colin Powell had a quiet word with the Emir asking him to tone down Al-Jazeera it jeopardized the American administration's relationship with the network. When the Kabul bureau was blown up a few weeks later, it was only logical to assume there was a connection between Powell's quiet word and the attack.

'When we feel the need to dump on Al-Jazeera we dump on both Al-Jazeera and the Qatari government and complain to both of them,' said the Department of State spokesman Dr Nabil Khouri. But if America has a problem with Al-Jazeera, it should approach the channel's executives, not the Qatari government. The BBC, financed by the British licence-payer, sometimes faces disputes with other countries, but the British government does not answer on the network's behalf and nor should the government of Qatar.

Targeting Al-Jazeera, by banning, bombing or criticizing it, has only served to rehabilitate the station in the eyes of the Arabs. Al-Mirazi explained why:

> The interviews we were given by the Americans, especially after the Afghan war, created some scepticism in the Arab world and drove people back to saying, 'There is something going on between those guys at Al-Jazeera and

the Americans. We don't accept their games, like when they say the American administration is angry with them or whatever. They are doing the jobs of Mossad and the CIA and the Israelis and the Americans.'

Even the Al-Qaeda tapes, people were saying, were doctored and given to Al-Jazeera in order to prove that 9/11 had been done by Arabs and Muslims. So sometimes if the administration thinks that it is punishing us by not giving us interviews, sometimes they are not punishing us but they are helping our image in the Arab world.

It is remarkable that until Al-Jazeera ran the Al-Qaeda tapes, American officials lauded the station for its free speech. The Department of State's Human Rights Report on Qatar 2000 says:

The government lifted formal censorship of the media in 1995, and since then the press has been essentially free of government interference . . . There were no reports of instances of political censorship of foreign news media or broadcasts of foreign programmes on local television over the past year. The Censorship Office in the Ministry of Information was abolished (together with the Ministry) in 1996 . . . Television and radio are state owned, but the privately owned satellite television channel Al Jazeera operates freely. During the year, radio and television call-in programs and talk shows criticized the Amir for meeting the Israeli Prime Minister at the UN Millennium Summit in September, and the government was criticized for allowing the Israeli Trade Office to remain open before the November Islamic Summit. Various government ministers are regularly criticized on a popular radio talk show.

How quickly the US administration changed its tune shortly afterwards, when Al-Jazeera started reporting the extent of the 'collateral damage' that American bombs were causing in Afghanistan.

America's attacks on Al-Jazeera not only run contrary to the position laid out in its own Department of State report: they also contradict American media policy objectives in other parts of the world. The Department has, for a long time, been pressuring Russia to open up its media to more Al-Jazeera-style television news and in June 2000, when the Russian government started imprisoning people of one sort or another who worked in the media, the White House and Congress fiercely condemned this attack on the free press: 'We agree that Russia's international standing will be severely damaged if the government lets stand actions that are intended to intimidate independent media and voices with whom it does not agree,' said Department of State spokesman Richard Boucher.

'I think for our purposes, we'll continue to make the case that a free and open press is an essential part of a democracy,' said Joe Lockhart, press secretary for US President Bill Clinton. On Capitol Hill, Congressman Christopher Smith stressed that, no matter what their political affiliation, all members of Congress were horrified at Russia's 'tightening of the noose' around the neck of the free press.

'Mr Putin – if he wants to be president of a democratic society – needs to understand that leaders in democratic societies are subject to criticism,' said Congressman Tom Lantos (Democrat, California). 'President Clinton has been subject to criticism. [Former US] President [Ronald] Reagan has been subject to criticism. And it's time for Mr Putin to grow up and understand that if he wants to run a free society, he will be subject to criticism.' President Bush has since frequently reconfirmed this commitment to free speech worldwide: 'This is the fight of all who believe in progress and pluralism, tolerance and freedom,' he said in a speech nine days after 9/11.

The American administration must come to terms with the reality that the proliferation of satellite news in the Arab world is an irreversible development. No one can stuff the genie back inside the bottle. Instead of squandering money on lavish advertising campaigns and glitzy new television networks showing happy

Muslims living in America, the American administration would have done a better job winning hearts and minds by spending more money on training a few more people to speak Arabic at a level where they could state their case on Al-Jazeera. The Arabs I met could not care less about happy Muslims living in America. Ideally, America should be able to field spokesmen regularly capable of taking part in debates in Arabic, which is admittedly not easy, due to the dialects and fluency of the exchange.

Despite a billion dollars spent on public relations, long-term investment in learning Russian during the Cold War means today there is a serious lack of Arabic speakers in the American administration. Incredibly, America has fewer than five spokesmen capable of advocating American policy in Arabic in a televised debate on Al-Jazeera. During the invasion of Iraq the American spokesman who appeared on Al-Jazeera, although a career diplomat, spoke through a translator – a clumsy PR mistake. If America cannot even answer the case against it, then what can it expect but to be trampled on in every argument? As Woody Allen said, 'Ninety per cent of life is just showing up.'

If Western governments cannot field the linguists to appear on Al-Jazeera, they would do well at least to watch it. Currently, no native Arabic speakers in the American or British intelligence services make it their business to monitor Al Jazeera's output around the clock. When I asked one senior British naval officer responsible for media liaison during the invasion of Iraq what he made of Al-Jazeera's coverage of the war, he told me, 'I had no one to watch the output for me, so I have no idea whether Al-Jazeera represented us fairly or not. In Doha there was a Jordanian guy hired by the Brits to watch TV stations and comment on the output. The result was that it was judged broadly balanced.'

Watching Al-Jazeera intermittently is not sufficient. In a region where gauging public opinion is notoriously difficult, Al-Jazeera's talk shows are a crucial weathervane of public political, social and religious opinion. Politics may be virtually non-existent in the Arab world, but television news is one place it can be practised and all the Arab news channels taken together can be studied almost like a parliament. Since most Arab TV reflects its respective government's position, together they can be read almost as a proxy forum for making and discussing foreign policy.

In November 2003 the former US Ambassador to Morocco and Department of State spokeswoman Margaret Tutwiler replaced Charlotte Beers as America's next Public Diplomacy Czar. 'Poor Margaret Tutwiler has just been given a fresh mandate to "sell" America to the world, as though we were a brand of toothpaste,' wrote former US Ambassador to Nepal (1981–84) Carleton S. Coon, Jr. 'The Bush administration is so convinced that spin can overcome substance that it would market toothpaste tasting like cow manure if it thought its advertising budget was sufficient. Tutwiler can only succeed if we change the product.'

Sure enough, less than six months later Tutwiler announced her resignation. It was another bitter blow to the Bush administration's PR campaign and since it was quite unexpected, and due to the handover of sovereignty in Iraq and the US presidential elections, the post lay unfilled well into the following year.

The root of Arab hatred towards America today has nothing to do with Al-Jazeera. When I asked Arabs from across the Arab world why they hated America so much they repeatedly told me the same thing: it is not a question of media; it is a question of foreign policy. Arabs see the Bush administration as an accomplice to crimes in Palestine and now the perpetrator of an illegal war and botched occupation in Iraq. They are angry that America props up oppressive Arab dictatorships with aid and trade when it could be supporting moderates, but above all, they despise America's one-sided policy towards the dispute between Israel and the Palestinians. 'Slavery was as much the fault of the cotton merchants of Massachusetts as it was the plantation owners of the South,' one Egyptian journalist told me, quoting Henry Thoreau in *Walden*, and so all Arabs implicitly connect the Israeli army in the Occupied Territories with the power in Washington.

The older generation in the Arab world still fondly remembers the occasions in the past on which America took a more balanced approach to the Middle East, for example when President Dwight Eisenhower intervened on behalf of the Egyptians against a joint assault by the French, British and Israelis during the Suez Crisis in 1956. Eisenhower took action despite the fact he was in the middle of a re-election campaign, and it did him no harm with the voters.

Thanks to the information revolution, Arab youth are not like their parents, who could scarcely make a telephone call to or from the Middle East or transmit any data in any form besides the Western alphabet. Arab teenagers are fast growing used to the Internet, as well as fax machines, satellite television, mobile phones, text messaging, voicemail, photos, audio and video recording, and all the other paraphernalia of modern communications technology, and they are fast learning to expect the same opportunities as their Western friends, with whom they keep in touch via email and the Internet. They are already well able to decipher political realities and are sophisticated at spotting propaganda. Unlike their parents, they have an internationalist outlook and a rights-based mentality. Their sense of injustice at what is happening in the Arab world today is neither cynical, nor naive, but ethical.

For Arabs everywhere, everything America does in the Middle East today is seen through the prism of Palestine. Washington is blamed for blocking attempts to find a 'just and lasting peace' between Israelis and Palestinians, for freezing the road map to peace and for supporting an extremist Israeli government that is in contravention of international law. When President Bush calls Israeli Prime Minister Ariel Sharon 'a man of peace', all the advertising expertise of Madison Avenue will not help him win Arab hearts and minds. You cannot polish a turd.

'If the American administration wants Arab support they should change their policy on the Palestinian issue,' was the blunt view of Al-Jazeera's bureau chief in the West Bank, Walid al-Omary, who explained:

They have supported an extremist government in Israel. They have supported nothing of the Palestinians'. The

Arabs have no reason to like America. The Arabs have suffered under the Americans more than any other nation. Americans support regimes in Arab countries who are against their own people.

If America changed its policy, Palestinians would forgive America. They know America holds the key. If the Americans tell the Israelis to withdraw from the West Bank, they will withdraw within a few days. In the last closure around Arafat, which was in September 2002, he was really in danger of his life. The Americans told the Israelis to leave the Arafat compound within two hours – the Israelis were out in twenty minutes.

A deeply revealing poll conducted in 2002 by the American pollster Zogby International illustrated graphically the significance of the Palestine issue to Arabs. Three thousand eight hundred Arab adults from eight countries were polled about their values, political concerns and outlook on the world. When asked to rank ten concerns in order of importance, they rated 'civil and personal rights' first, healthcare second and the rights of the Palestinian people third. Concern for Palestine ranked higher than an individual's personal economic situation and their concern for moral standards. The Arabs polled who cared most about Palestine came from Morocco and Saudi Arabia. Jordanians, it turned out, were no more concerned about Palestine than other Arabs.

'After more than three generations of conflict, the betrayal and the denial of Palestinian rights, this issue of Palestine appears to have become a defining one of general Arab concern,' Zogby's poll concluded. 'It is not seen in the same way as "the general Arab situation", nor does it appear to be viewed as an issue of foreign policy as in "relations with non-Arab countries". Rather, for our respondents, the situation of the Palestinians appears to have become a personal matter lumped together in a basket of other issues like civil rights and health care and ahead of more general concerns like moral standards or the state of their country's economy.'

For Arabs, the conflict in Palestine has become an existential issue, a touchstone for their pitiful situation in the world today. The daily images that come out of the conflict impress upon them recurrent feelings of helplessness and betrayal at the hands of the West. Until America resolves to make peace between the Israelis and Palestinians it can expect no popular support in Iraq, Afghanistan or anywhere else in the Arab or Muslim world.

If American policy makers continue without sparing a thought for the impact their policies might have on foreign opinion, they can only expect more terrorism. If America does not address the issues that matter most to Arabs, then there are others who will: like Osama bin Laden. 'America will never dream of security or see it, before we live it and see it in Palestine; and not before the infidel's armies depart the land of Muhammad,' he said dreamily on 7 October 2001, pointing his finger at the lens of the camera. Millions were watching.

Until there is peace in Palestine, impressionable young Arabs will continue to be attracted to violence and terrorism as a means to resolve the situation the only way they think possible. 'The main question is not about Al-Jazeera,' the network's reporter in Amman told me. 'The question is, are the United States and the West doing enough to promote democracy in the Arab world? The truth is that they are still supporting, protecting or tolerating some dictatorships in the Arab world to look after their own geopolitical or economic interests. If America changed its policy towards Palestine you would see American flags flying from every rooftop in Amman tomorrow.'

Unfortunately, rather than unearth the real roots of the problem, the current American administration chooses to blame Al-Jazeera for the phenomenal hatred Arabs feel towards America today. The real problem, America's unflinching support for Israel, is only ever spoken about in a formulaic, politically correct way, devoid of meaning. Terrorism is blamed solely on the Palestinians and discussion of any possible connection between the invasion of Iraq and America's policy towards Israel remains strictly taboo. When such a distorted political ideology is combined with a derisory cultural understanding of Middle Eastern societies, it is no wonder the world is in a mess.

The former US Ambassador to Nepal, Coon, wrote:

> It is truly a situation comparable to the parable about the emperor that has no clothes. The 'Israel right or wrong' gang in America has managed to impose such a complete embargo on any rational discussion of the subject that in order to find any intelligent analysis of the Israeli factor you have to turn to Europe, or to Israel itself, where the liberal opposition in that country can still raise its voice. American gentiles have been bludgeoned into the notion that any attempt to relate recent Israeli expansionism to American interests in the region is, horrors! anti-Semitic and there-fore completely reprehensible and anti-American. And every time some American Jews try to raise questions, they are accused of undermining Israel's security. It's amazing, how unfree our vaunted free speech has become on this issue.

Today the media is too often an agent of recrimination and hate. In serving its viewers, the media on both sides aggravates the differences between the two cultures, while significant commu-nication between the two camps remains minimal. When Americans and Arabs meet one another, they shake hands, do business and interact, but they do not communicate in any mean-ingful way. The most famous Arab Muslim in America is Osama bin Laden.

The frayed relationship between the West and the Middle East has never been easy, but after 9/11 there was a fleeting window of opportunity for both sides to come to understand one another better. This window closed with the invasion of Afghanistan. Since then it has often been glibly stated that Al-Jazeera and the rest of the Arab media is shaping Arab public opinion towards the West for the first time. But Arabs have been mulling over the pros and cons of democracy for almost two hundred years: what is meant is that today Arab public opinion matters for the first time.

11

Watching from the West

Since it began in 1996 Al-Jazeera has been steadily expanding. First it gradually became a twenty-four-hour broadcaster, then, in January 2001, it added an Arabic-language website, followed by a sports channel, a text-messaging service, a channel dedicated to live events, websites in Arabic and English and a tri-lingual news service distributed by mobile phones.

On 9 September 2005 Sheikha Moza bint Nasser al-Misned, the Emir's irrepressible second wife, inaugurated her latest educational project – the Al-Jazeera Children's Channel. It is the first Arabic-language channel dedicated to children and produces more of its own programming than any other children's channel worldwide – over 40 per cent. It began with an initial staff of two hundred and thirty five, all based in Qatar, and is aimed at children aged three to fifteen world-wide. At the launch, the Executive General Manager of the new channel said that Al-Jazeera Children's Channel would specifically target Arabic-speaking children in North America, and that an English-language children's channel was now being planned.

Over the years, the number of news bureaux worldwide has grown, and the network's bureaux in London and Washington have steadily increased in size. Today Al-Jazeera broadcasts several shows live from either Washington or London each week. By focusing on a global audience, Al-Jazeera has become increasingly popular in the West.

This popularity has had a profound impact on Arabic-speaking communities living in the West. There are an estimated 1.8 million speakers of Arabic in the US, some four hundred thousand in Britain and just under eight hundred thousand in Germany. I travelled to Dearborn, Michigan, the heart of the Arab-American community, to find out how the rise of Al-Jazeera had affected the Arab expatriate community there. I found that although Al-Jazeera plays an even bigger role in day-to-day life than it does in the lives of Arabs living in the Middle East, its sudden rise has also produced some unexpected social problems.

Dearborn is a suburb of Detroit, Michigan. It has the largest concentration of Arabs anywhere outside the Middle East. If you keep your eyes peeled while travelling in the Middle East you might guess that Michigan plays home to a big Arab community: at Arab airports you often see Arab families wearing Michigan football jerseys or Michigan State University T-shirts. In the queue for the check-in desk at Cairo airport I saw a whole family, men, women and children, kitted out in black-and-white Michigan tracksuits.

Detroit is a dilapidated, rust-belt American city, grey, flat and windswept. Tourists do not visit much, except for some down-market casinos, a few grimy, greasy-spoon restaurants and the annual North American International Auto Show. Anyone who makes any money doesn't stick around for long, partly because of the city's worldwide reputation for violent crime. The murder capital of America in 2001, Detroit was narrowly beaten into second place by Washington in 2002 and 2003. Besides a steady economic decline, 'Motor City' has offered the world Motown, techno and, more recently, rapper Eminem.

Driving around Detroit – which is the only convenient way to get around as the big car manufacturers bought and dismantled much of the public transport system – you notice that houses in the centre of town have their windows boarded up, factories sit abandoned, their windows smashed, and land that should hold businesses is now covered in knee-high grass barely concealing the rusted husks of burned-out cars. Central Detroit has not even got the basic fast-food staples, like Burger King and McDonald's, we have come to expect in every American city. The opening of a new branch of the International House of Pancakes made the evening news.

Dearborn, the prosperous Arab suburb, is just a few miles west of downtown Detroit. Covering twenty-seven square miles, it was once known as the heart of the Ford Motor Company and the legend of Henry Ford still looms large over every public park, library and community college. Today Dearborn has a thirty-thousand-strong Arab community – about a third of the total population – dominated by Lebanese and Iraqis, and has become one of the more desirable parts of the Detroit area. The main street, Warren Street, is lined with businesses signed in Arabic – cafés, automotive repair shops, legal firms, dental practices and supermarkets. Unlike the rest of Detroit, Dearborn is relatively safe and there are no homeless or drug dealers lurking on street corners. There are also a dozen mosques, including America's largest, which stands beneath a $15-million dome sprouting out of Ford Avenue. Walking down Warren Street, you have to remind yourself you are in Michigan. Men and women wear Arab clothes, flowing white *dishdashas* or black headscarves. It is also the probable location for Al-Jazeera's next American bureau.

Dearborn has a history of racist violence. Throughout the 1930s racism, poverty and poor labour conditions at the Ford car plant sparked a number of riots and murders. Ford himself was a notorious anti-Semite who blamed international Jewry for the world's wrongs. His own newspaper, the *Dearborn Times*, printed *The Protocols of Zion*, an infamous anti-Semitic text fabricated in Russia at the end of the nineteenth century that describes a Jewish plot to take over the world.

In 1943 a brawl broke out between white sailors and local blacks that spiralled into a riot engulfing much of Detroit. Eighteen hundred people were arrested, hundreds were injured, thirty-four people were killed and millions of dollars' worth of damage was done. In 1967, after Detroit police raided a 'blind pig', an illegal after-hours drinking den, riots broke out between poor urban blacks and white police. The rioters set fire to buildings and looted businesses of everything of value. Forty-three people died.

Dearborn, in those days, was a 'closed' town which had a segregated population of white Italian and Polish immigrants. Mayor Orville Hubbard, the fat, folksy 'dictator of Dearborn', stood with a gun on the city line between Dearborn and Detroit, to stop the hordes of rampaging black rioters he feared would be sweeping into his town on a looting spree. Hubbard was the most outspoken segregationist of his era outside the Deep South; his slogan 'Keep Dearborn Clean', which actually meant 'Keep Dearborn White', ensured he remained the town's mayor until 1982, after thirty-six years in the job. It is a testament to his legacy that Dearborn remains the only city in America that still does not celebrate Martin Luther King Day.

If Mayor Orville Hubbard could see what Detroit looked like today, he would roll over in his grave. The Italian and Polish immigrants, the first generation of whom arrived in the south of Dearborn to work in the factories in the thirties, have upped and moved outside the Detroit area, and in their place is a muddle of Arabs from across the Middle East, who are following exactly the same socio-economic path two generations later. There are Palestinian Christians in Livonia, Yemenis in Hamtramck, Iraqi Chaldeans in Southfield and Warren and Syrians in Macomb County. Of the three hundred thousand Arab-Americans who live in metropolitan Detroit, Dearborn is the heart of the community.

Most of these Arabs are recent immigrants. Many came to America as political exiles, fleeing persecution at home. Some came to work at Ford, but others were professionals bringing with them skills, money and prosperous family businesses, which have helped make Dearborn richer and safer than Detroit, which starts just a few miles east, at the other end of Warren Street.

Dearborn is still the first port of call for most Arab immigrants arriving in America today.

The day I arrived in Dearborn was the tenth day of the Muslim month of Muharram, when Shiites celebrate the Ashura festival. This is a holy day when Shiites remember Hussein, a descendant of the prophet Muhammad, who was killed at Karbala, a town in present-day Iraq. Hussein's death crushed hopes that it might be a descendant of Ali, the prophet's son-in-law and cousin, who would become the leader of the Islamic world. Hussein was Ali's son and his death and subsequent martyrdom cemented the difference between Sunnis and Shiites for all time. Shiites commemorate this tragedy with a great public show of mourning: ritualistic displays of anguish, self-flagellation, sometimes with whips and knives, for the pain Hussein's death brought upon the Muslim world, Shiites believe, can only be expressed through intense physical pain.

This year Ashura fell on Easter Sunday. The streets of Dearborn were deserted except for a thousand American-Iraqi Shiites slowly parading their grief through the town. They were lamenting loudly as they passed the white picket fences of American suburbia where American flags fluttered on the lawns. As I walked to the front of the parade, I passed first the women at the back, all dressed head to toe in black. Some were pushing prams, others were beating their chests in anguish. As I approached the front of the crowd, I could hear amplified prayer chants being belted out in Arabic over loudspeakers. The speakers would crackle out a prayer, then the crowd would all shout it back, twice as loudly. The men and boys at the front were flagellating themselves or beating their chests even more vigorously. Leading the prayers was a young imam with a neatly trimmed beard, flowing grey robes and smart white turban. His microphone was hooked up to speakers in the back of a slow-moving car, decorated with sheets embroidered with religious messages and hand-painted pictures of the martyr Hussein. Young boys with bandannas waved flags, red, green and black.

Some of the flags were sprayed with red paint to look like blood.

Detroit's police had turned out in force for the event, but their job consisted only of keeping the women at the back from trailing too far behind, and stopping the traffic coming in the opposite direction. Apart from all the vigorous self-harm, it was a peaceful demonstration of piety. Eventually the procession drew to a halt in a park, next to a scrubby, deserted children's playground. The imam stood on the roof of an SUV and addressed the crowd through a microphone. It was cold and windy and the feedback from the loudspeakers made it hard to hear everything he was saying, but the large crowd stood quietly and listened obediently.

Shouting to make himself heard, the imam called the crowd to prayer, alternating between Arabic and English. 'Jesus and Mahdi, we have been told, are the saviours of this world,' he chanted to the crowd. By 'Mahdi', or 'the divinely guided one', he meant Hussein. The crowd chanted back at him.

I was interested to see if he was going to make a political speech. That day there had been fierce fighting in Karbala, the town where Hussein had died in AD 680, between American troops and an upstart Iraqi cleric and his religious army. No politics were mentioned, only a prayer for peace in Iraq, a call for early elections and an annunciation of the unity of all religions. As the imam spoke, the wind billowed out his long robes, making him look like a wizard at some necromantic summoning.

At a similar Shiite celebration at the end of the Iraq war, an Al-Jazeera news crew had to be rescued by Detroit police from a crowd of fifteen hundred angry Iraqi Shiites who thought the network had been too sympathetic to Saddam Hussein. A year later I was keen to find out what American Iraqis thought about Al-Jazeera now.

Talking to members of the assembled crowd that day, I learned that although Iraqi Shiites in Dearborn used to suspect Al-Jazeera as too pro-Saddam, since the end of the war their opinion of the network had changed. They thought it had reported events accurately and fairly, especially Iraqi civilian casualties. The station was regarded as an important counterbalance to the propaganda power of the United States. Only Al-Jazeera would be sure to hold the coalition to the promises it had made to the Iraqi people.

Recently Al-Jazeera had been liaising between the Iraqi insurgents and the American soldiers over a ceasefire. This struck the men I spoke with as fearless. Al-Jazeera's exclusive footage from the recent fighting in Karbala had also impressed them. Although no one told me they agreed with Rumsfeld's accusations that Al-Jazeera was responsible for inciting resistance in Iraq, no one criticized the American administration. No doubt, the men said, the network was under immense pressure both directly from the American administration and indirectly from the Qataris, to tone down its footage, but hopefully it would be able to resist the pressure and carry on with its work.

'Al-Jazeera is the most popular channel around here,' one man told me. 'All the satellite dishes you see around here,' he said, gesturing at the rooftops of the houses standing at the edge of the playground, 'they are all glued to Al-Jazeera.'

'Al-Jazeera is a media revolution in the Arab world,' said another. 'People were just starving for this kind of coverage and this kind of media. So when it first came out, within a very short period of time it was in every home. People were watching it constantly, participating, calling it, because they heard things they never thought they'd hear in their lifetime on a major network, or what's become a major network.'

The next day I met up with the imam who had been leading the prayers through the crackly microphone. Besides being a respected religious leader locally, he was well connected to the Shiite community in Iraq. He had fled Iraq years ago, where he had worked as an aircraft engineer, to come to America. Saddam's men tried to get to him and they persecuted the family he left behind. Since the demise of the regime he had met Bush's cabal to advise on policy and had travelled back to Iraq as part of an advisory council.

The imam took me to lunch on Warren Street. He looked

imposing in the same long, grey gown and white turban he had been wearing at the Ashura festival in the playground. We spoke about the community in Dearborn and events in Iraq. He was ineffably polite, but our conversation was interrupted every couple of minutes by well-wishers on neighbouring tables, wanting to congratulate him on his rousing speech.

'Al-Jazeera,' he explained as we picked from a delicious Middle Eastern spread that came in American-sized portions, 'is like bin Laden or Saddam Hussein. It was an American creation and now it's running wild.' 'You mean like Frankenstein's monster?' I asked. 'Exactly, like Frankenstein!' he snapped. A man came to our table to thank him for the Ashura festivities. The imam quickly blessed him, before turning back to me and saying, 'A year ago all the Shia here in Dearborn were sure that Al-Jazeera had been in the pay of Saddam, but recent events in Iraq had made them reconsider. Now we think it is doing a respectable job, but we have not forgotten how pro-Saddam it was. Al-Jazeera is still on probation.'

He spoke about the Iraqi community in Dearborn all afternoon. Iraqi Shiites in Detroit, I learned, feel a deep sense of gratitude to America for getting rid of Saddam Hussein. At the last US Army recruitment fair the hall was packed with Shiites from Dearborn, who saw a job in the army as the perfect ticket back to the country they had left years ago.

At the end of the nineties satellite television began replacing letters, photos and phone calls as the most popular way for Arab expatriates in Dearborn to keep in touch with home. Now the whole family could enjoy a little slice of home life collectively, in front of the television. Gradually satellite television edged ever more centrally into the lives of Arab-Americans. It is not just news, but a social event, a link to home and an important part of the integration process.

As I went on to meet Arabs of other ethnicities in the Detroit area, I found that Iraqis generally had more reservations about Al-Jazeera than other Arabs. Most people I spoke with regarded Al-Jazeera as one of the most trustworthy news organizations.

The first thing they had usually started watching on Al-Jazeera was *The Opposite Direction*, but they did not catch on to the news until the start of the second Palestinian intifada – except for the Lebanese, who began a year earlier, during the liberation of South Lebanon – and from then on they were hooked. They stopped seeking out international news on the BBC or CBC (Canadian Broadcasting Company) and just switched on Al-Jazeera.

People in Dearborn's Arab community felt they had a responsive relationship with Al-Jazeera, which they had never enjoyed with CNN or Fox or MSNBC. Many had either been on Al-Jazeera themselves or been interviewed in the street, or had called in to a show. Others knew correspondents personally and would socialize with them when they came to Dearborn. Still, some suspicions remained.

'I don't trust any of the media,' said the barber as he trimmed my moustache. Arab barbers are supreme at tackling moustaches. 'But I trust Al-Jazeera more than any of the American channels,' he added, gesticulating with his scissors at a large, wall-mounted, flat-screen TV. Waiting customers sat gawping at Al-Jazeera playing soundlessly. The barber's shop was stylish and snappily lit. The barber, who was Lebanese, told me how he had long dreamed of starting his own business in America and how proud he was to have finally made it. A typical Dearborn success story, I thought. 'Al-Jazeera's the best, but it still doesn't tell you everything,' chimed in the man in the next chair, who was having his hair washed 'The Israelis . . .' mouthed the barber to me, bulging his eyes cryptically.

Arabs in Detroit are just as fixated on politics as Arabs in the Middle East. Even the free local newspaper is all back-to-back foreign news apart from the local ads. Although some Arab-Americans I met, like my barber, had clearly fully engaged with life in America, others seemed to have spent decades waiting, ready to return to their native countries tomorrow.

The undisguised passion with which Arabs in Dearborn spoke to me about Al-Jazeera led me to suspect that perhaps it might be a disincentive for Arab immigrants to integrate. I decided to pay a visit to the Arab Community Centre for Economic and Social Services (ACCESS) to find out what they thought.

ACCESS helps Arab immigrants in the Detroit area tackle all sorts of social problems, from sorting out visas to translating legal advice. I met three ACCESS community workers to speak about Al-Jazeera: Ghaisaa, Mas'oud and Abdul. Ghaisaa and Abdul both had a high opinion of Al-Jazeera and watched it all the time; Mas'oud less so. 'I feel proud when I see Al-Jazeera,' said Ghaisaa. 'I like the idea that Arabs are making history with their own news channel,' she said. The fact that her government seemed to have a serious problem with the station's output did not bother her. 'It's a challenge for those who try to hide the truth,' she told me.

Abdul, a Palestinian, had recently appeared on Al-Jazeera himself, talking about the effects of torture in the Detroit community. He had himself been tortured and he had been setting up a social programme at ACCESS to help rehabilitate other torture victims. After Al-Jazeera ran a piece about him and his fledgling programme, several psychologists and medical specialists called him from the Arab world asking for advice about setting up a similar centre.

I asked the three whether they thought Al-Jazeera helped or hindered Arab integration into American life. They all agreed that, to Arabs in Detroit, Al-Jazeera is often more than just a news channel. It was a lifeline to back home and, for people without their own satellite dish, sometimes even a social event. ACCESS used to have Al-Jazeera playing on the television in the waiting room, they told me. When this was replaced by Arabic educational programming, a stream of clients' complaints soon forced them to turn it back.

Abdul said watching news of the intifada made him feel depressed, homesick and guilty. Ghaisaa countered that by saying this had nothing to do with Al-Jazeera, but was simply the natural consequence of watching the news these days. Abdul said that as part of his investigation into the after-effects of torture he had recently completed a local survey on grief, loss and bereavement. The results had shown that among Arab-Americans who had been bereaved, those who retained something of their own culture – like watching Al-Jazeera – fared better than those who did not. It was a myth, he added, that watching English-language television helped immigrants learn English.

It was agreed that although some Arab immigrants in Detroit watched Al-Jazeera obsessively, which in turn contributed to social problems like homesickness and depression, the net effect of Al-Jazeera on the Arab community in Dearborn was beneficial. The two new weekly shows about American politics, *From Washington* and *US Presidential Race*, had been particularly helpful for new immigrants, who usually had no experience of how a democracy functioned.

This was a view I heard reiterated by other people who worked in the Detroit metropolitan community. Dr Michael Harmaneh, a Jordanian-American physician from Texas, who had worked for the Arab-American Behavioural Health Department before leaving to start his own private health group specializing in behavioural healthcare and substance abuse services, told me that whether it was Al-Jazeera's fault or not, the Arab community in Detroit faced a barrage of social and mental heath problems.

Many Arab immigrants coming to America were already suffering serious psychological stress. Iraqis had often been tortured; Palestinians had spent years living under the gun. For all the Arab immigrants, the transition from life in the Middle East to life in America was a traumatic one and after 9/11 their situation was aggravated. As a result, Dr Harmaneh told me, the Arab American community suffers disproportionately from a variety of serious mental health conditions, including depression, anxiety and schizophrenia. Many Arabs became compulsive gamblers in Detroit's insalubrious casinos; others, unable to speak English, became reclusive and lonely. But Al-Jazeera, he opined, was not to blame. Far from hindering integration, it helped alleviate the strain of fitting in and actually served to educate Arabs about life in the West.

An accountancy student from Djibouti that I met in Dearborn's Starbucks put this point to me succinctly. When I asked him whether Al-Jazeera stopped people in Dearborn integrating, he replied, 'No way. Al-Jazeera brings important new things to this country. America is made up of people like me, coming here and bringing something from my culture, and Al-Jazeera is part of what I have to offer. I listen to it and it gives me ideas and I bring them to America. It's part of my contribution to America.'

But Al-Jazeera certainly contributed to the psychological stress of one unfortunate Arab-American immigrant I met in Dearborn. Ahmad Berry used to run a two-hour weekly Arabic-language TV show on cable called *Arabic Time Television*. This was watched throughout the metropolitan Detroit area for seventeen years – until Al-Jazeera exploded on the scene and unwittingly squished Berry's business.

I heard about Berry long before I met him. 'You're writing a book about Al-Jazeera? You gotta talk to that guy, what's he called?' people would say to me. 'That guy who used to run that TV channel . . .' It seemed that once upon a time *Arabic Time Television* had enjoyed a cult following in Dearborn. It was nothing too special, but it was in Arabic and that was important to people. Tracking Berry down was hard. Plenty of people knew him, but no one had seen him in months, years even, and his office phone number had long been disconnected.

When I finally got to speak with Berry, at first he was reluctant to tell me his story. He had been hiding away from Dearborn for the past eighteen months, depressed he said, after his business went bust, and he did not want to talk to anyone from the press. Eventually I managed to coax him out for dinner. Standing in the car park of the diner, I recognized him straight away. He looked in bad shape. We went inside the diner and sat down in a booth. Berry was a middle-aged man, with a faded aura and a crumpled suit. He chain-smoked cigarettes through dinner as he told me his story.

'For the last seventeen years we had two hours of television

show on prime time, which covered the Detroit metro. We used
to cover different events – political events, educational events,
the economy . . . We interviewed different doctors about health.
We covered school issues and events. We were very popular here
because it was good information about what was going on and
bilingual.'

Berry had run the whole show: he had been producer, director and host. 'My show was not funded by any group. I refused
to be funded by any political group or go with any party. I was
independent 100 per cent. I generated the income from advertising and everybody wanted to advertise with me because it
was a famous show. They miss it.'

I could see pride flare in his eyes as he spoke. For a second
Berry turned into a charismatic local celebrity. 'We interviewed
judges and politicians, people running for senate and congress,
you name it, we interviewed the lot of them. We won many
awards for serving the community from different organizations.
One of the awards came from the City of Dearborn.'

As Berry spoke to me, I noticed people on the other side of
the restaurant casually pointing us out before turning back to
their dinner. He told me:

By the beginning of the year 2000 satellite dishes started
bringing Arabic TV shows from the Middle East. After
September 11, people were watching the news, wondering what was going on here, what was going on in
Afghanistan, they wanted to know what was going on all
over the world. That gave a boost to Al-Jazeera and other
channels coming from overseas, but especially to Al-Jazeera,
as they came up with the idea of freedom of the press and
democracy of the press, and we are not used to that overseas. Most countries are under dictatorships and you can't
say much on the news, but Al-Jazeera were open and that
was a good sign. People used to like their talk shows because
they were controversial.

Al-Jazeera's burgeoning popularity would not have been a
problem except that *Arabic Time Television* aired through cable –
and Al-Jazeera aired via satellite.

'They did not want to pay for satellite and cable. Plus they
wanted to follow what was going on in Syria, what was going
on in Palestine, what was going on in Iraq, what was going to
happen in the Middle East, all the big questions . . .'

A teenage Arab waitress arrived at the table and interrupted
Berry as he was speaking. 'Hey, wait a minute, aren't you that
guy? I recognize you!' she said, pointing a chewed ballpoint pen
at Berry. 'You were on that show, what's it called? . . .'

Berry's problem was two-fold. He depended on local advertising, but after 9/11 there was a downturn in the advertising
market generally and many local businesses decided to cut back
on television commercials. The situation was made worse when
larger American advertisers started pulling their advertisements
from Arab television stations out of a perverted sense of patriotism.

'I am depressed as I lost my job. I had good relationships with
a lot of people, Arabic people and American people, and I lost
all that. I lost my show and I lost my income. It was not easy
for me,' Berry confided. 'I hate them. I hate all the satellite TV
channels coming from all over, but I respect them. I hate them
because they were the cause of me losing my business. But I
can't say anything bad about them because they did not do it
on purpose. They damaged my life. I dedicated my life to media.
I have three daughters and a wife and I do not know how I am
going to support them . . .' he trailed off. 'But they did it legally,
they have the right,' he added, lighting another Marlboro. 'I
stayed away for a while.'

Surprisingly perhaps, he still regularly watches Al-Jazeera, even
if the pleasure is somewhat bitter-sweet:

I like to watch a free and open media and Al-Jazeera is
open – they have dialogue. They bring two enemies at the
same table. Al-Jazeera are truthful. They have courage.

They show you the reality. The American government thinks Al-Jazeera is challenging it, but Al-Jazeera is just doing its job. They don't have an agenda against the United States. They don't. It's just truth hurts sometimes. But now I am back and I pray for peace for all over the world. I think the United States should come up with a resolution for peace especially between the Palestinians and the Israeli people. They should find a solution to this, and be fair to both parties.

Many Arab-Americans I spoke with in Dearborn – especially the Iraqis – were not as forthcoming as Berry, Dr Harmaneh, the staff at ACCESS or the imam. On several occasions when I walked into a café on Warren Street, I felt like a cowboy walking into the wrong saloon, stopping the conversation dead. Dearborn cafés are like coffee shops across the Middle East: full of bed-headed men spending the day hiding from their wives. Often I could see through the window as I walked up to the door that an animated debate about something on TV was in full swing, but by the time I had ordered my dinner the loudest noise was me slurping my tea. Everyone else in the place sat smoking pensively, wearing thousand-yard stares, or suddenly began intensively scrutinizing their fingernails. As soon as I walked out they sparked up again loudly.

Many Arabs in Detroit seemed more reluctant to speak than Arabs I had met in the Middle East. When people did agree to talk, I noticed they book-ended every criticism of America with loud declarations of patriotism. Even the community workers at ACCESS refused to be taped.

'Of course you find that,' one Dearborn community worker told me, strictly off the record. 'Since 9/11 and the Patriot Act people are afraid. Section 215C of the Patriot Act has seen thirteen thousand people deported without trial, including American citizens and green-card holders.' Section 215C of the Patriot Act gives the FBI the right to access previously confidential records in the hunt for terrorists.

Citizenship, I was told, had now been subdivided into grades and Arab-Americans had become something less than full citizens. People had been picked up at bus stops and deported without a trial or even the chance to make a single phone call or collect their belongings from home.

For some time, network executives at Al-Jazeera have been talking about the possibility of launching an English-language version of the regular Arabic Al-Jazeera channel, along with an Al-Jazeera magazine and documentary and business channels, but these plans have consistently been delayed. The idea for the English channel was first announced as far back as 1998, but nothing much was done until 2002, when Al-Jazeera announced plans to start dubbing the Al-Jazeera Arabic news, commentaries and current affairs programming into English, using live translators. The talk shows were always going to be more difficult. 'First we will do the dubbing. Then, based on the feedback we get from the audience in the West, we have a plan to do an English-language channel,' said Ali Muhammad Kamal, marketing director of Al-Jazeera, in November 2002. 'We are trying to reposition Al-Jazeera as a global channel and not a pan-Arab channel,' he added. 'A lot of people watch the BBC or CNN as a credible source of news. We are trying to dent this credibility and relaunch as a more international channel.'

The huge impact Al-Jazeera has already had in the West, despite the disadvantage of being broadcast in a regional language few Westerners understand, shows that there is a hunger for the Arab perspective in the wake of 9/11. 'People are interested across Europe in Al-Jazeera,' says Muftah al-Suwaidan, executive director of the London bureau. 'Everywhere we go people say, when are we going to have English Al-Jazeera? So the interest is there. I know it is going to be a challenge, but this is the first channel in the history of broadcasting to tell the Arabic and Islamic perspective to the Western people. We feel it is a challenge and that we should do it.'

By broadcasting in English Al-Jazeera will fulfil its ambition of becoming a truly international news organization, on a par with the BBC or the Voice of America. The new channel hopes both to bring English speakers a fresh perspective on world events and simultaneously to throw open a window on to the Arab world.

'I believe after September 11 the Western world has become much more interested in issues pertaining to the Middle East,' said Al-Jazeera spokesman Jihad Ballout, 'and because of our achievements at Al-Jazeera this has, I think, heightened interest and the need for an alternative source of news. I think Al-Jazeera has established itself – even the Arabic language – as a credible alternative source of news on issues pertaining to the Middle East which is now at the very core of Western thinking.'

With so many millions of potential viewers, another important reason for Al-Jazeera to start broadcasting in English is the possibility of raising revenue from American and European firms through advertising. Thanks to the *de facto* Saudi embargo and despite Al-Jazeera's huge viewership, the network has still never turned a profit and is not expecting to start any time soon.

Although short Arabic news bulletins have been transmitted in various foreign languages before by terrestrial television channels, and Egyptian Live TV even once offered a partial satellite news service, this is the first time an Arab television news outfit has transmitted twenty-four hours a day in English. Even before details about the new channel have been made public, there has already been rampant speculation in both the Western and Arab press.

'Al-Jazeera, the popular TV station with its cheery cast of characters such as Osama bin Liner and his merry friends Saddam and Comical Ali, is on its way here,' chuckled a *Sunday Times* editorial. 'I believe our TV could be much improved. Instead of *Pop Idol*, how about *Mullah Idol*, as finalists battle it out in a mosque singing chants about Allah? At least *Middle EastEnders* wouldn't have all that maudlin drinking and dribbling in the Queen Vic. Nor would TV be so materialistic: how about *Who Wants to Be a Suicide Bomber?* Or *What Not to Wear* (anything but a burqa, really)? Tired formats could be refreshed: "You are the weakest link, goodbye" – cue for death by beheading.'

Why the new channel has been delayed is not clear. Sources within the Al-Jazeera Arabic service indicated that it has been difficult finding the right person to be the managing director of the new channel, because they want a Westerner, not an Arab, but other reasons have also been put forward. One Qatari I spoke with, an adviser to the Emir, was adamant the delay was the result of American political pressure. The English-language website had proved so troublesome during the Afghan conflict, he pointed out, that the last thing America needed now, with faltering support for their Middle East initiative, was Al-Jazeera in English.

Operationally, the new English-language channel will be much cheaper to set up and run than the Arabic service. Just as the BBC and the Voice of America Arabic service has a small Arabic language department within an overwhelmingly English-speaking organization, Al-Jazeera International will use the network of bureaux for the Arabic channel, which are already in place, only with Anglophone correspondents. BBC World is the John the Baptist for Al-Jazeera in English.

'The English-language channel will be run along the same core values that Al-Jazeera has been run on since 1996,' said Jihad Ballout. 'It is not going to be a mirror image of the Arab one. It has a different target audience to the Arab one. In terms of professional core values and integrity, 'The opinion and the other opinion will always be the guiding light for whatever media venture we get into. The core will be news – political, strategic news. Of course there will be economic news as it's the other face of politics. They will have some kind of sports bulletin in English, but perhaps not covering so much Qatari football league as Premier League. One of our objectives is to communicate with the West in its own language about issues pertaining to the Middle East as a direct, credible, alternative source of information.'

There is a sense among the Al-Jazeera staff I spoke with that, now that all the American networks are concentrated on the political right, there is a vacancy at the more liberal end of the spectrum. Al-Jazeera staff believe they can capitalize on this and the recent rise of left-wing media figures in America, like Michael Moore, Howard Dean and the liberal radio station Air America.

'If I am broadcasting to Americans I would give them what they are not hearing,' said Hafez al-Mirazi, Washington bureau chief. 'People who are marginalized, for example, and don't get a chance to be heard, people in the Arab world, for example, or people like Noam Chomsky.' Al-Mirazi believes Al-Jazeera should bring Americans Arab voices, the same way that Al-Jazeera brings Arabs American political voices. 'The people from Washington on Al-Jazeera, like Richard Perle and people, we get them as it is important to get the Arab audience to know about them we need them to learn about America and these voices even if they object to it. In America, people already know these voices, but they are missing some other people in the debate. And we would make sure those people would have their place.'

One example of this strategy came during the run-up to the US presidential elections. The Arab-American community had grown particularly interested in Democratic presidential candidate Dennis Kucinich, who, amongst other things, had pledged that if he was elected we would repeal some of the most intrusive aspects of the Patriot Act. Since Kucinich was a rank outsider in the overall scheme of things, he received little airtime on the major American networks. Seeing an opportunity, Al-Jazeera organized its own interview with him, during which he took questions from a group of Arab Americans.

The new Al-Jazeera English-language channel was finally formed in 2004. Called Al-Jazeera International, it will start broadcasting globally in mid-2006. Just like its Arabic sister channel, it will be a twenty-four-hour operation with headquarters in Doha, but the new channel will also have subsidiary broadcast centres in Kuala Lumpur, London and Washington DC.

The managing director of the new channel will be Nigel Parsons, a Brit with thirty years' experience in the broadcasting industry. He started his professional life as a newspaper journalist, as an apprentice reporter at the *Cambridge Evening News* and then at the *New Zealand Herald*. He later moved into radio, working for BBC Radio channels 1 to 4, and then into television, where, after working initially as a cameraman in South America, he later became involved in several successful TV start-ups including the Swiss EBC and Italy's Telecampione. At Worldwide Television News he was in charge of opening up Eastern European and former USSR markets and he instigated the first international agency news feed to Central Asia and Eastern Russia through Intersputnik. Before he was appointed as Managing Director of Al-Jazeera International in August 2004, he was the Director of Associated Press Television News.

The rest of the staff appointed at Al-Jazeera International so far have been drawn from across the world. Other key recruits include Morgan Almeida, Director of Creative Design, formerly with the BBC and CNN; Steve Clark, Director of News, formerly a controller of Factual Programmes at ITV; Paul Gibbs, Director of Programming, formerly responsible for the BBC's Business Breakfast and Working Lunch; Steve Jedowski, Director of Technology, formerly the Deputy Chief Engineer at BBC Worldwide; and Lindsey Oliver, Commercial Director, formerly Director of Networks at CNBC Europe.

Some of the presenters will already be familiar to Western news junkies. Riz Khan, who helped launch BBC World Service Television news in 1991, before being headhunted by CNN in 1993, has been poached by Al-Jazeera International to host an interactive news show called *Live Daily from Washington DC*. In the show, Khan will interview a variety of world leaders, newsmakers and celebrities in a question-and-answer format driven by viewer participation. Callers will get to put questions to guests through Khan. 'Imagine, a person at any level in society, in almost any country, having the chance to talk directly with a president or a prime minister, or even a global celebrity. It's a wonderfully honest and equal opportunity for people – something still uncommon in broadcasting,' said Khan.

Sir David Frost, a long time BBC stalwart, signed up with Al-Jazeera International shortly after leaving his long-running *Breakfast with Frost* BBC 1 show. During his time at the BBC the veteran broadcaster interviewed the last six British prime ministers plus the last seven US presidents. 'I love new frontiers and new challenges,' said Frost upon signing the deal, adding that Al-Jazeera International had guaranteed him 'total editorial control'.

Former *Tribune* editor Mark Seddon was hired as Al-Jazeera International's UN correspondent and will be based in New York. Cannily, and not a little controversially in America, the new English-language channel has also signed up the former US Marine captain who was Al-Jazeera's military liaison officer during the Iraq war. After the movie *Control Room* was released, Rushing left the Marine Corps, disenchanted with its media management. 'In a time when American media has become so nationalized, I'm excited about joining an organization that truly wants to be a source of global information,' said Rushing. 'I witnessed during the war how the US media was co-opted by the US government's messaging. I am proud to be part of a news network that believes in the power of the un-spun truth.'

At the time of writing, the show formats are still a closely guarded secret, though it is not expected that they will bear much resemblance to the shows that run on Al-Jazeera's Arabic-language service.

Since much of Al-Jazeera International's programme output will be manufactured in the four news hubs, the network hopes to present a truly international perspective on world events. Programming is set to be documentary-heavy, with an emphasis on the same kind of serious topics featured on the Arabic-language service like religion, politics, technology, culture and women's issues, as well as on world economic development and trade. A large part of the new programming will come from independent production companies, providing unprecedented opportunities for freelancers all over the world.

One thing that looks set to separate Al-Jazeera International from other Western news networks is the emphasis the new channel will place on developing world issues. Doubtless the new channel will also gravitate towards Middle Eastern topics, playing both to viewers' expectations and also to the network's strongest suit: the company's formidable reputation and contact database in the Middle East region. With Al-Jazeera's access and standing, it would be easy to imagine innovative documentaries on topics like the democracy movement in Egypt, for example, or on Palestinian refugee camps, both of which would be of considerable interest to a Western audience.

Al-Jazeera International's plan to station its headquarters in four different locations – New York, London, Doha and Kuala Lumpur – will also differentiate it from any other twenty-four-hour news channel. Each location will be responsible for one section of the news day and will concentrate on the audience living in its particular time zone. So, for example, the New York bureau will target an audience living in North America and during peak viewing-time in America, meaning that from six o'clock in the evening until midnight East Coast Time, the New York bureau will govern much of the programming output. At midnight East Coast Time, when the New York bureau knocks off, the office in Kuala Lumpur will pick up the ball, broadcasting to an Asian evening audience, until it is Doha's turn, then London's, and so on.

If all goes to plan, this strategy will make Al-Jazeera International the first truly global network, while still managing to keep a regional perspective. It should foster a healthy sense of competition between the four regional headquarters. It will also eliminate the need for a night shift, which, as anyone who has done it can testify, is a welcome breakthrough.

If it all goes wrong, on the other hand, then it could end up a chaotic, confusing mess, at home nowhere and out of touch with audiences everywhere. Trying to be all things to all men, based in four different time zones, is likely to stretch organizational abilities, as well as resources, to the limit. There is a reason why the BBC and CNN have single headquarters, in London and Atlanta respectively.

Before Al-Jazeera in English can make any impact at all, it has to be comprehensively distributed. This could prove to be an insurmountable hurdle, especially in America. Its distribution involves striking a deal with one of the major media companies and that is a question of politics as much as money: Comcast and AOL, for example, currently run the cable connections to about half the households in the US.

Most Arab-Americans I spoke with were pessimistic about Al-Jazeera's chance of securing nationwide distribution in America. 'There is no way they will be able to broadcast it. It will be like the Patriot Act – the lobbyists will force through legislation to stop it taking place,' one of the ACCESS staff assured me.

'What is more likely to happen in the United States is that cable distributors just won't carry it,' said Molly McKew, from the American Enterprise Institute. 'If it is the English interpretation of what is available in Arabic right now, I think most cable providers will just choose not to carry it.'

Al-Jazeera recognizes that distribution is likely to be a problem. 'The first challenge will be to distribute the signal. It is a tough job to be on cable,' said Washington bureau chief Hafez al-Mirazi. 'Distribution is a problem in America. The cable system is so complicated and so decentralized you have to go to each county and each part of the city even and persuade them to carry your signal. With the Al-Jazeera image and all of that stuff . . .' he shrugged. 'If we do get distribution it will be positive as it will allow people to judge Al-Jazeera fairly, not from the critics. They will be able to see what the station is carrying.'

The network has already run into obstacles trying to obtain a licence to broadcast in Canada. Its licence request was presented to the Canadian Cable Television Association (CCTA) in March 2003. This was not submitted by the station itself, but by a Quebecois communications company called Vidéotron that supplies a range of satellite and cable channels in Canada.

In July 2003, alert to Al-Jazeera's controversial content, the Canadian national broadcasting regulator decided to solicit opinions from the public. On hearing of the application, the President of the Canadian Jewish Congress (CJC) wrote a letter to the secretary-general of the country's Radio, Television and Telecommunications Commission expressing his firm opposition to Vidéotron's request for an Al-Jazeera broadcasting licence, even for paying subscribers. Al-Jazeera, he wrote, 'offers programming that is virulently anti-Semitic and racist and likely to contravene Canadian law'.

'CJC strongly opposes the applications by CCTA and Vidéotron to add Al-Jazeera (the Qatar-based, Arabic-language satellite service) to the list of satellite services eligible for digital distribution in Canada,' his letter said, continuing:

> CJC submits that Al-Jazeera's programming content contains hate propaganda, in contravention of Canadian laws and broadcast standards. As detailed in the attached submissions, it is CJC's view that Al-Jazeera has demonstrated a pattern of airing virulent and dangerous hate propaganda and/or contemptuous speech, largely targeted at the Jewish people. On Al-Jazeera, Jews are frequently characterized by hosts, guests and terrorists as a duplicitous, corrupt, world-dominating conspiratorial force; rights of Jews, individually and collectively, and their physical security are threatened; and Holocaust denial is commonplace. Suicide bombings are encouraged, while terrorist groups – including those outlawed by the Canadian government – are lauded.

Other Jewish groups joined the petition. The Canadian regulator's decision is still pending.

Al-Jazeera will not have such a distribution problem in Britain, where regulatory laws are different and where contemporary research suggests that Al-Jazeera in English would find a ready audience. Ethnic minorities, including Arabs, living in the West have grown disenchanted with Western news. The Broadcasting Standards Commission, Independent Television Commission, British Film Institute, Open University and others commissioned a study into how ethnic minorities living in Britain viewed television news in the days and weeks following 9/11. Although the study found no tangible evidence of bias, it found that British Muslims perceived a bias and had other deep reservations about how the mainstream British news was presented. The report concluded: 'A deep lack of trust in British and American TV news was evident in the views expressed among British Muslim informants. The most common complaints concerned lack of challenging debate and analysis, sensationalist reporting, limited and limiting perspectives, and perceived anti-Arab and anti-Muslim bias.'

Alienated and seeking an alternative perspective, many British Muslims already look for news from other sources. Young British Asians are prolific Internet users: 8 per cent regard the Internet as their primary source of news. Asian homes in Britain are twice as likely as non-Asian homes to have Sky Digital or cable TV and are more likely to own other up-to-date media technology and have Internet connections. A remarkable 87 per cent of British Asians already have access to Al-Jazeera via their connection to Sky.

'Al-Jazeera is hugely popular among Arabic-speaking viewers,' the report noted.

It is seen as offering relatively uncensored news when compared with 'western' TV news channels, and hence as an emancipatory new force in transnational Arab affairs, enabling Arabs and British Muslims more generally to participate in diaspora public and political debate more actively. Al-Jazeera, it is claimed, assuages the feelings of impotence felt by many with ties to the Middle East . . .

All other Arabic services come far lower in viewers' esteem
. . . Al-Jazeera is seen to compensate for Western TV's
failure to cover the second Palestinian intifada fairly . . .
Now Al-Jazeera is helping to create a *'consensus narrative of
the entire Arabic world'* [italics in original] . . . Unsolicited
by the researchers, many called for Al-Jazeera to develop
services in English and other European languages.

The study's findings showed that Asian viewers were leaving BBC,
ITN, Channel 4 and Sky for minority channels – notably Al-
Jazeera. Although there was no suggestion in the regulator's report
that Al-Jazeera was biased or in any way a corrosive influence
on viewers, it recommended steps be taken to try to keep ethnic
minorities watching the mainstream television news channels.
'The news media should redouble their efforts to engage with
Britain's ethnic minorities,' declared a second, follow-up report,
conducted in October 2002 by the Broadcasting Standards
Commission and the Independent Television Commission. 'This
is in their own business and institutional self-interest, but it is
not currently happening at a convincing pace.'

As a result of the findings in these reports the Communications
Bill, which established Ofcom, the powerful new regulator for
the British communications industry, was changed to extend the
regulator's duties to cover the interests of ethnic minorities.
Originally the bill ruled that Ofcom was responsible only for
'the different interests' of people in different parts of the country.
From then its duty was changed: now it was to the 'different
ethnic communities within the UK'.

Despite the change in the law, the BBC Governors' annual
report the following year revealed that the BBC was continuing to haemorrhage British Asian viewers. 'Extensive efforts have
been made by the BBC this year to understand ethnic minority
audiences better and we look forward to more output that serves
cross-cultural interests . . . It is disappointing that despite these
efforts, there is little evidence so far that the BBC is attracting
more people from ethnic minorities to its output. The reach

and share of both BBC Radio and BBC Television among ethnic minorities has decreased slightly . . . The BBC faces intense competition for this audience from the huge range of niche commercial services.'

Al-Jazeera's plans to expand come at a time when the mainstream American television news channels are in the hands of an ever-smaller number of media companies. There are only five independently owned national television news outlets in America and if ABC and CNN merge, as has been mooted, this goes down to four. With the nation's political conversation in the hands of so few, minority tastes that cannot guarantee massive ratings have been marginalized.

Yet at the same time the number of alternative or international media choices in America has expanded exponentially, owing to satellite and cable technology and the Internet. The average American household has eighty-nine channels and nearly a third of American homes have either cable or satellite television. This explosion of alternative media seems to have neutralized the American television regulator's fears that too much media power is in the hands of large media conglomerates and so even more deregulation looks likely. 'When I look at the trends in television over the last twenty to fifty years, I see a constant and increasing explosion in variety,' said Michael Powell, the chairman of the Federal Communications Commission, who is against structural regulation of the industry by the government. 'In the purported golden age of television there were three networks.'

If the American regulator decides to relax ownership laws further, one company will be allowed to own more stations nationwide, as well as newspapers, radio stations and broadband Internet services. American news will become even more homogeneous and more people, Al-Jazeera hopes, will be looking for alternative sources.

Many Arabs both in the West and the Middle East believe the new channel will have an important impact on the politi-

cal situation in the Middle East. In particular I found great hope
that Al-Jazeera in English might help resolve the conflict between
the Israelis and the Palestinians. That conflict is, after all, as much
a battle fought in the corridors of Washington as on the streets
of Gaza. Even the Arab League has noted that Arabs in America
have been remarkably hopeless at making their case, even when
they have the moral high ground. By contrast, the Israeli PR
machine lobbies extremely efficiently in Washington. The Arab
League suggested creating an Arab version of CNN to redress
the balance, but now some are hoping it will be Al-Jazeera in
English that will serve to influence the West.

A combination of factors, including 9/11, the war in Iraq,
the failure of the road map to peace and the introduction of
the Patriot Act, has forced the Arab community in America to
coalesce as a political entity. Al-Jazeera in English might accelerate this process, drawing in second- and third-generation Arab
immigrants as well as other previously unaligned Americans. This
could turn into a potent political force. There are already more
Muslim than Jewish voters in America and they are concentrated
in swing states, like Michigan, Florida, Ohio and Pennsylvania.
In the 2000 elections 46 per cent of Arab-Americans voted for
George Bush, while 38 per cent voted for Al Gore – Arabs naturally share the same conservative ideals as the Republican Party
– but after 9/11 they find themselves reluctant to vote for the
government that introduced the Patriot Act and lied about WMD
to win support for an invasion of Iraq. Now that this group
have become floating voters, American politicians are appealing
harder than ever before for the Arab vote. In the run-up to the
2004 elections, polls indicated that only 24 per cent of Arab-
American voters would vote for Bush rather than John Kerry,
not because they were enamoured of Kerry, but simply to unseat
Bush.

Even Palestinians I spoke with had faith that once Americans
saw that they were supporting an apartheid system and the collec-
tive punishment of a civilian population, they would start demanding a more just foreign policy from their government. Arabs

understand that often in America the truth of a situation is less important than how it is presented on television. If Al-Jazeera could convey the facts, not the stereotypes, Americans would surely be outraged at what was being perpetrated in their name.

'People in the West do not know the facts,' one Jordanian politician told me solemnly over a plate of rather luminous orange *kanafi*. We were speaking in a café in the centre of Amman which specialized in sticky pastries and sweets. It was, he had assured me, the best *kanafi* in Jordan. 'I believe in five years everything will have changed in Europe and America if Al-Jazeera starts broadcasting in English. It will be very, very important. And I believe in the long run they will do it in Spanish and in German and in French and it will be the most popular station in the world. For the Western people it will be extraordinary for them. It is exactly likely having an Arabic army invading the United Kingdom or the United States. They will try to stop it, of course.'

Even Al-Jazeera's staff believe that the problems in the Middle East are partly attributable to Western ignorance. 'Americans don't know what is going on in the West Bank because they don't want to know,' said Walid al-Omary. 'They don't even know where the West Bank is. I was at a conference and they have no idea. The West Bank is smaller than Washington DC.

'I hope that Al-Jazeera in English has an important effect. We need to change the Arab image. We don't hate American people. We are the same. We hate policy. Palestinians do not hate American people. Most of the people, here in Ramallah espe-cially, emigrated to the US. They just hate the policy of the administration. They are victims of policy.'

Nor is it only Americans who might benefit from some lessons about the Middle East, as Jihad Ballout explained to me:

In certain parts of Latin America, mainly Argentina and Brazil, where there is a big community of Arabic expats, until recently Arabs were still called Turks. This is because they are Muslims and because they come from the Middle

East and as far as they are concerned, the Middle East is Turkey. Very little is known about the difference between being Turkish and being Arab, culturally or politically.

It goes deeper than that. Islam is being portrayed not in its proper essence. A lot of scholars believe women in Islam are provided for adequately in terms of rights and responsibilities. It is only the way that certain people interpret Islam, which puts women in such a secluded position. Not many people in the States know that Islam since its inception has provided for a form of democracy and consultation.

The West does not know that or appreciate the real value of it. So perhaps we can redress the balance in terms of exchange of information. If people don't consider all Arabs as being Turks – with all the negative connotations of the term, oppressors invading Western Europe, hating Christianity, fighting the crusades and so forth – perhaps people would be more prepared to accommodate Arabs and give Arabs the benefit of the doubt and not jump to conclusions or have a preset mind as to issues, and Islam the same.

Ballout has faith that the media can change, not just confirm, opinions. 'I am not in the guessing game, but I can tell you what I hope to do: I hope to build this communication bridge between East and West which has always been unidirectional – i.e. from West to East,' he said. 'I want to redress this matter and get another direction on matters pertaining to the Middle East. I am hoping that people perhaps will start appreciating the cultural difference – and there is a cultural difference, let's not kid ourselves – this is what makes different people unique. Politically speaking, it must have an effect if societies start changing their minds and start accepting other cultures.'

Not everyone is so optimistic. Rami Khouri, executive editor of Lebanon's *Daily Star* and a member of the US task force on policy in the Arab world, told me:

I don't see Al-Jazeera being a hit in English. The key part of Al-Arabiya, Al-Jazeera and others is that they are a reflection of the Arab world in Arabic. This is the big issue – the importance of the whole political debate being in Arabic is vital. This is why CNN in the Arab world has not had the political impact it might have had. Imagine if it had been the other way around. Imagine if after the Gulf war in 1991 CNN had said, 'What we really need is an Arabic service.' Where would Al-Jazeera have been then? It would have been much harder, much tougher. The key to Al-Jazeera's success has been being in Arabic. They will find it hard to make money and make it work.

Even some of Al-Jazeera's staff expressed reservations to me about the new channel. Some fear that any insensitivity towards Arabs or Muslims on the new channel will be picked up by the network's many Arab critics and used as a weapon to attack the Arab-language news network. Al-Jazeera may be the most popular Arab-language news network, but trust between viewers and broadcasters in the Middle East is always fragile. Al-Jazeera's Arab journalists are rightly proud of the brand they have strived so hard to build and now they are concerned that by expanding that brand they will inevitably become more vulnerable. Others fear the competition, as Al-Jazeera will no longer be vying for viewers with bumbling Arab state broadcasting stations but with dynamic Western media conglomerates.

'Are we ready yet to go out and address a different market?' worried Yosri Fouda. 'When you go out and you find the likes of CNN and Sky and the BBC and MSNBC, ABC as your rivals – it is not exactly the same as when you are contesting against Egypt TV or Lebanese TV or Saudi TV. It is a completely different ballgame,' said the presenter of Al-Jazeera's *Top Secret*. 'I really feel that Al-Jazeera in English will be out, not necessarily because there are so many English-speaking people out there who are really interested in knowing what takes place in the Arab world, as much as there are people who are interested in what Al-Jazeera in Arabic is all about – and this does not sound to me like the right reason.'

In particular, Fouda is concerned that the focus of the new channel is too much on Britain and the US, when most of the new viewers will come from non-Arabic-speaking Muslim countries:

> I wish our colleagues who work on it every success but I still think it is coming out for not exactly the right reasons. I might understand that people who live in, say, Pakistan, Indonesia or Africa who can't understand Arabic, share a lot with people who live in our part of the world, in terms of the imbalance of the flow of information. Al-Jazeera in English might be useful to them. But what I can't understand is that the main focus seems to be on people who live in the West. I don't think that people who live in the West actually need anything new. You guys have more than enough media outlets to tell you about what is happening in the world. We in the Arab world, in the Muslim world, still need more and more in our own language.

Fouda is right. The biggest effect of Al-Jazeera in English will be felt in Asia, where many more people speak English than Arabic. Pakistan has 140 million Muslims and Indonesia, the world's most populous Muslim country, has a population of two hundred million Muslims, many of whom will be interested in following events in the Arab world, in Palestine, but above all in Saudi Arabia, closely. The fact that one of Al-Jazeera International's headquarters is in Kuala Lumpur – traditionally regarded as a news backwater – underlines clearly the importance of the non-Arab Muslim audience to the new channel.

One obvious social group that might seem like potential viewers of the Al-Jazeera English-language channel are second-generation Arab immigrants who do not speak Arabic. In many

Arab families living in the West, the parents or grandparents still speak Arabic fluently, but the children have been inculcated into Western culture to such a degree that, although they are still interested in the politics of the Middle East, they no longer speak the language. There are plenty of Arab families, from Glasgow to Detroit, who fit this description and for them the new channel could be important. But Al-Jazeera hopes the new channel will reach out to viewers beyond the Arab community.

'The profile of the viewer?' said Ballout. 'Of course, in addition to a great deal of Arab expats – second-, third-, fourth-generation expats who don't speak Arabic and are interested to know what is happening back home – I believe a lot of indigenous Westerners will be interested. Professional people, business people, people who traditionally have to wait for translations to be provided for them on news pertaining to the Middle East, but, as important, Western political people.'

'Anyone is targeted who does not speak Arabic – everyone!' enthused Mostefa Souag, the London bureau chief. 'You couldn't ask for better than the BBC, but people like to look through different windows and see with their own eyes. Any event can be seen from different perspectives and so impact in different ways. British people will like to see how a Middle Eastern station in English presents the news, not only about the Middle East, but about Britain itself. I have been to Germany and France and people say to me, "When are we going to get a chance to watch you in English?" because English is the first language of the world now. People are interested everywhere.'

Not everyone is so convinced about the new channel's appeal. 'I think there is the potential that it could have some kind of role among the more hippie-leftist anti-American regime policy California-style crowd,' said Molly McKew crisply.

I think that is definitely a possibility. People who in their everyday life in the United States, who are very liberal and not particularly informed on foreign policy, but occasionally dabble in their interest for it – those are the ones

who are more likely to be sympathizers of fundamentalist Islam.

There are a lot of Americans who are totally anti-Israel
and support Palestinian causes – you know the people who
went to Iraq before the war and tried to act as human
shields and that kind of thing. I think there may be a small
window of young American disillusioned leftists – they
might watch it – but I don't think it will have a very large
impact, or a very large audience, and I don't think it would
be for a very long time. I think it will be a flash in the
pan. It will be inevitable that Al-Jazeera's coverage of an
event will be so anti-American and so just non-moral and
non-human that it will just turn people against it.

Undoubtedly, Al-Jazeera has an image problem in America.
Although it has become a household name, it has not always
been for the right reasons, as Abdul Rahim Foukara, Al-Jazeera's
New York correspondent, knows well. He found recently that
some New Yorkers still assume there is more to Al-Jazeera's
relationship with Osama bin Laden than the station lets on.
'There is that perception that Al-Jazeera may be connected to
bin Laden,' he told me. 'Among Americans who think that,
obviously having an English-language channel is not going to
meet with an enthusiastic response. I cannot put a percentage
obviously on the number of people who think in that way. I
don't have any statistics. No one knows. But obviously there are
people out there who feel that way.'

Preparing a piece to commemorate the anniversary of 9/11,
Foukara decided to interview a survivor. Foukara is originally
from Morocco, but spent years at the BBC and speaks perfect
English in a dark-brown voice. His producer gave him a list of
survivors. He chose a name at random and gave them a call. 'I
looked at the list and I saw a Spanish-Latino name and I thought
maybe that's a good place to start,' he said, speaking to me in
his office in the UN building. 'When I called him, I told him
who I was and who I represented and there was a pause. He

was silent for ten or fifteen seconds. And then he said, "You know what, for the kind of associations that you have, you have such a cheek calling me, knowing that I survived 9/11."'

The man then poured forth a torrent of allegations about Al-Jazeera's connections to terrorism and Osama bin Laden. For about an hour Foukara tried to convince him that this was simply a human-interest story, that it had nothing to do with politics and that it was not fair to link him or anyone else at Al-Jazeera to bin Laden. The man was unsure, but eventually he agreed to take Foukara's number, have a think about it and call if he changed his mind.

At two o'clock in the morning Foukara's phone rang. It was the 9/11 survivor. 'I can't sleep,' he said. 'You'll have to tell me how you found out my name and my phone number.'

'Look,' said Foukara, 'there's a lot of stuff in the public domain on the Internet. I got one of our producers to do some research and she put stuff together and we came up with lots of names. If you look on the Internet you'll be surprised what you come up with.'

This seemed to satisfy the man, so Foukara arranged to do the interview the next day. Then, at the last minute, he called back: he had changed his mind again and he was cancelling. He was uncomfortable with doing the interview because he perceived there was some connection between Al-Jazeera and Al-Qaeda.

'There are a lot of people, here in America and especially in New York, in whose perception we are associated with bin Laden and the tapes, and they think that Al-Jazeera is basically the mouthpiece of bin Laden and they wouldn't touch it with a barge pole,' Foukara told me. But at the same time there were occasions when working for Al-Jazeera opened doors.

'When we went out before the war to cover the anti-war rallies, the reaction that we got from a lot of Americans in that category of people who opposed the war was absolutely phenomenal, very positive. They know the Al-Jazeera logo, they see it, they seek it out, they come to us and invariably their request is, "We want to talk to you, and we want you to tell people in the Arab world or the Muslim world or wherever your audience is that we are not all for the war, and we want you to reflect the diversity of America." So you get both sides of the spectrum.'

Ironically, Foukara thinks that Al-Jazeera's polarized and risqué reputation may be exactly what saves the English-language channel from the same fate as the BBC in America:

> The BBC has been trying to secure a market in America for years and years. They've tried different things and different programmes and different formats. My understanding is that the BBC have come to accept that they can secure a niche market but they cannot really secure a widespread audience.
>
> You could either argue, 'Well, if the BBC have all the resources and the name and haven't been able to make a breakthrough in America, what about a channel that's an Arab channel, that has certain associations in the minds of some Americans?' But the flip side of that argument is that precisely because of that people will want to know, there's enormous curiosity about the channel, and that the obstacle at the moment is Arabic and if you put it in English it seems to me you may be quenching a lot of thirst. All publicity is good publicity.
>
> Only on very, very few occasions does someone say to me, 'Al-Jazeera? What's that?' Most of the time people know the channel. Most of the time they're either leery or they're incredibly warm. It's a polarized response.

The BBC is not the only well-established brand that has had surprising trouble making an impression on the American public's consciousness. The National Geographic channel was launched off the back of a similarly strong brand and there were high hopes it would soon expand with its quality documentaries. No expense was spared in the launch, but distribution turned out to be a problem and backers found that when a channel comes buried in a package of dozens of others, making an impression can be much harder than expected. Al-Jazeera in English could find itself on a bouquet of fifty other channels, making widespread US popularity unlikely.

Given Al-Jazeera's turbulent relationship with America, guessing the popularity of the English-language channel may seem impossible. But few are more qualified to try than Arab-American pollster, lecturer and consultant on the Arab media, John Zogby. Zogby is the President of Zogby International, which has polled for Reuters, Fox, NBC News and many other high-profile media companies and has a reputation for sharp accuracy. In the 1996 US presidential elections Zogby had the most accurate result of all polls, coming within 0.1 per cent of the final result. I met Zogby in Washington to find out what he thought lay in store for the Al-Jazeera English-language channel.

'Al-Jazeera in English is almost like the anti-news. It is going to be like the Big Bad News. And it is going to have a cachet. It is going to be very chic,' he prophesied. 'It is going to have a decent-sized American audience. There is a small but growing group of people who are curious about the other side, who are curious about the Arab world, with a strong sense that they are not getting what they need to get from American news broadcasts. There are more and more news broadcasts, but less and less news in the United States. Cable does a wonderful job on breaking news but after that it is just filler with people just shouting at each other.'

Recent events, Zogby said, had driven a growing minority to distraction with mainstream American satellite news:

People are going to the BBC for Iraq war coverage and are saying, 'This is not what I am getting on CNN! We're getting cheerleaders!' Now I am not in on the plan with Al-Jazeera but I assume they will know how to appeal to an American audience so they will have the right kind of glitz and the right kind of guests and language and so on.

But the thing is, they are going to be the big bad boy in town and the cachet is going to be, 'I don't watch Fox shit, I get my information on the Arab world from Al-Jazeera.'

There are two distinct markets for Al-Jazeera in English. One is going to be American Americans – regular white Americans – and the other is going to be Arab-Americans who either don't speak Arabic or are the children of immigrants. 'I want to hear what is going on in my parents' country but I want to hear it in English.' Al-Jazeera has a market here in the US in the tens of thousands, mainly Arab-Americans. My gut sense tells me it may hit MSNBC proportions, meaning a hundred thousand, or a hundred and fifty thousand – but understand that a hundred thousand with a point of view is a whole lot different to an amorphous mass of a hundred thousand viewers, because a hundred thousand with a point of view becomes a cohesion. It becomes possibly a force. That is different.

Already it has become clear that many discerning, internationally minded Americans, still smarting over the issue of the non-existent WMD and increasingly anxious about the seemingly endless conflict in Iraq have begun to look further afield for their news. The BBC and CBC have both seen their ratings in America go up since the invasion of Iraq. This means the BBC is all the more anxious about Al-Jazeera International, which threatens to take their newly acquired American audience. When I addressed a crowd of BBC journalists in the spring of 2004 at the annual BBC news conference, I found everyone asking the same questions: How many people will switch from BBC World to Al-Jazeera International when it starts up and what can we learn from Al-Jazeera's Arabic service right now to stop this happening?

The BBC are right to be worried. Around the world, many people still choose the BBC as the most trusted name in English-language news, but the BBC World Service Television news today is chronically underfunded, dilapidated, repetitive and often simply a shambles. Currently, the only alternative for English-language news globally is CNN International, which is conspicuously American and blatantly commercial, with seemingly endless advertisements and breaks that even interrupt the news and weather.

It is not impossible to imagine that a few years from now Al-Jazeera International could eclipse the BBC and CNN International in some parts of the world. Probably not in America, but in countries like Pakistan, Indonesia, Malaysia and Afghanistan, where anecdotal evidence suggests that even if people don't speak Arabic, they already recognize that little calligraphic teardrop logo as an incontrovertible stamp of authenticity.

One thing is clear: Al-Jazeera's turbulent history shows no sign of slowing down. As long as the Middle East does not run out of news, Al-Jazeera's relevance looks guaranteed. In future the network can be expected to produce and export more Middle Eastern news and current affairs, not just to Arab and Western news outfits, but increasingly to partners in the Far East, Russia and Latin America.

'Al-Jazeera has been so good to the Arab media and the Arab environment in general that I do not think even our worst detractors would like us off air,' Jihad Ballout told me breezily. He is wrong: it is not hard to imagine Al-Jazeera being shut down. This would be a great pity, not just for the hundreds of people it employs, or the millions who depend on Al-Jazeera regularly for their news, but for free speech in the Arab world.

One US Department of State representative told me he thought the world would perhaps be a better place if Al-Jazeera ceased to exist altogether. 'To a certain extent we believe in the freedom of the press but this isn't the press,' he said. 'They don't seem to have an agenda or their agenda seems to be to incite. It is equivalent to shouting fire in a crowded theatre every single day. It's very much a tabloid and I think it increases the odds of terrorism acts.'

This point of view is not uncommon in Washington. 'I personally have no use for them,' said the AEI's Molly McKew. 'If they have the equivalent of what is on Al-Jazeera now, in English, in the United States, I would mobilize the American government to destroy Al-Jazeera.'

A more likely possibility than being blown up or shut down is that Al-Jazeera will one day be gobbled up by one of the world's giant media conglomerates. In the past network spokesmen have stated that any offer would be considered, as long as the buyer will guarantee editorial independence – a major problem for many buyers, both inside and outside the Middle East. Besides, as long as the Saudis maintain the embargo on advertising, Al-Jazeera is not very commercially attractive. But the Middle East has a youthful population which holds enormous promise for advertisers. If something were to happen to the Saudi government or its advertising embargo, Al-Jazeera would suddenly shoot up in value.

Until that day comes the network's executives are banking on the English-language channel turning enough profit to keep them in business. 'Al-Jazeera has got to be self-sufficient in order to guarantee its independence in the long run,' Hafez al-Mirazi stated adamantly. 'Until now the whole of Al-Jazeera has been dependent on Emir Hamad of Qatar, who has views on modernization. There is no guarantee whatsoever that if there is any change in his approach or in the government or in anything whatsoever, that Jazeera will continue to be there.'

Like every modern news network, Al-Jazeera is occasionally guilty of sensationalism, trivialization, desensitization, overuse of emotionally charged phrases, sentimentalization and presenting news without context. Often breaking the news seems even more important than the news itself. But Al-Jazeera has reversed the flow of information so that now, for the first time in hundreds of years, it passes from East to West. Thanks largely to Al-Jazeera, television programming in the Arab world is now audience-driven, not programmer-driven, and that also is a fundamental change. A media monopoly has been replaced by a screaming plurality of voices. Although not everybody in the Middle East has a satellite dish, in order to remain relevant and win viewers with access to both satellite and terrestrial signals, state programmers have had to change their style of news completely – so even the poorest viewers have benefited from a raised standard of news.

If, with the launch of the English-language channel, Al-Jazeera successfully manages to prise viewers away from the BBC World Service and CNN International, the network will do what it has for so long desperately dreamed of doing: it will lose its reputation as an enfant terrible and join the ranks of the world's most prestigious news organizations. From there we can expect to see a full bouquet of other Al-Jazeera channels sprout forth, besides the new children's channel, including documentaries, drama, music, sport and movies.

If, on the other hand, the English-language channel is a flop, then besides the Emir's money being wasted, the hard-won reputation of the Arabic-language service will be tarnished and the Al-Jazeera brand forever compromised. With hungry rivals like Al-Arabiya snapping at its heels, Al-Jazeera may fade back into obscurity, memorable only as a phenomenon that briefly flowered and changed the Arab world for ever, before disappearing as quickly as it bloomed – like Nasser's Sawt al-Arab radio station. For Al-Jazeera the stakes simply could be no higher.

Whatever happens, we cannot turn back the clock. The information age is upon us and in the century ahead we can expect only more Al-Jazeeras, adding to an ever-greater torrent of information, as regional ideas spread around the world and become global. Things will never be how they were before. 'Freedom is like death,' Yosri Fouda once told me. 'You cannot visit death and then come back from it.' And that is what has happened in the case of Al-Jazeera. The door has been opened, and now no one can close it.

Index